ɔɔ8-ɔ6

W9-ASM-063

TWENTIETH CENTURY MUSIC

100

ALSO BY
Peter Yates

•

A SHORTER POEM BOOK

AN AMATEUR AT THE KEYBOARD

TWENTIETH
CENTURY
MUSIC

*Its Evolution
from the End of the Harmonic Era
into the Present Era of Sound*

BY

PETER YATES

Pantheon Books

A DIVISION OF RANDOM HOUSE

NEW YORK

FIRST PRINTING

© Copyright, 1967, by Peter Yates
All rights reserved under International and Pan-American
Copyright Conventions. Published in New York by Pantheon
Books, a division of Random House, Inc., and simultaneously
in Toronto, Canada, by Random House of Canada Limited.

Library of Congress Catalog Card Number: 65–10015

*Manufactured in the United States of America
by American Book–Stratford Press, Inc.*

DESIGNED BY JAIME DAVIDOVICH

REBIND 780.904
y27t

Music

Acknowledgements

The author wishes to thank the following authors, or their representatives, and publishers for their kind permission to quote from copyright material:

Basil Blackwell, Publisher, Oxford, and Macmillan and Company, New York, for excerpts from Ludwig Wittgenstein, *Philosophical Investigations*.

Bollingen Foundation, for excerpt from Étienne Gilson, *Painting and Reality*, Bollingen Series XXXV–4. Copyright 1955 by the Trustees of the National Gallery of Art.

John Cage and Wesleyan University Press, for excerpts from *Silence: Lectures and Writings*, by John Cage. Copyright © 1961 by John Cage.

Gilbert Chase and McGraw-Hill Book Company, for excerpt from *America's Music*, by Gilbert Chase. Copyright 1955.

Mrs. Sidney Cowell and Oxford University Press, Inc., for excerpts from *Charles Ives*, by Henry and Sidney Cowell.

Robert Craft and Farrar, Straus & Giroux, Inc., for excerpts from Robert Craft, "Music and Words," in Minna Lederman, ed., *Stravinsky in the Theatre*. Copyright 1949 by Dance Index-Ballet Caravan, Inc.

Doubleday & Company, Inc., and the Trustees of Princeton University for the Program in American Civilization at Princeton University, for excerpts from Susanne Langer, "The Social Influence of Design," in Laurence B. Holland, ed., *Who Designs America?*

Farrar, Straus & Giroux, Inc., for excerpt from Walter Piston, "Stravinsky's Rediscoveries," in Minna Lederman, ed., *Stravinsky in the Theatre*. Copyright 1949 by Dance Index-Ballet Caravan, Inc.

Farrar, Straus & Giroux, Inc., and J. M. Dent & Sons Ltd., for excerpts from James Day, *Vaughan Williams*. First published by Farrar, Straus & Giroux in 1963. Also for excerpts from Edward Lockspeiser, *Debussy*. First published by Farrar, Straus & Giroux in 1952, in their Master Musicians Series.

Forum voor architectuur en gebonden kunsten, Amsterdam, for permission to quote from their issue of May 6, 1964.

Grove Press, Inc., for excerpts from Antonin Artaud, *The Theater and Its Double*. Copyright © 1958 by Grove Press.

Lawrence Hanson and Random House, Inc., for excerpts from *Prokofiev: A Biography in Three Movements*, by Lawrence and Elisabeth Hanson.

Harcourt, Brace & World, Inc., for excerpt from "East Coker," from *Four Quartets*, by T. S. Eliot.

Harvard University Press, for excerpts from Aaron Copland, *Music and Imagination*, and Paul Hindemith, *A Composer's World*. Copyright, 1952, by the President and Fellows of Harvard College.

High Fidelity, for quotations from articles and reviews by Edward Greenfield, Eric Salzman, Max Wilcox, and Igor Stravinsky.

Music

Holt, Rinehart and Winston, Inc., for excerpt from Victor I. Seroff, *Maurice Ravel.* Copyright, 1953, by Victor I. Seroff.

Alfred A. Knopf, Inc., for excerpt from Mosco Carner, *Puccini: A Critical Biography.*

McIntosh and Otis, Inc., and G. P. Putnam's Sons, for excerpts from Victor I. Seroff, *Debussy, Musician of France.* © 1956 by Victor I. Seroff. Reprinted by permission of McIntosh and Otis, Inc.

W. W. Norton & Company, Inc., for excerpts from Jay Leyda and Sergei Bertensson, eds., *The Musorgsky Reader.*

Oxford University Press, London, for excerpts from *Heirs and Rebels,* by Ralph Vaughan Williams and Gustav Holst.

Oxford University Press, Inc., for excerpt from Norman Malcolm, *Ludwig Wittgenstein.*

C. F. Peters Corporation, for excerpts from John Cage, *Compositions.*

Mrs. Gertrud Schoenberg, for excerpts from Arnold Schoenberg, *Style and Idea.* Permission granted by Gertrud Schoenberg (for U.S.A. only).

Mrs. Gertrud Schoenberg and the Free Press of Glencoe for excerpts from Josef Rufer, *The Works of Arnold Schoenberg, a Catalogue of His Compositions, Writings & Paintings.* Permission granted by Gertrud Schoenberg (for U.S.A. only).

Simon and Schuster, Inc., for excerpts from James R. Newman, *Science and Sensibility.*

Halsey Stevens and Oxford University Press, Inc., for excerpts from *Béla Bartók,* by Halsey Stevens.

Igor Stravinsky, Robert Craft, and Alfred A. Knopf, Inc., for excerpts from *Themes and Episodes,* by Igor Stravinsky and Robert Craft.

Igor Stravinsky and W. W. Norton & Company, Inc., for excerpts from Igor Stravinsky, *An Autobiography.*

The Viking Press, Inc., for excerpts from Claude Debussy, *Monsieur Croche, the Dilettante Hater.* Copyright 1929, 1957 by The Viking Press, Inc.

John Wiley & Sons, Inc., for excerpts from Max Kaplan, *Leisure in America.*

Thanks are also due to:

Sister Emily Marie Bryant, S.P., for permission to quote part of her dissertation, *The Avant-Garde Character of Charles Ives's Music Exemplified in Representative Vocal, Chamber, and Symphonic Works.*

John Kirkpatrick, for permission to quote from his *A Temporary Mimeographed Catalogue of the Music Manuscripts of Charles Edward Ives.*

Harry Partch, for permission to condense and quote his description of his musical drama *Delusion of the Fury.*

To Igor Stravinsky, Virgil Thomson, John Cage, Ben Johnston, Lejaren Hiller, William Malloch, Eric Salzman, Gordon Mumma, Roger Reynolds, Ivor Darreg, Gerald Strang, and Earle Brown, for permission to quote from reviews, letters, and conversations.

Dedicated in affection

TO Harmony Ives

TO Gertrud Schoenberg   TO Vera Stravinsky

TO Sidney Cowell   TO Louise Varèse

AND TO Frances

CONTENTS

INTRODUCTION

The Preface to this book has been scattered through it, in comments, short lectures, and asides. The book does not pretend to serve scholarship by studying the music of the last hundred years as if it were an ossuary to be fitted together bone by bone. I am not convinced that such study can tell us more about what has happened, although it would supply more information about individual works; there are in any case others who are able to do that task better than myself. Fifteen years ago, when I first tried to write this book, my wise friend, the composer Ingolf Dahl, after reading the 150 pages which had brought me only to the first years of the century, advised me to write my book as I write articles about music, for the common reader, and avoid "musicology." I have tried to follow his advice.

My purpose is to follow the evolution of music into and through the twentieth century to the present day, and in so doing to assemble an esthetics which will serve the listener to break through the confusion caused by those who do not understand, by those who do not wish to understand, and by those who deny what has been happening in music. No argument has ever persuaded esthetic evolution to return whence it came and do otherwise than it has done.

If sometimes music itself may seem to be the hero of my history, I do not imply that music thinks for itself. Music evolves only by the skill of discerning and creative human minds to perceive its necessary course and follow that, as an explorer seeks his way by discovering fords and mountain passes. The unknown is the antagonist, and the heroes are the exploring composers who by rightly making their way into and through the unknown are able to chart it for us and make it known. Instead of geographical charts, they give us works of art, that when we assemble them offer us a broad picture of the successive landscapes these explorers have passed through on their ways.

Music so thought of is not conceived as entertainment but as a steady advance into new means and potentialities able to be used for musical creation. The beauty comes afterwards in our perception and appreciation of the new musical landscape, its fertile abundance or bare grandeur, and the multitude of its distinguishing shapes, vistas, and intelligible relationships. There is also the intangible *presence* of the landscape, one's feeling towards it, one's emotional and spiritual responding when one is present in it. Each landscape is at once a discovery in nature and a creation of the human mind, which perceives and enters into and partakes of it. The "great" work is the more fertile and abundant, surrounded by bare peaks. Yet a small valley may be the only pass between two enclosing landscapes.

The term *creation,* the idea of "creating" a work of art, are modern, signifying the individualism and isolation which have become, in our minds, inseparable from the artistic effort. Craftsmanship, the excellent performance of a skilled job, is by the same amount lessened. In using the words *creation, create, creative,* I include both the individualism and the workmanlike craft.

Although the book offers no categorical ranking of composers by better or worse, it does discuss the limitations within which a composer works and the consequences of these limitations, as well as the peculiar and special gifts and means by which some composers have overcome and gone beyond the limitations which prevented others from like accomplishment. In a few instances I have made specific judgements, not with the intention of reducing the composer but to give evidence how the character of the creative mind, as revealed in the work of the artist, can impose constricting and destructive handicaps. The reader need not agree, and it would be better if he did not, since the composer's work is there for his use as well as mine, and the reader as conversationalist, listener, or student should return always to his independent judgement.

The book is as a whole, therefore, a survey of the evolution of music from the end of the Harmonic Era to where we are at present in the new Era of Sound. In such a survey harmonic analysis would be inoperative or misleading: an acquaintance who is writing a harmonic analysis of twentieth century music admits that his close study ceases along the curiously curving evolutionary line where harmonic music, capable of such analysis, veers over towards sound. The work of Ives, the mature music of Schoenberg, the still later music of Stravinsky are beyond his purview, as is all that is happening in music at the present time. For this newer music of sound we have developed so far no competent language of analysis.

"Never before have composers been so unprepared by their schooling," Igor Stravinsky commented in an interview. "The compositional techniques still generally taught are about as useful as spare parts for machinery last manufactured about seventy-five years ago. . . . The contemporary composer's very writing desk is in a jumble. At no other period has notation itself fallen into such chaos that composers were able to confuse notational gimmicks and musical invention. Truly, contemporary music, the life of it as well as the art, is a complex affair. . . ."

The composers mentioned in this book have participated directly in the evolution of twentieth century music; they do not include all the composers I have known in person, nor all the friends whose music I have enjoyed, nor all the composers whose work I admire and wish to hear. I have included nobody to flatter him, nor excluded anyone for spite. My method has been elimination. There have been many composers in every period whose compositions, however valuable, did not contribute to musical evolution. Many would think this a virtue in them, but it is not to my purpose.

I have not attempted an evaluation in absolute terms of the large body of unquestionably great music which has been composed during these years, certainly one of the most significantly productive periods in the entire history of music. Such an evaluation would have required a quite different and larger book than this, and several works which I have only referred to would have been given much larger space. Such works of absolute musicianship stand by themselves, apart from the musical evolution

occurring around them. I have discussed each composer in relation to what he has contributed to the changing courses of music
during this period; I have tried to avoid any comparative analysis
of ultimate worth.

There have been and are several important centers of musical
activity—I think particularly of Warsaw, Poland, at the present
time—replete wih adventurous composers and new compositions, that I have not mentioned. What is being done there is
being done also, and in part stems from what is being done, by
composers in the United States, with whose work and history I
am better acquainted.

*The book is not about my opinion of composers, though my
opinion inevitably enters into it, but is a discussion of musical
evolution during the last hundred years, in language not simplified for but directed to the common reader.*

As in all my writing about music, I have not used notated
examples, which, although they may show *how* something has
been done, are usually too short to make clear *why*.

My first acknowledgement of gratitude must go to the many
composers and musicians who have educated me by their example and in correspondence and conversation.

When listening to a composer talk, one should give less attention to the oratorio he performs before himself and before the
public—this defensive-aggressive material is changeable and suspect—listening instead for those moments of concentrated statement when the creative mind speaks. These are the moments of
revelation, if one can discern them. Igor Stravinsky, pacing the
room after hearing for the first time a solo *shakuhachi* (the
Japanese bamboo flute) play ancient temple music: "It is the
farthest from us." In that searching ear the microtonal subtlety,
the dramatic breath sound, the continually inflected melody, each
so unlike our own tradition, set in perspective the still unrealized
prospect of our music, that one hears now coming to realization.

But such experience might never have been drawn together
into a book, if John Entenza had not risked permitting me to
begin writing about music in the magazine *Arts and Architecture*.
That first short article, published in November 1940, was about
Charles Ives, and the first sentence brought together the names of
Ives and Schoenberg. I began writing this book then, in an
editorial freedom granted to few writers about music, and during

more than twenty-five years the sequence of gradually enlarging articles seldom missed a month.

My second acknowledgement of gratitude belongs therefore to John Entenza, whose trust, encouragement, and loyalty, whose deliberate editorial policy of noninterference, gave opportunity for a freedom of discovery which would not, I believe, have been granted elsewhere. This statement of gratitude would be incomplete if it did not speak also of the help and friendship given to me and to many by his two assistant editors, both now gone from us, "Brownie" and Susan Jonas.

I am grateful also to his successor as owner and editor of *Arts and Architecture,* David Travers, who without deviation has continued the same policy.

My third acknowledgement of gratitude is to the many friends who shared for fifteen years (1939–1954) the performing adventures of our Evenings on the Roof chamber concerts in Los Angeles, and to Lawrence Morton and the musicians who have continued them to the present time in the Monday Evening Concerts. Here we have tried for our own experience the literature of music.

I thank finally the several friends and composers who have read the manuscript of this book in whole or part and contributed of their own knowledge to its improvement; to Gerald Gross, who first proposed my writing this book, and to my editor, Paula McGuire; and to Dely Katigbak, who at a crucial time decisively gave my plan a sure direction by rearranging the order of the first chapters.

A Ford Foundation award, under the program for reporters, editors, and critics, enabled me to travel freely, before completing this book, to meet American composers and poets.

PART I

"During the seventeenth century all roads lead to Bach; during the nineteenth century, to Schoenberg."

—An Amateur at the Keyboard

I

MUSIC AND SOUND

Professional thinkers about music, until recently, have thought of *music* as one thing and *sound* as something else.

Technical talk about sound as a musical phenomenon starts with the Greek philosopher Pythagoras, who believed that he could establish a principle of order in the universe by expressing all relationships among the parts of things in simple whole numbers. In his experiments Pythagoras discovered that such relationships do exist among the perfect (acoustically correct) intervals of tones obtained by plucking a stretched string.

Tones and the intervals between them have been from that time until very recently the material of music. Music is, in that meaning, ordered sound; the written tones are notes.

Whatever sound could not be so ordered or written out in some notation was thought of as unmusical. Random or accidental sound was noise.

There is a double distinction. Music as ordered sound has implied both that the tones and intervals are in an agreed acoustical relationship and that a human mind has chosen to assemble and place them in deliberate order. Random sound, or noise, has implied that the elements of the sound as it is heard are not in an agreed acoustical relationship, because the accident of their being heard together was not governed by a deliberate human choice. This second distinction is no longer true; composers today are making music by deliberate use of random sound, or noise.

A good many cultivated musicians of the Western European tradition still hold to the opinion that any tones not set in order according to the system prevailing in Western European music cannot be music, thus ruling out nearly all types of highly developed Asiatic music as merely "primitive." As the result of what is now happening in music throughout the world, the Western European tradition may soon seem to be as "primitive" as any other tradition.

I call our musical tradition "Western European" because, although the tradition reaches back to ancient Greece, it grew to maturity in Western Europe, in Italy, Spain, France, Germany, the Netherlands, parts of Scandinavia, and England. The Byzantine and Slavic traditions of music grew separately from the same sources.

For Pythagoras, music began with the acoustically correct intervals, or perfect concords, especially the correct octave, the correct fifth, and the correct third. For us, music begins with the acoustically imperfect intervals, or discords, of the equally tempered scale.

The root of the matter is that if you reduce any set of acoustically correct intervals to approximate the twelve notes of an ordinary octave scale, the upper limit of the acoustically correct scale will exceed a correct octave by about a quarter-tone. This difference is called the *Pythagorean comma*. To fit the twelve notes into the octave, you distribute the difference of the Pythagorean comma by narrowing some of the intervals, making these intervals discordant. This is called *tempering* the scale. Any tempered scale contains some perfect and some imperfect intervals.

Until the sixteenth century, music was composed around the concordant rather than the discordant intervals of the scale. From the sixteenth century until the present time, music has been composed around the discordant rather than the concordant intervals. The distinction is fundamental to the evolution of Western European music, and it is generally ignored.

Until the sixteenth century, music had been composed around that instrument of infinitely *variable intonation*, the human voice, which could when necessary adjust pitch to preserve a concord which would otherwise become a discord. At this time there was no *scale* in our meaning of an exact series of fixed pitches. There was instead a mode, or melodic series of unequal intervals, including tones of mutable pitch; the performer adjusted these mutable tones by microtonal deviations to satisfy the harmonic requirements of the melody.[1]

After the sixteenth century, music began to be composed around the *fixed intonation* of the keyboard instruments. A new system of relatively fixed, unequal intervals, called *meantone*, came into predominance throughout European music. This intervallic system of fixed pitches governed the harmonic grammar of European music for more than two hundred years, roughly 1600–1800.

Our own system of fixed pitches, *equal temperament*, has lasted only 150 years and is already in advanced disintegration.

In meantone, every key has a slightly different intervallic pattern and therefore a distinct harmonic coloring. Every modulation alters the harmonic coloring and therefore in some degree the emotional character (*affect*) of the music. The unequal intervals of meantone provide a greater degree of tonal inflection within a single key than is possible within a single key of equal temperament.

Equal temperament solves or escapes the problem of the Pythagorean comma by dividing the octave into mathematically equal intervals, all equally imperfect and all equally discordant. Only the octave interval remains acoustically correct and concordant. In equal temperament all keys sound the same, though our innate sense of melodic concordance will often cause in us a feeling of key-relationship. That is why players of string instruments still adjust the intonation or pitch, when playing, to improve the harmony. A pianist cannot do this.

❀ Helmholtz noted that the violinist Joseph Joachim, when playing without accompaniment, altered the pitches to correct just intonation. Arnold Dolmetsch remarked of the Flonzaley Quartet that they played in just intonation. The New Music Quartet and the LaSalle Quartet performed works for string quartet by Lou Harrison and Ben Johnston in exact just intonation, as the composers wished. Rudolf Kolisch, Schoenberg's brother-in-law and one of the great performers of twentieth century Viennese music, insists that one should play in exact equal temperament. Edward Greenfield wrote of the Hungarian Quartet: "What was their secret, I asked, in achieving such perfection of intonation . . . ? They were quite agreed that the main point was their conscious decision to play in the evenly tempered scale. 'The size of a third has been a matter of argument in the Hungarian Quartet for thirty years,' Szekely said half in jest, but Koromzay put it more practically: 'We hate playing in the tempered scale, but we just have to.' "[2]

Recent experiments have shown that string players and singers now tend to alter the pitch in the opposite direction, toward increased dissonance. An example would be the widened thirds in the Robert Craft recorded performances of Gesualdo madrigals, which would have been originally in just intonation with mutable tones. Historians formerly described these madrigals as too dissonant to be acceptable; now our taste for brilliance causes singers to increase the discordance. Roger Reynolds told me that in Italy his piano was tuned by a tuner who had worked many years for Toscanini. The octaves and fifths were in such perfect concord they sounded like one tone, while the major thirds were brilliantly wide—not equal temperament but the medieval Pythagorean! A vocal instead of a keyboard temperament.

Here it would be well to point out that the *well-tempered* tuning used by J. S. Bach is not the same as equal temperament but a distinct tuning of unequal intervals, which keeps some of the modulatory coloring of meantone but permits playing in full chords with both hands in all keys. The tuning of instruments did not change throughout Europe as soon as J. S. Bach, a composer of slight immediate influence, issued his *Well-Tempered Clavier*. If so, the change would have been to well-tempered, not to equal temperament.

In January 1966 Margaret Fabrizio in San Francisco performed Bach's *Art of Fugue* on a well-tempered harpsichord. One critic emphatically preferred this version over the more usual arrangements for a group of instruments, because of the increased tone coloration and the sense of freedom from the prevailing D minor.

Modern harmonic theory is based partly on the simple arithmetical relationship of concordant intervals established by Pythagoras (but applied instead to our discordant intervals), partly on the modulatory coloring among the *unequal* intervals of the scale in meantone (which went out of music about 150 years ago), and partly on rationalizations of these conflicting systems in terms of the tuning we use today, equal temperament. Harmonic theory, as we learn it, is made up of three mutually exclusive sound-systems, which are taught as if the three were one.

Today we hear performed in equal temperament the choral music of the medieval and Renaissance periods, which was meant to be harmonized by acoustically correct concords, and the music of the seventeenth and eighteenth centuries, which was meant to be heard in the changing key-coloration of meantone. In equal temperament, all sounds alike.

With equal temperament, all intervals being alike, the differences among the keys vanished. These differences continue to exist in theory, but no ear can hear them. A key can be identified by its starting note but no longer by its distinctive coloration. To replace the vanished key-coloration, harmony was made thicker and heavier, until key-relationship, too, disappeared, swallowed up in practice by a single chromatic harmony consisting of all the notes in the octave. Harmony survived as a system of rationalizations. Dissonance lost dramatic relativity, because all music was now heavily dissonant. Therefore enharmonic change ceased to signify. "The conceptions of 'related' and 'foreign' keys vanish," Busoni wrote in his *New Esthetic of Music,* "and with them the entire intricate theory of degrees and relations. *We possess one single key.* But it is of most meagre sort."[3] That is where music had arrived at the start of the twentieth century.

Debussy exposed the theoretical impasse of music at the start of the twentieth century by dispensing with the traditional harmonic formulas. Schoenberg resolved it by showing that, since only the chromatic relationships remained valid in practice, a new single "key" of the twelve tones should be accepted and a new twelve-tone method of musical grammar should be derived from it.

Schoenberg's twelve tones, however, are no longer the key-related notes of previous musical theory. For Schoenberg, C sharp "is nothing else than the exactly measured half step between d and c, without any relationship to harmonic questions."[4] But since these exactly measured notes are to be thought of only as a gamut of equal-tempered sounds, there is no reason why other gamuts, of tones, sounds, or noises, should not be substituted for them.

Two American composers, both of whom studied with Schoenberg, have extended this theory along contrary paths. Lou Harrison said that when Schoenberg had reduced all harmony to a single key of the twelve tones, he should have gone farther and retuned the intervals to their exact acoustical relationships in just intonation. That is one thing that Harrison has done.

Joseph Yasser, advocating his own scale of nineteen-tone just temperament, made a similar proposal to Schoenberg in a letter. Schoenberg replied: ". . . to be musical means to have an ear in the *musical* sense, not in the *natural* sense. A musical ear must have assimilated the tempered scale. And a singer who produces natural pitches is unmusical. . . ."[5]

This confusion of purposes can no longer be maintained in the new Era of Sound.

John Cage said to me that when Schoenberg had emancipated the dissonance, he should have gone farther and emancipated music from its notes. At that time Cage had already composed for the prepared piano, creating exactly measured artificial tones which sounded instead of the notated tones.

The need of European composers to cling to a formalized grammar which would take the place of the disintegrating key-system gave sufficient persuasion for them to believe they were still within the domain of key-tonality even when for the ear they had gone beyond it. A positive substitute for harmonic grammar was felt to be necessary; therefore Schoenberg invented the tone-row, the "method of composing with twelve tones related only to one another," a grammar and syntax of the emancipated dissonance.

Schoenberg's opponents contended that he was destroying music. Schoenberg himself and his most closely allied friend and occasional pupil, Anton Webern, while insisting on the necessity of their actions, also viewed the prospect gloomily. Webern had broken with the immediate past of Germanic music more rapidly and decisively than Schoenberg. In his early Quintet for piano and strings one can already hear nodes of pure Webern breaking away from the surrounding conventional material. Webern has put vividly in words the tense awareness of their experience: "It was a hard struggle; inhibitions of the most terrifying kind had to be overcome; there was an anxious questioning: is that really possible? As if the light had given out—that's how it struck us."[6]

Charles Ives, born a month after Schoenberg, had been educated by his father, a pragmatical-experimental Yankee band-master, to feel neither the obligation nor the loss. Ives was more concerned with the character of his music than with theoretical explanations. Ives anticipated the emancipation of the disso-nance. He broke the rules against successive perfect consonances, so that it may also be said that he emancipated the consonance. Ives wrote music of great interest which contains microtones, incompatible rhythms, and noise; he welcomed what was later to be called "indeterminacy" and deliberately composed what would be called "mistakes."

Ives wrote a memo to his copyist: "Mr. Price. Please don't try to make things nice. All the wrong notes are *right*."[7]

That is where music is now going.

2

SILENCE AND THE FIELD
OF SOUND

Music is composed of sound and silence. The art of music is a peculiar and purposive skill in combining sounds and silence: peculiar in that it must convey some awareness of perceptible and reasonable order by whatever means the composer—or an improvising performer—feels called on to use; purposive in that the composer feels himself summoned by necessity to use these means. In the work of a genuinely creative composer the necessary means come first; the justification, technical, rational, irrational—or, as one might say of inspiration, superrational—follows. Schoenberg explained what he had accomplished after he had done it; Ives wrote his *Essays Before a Sonata* at the end of his active musical career.

Wherever life exists there is some sound. Even in an anechoic chamber, a room designed to eliminate sound reverberation, as John Cage discovered, one hears the sounds of one's own body. All music must contain silence, to be distinguished from an undifferentiated continuum of sound; the composition of silence is no less significant than the composition of sound. Schoenberg said of a famous performer who failed as a composer: "He has only the one fault: he does not know how to stop." The amount and placement of silence may be required, too, by acoustical phenomena; if a composer—or performer—does not accept these conditions, the music will not be adequately heard.

✿ The famous—or, as many insist, infamous—composition *4'33"*, by John Cage, known as the "Silent Sonata," four minutes and thirty-three seconds during which a pianist at the piano or several musicians with their instruments sit as if in readiness to play but produce no sound, has many philosophical, sociological, psychological, emotional, and critical implications, concerning among other matters the relation between performer and audience, between expectation and the defeat of expectation, whether or not one chooses to call it music. An audience which does not know what to expect may become hysterical; one that knows what to expect may receive the experience with appreciation, as it would receive any other well-known historic or "classic" composition. Cage's art is, in the Zen tradition, which has liberated him from many of our habitual fallacies, at once reverent and comedic; it expects that one will receive the unexpected with an undifferentiated attention and enjoy with a smile whatever one discovers. As music, *4'33"* supplants sound not by silence alone but by whatever sounds occur in the presence of the musicians during the four and a half minutes. (When I performed it for an audience at Antioch College, the silence was so complete that the recording engineer, who was taping the lecture by remote control, cut off the tape, thinking the lecture ended.)

For any student or critic of esthetic phenomena—that is to say, of what the mind does in the presence of art—the "Silent Sonata" is a work of primary relevance. It is, like any other effective work of art, an invitation to fresh and individual esthetic experience.

Silence is the absence of sound in which sound occurs; in musical tradition it is the absence of musical sound. One may describe sound as a two-dimensional field or continuum, bounded and defined by silence, having four boundaries, which I shall indicate by geographical directions.

On the south is the *continuum of fundamental pitches,* a linear continuity of sine waves (fundamental pitches without overtones) from the lowest to the highest audible sound.

On the north is *white sound,* the undifferentiated tonal spectrum, corresponding to white light. From white sound one can filter, by electronic means, any desired combination of overtones. The combining of fundamental pitches with overtones underlies the field of *timbre.*

On the east is *noise,* the totally random or inchoate mingling of sounds.

On the west is *just intonation,* the acoustically correct intervallic relationship of tones. Between just intonation and noise is the field of *temperament,* the deviating of tones from an acoustically correct relationship towards discord and noise. The five principal divisions of the field of temperament are just intonation or concord (acoustically correct intervallic relationship), consonance (where the relations are slightly incorrect), going on into dissonance (where the relationships recede farther from acoustical correctness) and so into discordance (where the acoustical

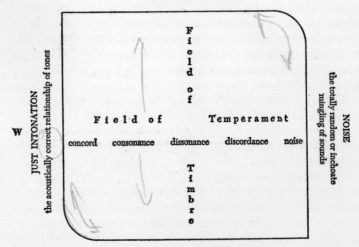

N

WHITE SOUND

the undifferentiated tonal spectrum
corresponding to white light

JUST INTONATION
the acoustically correct relationship of tones

W

Field of
concord   consonance

**F
i
e
l
d

o
f**

Temperament
dissonance   discordance   noise

**T
i
m
b
r
e**

NOISE
the totally random or inchoate
mingling of sounds

E

CONTINUUM OF FUNDAMENTAL PITCHES

a linear continuity of sine waves (fundamental
pitches without overtones) from the lowest
to the highest audible sound

S

relationship is rejected in favor of arbitrarily derived sounds) and noise (which cannot be indicated by notes).

A third dimension of sound is qualitative and dynamic; it includes duration, amplitude, attack, decay, crescendo, and diminuendo.

A fourth dimension enters with drama or play and involves audience participation. We are familiar with the situation in which the audience, however appreciative, sits inactively while the performer performs. We are less aware of the situation where audience and performers are intermingled, though it is the commonplace of many games and of ritual.

Sound may have other dimensions. We no more comprehend or command the evolving art of sound than composers of the seventeenth century comprehended or commanded the evolving art of vertically related harmony.

The simple plane figure indicating the principal dimensions of the field of sound is not a definition but an outline, the starting-point of a discussion—a field of art to be entered by expanding creative and imaginative experience. Specialists will qualify each dimension.

For example, the two curved corners of the diagrammatic field indicate that the four boundaries are in fact only two dimensions, each shown in two distinct significations. The *continuum of fundamental pitches* and *just intonation* are contrasting expressions of the one sound-dimension: the former signifying a continuous flow of pitched sound between the high and low audible dimensions; the latter signifying a series of acoustically related points (or notatable tones) derived from the overtone series along the same curve.

In the same way the rounded corner where *noise* meets *white sound* signifies, in the simplest terms, that white sound is the most inclusive noise, whereas noise is any inchoate mingling of sounds.

Just intonation has been during the last three centuries the most neglected dimension of the field of sound, though it has been known in precise mathematical statement and musical usage for 2500 years. The theoretical reassertion of just intonation by the seventeenth century Dutch physicist Christiaan Huygens, by the nineteenth century physicist Hermann Helmholtz, and by other devotees whose ears rejected the obvious imperfections of equal temperament, was realized as a practical mode for composition by the American composers Harry Partch and Lou Harrison and the Dutch physicist Adriaan Fokker.

The revival of just intonation reopened the art of concordant sonority which went out of vogue with the change from polyphonic to monodic music at the end of the sixteenth century—or, more simply, from a music of flexible pitches centered around the human voice to a music of fixed pitches centering around the keyboard instruments. There is no one absolute scale of just intonation. The fixed-pitch scales devised by Harrison (12 tones in the octave), by Joseph Yasser (19 tones in the octave), by Fokker (31 equal-tempered one-fifth tones in the octave), should be distinguished from mutable just intonation by calling them *just temperaments*. Partch's 43-tone scale is a just intonation of unequal fixed-pitch intervals. The quarter-tone scale (24 tones in the octave) is a microtonal equal temperament.

The microtonal scales devised by Fokker (from the writings of Huygens) and Partch enlarge the range of harmony and require the adaptation of standard instruments or the invention of new instruments to play them. Harry Partch has been the most creative innovator of new instruments during the century since Adolphe Sax.

John Cage brought the continuum of fundamental pitches into music in 1939 with the composition of his *Imaginary Landscape No. 1*, using two records of this curve in electronically generated sound made by a telephone company to test its lines, plus a tam-tam and a piano played with one hand while the other hand damps the strings. The composition was recorded directly on a phonograph record. This is the first surviving successful electronic composition.

Electronic sound-generation is also the source of white sound, from which any combination or range of exact tones or sound bands may be obtained by filtering.

Musical theory has never decided at what approximate degree of acoustically incorrect relationship tonal concordance ceases to be musically acceptable consonance and dissonance and becomes instead discordant noise. Because the scale of equal temperament is discordant (except the octave), the acceptance of dissonant tonality has been steadily widening to include outright discord. Beethoven's compositions would have seemed to Palestrina more noise than music, as indeed they seemed to many of Beethoven's contemporaries. The harmonies of Debussy or Richard Strauss would probably have angered Beethoven.

One can recognize the shouting and beating on shields of barbaric warriors as a noise-music. Noise as a musical dimension of sound was not unknown to Beethoven; Charles Ives used it positively in several compositions. It is doubtful that either Schoenberg or Stravinsky, in 1912, would have accepted as music the principal compositions conceived by Charles Ives between 1895 and 1912 (the year of *Pierrot Lunaire* and *Rite of Spring*). The noise-music initiated around 1907 by Marinetti and Russolo is, in description, comparatively superficial.

John Cage began the composition of a strictly noise music with his *Williams Mix* (1952), put together on tape by combining six categories of tape-recorded sounds, and the still more intricately noisy *Fontana Mix* (1958). Most musicians and audiences do not yet recognize noise-composition as music.

Consonance and *dissonance* are in practical usage degrees of concordance, consonance being a more nearly correct and dissonance a more deviant concordance. Practical usage twists theory to its purposes: the major third in equal temperament is a severe dissonance; harmonic theory defines the major third in equal temperament as a consonance—as indeed it was during the two hundred years of the predominance of meantone temperament.

❀ Some composers and theorists, among them J. S. Bach and Gottfried Silbermann, the instrument-builder, slightly widened the major third when tuning meantone, thus also widening the very narrow fifth. Because meantone with a correct third is very easy to tune accurately and the deviant tuning is not, we may assume that this practice was not general. Professional tuners today likewise slightly alter the exact equality of the intervals in equal temperament for harmonic advantage. Professional tuning came into existence with equal temperament.

At the present time the distinctions among the various degrees of tonality and sound—concord, consonance, dissonance, discord, random sound, and noise—are being reduced to a continuous field of musical possibility. Our ears, which have been trained to accept as music only the field of relationship and contrast between consonance and dissonance, are already beginning to hear as musical the distinguishing characteristics of the entire field of sound. Our awareness of microtonal differences is being sharpened by our discovery of the highly developed microtonal traditions of Asiatic music, and by our experiments in electronic music. Most of us accept as musical much noise to which we are accustomed (hall reverberation, imperfect acoustics, the slighter distortions of sound by record and tape equipment, incorrect orchestral intonation, audience stir, and so on), which we do not identify as noise. The stir of an audience, taped with the music at a live performance, can add excitement to the musical sound.

The third dimension of sound consists of the shaping elements which qualify the nature and dimensions of the individual sounds. The third dimension of sound, which includes duration, amplitude, attack, decay, crescendo, and diminuendo, intersects with temperament and timbre to form what composers of electronic music call the "sound envelope."

Understanding this, we can consider with less superstitious fear the advent of the electronic computer as a composing instrument. In the same way that medieval and Renaissance music had at its center the human voice, and music of the Harmonic Era had at its center the keyboard instruments—organ, harpsichord, piano— the new Era of Sound will have as its center the computer. With the computer a composer can indicate precisely at every point the exact characteristics including the sound envelope his music requires; he can bind these points together in any degree of complexity he wishes. But exploration of the sound envelope, of the entire field of sound, is at present still experimental and very incomplete.

The fourth dimension, drama, play, theatrical action, and audience participation, though as ancient as the use of sound for any musical, ritualistic, or dramatic purpose, has to do with the nature of the sound as an agent of group relationship and not with its quality or nature as sound.

All of this may seem to the uninitiated reader almost impossibly difficult to comprehend. It is really not so. Having these ideas in mind while listening to a great variety of music of many periods and traditions, and especially to the extraordinarily varied music of our own century, will ease much of the difficulty. One purpose of hearing music is to enlarge our capacity for listening. An understanding of these concepts in these relatively simple terms is essential for anyone who wishes to understand what has been happening in creative musical experience during the present century and, particularly, what is happening in music at the present time.

3

INTONATION, PITCH, AND SCALE

The earliest musicians beat their music on logs or drums, plucked it on bowstrings, blew it through flutes or whistles, and chanted and shouted. The variety of musical instruments is great, though the number of types is limited. Freely pitched percussion at two or more contrasting levels can have esthetic meaning, as it can convey messages (Morse code and the computer use only two message symbols). Drums are said to "speak" by microtonal changes of pitch and timbre. Indeed the sound of primitive instruments often resembles the quality of a speaking voice. Neither music nor communication by voice requires exactly pitched tones, though more nearly so in Chinese than in English. Music originated in the ordering of noise.

A sense of exact pitch comes normally from training and habituation; a rare few have it naturally. Many accustomed listeners, like myself, do not have it at all.

The acoustical relationships among exact pitches are a fact of nature. These relationships can be shown visibly and measured by the proportionate vibrating of stretched strings, as Pythagoras demonstrated, and the proportions can be expressed as arithmetical fractions.

❀ All musical relationships can be stated in terms of a numerical system. It is now possible for a composer to write music in terms of numerical relationships and feed this information, with supplementary dynamic, rhythmic, and other expressive instructions, into a computer equipped with sound-generating means and recording tape, which, after two or three passes of internal translation, will produce in sound the exact music the composer ordered.

It is a fundamental fact for music that the ordinary ear hears most accurately those intervals which have the simplest arithmetical relationships in just intonation. The music of nearly every highly developed culture, except our own music of the past three hundred years, is built around a melodic scale of unequal intervals in approximate just intonation—but using a variety of different intervals and tones. The basic scale of European music, accepted by Pythagoras and the majority of subsequent theorists, comprises an octave of twelve tones in just intonation.

Just intonation can be sung or played in more than one key with modulation among keys only so far as the musicians are able to keep in mind and make whenever necessary the correct pitch adjustments of the mutable tones. Daring chromatic experiments by such sixteenth century composers as Gesualdo, using all twelve tones, were not beyond the capacity of gifted amateurs to perform them. But Gesualdo composed in mutable just intonation, so that the vertical relationships were consonant. His madrigals were in such demand that they were many times reprinted.

Musicians and amateurs gradually turned from these established skills of consorted music to a new interest in accompanied solo music for voice and to developing a wider range of keys and possible harmonic modulations in the playing of keyboard instruments. To accomplish this, they needed a new tuning, having tempered or slightly incorrect intervals in place of the correct intervals. These tempered intervals would provide acceptably consonant relationships instead of the correct concordant relationships. For this purpose they invented the method of temperament known as meantone.

Meantone supplies a range of eight keys—or nine, by altering the G sharp or A flat at the end of the tuning cycle (tuned from C) to give the correct major third with E or C, making available the keys with signatures up to three sharps or three flats. Meantone retains the principal just (correct) major thirds but tempers the fifths by tuning them considerably narrower than the fifth of equal temperament. Meantone can be tuned very easily and accurately by ear, the correct thirds giving an exact check on the narrowing of the fifths. The combination of concords and dissonances furnishes a rich and melodious voice-leading and distinction among the parts in vertical harmony.

Most especially, meantone provides a built-in registration or scheme of harmonic color-change by modulation, since each key has a different pattern of just and tempered intervals, which imparts an identifiably distinct coloration to its harmony.

There is also the less recognized advantage, that by a discreet introduction of dissonant (incorrect) relationships the composer can widen the emotional significance, or *affect*. The sound of such incorrect relationships was called "the Wolf," meaning a dissonance to be avoided because the discord "howled" in the harmony. Wesley Kuhnle has demonstrated in his *History of Tuning on Tape* that J. S. Bach, in the second movement of his *Capriccio for a Departing Brother*, introduces "the Wolf" to hint of "The Dangers of Foreign Lands," as the movement is entitled, a hint which his listeners would not have missed. Mr. Kuhnle has shown a similar affect in the passage describing the death of Goliath, immediately after the flinging of the stone, in Kuhnau's *The Battle of David and Goliath*. These meantone affects became still more common in clavichord playing, by a slight raising of the flexible pitch. The controlled dissonant affects are in the nature of the tuning and the instrument.

Mr. Kuhnle has shown also how J. S. Bach and Domenico Scarlatti explored further extensions and adjustments (*accords*) of the meantone tuning beyond the generally accepted convention, proving that well-tempered tuning or equal temperament were not the only possible alternatives for the expansion and evolution of harmony.

C. P. E. Bach wrote that his father could tune a keyboard instrument so that it could be played in full chords in both hands in any key. This is the well-tempered tuning, obtained by progressively narrowing the fifths to the midpoint of the tuning cycle, but so slightly that the narrowest fifth of well-tempered was not so narrow as the meantone fifth, and then progressively widening them in the same proportions to the end of the cycle. The temperament accomplishes in playing what C. P. E. Bach claimed for it, but, since it is very difficult to tune accurately, well-tempered did not come into wide use. Wesley Kuhnle's studies and my own examination of the literature indicate that both Mozart and Beethoven used well-tempered for their composed sonatas but not for their improvised variations, which are still intended for meantone, probably because the composer usually improvised on an instrument not his own that retained meantone tuning. Beethoven definitely abandoned both the meantone and well-tempered tunings soon after 1800. Mr. Kuhnle has demonstrated that Beethoven's early *Preludes Through All the Keys,* opus 39, were composed for a well-tempered instrument.

Well-tempered tuning retains some of the individual key-coloration which any composer of that period would have been reluctant to surrender. The next change, to equal temperament, probably occurred to enable all the players in an orchestra to perform music beyond the harmonic range of meantone. To tune all the instruments of an orchestra to well-tempered would have been very difficult, if not impossible. From this time orchestral coloring (orchestration) replaces key-coloration as the means of emotional affect. Pianists began learning how to play the piano to imitate orchestral affects.

At some time during this period the modern orchestral convention of tuning from an A furnished by an oboe supplanted the general previous habit of tuning from C.

Except the demonstrations of Wesley Kuhnle's *History of Tuning,* there is no literature which clarifies the modifications and adaptations of tuning during the period when meantone, well-tempered, and equal temperament were in parallel use, the high period of our classic music. We do not know when wind instruments were modified to enable them to play in equal temperament instead of meantone. We have never really investigated the fundamentals of harmonic relationship—neither the tunings nor the intervals—of our European classic music. For lack of documentation, musicologists and students have so entirely avoided the subject that the majority are unaware the problem exists. The lack of documentation does not prove that nothing happened; it proves only—as some students are declaring—that the documentary method is inadequate.

The changes of tuning, first by a few composers to well-tempered and some time later by the great body of musicians to equal temperament, brought into common use all twenty-four keys, vastly widening the harmonic scope of modulation. Instead of the meantone distinction between a correct G sharp and a correct A flat, only one of which could be tuned on a single set of strings, one enharmonic tone, neither a correct G sharp nor a correct A flat, served for both. Beethoven soon revealed the dramatic result which could be achieved by modulating, say, on G sharp and then enharmonically foreshortening the expected lie of events by continuing on the same note as if it were A flat.

In spite of the unprecedented modulatory gambits which a great composer could bring off dramatically in equal temperament, the chief reason for and the affect of modulation ceased to exist with the vanishing of any audible distinction among the keys. Composers tried to make up the difference by orchestral coloring and increased brilliance. At this time the old violins were rebuilt to increase their volume, and the stronger Tourte bow was invented. Orchestration appeared as a major element in the art of music.

4

CHROMATICISM

The sound clash of dissonance goes far back in music: the sistrum; the pipe with two reeds tuned slightly apart for brilliance; the *acciaccatura*, a tone outside the harmony which is played with the tone or chord and at once released; the chromatic slide or scale as an embellishment; the dissonant *appoggiatura* which delays the resolution of the harmony.

Chromaticism results from the beating of dissonant interval relations, the same beats a piano tuner counts when tuning the dissonant intervals of equal temperament on a piano. During the seventeenth century, as the vertical relationship of harmony was emphasized, composers began notating chromatic clashes which were no longer linear and mild as in the *Chromatic Fantasy* by Sweelinck but inserted in the chord for increased brilliance, by lines indicating where the chromatic tones are to be added as acciaccaturas, according to the practice of d'Anglebert and François Couperin. In the more improvisatory white-note Italian music, chromatic embellishments were sprinkled like pepper by the player to his taste. The *Sarabande* of J. S. Bach's Sixth Partita follows the French practice; his *Chromatic Fantasy* expounds the Italian practice. Bach also wrote out many passages which are too decisive to be left for improvisation. Bach's chromatic harmony, no longer applied as an embellishment but instead integral to the composition, gave the revolutionary impetus that in the course of the nineteenth century would break up and eventually destroy the harmonic system. Mozart discovered the force of chromaticism at the full of his maturity; Beethoven knew it early and reinstated it in more drastic style in his later music.

In this regard Chopin learned from both Bachs. His harmonic innovation consisted in giving to the dissonant acciaccatura an equal notation and harmonic right. Seconds, sevenths, and ninths were now welcome not merely for their clash of dissonance but as extensions of formal harmony. Here was the "new music" of the nineteenth century.

Liszt and Wagner, borrowing from Chopin, extended the chromatic medium at some cost to its extraharmonic integrity. But Chopin clung to his strict basses, even while inserting extraharmonic "wrong notes," which his editors afterwards corrected. Liszt abandoned the strict bass whenever it pleased him to do so, seeking by the increased brilliance of slightly clashing dissonances to make up the loss of modulatory color; he inaugurated the extratonal coloristic style which is called *impressionism*, to be followed in this direction by Debussy, Ravel, and Bartók. Wagner took over the expanded harmony of Chopin, the orchestration of Berlioz, and the extratonal freedom of Liszt; when reduced by transcription for piano his harmony sustains his music less well than Chopin's. A surge of instrumentally voiced, chromatically oriented melodic counterpoint tending to dissonant polyphony made the vertical relationship the weakest link, soon to be swept away by the shifting tonality of tone-centers.

Chopin saw that the contrapuntal harmony of Bach and Mozart sufficed for their music, that Berlioz's weak counterpoint and Liszt's impressionism did not suffice. Chopin believed that the orchestral component had already become too great in Beethoven's piano sonatas. The majority of Chopin's contemporaries, among them Mendelssohn and Schumann, slackened their counterpoint without materially improving their orchestration.

Chromaticism, which had been formerly an extraharmonic device within the key-coloration of meantone, took on in Beethoven's composing a more decisive role, until in his later compositions the brilliance and clash of dissonances came to seem, as they are still felt to be, the ultimate musical embodiment of spiritual drama. In Beethoven's last works the chromatic acciaccaturas and shakes become extended trills, powerful sustaining members of the enlarged harmonic structure. Beethoven's music did not need orchestral coloring like that of Berlioz, because chromatic contrast and brilliance were built into his harmony and became its final means.

To say that chromaticism increased to make up the loss of meantone key-coloration will not suffice, though it is the most pertinent generalization concerning the musical developments of this period. The revolutionary increase of contrapuntal chromaticism within the conservative formality of the music by J. S. Bach broke through the harmonic boundaries of meantone. The implications of Bach's chromaticism exceeded any theoretically consonant formula, either in well-tempered or in equal temperament. The last compositions by Beethoven carry forward these chromatic implications to an extreme which was not widely accepted, outside a coterie of skilled admirers, until the twentieth century. Chopin's chromaticism, although it went less far than that of Bach or Beethoven, prepared the public ear to receive, after three-quarters of a century, the full impact of their art.

5

HARMONY

Although the increase of chromaticism seems to be, in retrospect, the main line of musical development between 1750 and 1900, few musicians during that period would have thought so. Throughout the entire three hundred years of the Harmonic Era, melody and accompaniment remained the principal style of composition, and in harmony consonance kept priority over dissonance.

The tradition of consonance was established, especially in Italian music, during the high polyphonic period of just intonation, but the rules applied to concordance rather than to relative degrees of consonance and dissonance. When tuning changed to meantone, concordance survived only at the octave and major third, the other intervals of the scale being discordant. Dissonance brought into music, as at an earlier time perspective had brought into painting, a new possibility of sharp tonal contrast, a new sense of tonal relationship in depth, and an unprecedented awareness of tonal drama. From these eventually emerged the great textural and structural forms, the tensions and sustaining levels of a steadily enlarging classical music.

🏵 Harmony, like every term in music, includes wide, imprecise, and contradictory meanings. It is, essentially, the vertical relationship of tones simultaneously sounded. In traditional usage, harmony distinguishes those vertical relationships which observe certain agreed rules or technical conventions. For horizontal, linear, or melodic harmony there is no distinguishing term. I use "melodic or horizontal consistency." The distinction becomes quite evident whenever a composer tries to "harmonize" by conventional procedures a genuine folk melody. The twelve-tone row is a horizontal melodic consistency twisted in vertical relationships which are derived from the twelve-tone consistency of the row. A row of any number of notes can have an equally valid horizontal consistency.

Italian musical theorists took as their model the concordant polyphonic counterpoint of Palestrina. In *polyphony* the vertical harmonic relationship is subordinated to the polyphonic distinction of voices. In truly *harmonic* music the vertical relationship predominates. *Counterpoint* is an adjustment, among parts or voices, of the horizontal and vertical relationships, the balancing of melody and chord.

The formal Palestrinian counterpoint, little changed by translation into meantone and more recently into equal temperament, is still taught as conscientiously as the Greek plane geometry of Euclid. This is the counterpoint Beethoven did not have time to study and Schubert regretted that he had not learned. In practice, the rules of formal counterpoint were progressively rationalized to take care of harmonic events and provide for dissonant relationships which Palestrina's art had no reason to anticipate.

Composers accepted the priority of consonance over dissonance, with whatever practical modifications they felt to be unavoidable in their own usage, as the art of music. They seldom argued that the less dissonant relationships were not consonances, though they took care to avoid the more severe dissonances or discords which were called "the Wolf." Even those composers who explored the possibilities of unusual meantone coloration in extreme keys and unusual accords, like J. S. Bach and Domenico Scarlatti, or contributed to establishing the contrary line of chromatic dissonance, took pains to begin and end in acceptable harmonic consonance, though they might, after the manner of old Bach, render the consequences harmonically ambiguous. With Haydn and still more with Beethoven the temporary ambiguity of harmony and key became a part of the compositional humor and drama, the listener having sometimes to be helped home by the aid of several decisively reiterated tonics at the end. Such subversive skill and knowledge were reserved to a few composers. After Beethoven's death, melody and accompaniment, still in relatively simple consonant relationships, remained predominant.

Only in one important relationship had the tradition altered. The principle of *thoroughbass,* the clear and firm relationship between the harmonic structure of a chord and its bass, had been gradually giving way to the principle of *inversion,* in which the relationship of harmony, chord, and bass is no longer firm and clear. It became acceptable to establish a harmony independent of its bass and thereafter to move the bass as if in constant pursuit of the changing harmony.

In this way a general theory of *tonality* replaced the principle of thoroughbass. In tonality every tone is related, directly or indirectly, to a tonic rather than to the tone which serves to provide the temporary bass of the passage. The key-signature no longer establishes the prevailing tonality of a composition but may be constantly changed to confirm the temporary tonality of a passage or even dispensed with, the harmonic function altering with the change of tone which serves it, for grammatical and syntactic convenience, as a bass. This is the Wagnerian harmony, later borrowed and adapted to his own idiom by Debussy.

This tone-centered harmony became general and commonplace in twentieth century music. It is only a step in practice, but an important step, short of outright atonality. Conservative composers and musical analysts cling to it, as if to musical sanity. Hindemith, for example, in *A Composer's World,* asserts that tonality has become as fundamental to Western music as gravitational attraction to existence on the earth and proceeds immediately to ridicule the possibility that any "atonal" music can escape the "gravitational attraction of tonality." He goes on to explain that "atonal music disturbs the customer's feeling of gravitational attraction by combining so many different forms of attraction that his sense of location cannot adjust itself fast enough. So-called atonal music," he insists, "music which pretends to work without acknowledging the relationship of harmonies to tonics . . . cannot satisfy our desire for gravitational orientation. . . . Spatial dizziness is the result. . . . The innocent onlooker feels his inside turned into a pretzel-shaped distortion."[1] This is polemic, not criticism.

Modulation, which had its rationale in the distinguishably unlike affect of each meantone key, continued during the nineteenth century to be practised as a structural device, the variety of color being supplied now by the addition of chromatic tones, by enlarged orchestration with increasing differentiation of instrumental voices, and by harmonic impressionism or tonality without a strict bass. Harmonic theory argued against but belatedly rationalized, accepted, and soon took for granted these reaches of compositional proficiency beyond acoustical clarity into acoustically compromised dissonance. The final elaboration of these expanding chromatic devices occurred in the compositions by Richard Strauss and the early works by Arnold Schoenberg, where the relationship of the passage with its bass can still be discerned and rationalized, though the music proceeds as if in chromatic and melodic independence of any key. Strauss preferred a chromatic harmony interlaced by recognizable melodies; Schoenberg preferred a polyphony of constant melodic variation laced by chromatic harmony.

In Schoenberg's totally melodious First Quartet the key is D minor, but the texture is in fact dissonant polyphony. The harmony is from Wagner, the counterpoint out of Brahms—"Too thick!" Schoenberg said to me. "Too thick, like Brahms!"—the form is the first-movement form of Liszt's B minor Sonata, and one of the two expositions exactly follows the exposition of Beethoven's Third Symphony. The Quartet is an eclectic masterpiece comprising the full range of nineteenth century techniques. (This brief analysis of the First Quartet came from a taped talk by Schoenberg made for a program which he could not attend because of bad health. I have been unable to trace the original, and there was no copy of it in the Schoenberg library.)

As harmony began disintegrating towards incomprehensibility —that is, a condition in which nobody could understand what was happening until he studied it in score—composers tried to offset the harmonic difficulty by winding through the music some little tune or heroic motif that the listener could hang on to. The *Tristan* Prelude might seem harmonically mysterious, but once anyone has the hang of the tunes he needn't worry about it. In the third, or slow, section of his First Quartet, Schoenberg has wound his art around a little motif, a very beautiful one but so disguised by continual variation that few listeners recognize that this motif is also, note for note, one of the "Deep Southern folk tunes" of George Gershwin's opera, *Porgy and Bess,* written some thirty years later, the song "Bess, you is my woman now." You will also find anticipation of the same melody in earlier Gershwin (*An American in Paris*).

The rationalizations holding together these contradictory developments in one workable system are still being taught today in terms of the priority of consonance, while the trained ear has long since made the adjustment to receive as consonances harmonic relations that earlier composers would have dismissed as screaming discords. "The Wolf" of meantone has become the commonplace of twentieth century harmony.

Therefore, as Arnold Schoenberg eventually realized, it became necessary to emancipate the dissonance.

6

THE EMANCIPATION OF
THE DISSONANCE

The most fundamental insight for the subsequent course of twentieth century music is what Arnold Schoenberg, who had it, called "the emancipation of the dissonance."

Schoenberg said late in life that there had been at least a half-dozen composers besides himself who might have recognized and formulated this insight; he had always been astonished that none did so. Brahms, Debussy, Mahler, Strauss, or Scriabin, even Reger, might have done it. Charles Ives emancipated the dissonance in practice before Schoenberg but did not formulate it as a principle. If he had, no one would have heard him.

The emancipation of the dissonance consists in the recognition that the system of twenty-four major and minor diatonic keys, which had seemed to govern all music during the eighteenth and nineteenth centuries, and which had become in the art of J. S. Bach and Handel, Beethoven and Berlioz, a part of the esthetic firmament, had been supplanted by a single key of the twelve chromatic tones. The effect was to widen the field of esthetically acceptable dissonance to include, by implication, any possible melodic or harmonic combinations of the twelve tones.

During the harmonic period, consonance had been defined as the simple relationship of tones within a key and dissonance as the more complex relationships. Musical drama proceeded from the normal or agreeable relationships to the more extreme or less agreeable relationships and then returned whence it began. With the emancipation of the dissonance, these contrasts ceased to exist by relationship to an established system of keys and became more strictly acoustical, existing that is to say only in relation to one another. Schoenberg saw eventually that the twelve tones could exist in this new understanding only as twelve exactly placed sounds undifferentiated by key.

Afterwards, especially in his later years, it pleased Schoenberg to play with this double relationship by writing atonally while moving in and out of strict tonality, as if to show his critics how easily he could slip in and out of what they believed to be a musical straitjacket. Other critics then assailed him no less fiercely for "betraying" the new, liberated art of music he had established and validated. These critical "innovators," as they thought themselves, were still operating under the always temporary belief that there is a right way and a wrong way of composing music. Some hold that the right way is the way of tradition, and these unceasingly quarrel with those others who hold that the right way is the way of a particular innovation. Schoenberg, who thought any system of composing a poor substitute for the creative inspiration of his art, held both critical attitudes in equal disdain. His critics thereupon made fun of his belief in inspiration.

It had become evident to Schoenberg that the means of imparting order to chromatic musical relationships lay in the chromatic relationship itself and not in any continually more strained system of technical rationalizations between twelve-tone, single-key chromaticism and seven-tone, twenty-four-key diatonicism. Once this recognition had been creatively established—and the completion of his Quintet for Winds, Third String Quartet, Suite for Seven Instruments, Variations for Orchestra, and *Moses and Aron* left no doubt of that fact—there was no reason why a composer should not compose in strict diatonic key-relationship when it pleased him to do so, or in other variants of either system or both together, as such composers as Igor Stravinsky and Lou Harrison have since that time creatively demonstrated, adapting one's mastery of both systems according to one's own creative inspiration. Schoenberg had early done this in his canon for voices, *The Parting of the Ways*. Alban Berg demonstrated the same truth on a larger scale in his Violin Concerto. Many composers today use atonality independently of either method.

The emancipation of the dissonance did not outlaw diatonic harmony, or nontonal percussion, or pentatonicism, or the use of microtones, or any combination of them as creative means. It did no more and pretended to do no more than to free formal composition from any claims of key-relationship and to render it independent. As such and for that reason it could not be "betrayed."

By the same understanding, to insist that Stravinsky "betrayed" his art by including in it, however belatedly, what he discovered to be useful for himself in the art of Schoenberg is a critical absurdity.

Around atonality great battles of theoretical verbiage were fought, the dust and clangor of the warfare rather obscuring than clarifying the truth of the initial insight. The detractors argued that the human ear and the mind's capacity of musical apprehension, while capable of being stretched to any chromatic extreme of diatonicism, could not find order in an atonal music which excluded relationship to the diatonic keys. As usual, the argument centered more around terminology than upon what was able to be heard. The longest ears did the least listening.

Thus, during the first period of atonality, a time-lag occurred, while the new way of musical thinking gathered force against the resistance of all who would not accept it.

❁ Schoenberg resented and rejected the hostile term "atonality," saying that his music is composed of tones and therefore "tonal." But *atonality* is at least as meaningful as *cubism* in painting—a term originating in Matisse's disdainful *"les petits cubes"*—and more so than *Fauvism*—*"les Fauves,"* the wild beasts—pitched at, among others, Matisse. I shall use the term *atonal* without hostility and for no debatable precision but for what it signifies, in period, style, idiom, concerning which there is little doubt.

7

AN INTRODUCTION TO
ARNOLD SCHOENBERG

For some time Schoenberg's ability to create convincing atonal music went beyond his ability to explain simply what he was doing and why it was necessary. As conservative by nature as J. S. Bach but with an amateur innocence which Bach did not have, Schoenberg composed his new radical insights, at first tentatively and then with increasing assurance, as inescapable musical developments and tried afterwards to make clear what he was doing. In the course of the long argument the situation was reversed, and the explanations came to be taken as if they had been rules governing the composition of the music which preceded them. Though Schoenberg may have been sometimes confused by the chaos of miscomprehension and horrified rejection he had innocently but not unwittingly provoked, he never deceived himself by equating his explanatory handiwork with the finality of his composition.

When in later years despair on the surface seemed to overwhelm him, farther down the spiritual waters moved untroubled. The great sanity of his humor continued to break through his unrest. "Uncle Arnold played on the floor with us, like a child," Webern's elder daughter, Amalie Waller, said of her childhood. "We could not respect him, but we loved him the best." Many years afterwards, in Los Angeles, Schoenberg carried on a long correspondence, entirely of word-play, with the young son of composer Gerald Strang. Reminiscences of Schoenberg's humor abound among those who attended his classes and university lectures. Like a true comedian he could fall from wit to melancholy, or from melancholy to wit, in a moment, and one could never be sure when in despair he might not be laughing. His acceptance of an award of membership in the National Institute of Arts and Letters, accorded him at age seventy-three, is bitter as Timon, with a fighting swagger of laughter which shows him no misanthrope. "Personally I had the feeling as if I had fallen into an ocean of boiling water. . . . I have perhaps only one merit: I never gave up. But how could I give up in the middle of an ocean? . . . The credit must be given to my opponents. They were the ones who really helped me."[1] And in the letter of thanks to those who sent him their good wishes for his seventy-fifth birthday: "Once, when serving in the Austrian army, I was asked whether I was really the composer A. S. 'One had to be it,' I said, 'and nobody wanted to be, so I volunteered.' "[2] It was this humor which enabled him to follow biting criticism with forgiveness— "for he had," as Stravinsky wrote of him, "an exceptionally forgiving nature"—and to rise again out of an extremity of defeat. His humor opened to him regions of pure art-play closed to the self-seeking artist, which exceed the accepted meaning, and of course the derogatory meaning, usually applied to what he spoke of as "art for the sake of art alone." It is an art of spiritual innocence, as positive as sometimes impractical, when the play of mind, in lightness or after severe labor, even in defeat, smiles at itself, needing no other reassurance.

Never an easy man, perching in conversation at the front of his chair as if for flight, more open in discussion than in pronouncement, he loved greatly and was greatly beloved. During his first years in Los Angeles he wrote music plainly meant to give pleasure to performer and listener, his Suite for String Orchestra, his Violin and Piano Concertos, his arrangement of the Brahms Piano Quartet in G minor as a symphony, and later his Variations for Organ and for Band. All were repulsed, by performers and public, yet once more he set to work. In his last public appearance the affection of a large audience at last went out to him, but his music was still seldom played. Even today, when the authority of his mind and art circles the earth, the Los Angeles Philharmonic has not often programmed his music. In 1965, Stravinsky wrote: "Los Angeles . . . chose to baptize its new [Music] Center with the beer of Strauss's *Fanfare* and Respighi's *Feste Romane*. . . . To play Respighi instead of Schoenberg at the debut of a Los Angeles Music Center would be comparable to the unveiling of a bust of Lysenko rather than Einstein at the opening of a museum of science at Princeton. . . ."[3]

Like a more intelligent Siegfried or Parsifal, Schoenberg struggled to overcome impediments and to resist temptations not of his own making. As a conservative of the Germanic musical tradition, he believed that the way he had come inhered in that tradition and that the choices he must continue to make should no less decisively spring from that tradition. Apart from some preliminary borrowing from Liszt and a sidelong but clarifying glance at Debussy as an offset to Brahms, he proceeded into the future by radical analysis of the great composers of the Germanic past, seeking in them precedent and authority for the creative actions he felt called on to perform.

During the nineteenth century the Germanic musicians had bemused themselves by a pseudoreligious, pseudophilosophic sentimentality, believing that God spoke through the tragic utterance of Beethoven and the fallible human heart through Schubert, wherefore Schubert must be less than Beethoven; that Mozart, like the builders of rococo churches, was deficient in spirituality and lacked emotion; that J. S. Bach was the true source of correct contrapuntal workmanship but not tragic, lacking the romantic lightning-thrust of God.

These were never general propositions in the way that I have stated them, and it is doubtful that those who took them for granted would have stated them so baldly. Nevertheless, having disposed of the greater men hierarchically, one could dispose of theoretical questions analytically, always provided that one subordinated them to the hierarchic sentiment. Wagner's unquestionably German sensibility and the heroic scale of his somewhat hysterical epics made up for his Lisztian deviations, but the pure-German Brahms inherited the romantic mantle of the classically inspired, tragic Beethoven.

A very considerable residue of this religio-philosphical-nationalist Germanic sentiment survives to confuse musical understanding and criticism to the present day. There are still deeply earnest interpreters of musical meaning who declare that every figure of notes in a composition by Beethoven carries an exact significance

—as other persons fervently believe that the plays attributed to Shakespeare were written as a cover for concealed messages in code.

Schoenberg never entirely escaped the Germanic rhetoric or the passionate emotional irrationality of Wagner, which he renewed and concentrated in the instrumental tone poem *Transfigured Night,* the song cycle *Gurrelieder,* and the solo opera *Erwartung.* In later years he dismissed its verbalized equivalent as "poetry," putting such language outside the scope of responsible musical commentary, even to the extent of removing many beautiful passages from the text of his own *Harmonielehre (Theory of Harmony)* when, thirty-seven years after the first publication, it was translated into English. Portions of this excluded text in English appear in the early biography of Schoenberg by Egon Wellesz.

Like many Viennese intellectuals of this period, including Sigmund Freud, Schoenberg had a strong sense of the significance of word-play; he came under the spell of numerology; word relationships and numbers influenced his concepts. There was also in him, as among the Viennese Jews of that period who could not aspire to official recognition without becoming Roman Catholics, a powerful urge to an all-reconciling mysticism, which made the most of being a Jew, a Christian, and a German. There was also the darker alternative conception, in Mahler's contrary statement: "I am three times homeless: a native of Bohemia in Austria; an Austrian among Germans; a Jew throughout the whole world." The transcendency of Jewish spirituality in a Catholic culture, of Austrian Germanic culture in the midst of aggressive German nationalism, and therefore of race, spirituality, and ethos isolated by and against the mankind these would bless, bound them in tragic difference. Therefore Schoenberg revered the mind and art of Gustav Mahler, to whom he dedicated his *Harmonielehre.* He painted Mahler's funeral and composed the sixth of his *Six Little Piano Pieces,* opus 19, in the atmosphere of that event.

A vigorous and accomplished painter and draftsman, Schoenberg exhibited with the "Blue Rider" group in Vienna. Wassily Kandinsky, a leading painter of the group, discriminatively praised him. Over half of Schoenberg's paintings, drawings, and sketches are self-portraits, including parodies and grotesques, showing similar preoccupations as his music but less care for detailed skill. A painter's self-portrait is at the best a debate of the viewer with his image; this is noticeably true of Schoenberg's self-portraits. Whether he is painting his bald pate dropping below the edge of the canvas in the manner of a sunset—"the bald pate of Cassander" from the yet-to-be-written *Pierrot Lunaire*— or his face upturned in agonizing appeal, he does not flatter his appearance.

In these ways and for these reasons Schoenberg's creative life and work took on the form of a debate. His art became, in Stravinsky's eloquent description, "the passionate development of the argument," directed by inspiration but controlled by craftsmanship. Independent musical analysis drew him from Beethoven to Mozart, from the inspired rhetoric of Wagner to the detailed, intrinsic workmanship of Brahms—in his later years to admiring appreciation of the textural mastery in the last operas by Verdi.

The debate showed itself as an alternation of stylistic methods: the one aspect a romantic, inspired declamation, sentimental, prophetic, or mystical according to the authority of its substance; the other an almost note-by-note detailed analytic mosaic that foresaw the extensible complexity of any pattern of intervals. *Transfigured Night, Peace on Earth, Die glückliche Hand, Moses and Aron, A Survivor from Warsaw, De Profundis* debate truth between soul and body, war and peace, inspiration and reason, the absolute and the temporal, destruction and survival, man and God. Schoenberg's idiom was immediate, passionate; the musical ordering, his medium, objective as fugue.

Schoenberg was as natural a melodist as Schubert, but he required of melody the capability to combine with itself polyphonically, like the melodies of J. S. Bach, and an analytical clarity capable of the contrapuntal freedom with economy of Mozart. Schoenberg was from the start, not less in his early music than in his much later tone-row compositions, a polyphonist, for whom each note, in melody or accompaniment, should be ideally of equal significance and weight. The historical model of such composition is the *Art of Fugue,* the unfinished last composition by J. S. Bach.

Therefore in the progression of his music Schoenberg's thought reached backward to a period before the nineteenth century, though he never abandoned the Wagnerian rhetoric and the intrinsic, detailed workmanship of Brahms.

Schoenberg declared that he practised composition every day. He believed that the composer's art does not originate in or from his technical resources; his technique is simply a device for getting the work done as he wants it. When the hidden drive of his esthetic consistency appears to violate the stylistic formalities to which he is accustomed, a composer should trust himself to discover the new stylistic means his art requires.

His method of composition was not "experimental" so much as "exploratory." He commenced writing a new work by extending his daily practice of composition. He did not "have something to say" and put that into music. The composition grew, like a personal letter—not a business letter which is written to a formula— by a merging of idea and means. The idea was not necessarily a "subject"; it might be no more than an urgency, a feeling of command to write. All of us have this experience and think it no miracle, when we write a letter to a friend. If we write well, the esthetic consistency or content of the letter determines its exact form; we know how to begin and where to end.

With Schoenberg the incentive was often a poem, which he composed as a song. The sense of the words would carry him forward in search of the best means. He would explore the great variety of traditional devices, and at the point where none of these proved serviceable he would go beyond them. He did not go experimentally outside them; this experimental method was more natural to Schoenberg's American contemporaries, Ives, Ruggles, Varèse, Cowell, who did not share his reverence for tradition. Schoenberg's most unusual devices grow out of the Germanic tradition which he cherished; they do not violate that tradition but extend it.

8

IDIOM, CONTENT, STYLE

"What I give is the morphology of the use of an expression. I show that it has kinds of uses of which you had not dreamed. In philosophy one feels forced to look at a concept in a certain way. What I do is to suggest, or even invent, other ways of looking at it. I suggest possibilities of which you had not previously thought. You thought there was one possibility, or only two at most. But I made you think of others. Furthermore, I made you see that it was absurd to expect the concept to conform to those narrow possibilities. Thus your mental cramp is relieved, and you are free to look around the field of use of the expression and to describe the different kinds of uses of it."—Ludwig Wittgenstein[1]

Theorists, musicologists, and critics have tried many ways to explain the emergence of a distinctively new music around the start of the twentieth century; these theories usually fail by disregarding the fact that the evolution of music occurred—and still occurs—as an auditory, not a harmonic, phenomenon. Since we are now passed out of the Harmonic Era, the rules of harmony no longer apply to explain what is now happening. One may doubt that these rules furnished a satisfactory explanation even during the Harmonic Era.

The fallacy is in the belief that a composer selects grammatical or syntactical devices as a means of conveying "emotion," or his "message," or whatever he is presumed to wish to "express." Such devices exist and always have existed in any art in great profusion; the good maker uses them to his convenience but does not rely on them. Seventeenth and eighteenth century music was put together of conventional figures; we value a composer of this period not because he made his art a rhetoric of these figures but because he bent these figures to his individual purpose, so that hearing his music today we are scarcely aware of them.

The gap between a composer's idiomatic means and what he is presumed to wish to say can be bridged after the event, but a good composer does not bridge it, because for him no gap exists. What he wishes to say is what he does say in the idiom in which he says it. His early idiom, however derivative, will become his own and speak with his own voice.

The composer who wishes to follow tradition borrows conventional means to say what has been already said—and often better said—by others, because this sounds to him like music. Though he may explore and even invent new and original devices, the danger is that he will fail to develop his own idiom, the unmistakable assurance of his own voice and manner of speech. It is this manner of speech, this unmistakable idiom, that we signify in calling it by the composer's name: Palestrina, Beethoven, Verdi, Debussy.

Forms, devices, techniques are useful as designs or containers which set bounds to the natural expansiveness of the idiom. Whether accepted rigidly as patterns or permitted to shape themselves flexibly, these do not create the idiom; it penetrates, permeates, and adapts them.

The composer who wishes to be original will either borrow new means which seem to be the originality of his day or else try to invent similar means to convey or express what he believes he has in mind. The danger is that he will try to bridge the gap by the sound of his own voice as explainer: This is how I have done what I have done for this reason. Each work becomes a separate effort to possess rather than inhabit.

The attempt to bridge by words the gap between idea and means should be distinguished from the more fruitful theoretical report of what has been learned as a result of creative exploration.

A composer's idiom is his own manner of speaking as creative thinker, original as the sound of his own voice. His content is his esthetic consistency, saying what he has to say. A composer is not uniformly aware of the forces which make him what he is; they are a part of him. The consistency he must achieve if he is to become a composer, instead of a practitioner of his art, will be under his control exactly to the degree that he is able to direct his intuitive conditioning to its creative purpose. "One singular deception," says C. S. Peirce, ". . . which often occurs, is to mistake the sensation produced by our own unclearness of thought for a character of the object we are thinking."[2] The consistency, as it is achieved, matures within the composer as his content, what he has to say. The subject, not yet married to content, grows within the composer as an irritant, putting him to work; his manner of disposing of it will be his style for that work or that period. A true composer has no way of knowing whether what he does will be acceptable or great, and he will falsify himself exactly in the degree that he directs his attention to that purpose. He can only believe that what he does is right; success or failure cannot swerve him. Style follows content, the outward sign of the composer's growing inner consistency; the achieved consistency of the artist extrudes the idiomatic consistency of his style. Together they evolve.

Igor Stravinsky said to me of his *Three Songs by William Shakespeare,* in which he epitomized his discovery of Webern's music: "A good composer does not imitate; he steals." He does not display what he possesses; he secretes it in the inner esthetic consistency (his content), which extrudes it in the idiomatic consistency of his style. Hearing a work by a composer whom one does not immediately identify, one will sometimes detect passages which, starting in commonplace, are transformed by idiomatic decisiveness to convey the power of the mind that has converted them. Occasionally one can detect the source, as when Beethoven "swipes" from Clementi or Cherubini.

Some writers like to believe that the maker imposes his will upon the medium; it would be more true to say that he discovers his will within the medium, his will being the release of his content, responding to a subject, into style. There is finally the inspired, considered, yet often extrarational tinkering by which the content, the true maker, shapes, shifts, fits, pieces, works, and rejects the stylistic product to discover its unique individuality. At every stage of the process, chance, accident, the circumstantial envelopment of the sensuous mind impinging upon fact and abstract modify the style by unanticipated events. His art is not what an artist means to do but what he does, a type of secular revelation—it may expose the artist or become him—by which the creative mind learns more than its audience.

In every culture and period of art the method of composition is often the real subject. An external subject becomes significant as it is subsumed within the method of composition, the true subject, which is content ever pressing to be shaped in style. The "urgency" of art has little to do with any attachment to whatever narrative, melodic, referential, technical, or explicatory thread of subject matter is run through the design. The urgency is the continuous discovery of the composer's content within the abstract-factual pattern of cross-references of which distinctively in each particular work he has reshaped his style. Urgency in art occurs when content, having found the means to concentrate into style, thereby makes imperative every unexpected happening it enforces within the style. These are not chance occurrences but the central and directing eventualities of art. Ability to recognize these eventualities and accept them, putting aside the "correct," or reasonable, or explicatory alternatives, is the distinction of what we call genius. Words or any customary symbols will not usually tell what to look for; that is why works and lives of this quality are customarily vulgarized.

The truly skilled listener will seek to discern such occurrences as hints of the esthetic individuality which produces them; he will learn not to confuse these "errors," "accidents," "wrong notes," and "wrong ways," these "failures" of the composer to follow expected paths, with the more commonplace recognitions which are the mark of talent in his time. A professional critic should be particularly careful about this. When he discerns a consistency of deviation in such matters, he will begin to recognize the esthetic consistency which requires them; and in doing so he will serve as "posterity" to the better, though still unproved, creative achievements of his lifetime. But he must hear these things first: he will be able to "hear" by looking at the score only those combinations the sound of which his mind is able to anticipate; and so he may be led astray by slightly differentiated commonplace. He listens for what he expects instead of attending to what he could not expect and concentrating on that. A polished style will attract, unexpected idiomatic individuality repel him. For these reasons the accustomed listener, sophisticate, dilettante, snob, professional critic, is not usually among the first to recognize with admiration the individuality of a genuinely creative style. These more than any others will reject and fight it, because their habituated sensibilities cannot remain insensitive to it. Obvious originality is seldom more than slightly differentiated commonplace; one should guard against being deceived by it. Fear of the unknown is an important psychological factor; its effects should be noted and discounted in apprehending our reactions to unfamiliar surroundings, forms, habits, presences, events, works of art.

When Igor Stravinsky listens to a work he does not know well, you will see him with the score open before him, a magnifying glass ready to his hand; an unfamiliar chord or passage stops him; he takes up the magnifying glass and studies what has happened, then, satisfied, continues following along the page.

Any would-be artist may have the "makings" but not the achieved content. The best way to estimate the difference is to go around a large chronological exhibition of paintings by one artist, where one can study the artist's evolutionary growth by immediate comparison: one begins with ideas, styles, capacities, potentialities; one watches these converge, then fuse in a pervasive style, reflecting an individual content (not a subject). This content is what is being shaped, occasionally hammered, into style.

New words, new phrasings, novel subjects, changes of grammatical or syntactical device are of no more than incidental importance for the shaping of a content into style. The adventure of an artist's lifetime is in discovering his content as an abstract self, excluding false relationships which seductively encroach upon it and more or less purely transfiguring this content into shapes of his own style. If his abstract self fits him too easily, he will settle in it comfortably, lacking the subjective irritation which drives the creator: by this one can read the Book of Job as a metaphor of the creative spirit. The adventure also retrospectively influences the content, making it, paradoxically, more inclusive and more determinate. Whether the composer borrows forms by professing the mode of *Ulysses* by James Joyce, or inspiration by following figures in the paper, he will either craft his content towards the determining event of form or he will fail. However "indeterminate" the form, it is determinate within the "rules of the game" which produce it—a very important characteristic in regard to much composition of the present decade. Temporary, immediate success may prove a real failure, because the composer has chosen the contemporarily adventitious.

Whatever vagaries may beset the artist's living, his attitudes, his peculiarities, his moral or financial flaws or failures, his inability to think in good order outside his medium, do not essentially block his content; they do influence and may warp or block the flowing of content into style. Having achieved his content, the artist may never let down the continuing effort to project his content into style; otherwise he will parody himself. Thinking can precede or accompany or follow the pursuit of style, but an artist thinks of what he is doing as most of us do not. We think of what we are doing and what we should like to do and how to go about it and whether it is right or wrong, as well as of what others have done and are doing. We live in a creative confusion, but insofar as he has achieved a consistency of decision, a content, a true artist does not. Our confusion protects us from the decisive agony of concentration out of which flows the plastic material of art.

Content, as an individual consistency or mode, is derived from the common content and idiomatic consistency of the time, the tradition and the conventions of originality which distinguish the general thought and workmanship of the period. While the mind of the creative thinker is developing within this common content, his own consistency may assume new relationships, both positive and negative, contrary to the general understanding, opposed sometimes even to his own understanding of what is being thought about in his time. Projected into idiom and style, this unique consistency, though some may recognize it, seems to defy assimilation. Thus a time-lag results.

Concentrated in its idiom and divorced from the general derivative content of its time, the style of such a creator may seem for a long while unintelligible; yet at a farther distance it will be thought the style most characteristic of its period. It is far, Lord knows, from the wish of any genuinely creative mind to be not understood in its work, and for a time the work may remain hidden as if only the Lord knows what is in it. "Heifetz cannot play it. Nobody can play it," Schoenberg was mournfully boasting of his Violin Concerto soon after I first knew him. The violinist Jascha Heifetz emphasized the time-lag by performing at that time other new concertos, of a derivative vulgarity which did not show the performer to advantage or satisfy his audience.

One critic has set up a criterion that a composer whose work has not been popularly accepted within twenty-five years after his birth, death, coming of age, or some other date—it is immaterial—could not be a great one. When Mozart and Schubert died, few of their major compositions had been published; when Béla Bartók died, the bulk of his music was in print: each died in extreme poverty, and the money-making success of their creative effort began in each case after death. Worldwide appreciation of Beethoven's later compositions did not commence, outside a relatively small circle of admirers, until his music began to be recorded during the years 1925–1935; worldwide appreciation of Schoenberg's later compositions has commenced within the decade after his death, and the esoteric circle of his early admirers has expanded to include a majority of the world's composers.

Bach's *Saint Matthew Passion* lay secluded for a century, until Mendelssohn discovered and performed it; Bach's *Art of Fugue* and *Musical Offering* were first performed in 1927. Beethoven symphonies were not heard in Paris until 1828, the year after his death. Charles Ives's Second (*Concord*) Piano Sonata came to national attention in 1939, some twenty-seven years after it was written and eighteen years after publication; his Fourth Symphony was first heard completely some eleven years after his death and forty-nine years after he composed it: only now can one begin to anticipate the full weight of his influence.

Critics antagonistic to the creative activity of their lifetime continue to assert that Bach, Mozart, Beethoven, Berlioz, Brahms were popular composers while they were living, that by comparison Schoenberg, the mature Stravinsky, Ives, Bartók, and John Cage are without popular recognition, except in esoteric circles; this is an ignorant, when it is not a deliberate, misrepresentation.

Joseph Haydn was the most widely admired living composer of the classical era of European music; Igor Stravinsky has been the most widely admired living composer, without question, since the death of Debussy. Such admiration is not the final measure of a composer's authority or of the durability of his work, but it is one measure and it is ridiculous to deny it. After Schoenberg's death, the British magazine *Music and Letters* devoted an entire issue to statements by British composers dispraising him—a unique if a backhanded way of distinguishing a master from a bevy of his contemporaries who had not learned from him.

The roots of content are individual as the material is common; the subject is individual, the subject material common. "Failure to communicate," a fault critics customarily charge against any impressive work they fail to comprehend, may be the clue to a fresh content. Far from belonging exclusively to the composer or representing in isolation his inventiveness, the new content springs, vigorously or weakly, as weed, plant, or tree, out of an underlying esthetic responsiveness to new and still imperfectly realized conditioning forces. Such changes alter our relations with the cosmos.

To paraphrase a splendid sentence by J. Robert Oppenheimer: The adventures of art are adventures of content, involving discoveries of the inadequacy of our means of realizing nature, each time the modes by which our experience of nature is achieved become unfamiliar and strange.

> And so each venture
> Is a new beginning, a raid on the inarticulate
> With shabby equipment always deteriorating . . .
> —T. S. Eliot, "East Coker"

And the danger is to give up, to come down oneself into "the general mass of imprecision of feeling," the elegiac an excuse too late.

The artist tries to mediate among the modes of content and circumstance, with the wish, perhaps, to communicate, to convince, or to establish by this mediation a harmony (beauty), an apprehensible simplicity of relationship (texture, structure, form), or a concentration or diverse sequence of events to contemplate. The entertainment resulting from these adventures may be as slight as pleasure, as demanding as an exploration. If the means be the subject, the work of art deals with its innate problems, which are embedded in its content. When an external subject is overlaid upon this content, subject and all that deals with it in style become ambiguous. A great fuss can be made over any part of this.

The theory that art as beauty gives pleasure serves the dilettante as a presumed equivalent of the artist's delight in what he does. Pleasure and delight may both be wrongly based. The pleasure theory enables the dilettante to assert his liking and its causes as standards to oppose whatever he does not like because he has not learned to work with differently composed experience.

What gives immediate pleasure is our own tentative recognition of a type of artistic workmanship with which we have learned to agree. Thus many imitative and bad works please the habituated dilettante, while the permeating individuality of a new work of art throws him off and gives him no pleasure. Perception of a genuinely new relationship which is beauty begins with the creative mind; anyone can aspire to such perception, but to do so he must admit to attention many experiences which do not at first and may never please him. The majority of these experiences will fail ultimately and often at once; by opening himself, by himself working at the esthetic receiver's job, the viewer or listener develops in himself unanticipated capacity for discerning the "rights" and "wrongs" of the new experience.

The work of art does not change, only the capacity of the viewer or listener to receive and recompose it. The beauty exists, not in the object, but in the new, possibly complex relationship the object brings into being, which includes the receiver and which becomes beauty as the receiver takes his right part by learning how to recompose it. Beauty can also vanish when the receiver, realizing the limitations of the experience, wearies of it or rejects it.

❧ Let me quote here from "The Critical Function," a chapter of my earlier book, *An Amateur at the Keyboard:*

"Beauty consists in the relationships among events that occur in the presence of the human mind: through its sensibilities, which are passive; by its active ability to think. . . . Except through the attention of a human being, there is no beauty, though the elements of beauty may be present. Beauty is therefore also the result of spiritual attentiveness. We study, we train, we discipline ourselves to concentrate the attention beauty requires of us.

"No matter how good a performance or how great the composition, the listener must recognize and compose with *his* mind all that he is able to make of the opportunities that are given him. A few years ago only the exceptional listener could hear any work by Béla Bartók and make a composition of it. Today that is a common privilege.

"When an unknown composer places his wares before you, by means of a performance, it is you, not he, who must compose the composition. The performers may help or they may hinder you in doing so. . . .

". . . there is no such thing, in sound, as the absolute work itself apart from any performance There is only the remembered composition that each individual, in his own re-creative response, has tentatively composed and is able to call up by recollection. The score is only a design to be realized in performance. The critic, at least in part, criticizes his own re-creative capacity—himself."[3]

The great works of each period survive to become like facts of nature, representation that does not represent, explanation that does not need explaining, like the finger of God in Michelangelo's fresco reaching out towards Adam. Best approach them tentatively, in concentration, asking neither to be pleased nor to be entertained. Only then will the secular revelation offered to all men in their presence become sacred, free of dogma, yet like a liturgy a creative repository and symbolic representation of the human mind.

9

THE TWO HARMONIC TRADITIONS OF NINETEENTH CENTURY MUSIC

To comprehend what has been happening in Western European music since the sixteenth century, and more recently in the expansion of this tradition throughout the entire world, one needs to reconsider these events in terms of the entire field of sound rather than think of them, in the usual way, as the consequence of changes in harmony and notation. Thus we can approach the other musics of the world in a mutual field of reference, instead of continuing to think within our harmonic tradition as an isolate.

The nineteenth century was the period of the decline and disintegration of Western European harmony, which had attained its most complete formal expression during the eighteenth century. To say that harmony disintegrated does not imply that it "went to the bad" or that the compositions by nineteenth century composers were "inferior." Beethoven's later music had reached, by extraharmonic advance, a condition of harmonic disintegration at least equivalent to that of the more advanced music at the end of the century. The skills of polyphonic concordant harmony vanished during the sixteenth century quite precipitously, at the summit of achievement; to say this in no way detracts from the accomplishments of Vittoria, Palestrina, Byrd, Weelkes, Gesualdo, or Monteverdi.

Nineteenth century music was compounded of three distinct

sound systems, assembled in two distinct harmonic theories, which were rationalized as if the two were one.

The sound systems were: acoustically correct just intonation, the theoretical basis of formal counterpoint in concordant or consonant relationship; meantone, which retained correct intonation only at the octave and major third, the other intervals being unequal and more or less dissonant or discordant—the affective basis of key-distinction; and equal temperament, which retained correct intonation only at the octave, the other intervals being uniformly equal and discordant, as a result of which harmony, losing the acoustical basis and affect of key-relationship, evolved towards the unitary aggregate of single-key chromaticism.

The two harmonic theories may be designated most simply as the Italian and the Germanic.

In the Italian tradition of predominantly consonant vertical relationship, dissonance, whether as acciaccatura, ornament, or dramatic intensification, is applied as an embellishment, and modulation seldom travels far from the original key except to become established, with relative firmness, in another key. The resulting music, though it may be of great elegance, lacks tension and dramatic contrast; it fails conspicuously in the larger developments of sonata and symphony. It succeeds in opera, which consists for the most part of harmonically accompanied melody. The Italian tradition delays but requires resolution; the Germanic tradition makes much of the delay, preferring to imply resolution until chord or cadence nails it down.

The Germanic tradition is essentially dissonant, both horizontally and vertically. The melody breaks through into the accompaniment, and the harmony is continually being modified by changing vertical adjustments, which impart a continuous tension between the implications of unresolved harmony and the restraining influence of key. Acciaccatura, ornament, and dissonance are no longer applied as embellishment but become substantive with the melody; modulation becomes abstract drama, provoking a constant intensification towards climax; and the contrast of keys is no more meaningful than the transitions between contrasts. The Germanic tradition succeeds in sonata and symphony but less well in opera. Germanic opera since Mozart is essentially a dramatic symphony with voices.

Italian opera and Germanic opera are distinct, not because one is inferior to the other but because they embody contrary musical developments. The vocal traditions also are distinct: in Germanic tradition the voice must carry its part not merely against but amid the orchestra; in the Italian tradition the orchestra remains subservient to the voice. Throughout the nineteenth century the Italian vocal tradition retained its virtuosity of ornamentation and embellishment, which the growing Germanic taste was inclined to decry as artificial and superficial. This skill of elegant vocal display seemed to have become obsolete after the first decade of the twentieth century. Revival began in the later 1950s and continues to the present time in the singing of Maria Callas, Joan Sutherland, and Marilyn Horne—each of whom is no less capable of singing a major role in Germanic opera.

Accompanied song, a French and English tradition, and the Italian solo cantata kept throughout the eighteenth century the distinction between voice and instrument. The Germanic *lied*, arising in the early nineteenth century, quickly took on the character of the Germanic instrumental movement, the voice obbligato to the complex accompaniment. The melody kept its whole shape, or some variation of it, at each presentation. Following this design, the Schubert sonata and Wagnerian opera grew enormously extended; a similar plan produced the extraordinary lengths of the Bruckner and Mahler symphonies.

In the classic Germanic sonata and symphony, the subject ceases to be predominantly melodic and is transformed into an analytic theme or subject put together of short figures, capable of being taken apart and used separately or reassembled in distinctive melodies as the composer wished. A tune could be reduced to no more than its rhythm, and this rhythm might take on the harmonic body of another tune to produce new melody. The interchangeability of these analytic units resembles only superficially the interchangeability of whole motifs or melodies.

Many nineteenth century composers continued the habit of composing themes of short figures, but these figurative subjects are nonanalytic and retain their shape without analytic change.

The classic theme of Haydn and Beethoven is therefore distinct from the Wagnerian motif. Haydn composed, according to his purpose, in either Italian or Germanic idiom, but his usage tended increasingly to the Germanic. Beethoven, when occasionally he used the Italian idiom, for example in the Piano Sonata,

UNIVERSITY OF ILLINOIS MUSIC LIBRARY

opus 31:1, twisted it to his own complexity. J. S. Bach distinguished the Italian and the Germanic, as well as the French, styles of his period, but in use made them almost uniformly Germanic, setting under way a preference for dissonant ambiguity, which Beethoven in his later works made definite. Mozart moved with equal ease as an Italian or a German, capable of operatic melodies as harmonically clear and self-complete as any, and of analytic subjects which combine with the utmost flexibility into sonata or concerto. But the Wagnerian motif, though sometimes assuming the figurative or tuneful shape of an analytic subject, is in fact a nonanalytic melody, not always fully stated at each reappearance, the strands combining into polyphony less by harmonic than by instrumental distinction of parts.

A Rameau or Handel opera is almost continuously melodic, but the entire complexity of the work is in the voice or voices, the orchestra being almost entirely subordinate. A Wagnerian opera is no less melodic, but the complexity is symphonic, the voice seldom breaking free for a period of uninterrupted song. Until lately we had thought the Wagnerian the higher art, but the argument can be made that there is more good melody compressed into a Rameau opera than in an opera by Wagner, who merely repeats fewer melodies more forcefully and more often.

The French tradition vanished, like the British, though perhaps less noticeably, during the later eighteenth century. Between Rameau and Berlioz there is only Gossec. Berlioz was idiomatically weak German, from Gluck and Beethoven, but orchestrally the forger of the Wagnerian instrument. Chopin, Liszt, Gounod, Franck, Massenet, Saint-Saëns represent a new polyglot international tradition, which settling afterwards around the peripheral countries of Europe became nationalistic.

Even as it was losing prestige to Germanic music throughout Western Europe, the Italian tradition reappeared from Russia, where it had been uncritically domiciled for a century, to reconquer the popular appetite with the Tchaikovsky symphonies and the glamorous orchestral poems of "the Five" (Balakirev, Borodin, Cui, Mussorgsky, Rimsky-Korsakov—the first four amateurs).

Mussorgsky, an inspired amateur, filled out the Italian design with native Slavic melody, musically set conversational and declamatory Russian speech, and the clangor of bells, to create an art completely his own—so much so that, after his death, Rimsky-Korsakov softened the musical idiom to make it harmonically polite. It is not the harmony but the unique sounds of Mussorgsky's art that signify.

Over in France, Erik Satie, an anti-German like Mussorgsky, re-created and parodied simple Italianate harmony in such a way as to make it entirely individual and French. With Satie, and earlier in a few works by Chabrier, once admired but now nearly forgotten, the anti-Germanic revolt of twentieth century composition begins. A seldom popular, minority movement, it contributed to the American new music of the 1920s and the subsequent radicalism of John Cage.

A pupil of Rimsky-Korsakov, Igor Stravinsky adapted the Italian style and Slavic melody by adding to these whatever he could steal from the polyglot past of European music that was not Germanic, to become the most successful and popular composer of his lifetime; only after full maturity and again towards the end of his career accepting, first from Beethoven and finally from Schoenberg, the consequences of the Germanic chromaticism he had long avoided.

Technical criticism, having disparaged the work of Tchaikovsky for what it lacked of the Germanic, embraced the earlier work of Stravinsky for the same reason, but turned against him when his later works made clear that he had learned from Schoenberg. With these last works Stravinsky admitted the final dissolution of the Italian harmonic tradition.

The culminating victory of Germanic chromaticism was no less its dissolution. In the same decade when Stravinsky embraced the consequences of chromaticism, the Era of Harmony, with all its implications and directions, belatedly ended, already superseded by the new Era of Sound.

THE FIVE-PLUS-TWO IDIOMATIC
ORIGINS OF TWENTIETH
CENTURY MUSIC

PLUS A DIGRESSION ON THE AUDIENCE

Lines traced through history should be regarded skeptically, as one looks at an historic map, put together of information and misinformation, enforcing perhaps theological or political opinion, against the shorter-view accuracy of a mariner's charts. An inaccurate fact on a mariner's chart can sink a ship.

The lines are not facts; the accretion of facts without lines to direct them can be academically destructive. If the facts challenge the lines, the lines also challenge the facts. The most fruitful mythologies, from Plato to Freud, have come as a result of tracing lines through history. The seeming mythologies of Herodotus and Darwin have proved, after the accretion of new facts around them, to be surprisingly accurate.

". . . Planck once pointed out that whether a physical quantity is 'observable in principle' or whether a given question is meaningful in physics are not matters to be decided a priori. It depends entirely on the theory we adopt, for the theory shapes our instruments, our methods, our interpretations. We are not simply cameras or mirrors. It may be we can still save the notion of a line of demarcation between the observer and the thing observed; but, if so, at the line itself there is an uncertainty, an uncontrollable ripple, one might say, produced by the interaction of the seer and the seen. The new physics disenchants us as to the firmness and fixedness of substance." (*Let me point out the accuracy of that word "disenchants" in this scientific context. We are not so far as we had thought from sorcery and Merlin.*) " 'We no longer have absolute, completely determined entities, from which we can immediately read off the laws and to which we can attach them as their attributes.' " (*We are closer in sensibility to Heraclitus than to Comte.*) "The content of our empirical knowledge consists of no more than the 'totality of observations which we group together in definite orders . . . and which we can represent by theoretical laws.' Quantum mechanics does not deal with things whose laws we seek to discover; instead, from observation we constitute the things. Atomic physics deals with 'the nature and structure not of atoms but of the events which we perceive when observing the atom.' " (*The lines of observation accrete what we believe to be the facts.*) (James R. Newman: "Determinism and Indeterminism," from *Science and Sensibility.*[1] I have set my interspersed comments in italics to distinguish them from the quoted text.)

But a single fact correctly observed can alter entirely the consequences of our hypothetical lines. Such are the essential facts we should look for; the accumulation of factual data in a heap may accomplish no more than to seem to confirm an incorrectly observed premise or a false presupposition, that by being habitually restated is presumed to be a fact. Our schoolbook teaching of theory and history wallows in a morass of presumed facts.

In *An Amateur at the Keyboard* I wrote: "Five distinct streams of music mingle in the twentieth century keyboard art: the French, the Russian, the German, the inheritance of Liszt, and American experimentalism." Going beyond the keyboard art we discover two more, which did in some degree also influence keyboard music: the Oriental or Asiatic, and the Negro art of transformed borrowings which became *jazz*. These are the five-plus-two idiomatic origins of twentieth century music.

These are idiomatic origins; they are not forms or styles. They are not traditions but may become or participate in the formation of traditions. The idioms enter into and alter content, but the idioms too are altered.

These idiomatic origins of twentieth century music start coming to notice during the long lifetime of Franz Liszt; his compositions focus them in a wide, blurred lens.

Unlike J. S. Bach, Beethoven, and Schoenberg, whose work in each instance summarizes and completes a long period of musical development, transforming it and driving it with vast energy into the future, Liszt was a continuator, a rediscoverer and interpreter of styles, which pooled in him and spilled over, cutting no decisive channel. Nearly all the origins of twentieth century music may be found in his work but no established style, form, or tradition. The French, the Russians, the Germans inherited idiomatic originality from him. In America, Gottschalk and Mac-Dowell extended the Lisztian practice. He contributes to the notion of *difficulty* as an esthetic criterion: though it passed for showmanship with him, the notion of the difficult became monumentalized in the giant pianistic works by his contemporary Alkan and has continued as a confusing measure of judgement to the present day. Liszt contributed perhaps more than any other to popularizing the study and revival of folk music as an element in original composition, thus encouraging both the good and the bad elements of musical nationalism. Liszt's content, his esthetic consistency, was dispersed and weak, so that today, having passed beyond the reach of his idiomatic originality and being better informed than by his scholarship, we are more aware of his esthetic inconsistency or lack of content and therefore underrate his importance. Between Beethoven and Debussy, Liszt transformed the art of music.

Schubert also transformed it, by showing how whole, nonanalytic melodies could be combined into the larger forms of sonata and symphony, thus projecting the long wrestle of melody with counterpoint which culminated in the polyphonic solutions of Schoenberg; this stylistic and formal problem cut a decisive channel but influenced Germanic music almost exclusively.

Berlioz, Mendelssohn, Schumann, Tchaikovsky, and Sibelius neither fully faced nor solved the problem; their forms are loose-textured and repetitive, composed for the most part around nonanalytic, reiterative figures, which being assembled into tunes give the appearance of structure, plus a harmonic filling, like cornstarch in gravy, which thickens tonal coloration but keeps out of sight. The scherzo of Schumann's Second Symphony repeats the same short figure a hundred times—more than that, if you take it in slight variation. This simple method, which loses little

by performance in a keyboard transcription, permeated the nineteenth century European polyglot. The method pleases the casual
listener because it makes short demand on the attention; the mind
skips from one figure, tune, accumulative melody, or climax to the
next. Schumann's undoubted gift for genuine, relatively uncom-
plicated, songlike melody raises his music above the surrounding
and succeeding polyglot. Like Chopin and Liszt, he was an
originator of contemporary habits.

Sibelius, coming later, seems to have been aware of the need to
enrich the texture of this symphonic style, while avoiding the
Germanic alternatives of extreme concentration, as in Brahms, or
extreme length, as in Wagner, Bruckner, and Mahler. Sibelius
dwelt on the short figures, combining them to larger melodic
conclusions, simplifying the analytic process but throwing off
those analysts who look for a symphony to begin, one way or
another, with an exposition of its subjects. Considering his piano
compositions and his songs, it is amazing that Sibelius could write
for orchestra with a full and genuine symphonic grasp.

In fact, Sibelius's method was an improvement over the contrary procedure, too superficially derived from the classic symphony and Beethoven, of starting with two or more contrasting
subjects, that by reiteration bounce the music from climax to
climax. Plenty of this sort of music is being composed today, with
still some popular success. (The wrong idea of performing a Bach
fugue by emphasizing each re-entry of the theme has the same
intention and is heard in the same reiteratively emotional manner, ignoring most of the surrounding detail, which is compressed
into a sort of motor energy. This wrong way of playing Bach, and
the reaction against it, have had unreckoned consequences
throughout twentieth century musicianship.)

We have to keep in mind that the popular nineteenth century
audience, trained to the structural, textural, and harmonic sim-
plicities of Italian opera, the most fashionable music, and accustomed to listening intermittently in the pauses of conversation or when the house quieted to hear a well-known aria, only
very gradually developed to become the courteously quiet, patient, relatively intent audience to which we are accustomed. The
Viennese audience of Beethoven's lifetime preferred Rossini; at
mid-century, as Percy Scholes notes, the popular audience
thought Spohr the equal of Beethoven, if not a better composer.
Stendhal, though he admired Mozart, considered his music too

Germanic, too studied in comparison with Pergolesi. In the early 1890s, that vehement young music critic George Bernard Shaw was still crying up the worth of Beethoven in a symphonic repertory built around Mendelssohn and Spohr.

❀ Music became during the later eighteenth century and still more in the early nineteenth century a public art, spreading outward from the aristocracy of church and state, who until then had privately supported it, to the polite audience which attended church and theater in more cultivated centers (as we read in the career of Haydn), and then going on the road, as the Italian opera troupes had been doing already, to seek audience wherever people could afford to pay for music. Then and not later commenced the "lack of communication" between the serious composer and his audience which produced the first great crop of touring soloists, typified by the pianist Sigismond Thalberg and singers from Jenny Lind to Nellie Melba, who delighted their audiences by simple tunes and technical acrobatics. My own piano tuner of a few years ago was old enough to have toured America with a violinist who featured his skill in playing the violin upside down.

"Lack of communication" has been in reality a slow but steady increase in communication between the serious composer, his traveling representative the conscientious performer, and the slowly ripening public intelligence for music as an art on the same level as poetry, painting, and drama, which do not exist solely for public entertainment. As the level of concerned musical intelligence steadily rose and widened, the size of the residual audience correspondingly increased, that audience which looks to music as to other cultivated and fashionable skills—as it looks to horseracing, wagering, and professional athletics—for means of nonparticipative diversion. This audience has always rejected the unhabitual and demanding classic no less uncharitably than the unhabitual and demanding contemporary.

Within a decade after Debussy's death, his music was already more intelligible to the mass public than the Bach *Brandenburg Concertos*, which have since come to wide popular acceptance. The symphonies of Bruckner suffered outside Germany a longer rejection than the orchestral works

by Schoenberg. Chamber music of any period is still generally unwelcomed by the mass audience which believes it
has no trouble hearing the same types and styles of music
in symphonic guise. Impresarios, managers, critics, and other
professional upholders of "high musical standards," when
they sound off, seldom seem aware that they are defending
no more than roadblocks of contemporary fashion against
creative excellence.

Musical appetite and its ability to digest more concentrated food grows by opportunity to do so—not by anyone's
firmly held opinion that it cannot. This has been the lesson
of the phonograph. The new era of the phonograph has also
demonstrated that, while bad in quantity always drives out
good, the good lasts longer. It is the one consolation the
musical public offers the majority of great composers.

The composer dies, bequeathing his compositions to the
public that has seldom had the opportunity to hear them and
may scarcely know his name; the impresarios, managers,
critics, and other upholders of "high musical standards" in
their own good time will use for their uncomprehending purposes his music and his name—most commonly to beat down
the works of still newer composers.

In discussing musical appetites, tastes, and preferences,
the size of audience response, and the significance of "standards," one needs to have always in mind three classes of
musical interest: the small body of admirers whose appreciation of music tries to keep in touch with the work of contemporary composers, and through similar interest reinvesti-
gates and retrieves new music from the past; the dilettantes,
who are usually aware of the best but prefer the more easily
fashionable, especially when it comes to reputation, and for
the same reason rush in a body to admire new, fashionable
recoveries from the past—these are the most vindictive
against new composers whose work they are unsure of and
will not or cannot grasp; and the great residual mass of
listeners who receive all their tastes and opinions at second
hand.

The members of the first, small group make a composer's
life possible but often foment cliques and feuds around a
favorite composer against others of contrary style, whose
work they believe challenges their master's. The second,

larger group congregate around the temporarily popular composers, regardless of quality, while throwing their considerable experience and learning against any composer whose work seems to exclude them because they will not make the effort to penetrate it. The third group, in vast esthetic ignorance, follows its temporary leaders, who control the music business and award reputation with little or no appreciation of quality. Too many professional musicians and musical spokesmen, including educators and even composers as well as vocal spectators, are of the third class. With few exceptions, they will never be aware that they are of this class, because the rewards it offers are to them the most immediate proof of art.

Each listener has, in some degree, his choice of the three classes, according to his opportunities and the attention he brings to them. The great body of listeners is denied access to the first class by inability to keep up with current creative musical activity, since they seldom have opportunity to hear the most important new music in performance. They may do their best to belong to the second class of listeners, too often by parroting its favored names and prejudices; in general, having no particular drive to musical experience, they settle in the third, residual class, having their choices made for them and expecting only entertainment. These are the empty seats at any significant performance of unusual music. Though they will admit their ignorance of music, members of this third class are often very insistent about, and combine to enforce, their musical opinions. They believe that music should be performed for their benefit, at the habitual level of their "taste."

Polyglot signifies a confusion of languages. During the nineteenth century the Italian tradition had retreated to Russia, from which it re-emerged glamorous in Russian idiom; the Germanic tradition became an idiomatic wrestle of analytic and melodic structure. French music, during the century beginning with the war between the Germanic "Gluckists" and the Italian "Piccinists," had become the true polyglot. Because this style was not really French but centered around Paris, from which its composers of several national origins came and went, it might be better called *Parisian*. Its true master was Chopin, who came from Poland to Paris and lived there after 1831, with a long stay in Mallorca.

More than any other composer, Chopin successfully married the Germanic chromaticism with Italian harmony, while simplifying the dissonant trend from J. S. Bach through Beethoven. He stands for a large body of composers who, during the nineteenth century, less successfully attempted the same mixture. He influenced every idiom but had only one successor, the Russian Alexander Scriabin. Chopin's Polish nationalism, though it affected only a portion of his music, helped set in motion the rise of nationalistic composers throughout and around the periphery of Europe.

The great master of this Parisian polyglot was Franz Liszt, the innovator of modern polyglot virtuosity in every sphere of music. Hector Berlioz directed similar skills into his predominantly orchestral compositions, by techniques more related to instrumental sound than compositional substance. Berlioz created the modern orchestra, a polyglot medium as unlike the classic orchestra from Dittersdorf to Beethoven as the nineteenth century grand organ was unlike the organ of Bach. Berlioz added voices to the orchestra, but Wagner consummately wound voices and instruments together to create a passionate ritual of emotion, a musical realization of narrow psychological motivation as transcendent as irrational. For a century this new skill of orchestration concealed by its attractions the increasing vacuum of content throughout orchestral music. Only a few composers, among them Brahms and Bruckner, did not wholly or in part succumb to it.

The true French idiomatic originality began to appear during the last fifteen years of the century with the concentration of Parisian polyglot into French impressionism, influenced at first by Wagner and by Liszt and then revolting against nearly every type of non-French influence, particularly the Germanic. In France, to the present day, the Germanic, the Parisian polyglot, and the true French modern impressionistic tradition have existed side by side.

British music, although never idiomatically individual after the end of its great period and nearly dormant in the nineteenth century, incorporated equally the Germanic idiom and French impressionism. British music revived as British polyglot and has remained so.

At the same time a new influence appeared, which had nothing to do with the nineteenth century. Arnold Dolmetsch commenced the revival of the music, instruments, and performing styles that were in use before the orchestra and piano. The effect of this example penetrated European music, never in itself producing a new style but contributing to the rise of that broad archaizing tendency which produced among other manifestations the formalizing habit called "neoclassic." The Lisztian interest in transcribing older music, the scholarship of such musicians as Camille Saint-Saëns, the great activity of Germanic editors in bringing out editions of earlier European music, the vivid personality of Wanda Landowska and the rise to popularity of the twentieth century version of the harpsichord, which she invented, all contributed to this archaizing trend. The compositions by Ralph Vaughan Williams, though not strictly neoclassic, exemplify the twentieth century composite of modern, orchestral, and archaizing means.

American music, which had assumed some individuality before 1830, was swamped, as the British music had been earlier, by importation of European musicians and, with them, the current stylistic trends from Europe. In the same decade when Emerson was proclaiming the esthetic independence of America from Europe, the return of American art, including music, to entire dependence on European models swept away all but the vestiges of new beginnings. American musical individuality survived among the countryfolk and the illiterate.

A new American experimental tradition started full-blown in the writings of Herman Melville and Walt Whitman, in the Chicago architecture, and around 1891 in the *Variations on "America"* for organ by Charles Ives. During the 1920s, when Ives had already ceased composing, only a small group of musicians, among them Henry Cowell, recognized the importance of his work; his influence did not appear until after 1939 and is still growing.

Oriental or Asiatic music first entered European idiom when Claude Debussy and Maurice Ravel heard the Javanese *gamelan* at the Paris Exposition in 1889. Debussy began imitating the sound of the *gamelan* in his piano music, but the idea of a vertically related music without formal harmony, a melody of chords which do not modulate, a single nondiatonic scale without key-relationship, permeated his art. If the effect in such a composition as *Pagodes* is no more than a *chinoiserie,* the ultimate consequence was a new sound, impressionistic and pellucid. Debussy had not emancipated the dissonance or the consonance; he had prepared the public ear for the acceptance of those more drastic freedoms by emancipating music from the rules of harmony.

African music did not come to America as jazz, directly or indirectly. The Southern Negroes, retaining of their aboriginal music little more than a memory of its idiomatic rhythms, took up the popular music of their masters, the *chansons* of French Louisiana, the hymns and country-primitive part-singing of rural Protestant revivalism, adapting them to their own rhythms and melodic speech. White imitation of this Negro music in the minstrel show became ragtime, and the Negroes again translating to their own idiom made it jazz. Charles Ives incorporated ragtime into his new, extra-European composition, but jazz has remained, apart from a broad rhythmic influence, a distinct and independent American tradition. In spite of all that has been written about jazz, mostly socioeconomic-biographical surveys of relatively sophisticated urban jazz, it has never been adequately documented as a distinct musical idiom, and much that might have been known about it, for example a careful documentation of its rhythms, has been lost, except as information may still be obtained from early phonograph records.

The belief that jazz is the unique American contribution to music is incorrect. The American experimental tradition stemming from Ives, Ruggles, Cowell, Varèse, Partch, and Cage is also an indigenous creation. Jazz developed and has evolved in America by its own separate paths, with its own idioms and tradition, confused with but never becoming a part of any other music, popular, traditional, or American experimental. In derivative style it influenced Parisian music as well as American. Stravinsky's "rag" (*Ragtime, The Soldier's Tale*) is early European jazz, probably never better performed than by Stravinsky himself when he recorded the inimitable *Piano-Rag Music*. Aaron Copland tried and failed to capture jazz for art, notably in his Piano Concerto. The reverse happened; jazz imposed art-form on his Piano Variations and *Music for the Theater*. Copland did not let this happen again; the result was too shockingly bare of melodic propriety and different from American expectations. The Piano Variations remain an unduplicated masterpiece. No other composer in that line has been so fortunate. But knowledge of jazz as a competing or contrasting music has effected deep and by no means obvious changes in the nature of American melody and rhythm.

From our present distance we are able to see jazz as an individual and serious art, never really well known except among a small circle of predominantly Negro musicians, for whom it took the place, one might hesitantly suggest, of an articulate emotional speech, an outward expression which could not be repressed. These musicians did not theorize about jazz; they "blew" it, in the same way that J. S. Bach composed in music his ideas of musical education and his theological conceptions. Jazz in its best manifestations has remained as remote from popular vulgarity as any other serious music, continually reasserting itself against the flood of commercially vulgar tune-writing that has presumed to use its name.

In our Western tradition, folk and popular music, however widespread and self-sufficing, have in the end always remained subordinate to the continuity of art music, to which they have imparted a renewed vitality. The recent discovery in depth of Oriental music has had a similar revitalizing effect on Western musical form.

II

"A NEW LANGUAGE . . . THE FIGHT AGAINST ROUTINE"

In December 1877, Pyotr I. Tchaikovsky wrote a letter of musical criticism to his devoted correspondent, Nadezhda von Meck. It is only in part the sort of letter that, from our distant vantage-point, we should have expected him to write.

"A Mussorgsky, for all his ugliness, speaks a new language. Beautiful it may not be, but it is fresh. . . . Our ugliness is, at any rate, better than the pitiful impotence, masked as serious creative power, of Brahms and other Germans. They are irreparably evaporated. . . . In France, on the other hand, there are strong progressive forces. Berlioz, it is true, is only now, ten years after his death, beginning to be performed. Nevertheless, many a new talent and many an energetic warrior has entered the fight against *routine*. . . . In their aspirations toward novelty, the French are not as daring as our innovators. But they don't transcend the limits of the possible as Borodin and Mussorgsky do."[1]

After Debussy had listened to the Oriental musicians who played at the Paris Exposition in April 1889, his early infatuation with the music of Wagner soon ended. In later years he compared this experience with the rites of opera at Bayreuth.

"The Annamites present a sort of embryo of a lyrical drama, influenced by the Chinese, where one recognizes the form of a tetralogy; only they have more God and less decor. . . . A small clarinet passionately directs the emotion, a tam-tam creates a terror . . . and that is all! They do not need a special theater, nor the hidden orchestra. Nothing but an instinctive necessity for art, ingenious to satisfy, not a single trace of bad taste!"[2]

Harmony was disintegrating, and from both sides of Europe its formulas were being challenged. Wagner, who claimed to be the inheritor of Bach and Beethoven, towered over Europe in such menacing authority that the best young composers of the peripheral countries suddenly turned nationalistic Davids, with homemade slingshot and native pebble, firing away at the admired, almost venerated Germanic monolith.

The Germanic composers were not popular in our sense of popularity; they were the great figures by whose measure all seriously intended music should be judged. Already, in Germanic estimation, Brahms was taking his place among the colossi, to be followed after the customary critical warfare by Richard Strauss.

The lesser composers, as always academically compelled, made pilgrimage to Bayreuth but turned by preference away from Wagner, like Edward MacDowell and Carl Nielsen, to the more manageable formulas of the polyglot tradition and the simpler lyrical example of Edvard Grieg. And one hears the grotesque spectacle of Nielsen, in Germanic-polyglot costume, trying to capture the spirit of Borodin's *Polovtzian Dances*. Or the muttonchop complacency of Edward Elgar, a genuine melodist capable of the *Enigma Variations* and the splendid Violin Concerto, who could not apprehend the significance of Debussy or rise above the flat sentiments of his time in attempting his major intellectual effort, *The Dream of Gerontius*. Elgar was pleased to have his music commended by Richard Strauss. The most eminent American composer-pedagogue, Horatio Parker, who taught among others Charles Ives and Roger Sessions, felt himself complimented when one major work, his oratorio *Hora Novissima*, a superior pudding of well-derived formulas from the best European masters of three centuries, was accepted for performance by the Three Choirs Festival in England.

So there was throughout music, during the later decades of the nineteenth century and well on into the twentieth century, a three-way tension. The Germanic composers, though aiming at the heights, adulterated and compromised their art with emotional and melodic formulas and hyperbolic gestures; in that respect Wagner may be seen as a Germanic Bernini (the great figure of the Italian Mannerists, sculptors, painters, and architects who exaggerated posture and the symbols of emotionality in the century after Michelangelo).

The younger French and Russians, denying the further validity of Germanic abstraction, sought instead a music of immediate human reality, spiritualized but able to speak to the feelings as directly as a human voice. The newer polyglots, as indefinite in purpose as in tradition, clung as in every generation to the outworn academic formulas—which survive as formulas for the teaching of composition to the present day—relying on title, sentiment, and heroic posture to bring off their larger intentions, while they succeeded in a small way with bread-and-butter virtuosity and charming lyrical pieces. The polyglot at this period turned to Schumann as the mannerist to Beethoven.

As the chief new composers were preparing to abandon Wagnerism, the popular audience was discovering it, a vogue which did not end until the Second World War. Riding the tide of Germanic imperial inflation, the Germanic composers appeared to ride with equal superiority the Wagnerian musical inflation.

Anton Bruckner did so quite naturally, because the academic severity of his nonanalytic symphonic form permitted no shortcuts. His music was at length not because he padded it, as the polyglot symphonists padded theirs, but because he did not pad it. He composed into his symphonies everything that his material compelled him to say, in full sentences and one sentence at a time. His art steadily matured, but the esthetic consistency did not vary; it could run thin but never soft or cheap. (In the ruins of Berlin, surrounded by the Russian armies and already under bombardment, a last audience walked through the rubble to hear the Berlin Philharmonic play Bruckner's unfinished Ninth Symphony, like a farewell to all that had been best in the Germanic spirit.)

Friends of Bruckner, believing to do him a favor, cut large sections from his symphonies to reduce their length. The effect was to make them seem longer; the listener, unable to follow the argument intuitively sentence by sentence, was soon confused and floundering.

In his Masses, Bruckner's severity preserved him from the decorative inflation which had gradually reduced sacred music to the level of sentimental opera—not the level of Verdi's *Requiem,* which is the equal of the greatest opera, but the level of Charles Gounod's tawdry-cheap but once beloved *Saint Cecilia Mass*. Each section of the Mass has something to say, and Bruckner forcefully said it, without Bach's theological exposition of each clause or Beethoven's dramatic supererogation.

For these among other reasons Bruckner's music has survived the Wagnerian decline, as it is surviving the decline of Strauss, and we hear it today as the composer meant it, scarcely noticing the touches of Wagnerian orchestration, because of which Bruckner, who admired Wagner's music, was formerly dismissed as a Wagnerian imitator.

Gustav Mahler, the greatest of Wagnerian conductors, learned his symphonic style from Bruckner, dismissing the work of Brahms as unworthy of emulation. The learning did not involve imitation; Mahler, the torn Jew, could not share Bruckner's rooted peasant faith. Instead of Bruckner's heaven-reaching unison octaves and affirmative chords, Mahler's music is an argumentative and clamorous counterpoint, incompatible subjects forced by will to combine in all positions with orchestral cadenzas of heaven-shattering, despairing violence announcing catastrophe before the ultimate apotheosis and resignation. They are most alike—and Anton Webern in his minuscule the same—in turning for peace to symbols of the Austrian countryside and sweet country tunes; with Webern a hint of unresolved melody suffices. Mahler's orchestration contains a little Wagner but more Bach, from the keyboard works he read devotedly, counterpoint somewhat after the manner of Liszt in his *Faust Symphony* but with more elegance and in far greater variety. It is curious to observe how little the style of the large-scale nineteenth century composers resembled Beethoven's, even when they deliberately imitated some portion, as they often did, of Beethoven's Ninth Symphony. Even for Brahms, who labored to revive it, the analytic style of the Germanic classic symphonists was a lost art.

So that when Schoenberg, trying to preserve the Wagnerian orchestration, which he had mastered more thoroughly than Strauss, and toughening the musical fabric with tight Brahmsian counterpoint, was driven towards a melodious and potentially more dissonant polyphony, he was able to confirm from the usages of Strauss and Mahler what he had learned by study of Mozart and Bach, the multiplex positioning of melodic themes. But whereas Mahler, as nervously determined as Bruckner was severe, insisted on writing full sentences, even if more than one sentence at a time, Schoenberg broke up and varied the repetition of the sentences, weaving them together to paragraph length.

It is this contrapuntal polyphony of continually varying melody which made Schoenberg's music difficult for his contemporaries, as it is still difficult for unprejudiced listeners today. Only *Gurrelieder*, which Schoenberg had completely composed in 1901 and orchestrated several years later, kept a sufficiently Wagnerian melodic looseness to be popularly successful when it was at last performed in 1910.

Atonality, which came about as a result of these procedures in chromatic harmony, was never the real issue. Schoenberg's early music is not more atonal than the developed idioms of Strauss, Scriabin, or Debussy, but it is larger and more compressed in musical scope and therefore more difficult to follow. Today the greater part of Schoenberg's early music, which seemed to his contemporaries unaccountably and unbearably dissonant, is in danger of sounding oversweet. The true difficulty of Schoenberg's music in any style at any period is to follow clearly the concentration of interwoven varied melody, as demanding note by note in the *Six Little Piano Pieces*, opus 19, as it is unrelenting in the Wind Quintet, opus 26, or the opera *Moses and Aron*—an entire opera composed around a single twelve-note theme.

Richard Strauss came to early reputation as composer and conductor, under the scholarly pianist and conductor of the famous Meiningen orchestra, Hans von Bülow. Strauss developed rapidly to become in young maturity the most successful of the Wagnerians—though he was as indebted for his orchestral writing to Berlioz and Liszt as to Wagner—drifting next towards the style of Verdi's *Falstaff* in writing *Der Rosenkavalier* and then back toward Mozart.

"In the final duet, between Quinquin and Sophie" (of *Rosenkavalier*), Strauss's collaborator Hugo von Hofmannsthal wrote him in 1910, "I was certainly hampered by the metrical scheme you gave me—but I have come actually to enjoy being bound down to a melodic form, since I see in it an approach to the old pre-Wagnerian style."[3] Among the radical Germanic twentieth century composers, Strauss first reverted to the neoclassic. Having no deep esthetic consistency to drive him forward, he could venture only so far as his uninhibited skill could carry him, then turn back. He resembles those heroic British mountaineers who almost made it to the top of Everest in overcoats and hats. So Strauss perished in his *Alpine Symphony*.

The aged Strauss, in his last writings when he was admittedly emulating Mozart, became once more the gifted, stylistically vague polyglot of his preoperatic adolescence. The concise assurance of his earlier tone-poems had melted into the Wagnerian inflation of his discursive, autobiographical symphonies. The concentrated psychomusical dramaturgy of his powerful if repellent operas *Salome* and *Elektra* had softened to produce the comic human portraits of the first act of *Rosenkavalier*, degenerating to the stuffed similitudes of the succeeding acts, a decline confirmed by *Ariadne auf Naxos*. Flashes of virtuosity still enliven the later operas. But the creative intelligence, which for a time had grown to match the unquestionable authority, died in Strauss in middle life. From then on he was a great talent groping.

The divergence between the high aims epitomized by Beethoven and the more accessible formulas of Berlioz, Liszt, and Wagner, between the polyglot compromises and the ambition of an artist who understood these compromises too well to wish to confine himself by them, made Strauss at once successful and reticent, a true lover of his art—as he proved lifelong by his conducting—but cynical concerning human motives, too often content to produce by his own means the "sudden crash," which, he told the young Stravinsky, astonishes the crowd. "After that they will follow you and you can do whatever you like."[4] His facility in descriptive music led him astray from musical significance. He, before Schoenberg, should have understood and followed up the emancipation of the dissonance, but it is doubtful whether his mind ever questioned the rules which he stretched past breaking-point. He clung to the harmonic rationalizations of dissonance as he clung to popularity, until his music, in its more complex working, veered over into sweetened, acoustically chaotic noise—for a conspicuous example, the fugue of the *Domestic Symphony*.

Secure in his position as a great composer, his compositions and himself as conductor always in demand, Strauss never had to "face the music" until it was too late. When the fertility of his invention ran out, he continued inventing.

When a composer has risen early in life to so much fame, has had his major works constantly performed in concert halls and opera houses throughout the world, and is besides one of the chief executive musicians of his time, director of the opera houses at Berlin and Vienna and a principal conductor, his career and reputation will be burdened by the laurels of those who adulate success and bruised by the envious. Strauss was his own first severe critic; in early maturity he frowned at performances of his chamber music and the *Burleske* for piano and orchestra. In later life he tried to repair his early *Serenade* for 13 wind instruments and returned to the slack preciosity of adolescent skills now grossly out of date. Against servile music directors who would trim music, his or another's, to satisfy prejudice or fashion, he was a vigorous and unyielding enemy. With the Kaiser, who disliked his music but could not disown his reputation, with the Weimar Republic, and again with Hitler, Strauss urged legislation to protect a composer's works from exploitation and to extend the copyright period to fifty years. He won from Hitler, over Goebbels's conspiring interference, the fifty-year copyright. In spite of severe pressure he would not renounce Stefan Zweig as his librettist. He was forbidden to leave Germany, and his eightieth birthday was officially ignored because of statements found in his letters to friends outside Germany.

He was also generous: "It is better for twenty to be regarded too highly than for one to have the way barred to him. Sufficient that a man has the will and the ability to do something." Throughout his career he prepared and conducted programs of music by his contemporaries. He steered Schoenberg to employment at the Stern Academy in Berlin, unaware that this young contemporary had already solved the technical problem of his lifetime. Schoenberg's *Erwartung* combines the best of Wagner and of Strauss in a half-hour of unrelenting, passionate melody, compressing as much music in a few measures as Wagner or Strauss could write down on a page. Alban Berg's *Wozzeck* and *Lulu* and several operas by Hindemith and Schreker testify to the continuing dramatic authority of Strauss, in the psychomusical mode he abandoned.

For all their many deviations, the Germanic composers stayed true to the continuity of their tradition, passing it on from Beethoven and Schubert, through a century of nationalistic assertiveness and esthetic compromise, to renewal in the art of Mahler, Hindemith, and Schoenberg. The formulas had changed, but the Germanic routine had never ceased. Schoenberg believed that he could find in Germanic music alone validation for each of his seemingly unprecedented procedures.

Béla Bartók in the same way found his most radical innovations by a minute analytic disintegration and reconstitution of the procedures of Balkan, Turkish, and Arabic folk music. He analyzed thoroughly and reconstructed acutely to create passages capable of constant alteration and growth in abstract forms.

For the innovating Russian and French composers tradition provided a non-Germanic medium, the old Italian harmony, orchestrally colored after Berlioz and Wagner but deprived by Liszt of the firm rooting in thoroughbass which gave Chopin his strength. Chopin was the last composer to take full advantage of the eighteenth century, the last classicist who could not be called a "neoclassicist."

The other non-Germanic, alternative formulas were all polyglot. The Russian composers honored Bach and Beethoven but preferred Weber and especially Schumann. They studied these works at the piano, applying what they learned to a Russianized version of Italian opera, for which the few works of Michael Glinka served as nationalistic model. The overtures to Glinka's operas furnished an orchestral style, supplemented by imitation of Berlioz, Weber, and Liszt. John Field, a pupil of Clementi, created during his long stay in Moscow the Russian piano style, simplistic and decorative. The combination of styles jelled and set, to become for a time the most popular art-music of the Western world. In the United States particularly, audiences are still swayed by it.

The virtues of this style are most evident in the mature works by Tchaikovsky, each movement charged with melodies or tunes carefully fitted to present a recognizable emotion and dramatic shape. Color, subtlety of design, programmatic intention were never permitted to clutter or conceal strict formal progress and thematic relationship. If Tchaikovsky's art did not go deep, it was unfailingly emotional and strictly consistent at an esthetic level the popular audience could reach.

The vices of the Russian innovative effort are all too evident in the tone-poems and symphonies by Balakirev, Borodin, and Rimsky-Korsakov. Originality begins in derivation and therefore initially lacks content. Mily Balakirev, the chosen disciple of

Glinka, a true teacher and experienced musician as well as a close student of Russian folk idiom, created a genuine Russian sound and a whirling verve, which reappear throughout the music of his younger associates, the members of "the Five." Balakirev's thematic fragments, however "ethnic" or truly Russian in origin, grow by simple imitation and repetition, the common polyglot procedure of lesser nineteenth century symphonists. He had a Berliozan flair for coloristic orchestration and for keeping things going by the persistent rising and falling of figures building towards crescendo and the inevitable cymbal-clash. In middle life Balakirev withdrew from his circle of admirers, abandoned music, and became a devotee of Russian pietism.

Borodin achieved a few times the melodic essence of a movement in well-combined themes. Some of the music for *Prince Igor* was thought to exceed the limits of harmonic propriety; today it sounds theatrical and provincial.

The perils of innovation are seen most clearly in its comparative successes, for example Rimsky-Korsakov's *Antar Symphony,* which Debussy warmly greeted, and *Schéhérazade,* each a symphony made up of tone poems with explicit narratives. Although several of his works are still performed and heard with pleasure, Rimsky-Korsakov's music would have little importance for the twentieth century if he had not been the teacher of Serge Prokofiev and Igor Stravinsky.

A second associate of Glinka, Alexander Dargomijsky, though his music is little known outside Russia, went beyond the Russian sound to create a new type of operatic declamation. In his chief work, an opera, *The Stone Guest,* he set to music the exact text of Pushkin's short drama of Don Juan. "The sound must express or echo the word," he insisted, and his example, though not fully successful, inspired other Russian composers with a new respect for drama, not merely as a libretto arranged to provide vocal set-pieces held together by dry recitative but as a dramatic unity, music reinforcing words.

Wagnerian opera the Russian composers unanimously detested; the idea of setting the voice as another instrument in a mass of orchestration did not appeal to them, nor the undramatic extension of the form which places the burden of the drama on the music. Dargomijsky saw more clearly than Wagner the possibility of a dramatic opera in which song is constantly subordinate to declamatory speech and action. It can be said that this development has grievously injured the true art of opera and impaired operatic song. Twentieth century opera has been at best a compromise between song and declamation, in which too often the persistence of the large Wagnerian orchestra prevents any clear understanding of the words. But Schoenberg, in *Moses and Aron*, turned even these conflicts to advantage.

❀ Opera was in its beginnings a national art, intended to be heard in the language for which it was written, the sound of the language governing the musical idiom. When traveling Italian operatic troupes performed at German courts, the audience was supposed to understand them in the original language. As the German popular audience for opera grew larger, German composers invented the *Singspiel*, vernacular opera in German with spoken passages as well as song, of which Mozart's *The Magic Flute* is the supreme example. The idea of opera in the vernacular may have originated in the English ballad-opera. Yet Handel, a German, wrote Italian operas in Italian for London listeners who did not know that language. He wrote his dramatic oratorios in English, because the text, being sacred, should be understood. Wagner reinstated the importance of the dramatic poem but drained the values of dramatic speech into oratory and abstract musical symbol, the leitmotif. Tristan and Isolde bellow their passion at each other in periods which scarcely permit a caress; only Brangaene in warning and King Mark in betrayal are human. The orchestral *Liebestod* lacks nothing of the operatic, except the unsurpassable instrument of the human voice. To understand the vast immobilities of Wagnerian drama one needs to memorize the leitmotifs and keep in hand a synopsis of the action; so one needs no German. The text is as abstract of human emotion as the sound is overcharged with it.

The influence of modern realistic drama, an art of dramatic conversation instead of declamation or poetry, has persuaded some listeners that the language of an opera should be understood by its audience. Opera, they contend, should be given in the language of the country in which it is performed. Dargomijsky's argument has succeeded too well.

The fact is that any composition of words and music is best heard in the language and with the words for which the music is written. The lyrics of Blitzstein's *The Cradle Will Rock* parody American popular song in the words of American vulgar speech. Debussy's words and their musical setting are one language. Wagner in French or English, Mussorgsky in Italian lose the musical coloration, inflection, and weight of the original speech. Yet a carefully prepared translation may in some instances fit the music so well that the composition does not suffer, and its effectiveness for the listener may be improved. Bach and Mozart can be sung in English to advantage.

Schoenberg told me that he wished the song-speech (*Sprechstimme*) of his *Pierrot Lunaire* to be in the language of the country where it is performed. In Italy he performed it in Italian and thought the color of the language perhaps more suitable for the atmosphere he imagined. He admired the excellent English translation by Carl Beier and Ingolf Dahl, which exactly fits the music yet imparts a lightness the work does not have in German. He regretted that his own recorded performance of *Pierrot Lunaire* was not in English. Writing about a proposed American performance of the *Gurrelieder*, Schoenberg stresses:

"ONE THING IS VERY IMPORTANT.
Make the performance in ENGLISH not in German. . . . There is no reason why it should be in German."[5]

Impresarios and musicians are best advised to ignore both the scholarly argument that any composition of words and music should be performed only in the composer's language and the popular argument that every work should be performed in the language of the audience. The decision in each case should be made according to the excellence of an available translation and its adaptability to correct reading of the music. Italian *bel canto* requires exact placement of the consonants and vowels to realize the correct tone and ornamental inflection of each passage. "I love you" is a correct translation of a "Ich liebe dich" or "Je t'aime," but rhythmically and in adaptability for singing they are quite unlike.

"The sound must express or echo the word." Sound echoing the word is an operatic commonplace, going back at least as far as the sixteenth century madrigal; but sound *expressing*, that is to say transmitting clearly the significance of the word, its meaning and connotation, with emotional and conceptual overtones, this is a new idea. (The idea would attain its ultimate realization, not in the work of a Russian composer or entirely in Debussy's *Pelleas and Melisande,* but in Alban Berg's *Wozzeck* and Schoenberg's *Moses and Aron,* where it is joined with an equally strict conception of musical form.)

Dargomijsky's dictum came immediately out of the enthusiasm and reverence of his young Russian contemporaries for the poetry of Alexander Pushkin. Just as Pushkin made, from Byron, Shakespeare, and his knowledge of Russian peasant speech, a new poetry and, though it was never successful on the stage, a new drama, which denied the formalistic precedent of the approved Russian literature—during his lifetime an edict was issued barring blank verse from the Russian stage—so Glinka and Dargomijsky created, in the spirit of Pushkin, a new music, from Berlioz, Gluck, and the music of the Russian folk, which denied the Italianate example of the prevailing Russian opera. (It was to this Italianate Russian opera that Stravinsky would return in writing his two short comic operas, *Mavra* and *Renard.*)

Glinka's *Russlan and Ludmilla* initiated the new style; Dargomijsky's *Russalka* and *The Stone Guest* confirmed it; each was the setting of a work by Pushkin. Borodin made an opera of Pushkin's *Prince Igor,* Tchaikovsky selected *Eugen Onegin,* Rimsky-Korsakov *Mozart and Salieri,* an interesting miniature opera, and *The Golden Cockerel.* But the most complete realization of Pushkin's Russian language and Dargomijsky's rule was achieved by Mussorgsky in his musical-dramatic setting of *Boris Godunov.*

"I want to say that if the expression in sound of human thought and feeling *in simple speech* is truly produced by me in music, and this reproduction is musical and artistic, then the thing is in the bag. . . . Whatever speech I hear, no matter who is speaking (nor what he says) my mind is already working to find the musical statement for such a speech."[6] So Mussorgsky wrote to Rimsky-Korsakov before composing *Boris.*

And in his autobiographical sketch, written in the third person shortly before the end of his life, Mussorgsky defines himself: "Mussorgsky cannot be classed with any existing group of musicians, either by the character of his compositions or by his musical views. The formula of his artistic *profession de foi* may be explained by his view, as a composer, of the task of art: art is a means of communicating with people, not an aim in itself." (This conception of a practical, communicative music recurred in Germany during the 1920s, in America from the late 1920s into the 1940s, producing some of the most characteristic American music; it underlies the American experimental tradition, no matter how difficult the composition, in the works of Ives, Varèse, Cowell, Roy Harris, Copland and Partch.) "This guiding principle has defined the whole of his creative activity. Proceeding from the conviction that human speech is strictly controlled by musical laws . . . he considers the task of musical art to be the reproduction in musical sounds not merely of the mood of the feeling, but chiefly of the mood of human speech. Acknowledging that in the realm of art only artist-reformers such as Palestrina, Bach, Gluck, Beethoven, Berlioz, and Liszt have created the laws of art, he considers those laws as not immutable but liable to change and progress, like the entire spiritual world of man."[7]

Whatever opinion one may hold of Mussorgsky's fragmentary work, there can be no doubt that he understood and had firmly in mind what he wished to do. The enthusiasm of his friends for his music reflected his own enthusiasm, but privately and critically they withheld praise for exactly the one quality which caused him to stand so high above them as a composer: his determination to achieve true Russian speech in music. César Cui wrote (*La Musique en Russie*): "M. Mussorgsky is a recognized master of declamation. In this he holds first place after Dargomizhsky. But his immoderate abuse of imitative accents unfortunately denotes too great a tendency to grasp and to produce external effects, to the detriment of musical sense. . . . His modulations are too free, and sometimes one might say that they only proceed along lines of pure chance."[8]

"The mood of human speech" is nearer the operation of chance than of correct harmonic modulation. Mussorgsky's practice, reformulated and restated by succeeding composers, has contributed as fundamentally as the theory or the work of any composer to the distinctive attitude of twentieth century composers and the character of their music. Only those composers who make a criterion of difficulty refuse his influence. The faults of the method appear, for example, in the style of Janáček—Bartók, working with similar material, corrects them—but the virtues far outweigh the destructive effect.

For a while Mussorgsky and Rimsky-Korsakov, who was fifteen years younger, shared a room and worked together, the younger, professional composer persuading Mussorgsky to modify some of his more extreme liberties. After Mussorgsky's early death at forty-four, Rimsky-Korsakov carried on this devoted work of editing and modifying his scores and orchestration. *Boris Godunov* is still performed more often in the modified version than in the original, which enthusiasts of Mussorgsky's music prefer.

Probably the best demonstration, in Mussorgsky's own words, of his freedom as he practised it is this paragraph from a letter to Vladimir Stasov, a writer and supporter of these new tendencies: "Maybe I'm afraid of technique, because I'm poor at it? However, there are some who will stand up for me in art and in this respect also. I, for example, cannot bear it, when the hostess, in serving a good pie which she has prepared and we are eating, says: 'A million *puds* of butter, five hundred eggs, a whole bed of cabbages, 150¼ fish . . .' You eat the pie and it tastes good, then you hear about the kitchen, and you at once imagine the cook, always dirty, a chopped-off chicken head on a bench, gutted fish on another, and sometimes side by side, and somebody's intestines peeping out of a sieve (as though the Prussians had honored us with their presence), and more often one can visualize a greasy apron, the same apron that is used as a nose-rag, and which later will be used to wipe the edge of the pie dishes, in order to clean them . . . well, the pie grows less tasty. There is in ripe artistic productions that side of chaste purity, that when touched by dirty paws, grows loathesome."[9]

This vivid imaginative ability to elaborate on the exact circumstance, to realize the abstract comment in immediately realistic visual figures, created *The Nursery, Songs and Dances of Death* —and, by reverse action, *Pictures at an Exhibition*.

One thinks of the similar outburst by Charles Ives, in the Epilogue to his *Essays Before a Sonata*, written at the end of his composing, his music still unheard: "A MS. score is brought to a concertmaster—he may be a violinist—he is kindly disposed, he looks it over, and casually fastens on a passage 'that's bad for the fiddles, it doesn't hang just right, write it like this, they will play it better.' But that one phrase is the germ of the whole thing. 'Never mind, it will fit the hand better this way—it will sound better.' My God! what has sound got to do with music! The waiter brings the only fresh egg he has, but the man at breakfast sends it back because it doesn't fit his eggcup. Why can't music go out in the same way it comes in to a man, without having to crawl over a fence of sounds, thoraxes, catguts, wire, wood, and brass? Consecutive-fifths are as harmless as blue laws compared with the relentless tyranny of the 'media.' "[10]

Here prose takes on the character of musical speech, with no need of accompaniment.

In the same letter to Stasov, Mussorgsky writes as Schoenberg might have written: "So do not tell me . . . why our musicians chatter more often about technique, than about aims and historical tasks—because this [the sterility of their symphonies] derives *from that.*"

Of Mussorgsky, Claude Debussy wrote: "No one has ever appealed to the best that is in us in deeper or more tender expression. He is unique and will remain so, for his art is free from artifice or arid formulas. Never was refined sensitivity interpreted by such simple means. It is like the art of an inquisitive savage who discovers music at every step made by his emotions . . . this form is so manifold that it cannot possibly be likened to the recognized or orthodox forms. It is achieved by little consecutive touches linked by a mysterious bond. . . ."[11]

In that last sentence Debussy touches upon the secret of his own art.

AN INTRODUCTION TO
CLAUDE DEBUSSY

"The thing, then, is to find what comes after *Wagner's time* but not after *Wagner's manner*," Debussy wrote to Pierre Louÿs. Wagner was "a great collector of formulas . . . he placed a period to the music of his time in much the same way as Victor Hugo did for poetry."[1]

Germanic music had a living growth of theory, however rationalized and often unreal, a living tradition with living masters; it was large enough to include Wagner and Brahms, big enough to take what it wished from other music and exploit the material as it pleased. French musical theory was a dry academic pedantry, polyglot and centering in Paris, lacking the melodic inspiration which the Russians and the peripheral nationalists discovered in folk music; the living French composers had not learned, as the Russians had, from Berlioz; orchestration could be reduced to a treatise; Liszt had taught them nothing of his creative vision. There was not even a clear tradition to react against. Debussy's first model was Jules Massenet, a former winner of the Prix de Rome; to win that prize himself was the official incentive to his composing.

Debussy saw through the polyglot inadequacy; he already possessed, in unformed ability, the alternative. "One winter evening of 1883, Debussy went to the piano to imitate the sound of the buses" in the street. "He played a sort of chromatic groaning, to which his friends and a few people who had stayed on from other classes listened mockingly. 'Look at them,' Debussy said, turning round. 'Can't you listen to chords without knowing their names?' . . .] At the piano we heard groups of consecutive fifths and octaves; sevenths which instead of being resolved in the proper way actually led to the note above or weren't resolved at all; shameful 'false relations'; chords of the ninth on all degrees of the scale; chords of the eleventh and thirteenth; all the notes of the diatonic scale heard at once in fantastic arrangements. . . . And all this Claude called . . . 'a feast for the ear.' "[2]

"What rule do you follow?" he was asked. Debussy answered, *"Mon plaisir!"*

He was already beginning the transition from formal harmony to sound. It was in this more than anything that he differed from Maurice Ravel.

The members of the Russian "Five" at that age had challenged the accepted formulas and worked out their new devices in close association and mutual criticism, surrounded and encouraged by intelligent friends. Debussy had a few sympathetic friends but no encouraging musical association. When he went to Russia as house pianist for Tchaikovsky's benefactor, Nadezhda von Meck, he was greeted as a "pupil of Massenet" and confined to admiration of Tchaikovsky and the Moscow school, hearing and learning little of the Petersburg "Five." Debussy took no pleasure in winning the Prix de Rome and felt himself confined during his stays at the "abominable" Villa Medici in Rome. His thoughts and letters from the day of his arrival were directed to escape. All his life he was trying to escape confinement. The heaviness and formalism of French music weighed on him: "I don't think I shall ever be able to put music into a strict mould. I'm not speaking of musical form; it's a literary question. I shall always prefer a subject where, somehow, action is sacrificed to feeling." It was then he discovered Wagner; he became a Wagnerian "to the pitch of forgetting the simple rules of courtesy,"[3] as he wrote later.

The revulsion was rapid, but memories of the Wagnerian orchestra did not soon leave his music. In Rome he marveled at the counterpoint of Orlando Lasso. "I should like to keep the melodic line lyrical," he wrote, "and not allow the orchestra to predominate."[4] A traditionless innovator, he was feeling his way to his own music.

"It's a literary question." Returned to Paris, he became an associate of poets, literary enthusiasts who had discovered Wagner and wished to create a vague, verbally orchestrated, symbolic poetry which would be the equivalent of music. Debussy thought rather of a music which would be the equivalent of poetry. He had heard Liszt play once at the piano and preserved the memory of his pedaling: "It was as if he were breathing." He became aware of Berlioz, but he preferred Rameau over Gluck or Wagner. He imagined a music that "will begin where the words are impotent; music is made for this 'inexpressible.' I would like it to appear as though it came from a shadow and that from time to time it will return there."[5]

"The intensity of expression should vary in degrees. At times it is necessary to paint in monochrome and limit oneself to gray tones. . . . I am dreaming of poems which would not condemn me to contrive long and heavy acts, poems which would offer me the scenes which move in their locality and character, and where the actors do not argue but submit to life and their fate."[6] He was to find such scenes, not so often in the librettos he considered and rejected, but in the poems of French poets from Villon to Verlaine which became the "scenes" of his great songs.

Debussy said this in October 1889, a few months after the experience of the Paris Exposition, where he had heard the Annamite drama and Rimsky-Korsakov had directed two concerts of music by the Russian "Five." Instead of the raw Russian color, Debussy preferred the Whistlerian refinement of monochrome, "scenes which move in their locality and character" like the Annamese musically accompanied dance-plays.

Debussy's musical art is a constant reaching towards a goal he foresaw, though he must adapt the means. He advanced as far by rejection as by innovation. His new art came to him slowly, a song, a piano piece, a poetic scene for instruments or for voices. He sought ideas, librettos, poems from his intellectual equals, complete understanding from his friends, and from women a loyalty he could not return. The ideas, librettos, poems were often unsuited to his needs; when understanding failed he rejected the friend; the women he lived with served but could not help or protect him. A lonely creator, he became an ever lonelier man.

Debussy's supreme achievement is to be found in his songs, as distinctive in style, though not in model, as the earlier French *chanson*—so artificial they are like no other music yet seem natural, because the music, the emotion, and the French speech these spring from are one idiom. He created a new French art of song, in which, though much imitated, he remains unequaled. Like his Germanic contemporary Hugo Wolf, Debussy fused words and accompaniment in a single experience. The sound is translucent, the experience evoked. Dowland and Purcell, Schubert and Wolf, Debussy and Ives are the great art-song creators of Western music.

This sense of the unified experience permeates his music. As an innovator he was no more than partially successful. For all the references and influences that entered into his music, his best creation is an atmosphere, a Whistlerian monochrome that can erupt with the lights and movement of *La Mer*, can wear an Oriental or a Spanish costume and does not disdain wit, which is capable of the formal linear clarity of the Quartet, the *Études*, of the mere hints of color, as if seen and heard from a balcony at a distance, of the prelude *Fireworks*, the sadness mingled with quiet savagery of the last sonatas, for cello, for flute, cello, and harp, for the violin.

Impressionism, symbolism, the qualities of contemporary French painting and poetry, came to him, perhaps almost unconsciously, through the "transcendental" accompaniments of Liszt, especially the large tone poems for piano, which Debussy deprived of their ponderous reiterated melodies, leaving only the little vestige of a tune, and transmuted into what painters call *chiaroscuro* or "tone."

Indeed, one might better speak of Debussy as Whistlerian rather than impressionist, since his color begins in flat washes rather than in anything resembling "pointillistic" instrumental clashes, and his shapes remain vague, though the line is more decisive than Whistler's. When he succeeded it was by the application of light rather than color, by contrasting linear emphases which show how nearly his art returned to the keyboard music of the clavecinists; like Couperin he relied on silence, interwoven with and as the background of each phrase. He probably came to and heard Couperin through Chopin, pianistically, with more contrasting emphasis and less registration by color than on harpsichord. He was seldom so sumptuous as Couperin can be in one of his large, slow overtures or a saraband. Therefore, when the time came to dedicate his *Études*, he could not decide between Couperin and Chopin but eventually chose to dedicate them to Chopin. Debussy thought of these as studies solving technical problems, but he wrote them in a style more resembling Chopin's Preludes or Couperin's, more improvisatory and less demonstrative than that of Chopin's *Études* or Liszt's. Because he omitted the solemn guidance of the tune usually threaded through these larger examples, his *Études* have never joined these others in the dumping-ground of pianistic virtuosity at the end of the typical recital program. One needs a special attitude to play them—and, as many believe, a more skilled audience to hear them.

Debussy resembled Whistler in his sensitivity to atmosphere instead of substance, the fall of a phrase rather than its character; in his sensitive yet often bitter and exacerbated criticism. There was the same danger, too, that in attempting any larger canvas his sensibility would waver between the sentimentally poeticized objects of Pre-Raphaelite taste and Manet's rationally objective vision. Nijinsky, dancing *The Afternoon of a Faun*, dramatized the conflict by applying to the atmospheric visual poem the concrete sexual gesture. But it was precisely on the larger canvas that Debussy most firmly set his mark, not with full-scale symphony and four-hour opera but in a series of unique works shaped exactly to his foreseeing taste: the orchestral tone poems that are not descriptive; the sustained songs, so completely realized in every detail that one should not sing or hear sung more than two or three of them at a time, because the concentration they demand is too exhausting; and his opera *Pelleas and Melisande*, musical poetry shaped to the sound and flow of spoken French.

Though Debussy appreciated the daring simplicity of Erik Satie, he did not venture so far into outright dissonance. His orientalizing taste preferred harmonies that chimed or rang to those which clashed. His harmonies, though freed from formal counterpoint and sequence, remain continually plastic within the whole body of each composition; he did not create them as innovations for themselves. He did not invent "chords without names" to show them off. By abandoning the theoretical rationalizations of his time, he avoided the heavily technical vulgarity of Strauss, smothered in rich orchestration. Though he deliberately embraced atonality before Schoenberg, he retained the traditional Italianate desire for vertical concordance, however laboriously he must seek it. His art demanded great daring but never to display it, so that his music seems in our ears less courageous than it is.

There was in him nothing of the Dadaist. His rejections were final, satiric, savage. His critical writings try to play with but instead mock and abuse the despoilers of music. His line of development and that of Satie were mutually exclusive. He had little use for but did not disdain the outright virtuosity of Ravel, was not above stealing from him. Some of their harmonic discoveries ran parallel: they both derived from Lisztian impressionism; orchestrated after the manner of Berlioz instead of Beethoven or Wagner; looked back for renewed clarity to the clavecinists Couperin and Rameau; and alike rejected the worn-out polyglot compromises they were trained in. Above all, they shared the poetic awareness of French idiomatic speech.

Ravel, in the neoclassic manner, ran toward polytonality, the brilliant clashing of two or more keys heard together. Polytonality is little more than the splitting of a composition between two or more still diatonically harmonic keys. Strictly applied, polytonality is not atonal. Debussy, having freed his harmony from diatonic rule and key, reassembled it most often around the whole-tone scale, which having six notes instead of seven in the octave, without semitones or triads to define harmonic relationship within the scale, seems both vague and sonant. This less dramatic harmony, more suitable to intimacy than to declamation, appears prophetically in Dargomijsky's *Stone Guest* and in the middle operas by Puccini. Whole-tone harmony is able to be at once atonal and more consonant than diatonic harmony, because the contrast between more and less dissonant relationships is not enforced by any sense of key. Whole-tone harmony avoids the drastic harmonic shifts of the tone-center compromise, which prefers confusion to vagueness. Debussy's music lacks the sharp contrasts which produce harmonic drama; all difference is muted.

Stravinsky was right in believing that he could outgrow Debussy. One can steal from him no more than a mannerism, for the most part the conveniences and limitations of the whole-tone scale and its vague harmony. Debussy's content, like his harmony and its idiom and resulting style, was self-complete and completed in his work. Difficult even to imagine what his next composition might have been, had he lived longer. Among his later works the ballet *Jeux,* alone, seems to point a further direction.

The last hundred years of the Harmonic Era lead to Schoenberg, but it was Debussy, during the decade before and after 1900, who effectively ended that era. He was the first composer of the new Era of Sound, though he would surely not have recognized himself by such a description. Debussy looked backward, while the young Ives looked forward.

THE NEOCLASSICISTS

WITH A DIGRESSION ON TRANSCRIBED MUSIC

Debussy's revulsion against Wagner concerned only himself; he did not turn entirely against Germanic music until after the start of the First World War. (At that time, Ravel, who was in military service, courageously upheld the right of such "enemy" composers as Schoenberg and Bartók to be heard in France.) Debussy did not lead but moved in habitual isolation within a larger anti-Germanic trend among French composers, which began with the founding of the Société Nationale de Musique in 1870, after the military defeat of France by Germany. Because the Société was established as much for patriotic as for musical reasons, its polyglot French founders merely reacted against Germanic influences but developed no common theory, idiom, or style.

These founders included Camille Saint-Saëns, César Franck, Vincent d'Indy, Gabriel Fauré, all professors at the Conservatoire or Schola Cantorum; unlike the pedantic majority of these faculties, they exercised a liberating influence throughout French music; d'Indy being at a critical period a defender of Debussy and afterwards, with Albert Roussel, teacher of the middle-aged Satie; Fauré, the principal teacher of Ravel.

Liszt had awakened these composers by his open-minded looking back to music of earlier periods. Germanic musicological scholarship and publication of earlier music set them an example. And it should be remembered that, although the general level of public audience response to music was lower than it is today, several pianists of the generation after Liszt, inspired by his example, became capable of a repertory which has seldom been equaled from that time until the present. (Wrong notes, in fact "cascades of wrong notes," as some reported of the playing of Anton Rubinstein, were less seriously regarded then than now.) Before his death at twenty-nine, Carl Tausig had memorized the entire classical piano repertory. Rubinstein's repertory included some pieces by the English virginalists of the late sixteenth century. Hans von Bülow performed in one series of recitals the complete piano works by Beethoven and in another the complete piano works by Brahms. His correspondence reports a recital consisting of Beethoven's *Hammerklavier Sonata* followed by the *Diabelli Variations.* Each of these pianist-composers transcribed the music of earlier centuries, with their own elaborations, to increase the repertory of virtuoso music for piano.

❀ The stuffy, snobbish, pedantic belief that transcribing music is a low habit and that such transcriptions are unfit for serious public hearing needs to be got rid of. Keyboard transcriptions served the same educative function during the nineteenth century that the player piano, phonograph, and recorded tape have served in the twentieth; these were the chief means by which students and amateurs acquainted themselves with the symphonic and chamber music repertory. The greater part of instrumental music in both the Italian and the Germanic traditions had been composed originally at—or, one might say, in view of—the keyboard, the lie of the parts adapting readily to arrangement for two or four hands. When the music was choral or operatic, the amateur and student readers seldom hesitated to sing as well as play it.

But the new orchestral style of Berlioz presented difficulties, and the new compositions by Debussy, a half-century later, even greater difficulties for anyone who wished to read them at the piano. Berlioz thought his music not in keyboard relationships but directly in the sound of instruments. Keyboard transcription did not seriously distort the generality of classic or romantic music, though in certain instances the effort to preserve the sound-character of an uncommon piece went beyond the capacity of any keyboard instrument, as when Beethoven transcribed for four hands his *Great Fugue*. This is probably one reason why Bach's *Brandenburg Concertos* did not have much currency during the nineteenth century. Keyboard transcription gives little of the subtle instrumental coloring of such a work as Berlioz's *Romeo and Juliet Symphony* or *The Childhood of Christ;* it makes harmonically too obvious the commoner Wagnerian orchestral polyphony.

Transcription as a skill lost reputation when audiences began tiring of that staple of the nineteenth century piano repertory, the fantasia with trivial variations and a great show of virtuosity on operatic themes: Lizt's *Fantasy on Mozart's Don Giovanni,* as further elaborated by Busoni, is perhaps the best, though not the most difficult, of these. The organ works by J. S. Bach, transcribed for piano, make a bigger show on that instrument than his compositions for clavichord or harpsichord; in transcriptions by Liszt and his successors, and particularly by Ferruccio Busoni, Bach's music became popular for the wrong reasons. "Bach-Busoni," though as a whole excellent pianistic workmanship, well founded in scholarly musicianship, became a term of reproach.

Orchestral composers in the same way began transcribing older music for the new instrument of Berlioz. Much of this was and for the most part still is badly done, for no better use than to enlarge the repertory with familiar music in the wrong setting at the expense of newly created compositions.

The distinction should be, as with any other music, by musical judgement instead of prejudice. Liszt's operatic fantasies or Gottschalk's folk-music adaptations are too good pianistic fun to be outlawed from the repertory. Bach-Busoni has perhaps served its purpose, and orchestral Bach-Stokowski, though in public hearing much still satisfies. Few would wish to sit through a public reading of a Beethoven symphony in Liszt's transcription for two hands at the piano, but the experience might enable us to grasp more readily the symphonic-length piano works by Alkan.

Any performance on modern instruments or in modern style of music composed for other instruments or earlier versions of the modern instruments (e.g. the violin or piano before 1800) or to be performed in a style unlike the modern is in effect a transcription, except that the stuffy, the snobbish, and the pedantic pretend there is a difference, because they wish to hear only the "original score," although the score they read from has usually been adapted by modern editing. For early scores in the tradition of *musica ficta* or with indeterminate juxtaposition of notes and bar-lines (for example, the original printed score of *Parthenia*), a "correct" modern edition, however carefully prepared, is an arrangement. Any seventeenth or eighteenth century scores are "arranged" in modern performance, however note-perfect, when the significant difference between *good notes* and *bad notes* ceases to direct by habit every turn of phrase. Every sonata or chamber work with *continuo* accompaniment arranged by the editor ceases to be the original score.

If the argument against transcriptions, that they are not originals but copies more or less distorted, is viable, then we must admit that, except in very unusual conditions, none of the music we hear that was composed before 1800, and practically speaking, very little we hear that is not of our time is an original; it is a copy more or less distorted. The sound of our symphony orchestra is not that of Beethoven's orchestra; the volume, attack, pedal, and overtone registration of the sound of our piano differs from Beethoven's. Liszt and Kalkbrenner changed the performance of Chopin's piano music in his lifetime. In each case, our method of performance is unlike the original. The same is true of our present-day playing of 1920s jazz.

What Étienne Gilson has written about "so-called reproductions of famous paintings"—and he applies the same argument against canvases which have been preserved by re-painting—applies also to musical compositions: that they "can do little more than to familiarize their public with the subject and the composition of these masterpieces, but when it comes to colors, which are the substance of paintings, they are likely to spread the misleading opinion that, provided their colors more or less resemble those of the original, a few differences in tone do not matter much."[1]

Transcription is an ancient musical skill, practical in use and never despised until now, very common in the sixteenth, seventeenth, and eighteenth centuries, the chief means of amateur and scholarly rediscovery of earlier music during the nineteenth century, and in the twentieth century an occasional achievement of art. Ravel's orchestral arrangement of Mussorgsky's *Pictures at an Exhibition* has established itself solidly in the repertory—from which, however, the "bleeding fragments," as Donald Tovey called them, of Wagnerian opera are slipping. Webern's transcription of the six-part *Ricercar* from Bach's *Musical Offering* is not a reproduction of Bach's instrumental sound but a landmark in new soloistic orchestral technique. Schoenberg's orchestration of the Brahms Piano Quartet in G minor is not overrated if one calls it a fifth Brahms symphony—and in orchestral diversity and instrumental subtlety it is the best.

Schoenberg's reason for transcribing the quartet was strictly musical. A recorded version had appeared, in which Artur Rubinstein performed the piano part as if it were a concerto. At the time, most of us thought it very fine. But Schoenberg heard how Brahms, in his long hesitation to commit himself to a symphony, had indeed written one in the G minor Piano Quartet, giving the bulk of the material to the piano. By orchestrating the piano part, which overweighs the quartet, Schoenberg created the lost Brahms symphony.

This is an exceptional case. Nearly all efforts to blow up works for smaller means by orchestrating them, for example the Schubert *Grand Duo* for piano four hands rewritten as a symphony by Joseph Joachim, have failed, for lack of creative skill in the orchestration. Transcribing music for another means requires as great skill as creating it. A beautiful example is Stravinsky's recomposed version for chorus and orchestra of J. S. Bach's *Canonic Variations,* the original for organ. Are the Stravinsky ballet scores *The Fairy's Kiss,* made of pieces by Tchaikovsky orchestrated or reorchestrated, or *Pulcinella,* elaborated from compositions by Pergolesi, to be called transcriptions, re-creations, or essentially new works?

Putting prejudice aside, it is better to perform a new work than a familiar one secondhand in an arrangement.

Music is constantly being made new; the notated score is only a guide. By recovering the notated compositions and styles of performance of other periods, using such skill and knowledge as we have to re-create them in some part as they may have sounded, we contribute to the present state of music nothing resembling a well-preserved sculpture or painting from another epoch. We create a fresh musical experience as integrally valid as we are able to make it, but it exists as music by its integral validity and not by its identity with the original work. The more we know about how such a composition may actually have sounded, the more integrally valid our performance and its usefulness for the ongoing of music. Players who merely fake such performance, and dilettantes and pedants who support them, do harm both ways. They interfere with a genuine adaptation to modern instrumental practice, while pretending that a very imperfect archaism is correct.

Imperfect archaism during the nineteenth century Gothic revival innovated a hideously pretentious architecture. It destroyed precious Gothic and Romanesque survivals to replace them with pretty, characterless improvements. It also built the British Parliament buildings at London and inspired John Ruskin to moral conclusions, amid many false esthetic judgements, which in turn inspired Tolstoi and Gandhi, both nearly impervious to esthetics, to moral action. It aroused William Morris to reinvigorate the hideous commerce of nineteenth century printing by the archaizing example of his Kelmscott Press; it stirred the tendrils of the *art nouveau,* while reviving a taste for simple furniture and cottage surroundings which has drastically improved the conditions of twentieth century domestic living.

We cannot imagine how Beethoven's late sonatas, symphonies, and quartets may have sounded when first performed, but we can revive the correct tuning of music not composed for equal temperament, we can rediscover the older instruments and the correct styles of playing them, we can vigorously explore the rhythmic teaching of earlier masters, all to advantage. Our serious note-players at present attempt none of this. Revival of old instruments, of the great variety of former playing styles and rhythmic conventions, will open our ears to fresh musical possibilities. We are able to comprehend more fully, as a result of such experiences, what is happening in music today. I have observed in lecturing on the history of European tunings that the listeners who respond most instantly to these microtonal distinctions are those who have trained themselves to hear the microtonal divergences of electronic music. They are also, in my experience, the most able to apply what they hear to their own compositions.

Neoclassicism came out of the archaizing adaptation of old idiom to new means, as demonstrated by Liszt in the third book of his *Pilgrimages* and his *Harmonies Poétiques et Religieuses*, in the same way that impressionism came from such extraordinary virtuoso innovations as Liszt's *Fountains of the Villa d'Este* and *Benediction of God in the Solitude*, where the accompaniment spreads over the keyboard to become the composition, threaded through by a recurrent tune.

Liszt's true heir in this direction was not Debussy but Maurice Ravel, who continued the direct line of Lisztian impressionism in his own *Fountains, Miroirs*, and *Gaspard de la Nuit*, while developing the neoclassic line of archaizing art, not so much in the late *Tombeau de Couperin* but more particularly in his entire feeling as composer. The archaizing tendency, which was little more than a solitary corner of the later works of Liszt, was fundamental to Ravel from the beginning. "If you have nothing to say," he declared, "you had better keep quiet, rather than repeat what has been already said well. If, on the contrary, you have something to say, this 'something' will never appear so clearly as in your subconscious infidelity to the model."[2]

"Subconscious infidelity": it is the true sign of distinction between mere archaizing, the better or worse sort of transcription, the academically faithful adhering to past models—so far as one's capacity permits—and the enforcing of one's own esthetic consistency, one's immediate content as a composer creating today, into the seeming habit of another art.

Or as Robert Craft has written of Stravinsky: "Living in an age where he could feel no development towards a common style, he was impelled, by an amazing self-awareness, to force his position, to establish his own relation with the maturities of the eighteenth and other centuries."[3]

The French professor-composers, in withdrawing from Germanic influence, sought alternative styles among the French and polyglot composers of their own century, with little more than a genuflection towards the great masters of genuinely French tradition through the medieval, Renaissance, and classical periods. It was Richard Strauss who transcribed for orchestra a suite of pieces by François Couperin.

For Debussy and Ravel the new French character was in the sound. Their vocal art created in effect a new French singing voice.

For Erik Satie the difference was in the attitude; therefore Satie, in a style of little abstract gestures, of seeming preciosity without purpose, went farther than the others in shaking off not only Germanism but reliance on the musical elaboration of the sound. He defined the "new spirit": "It teaches us to aim at an emotive simplicity and a firmness of utterance enabling sonorities and rhythms to assert themselves clearly, unequivocal in design and accent, and contrived in a spirit of humility and renunciation."[4]

It was for this understanding of the contemporary purpose in music that Ravel could speak of Satie, with Chabrier, as the two most "necessary" French composers. The expressive simplicity Ravel learned from Satie shows to utmost refinement in many passages of *Beauty and the Beast* and *L'Enfant et les Sortilèges*.

Neoclassicism was not in essence a return to the eighteenth century; it was, if I may use a curious terminology, a *purification of the polyglot*.

Having once appreciated the use of the term *neoclassicism* in this larger significance, one will not be confused by the enthusiastic turning back of Ravel to the Oriental and Russian music heard at the Paris Exposition which also awakened the imagination of Debussy, and at the same time to Chabrier, Gounod, Liszt, Chopin. Out of this mélange of sounds, forms well and ill digested, habits, conventions, idiomatic formulas and styles neither sharply distinguished nor discrete, Ravel composed with great effort a succession of increasingly well defined compositions, by no means of equal quality but unquestionably the stylistic idiom of a unifying intelligence, never fully mature but intensely musical. Towards the end of his career, Ravel's content, seemingly incapable of further growth, was running shallow. He would still write the best-selling *Bolero*.

In the same way, over a vaster field of reference, one will not be confused by Stravinsky's reverent turning back to the work of composers less gifted with scope of vision, strength, knowledge, consistency than himself: Tchaikovsky, Glinka, Gounod, Pergolesi. At the same time he turned away from the Russianizing idiom of "the Five," which had brought him his first reputation among the Parisian admirers of the "barbarians," as they called these Russian composers. The savage reception of *Rite of Spring* at the first performance, but more profoundly Stravinsky's distaste for the presumed "ethnic" connotations of a work which, in its strict dramatic objectivity, described a "pagan rite" but not the primitive barbarism of savages, a work which he had composed in a highly cultivated instrumental idiom to create the musical character of a far-off event realized in the almost abstract physical groupings of ballet, had brought Stravinsky to a crisis. Once more, in profound nostalgia, he would return to the Russian life, now irrevocably lost to him as an exile after the Russian revolution, in the totally disciplined ritual of *The Wedding*—an ethnic gesture but no ethnic music. There was nothing in this music but association to remind the listener of Balakirev, Borodin, or Stravinsky's heavy-handed master, Rimsky-Korsakov, whose work he understood so much better than the Parisian enthusiasts. As for Mussorgsky's idiom of Russian speech, Stravinsky preferred the more Italianate melody and harmonic directness of Tchaikovsky and Glinka.

Stravinsky preferred, indeed, the old *bel canto* Russian opera in Italian style of the generations before Glinka. An expatriate partly by accident, partly by taste, an exile perforce, he would weld materials from the junkyard of the European polyglot to create a melodic art not of orchestration but of instruments. In *The Firebird* and again at the opening of *Rite of Spring* he found for the bassoon its singing voice, an objective melodic character which even Mozart had not so well conceived for it. Stravinsky's art of liberated instrumental voices enabled him to break through the impasse of Russianizing raw orchestral color, and again out of the restrictions of the polytonal idiom, until at last in *Orpheus* he could sing as if freed even from his own drastic convention. Now the whole of European music after Monteverdi was at his command, except the Germanic art from Wagner to Schoenberg, which he still disliked and rejected. Within the next few years he discovered at last the mature music of Schoenberg. But it was not just the music of Schoenberg and afterwards of Anton Webern that he discovered, it was his own complete freedom from the tradition of the Harmonic Era, a defection that shocked, alarmed, outraged the great body of musicians who had looked to him as the chief defender of harmonic tonality against atonality and its consequences, which they believed would be harmonic chaos. Stravinsky was quite right, and so within their limited view were they: tonality is one area of the field of sound; the whole field is, in terms of tonality, harmonic chaos, requiring the invention of new disciplines to make it music. Stravinsky saw that the Harmonic Era had ended, and he went beyond it. After that, despite increasing handicaps of age, he continued composing his own content in his own style as satisfactorily as ever.

The other younger neoclassical composers wavered like their masters, Vincent d'Indy and Gabriel Fauré, between neoclassicism and the old romantic polyglot. D'Indy accomplished little to remember, but Fauré produced a large body of fine songs, prevailingly neoclassic piano pieces at once pedantic and limpid, calmly romantic orchestral compositions, and a Requiem Mass as fustian ornate in form, architecture, and color as a turn-of-the-century cathedral.

The still younger neoclassicists took their ideas from Satie, passing belatedly to occasional imitation of Ravel, whom they afterwards rejected, or rushed after Stravinsky, who quickly left most of them behind. The elder French composers, whom Fauré abandoned, drew in their strictures to oppose a development they had commenced but could not follow. Their Parisian institution, the Société Nationale, became the refuge of reaction, to be replaced by the new Société Musicale Indépendente.

14

THE ART OF MUSICAL PARODY

WITH AN INTRODUCTION TO *Erik Satie*

While the more widely recognized Parisian composers were translating the polyglot into the neoclassic according to their various abilities, Erik Satie went his way back and forth into the city from the suburb where he spent his later years, sharing with the most radical French poets and painters the creation of a new esthetic.

One might well call him the first true neoclassicist, citing as proof the bare simplicity of his early piano works, the *Sarabandes, Gymnopédies,* and *Gnossiennes.* He became, because of the purity of his rejections, the first musical surrealist. He transformed the polyglot into a small harmonic and melodic essence, twisting it on itself in little knots of harmonic variance, pointing up the seeming helplessness of this bare music—barely music, the ordinary musician still thinks it—with texts of equal-seeming insignificance and, throwing his influence against all formal masterpieces, including those of his admiring friend Ravel, took up the notion of *collage*, borrowed from the painters, to make compositions of street music, popular tunes, sounds, noises, disconnected and, one might think, directionless. In the midst of these almost private exercises, a figure liked, laughed at, admired but his music seldom performed except in semiprivacy, he returned in middle age for three years to the Schola Cantorum, where he studied formal counterpoint with Vincent d'Indy and

Albert Roussel. In the liturgical mood he wrote his small, lovable, and raggedly incomplete *Mass of the Poor*. Then, as if convinced that what he had learned was of no interest, he continued as before, producing in the continuation of his little music the one major work, *Socrate*, a setting for voice and small orchestra of three scenes from the Socratic dialogues in French translation. In that one work he showed, as if to illustrate his criticism of Debussy and Ravel, the beautiful skeleton of an ultimate neo-classic art—a vocal line the most sensitive to communicate emotion, Virgil Thomson has said, of any in European music, except the recitatives of Bach's *Saint Matthew Passion*.

Looking backward from today we can see that Satie was one of the four composers, with Schoenberg, Debussy, and Stravinsky, who made inevitable what is happening in music at the present time. Until now he has been more influential than Ives.

"Everyone will tell you that I am not a musician," he wrote in *Mémoires d'un Amnésique*. "That is true. . . . Do you know how to clean sounds? It is rather a dirty process. . . ."[1]

"With a united voice I cry: 'Long Live the Amateurs!' " He meant it. "All great artists are amateurs."

Musical parody is an aspect of art to be recognized and enjoyed by the appreciative listener. It is peculiarly an aspect of neoclassicism, where the composer presents in a fresh relationship a recognizable convention. Satie and Stravinsky, each to the scale of his art, have this parodic skill. It goes so deep into many of their compositions that the listener is hard put to it to decide where parody ends and the customary solemnity expected of music starts.

A parodist is one in whom the convention and his use of it play at cross-purposes: a skill-crossed consistency. Mozart understood musical parody but kept most of it to his letters, apart from several movements and one sextet he called *A Musical Joke*: if the piece is not played exactly in the convention it is not funny. Music that is meant to be funny is too often blatant; parody, because it retains the convention while teasing it, leaves the listener in two minds, aware that what he is hearing is not what it might seem yet is right because it pleases him. Not expecting to be amused, he smiles. J. S. Bach, who customarily introduces the Holy Spirit in an airy measure, is a sublime parodist: the Father authority, the Son sacrifice, the Spirit delight.

Why in such an example do I speak of parody? Because it is

the parody in such case which makes the statement, as Tintoretto by the parodic act of foreshortening appears to reveal the heavens. The rococo painter, having learned this trick of parody, paints heaven with a swirl through the roof which keeps the rain out. The statement is still there, more acute because against nature and reason, a trick of eye; so nowadays, though we see it as calculated, we are touched by it. For Bach this parody of the real is the outer garment of belief.

Beethoven was a consummate parodist and in his younger years amused himself with it in his improvisations; there are also superb parodies in the *Diabelli Variations*. His parodies are often large-scale compositions, or concealed within them, at moments coarsely funny, like Mozart in several of his letters, more often not so obvious; for Beethoven, as for Satie, parody was sometimes musical criticism. Chabrier wrote musical parody, but his humor, even concerning Wagner, did not preserve him from writing a solemn Wagnerian opera called *Gwendoline*.

Serge Prokofiev, in his younger years, wrote excellent musical parodies; they are humorous and funny but not critical. The best known is his *Classical Symphony*. It is one of Prokofiev's lighter compositions: one can say of his music, the lighter the more lasting. Stravinsky's parodic Symphony in C does not point fun in clever tunes but deliberately competes with the classical symphonic writers in their formal medium, while never relinquishing his own deeply implicated idiom.

Stravinsky's parody is seldom critical. *Petrouchka, The Soldier's Tale*, the duet between trombone and contrabass in *Pulcinella*, the entire scheme of *A Game of Cards*, and several passages in *Agon*—of course, the little concerto for violin solo with three trombones—are parodies. *The Rake's Progress* glitters with parodic chuckles.

Schoenberg also is a parodist, and funny, if you know where to listen. There is parody in his *Satires*, in that great instrumental comedy, his Suite for Seven Instruments, and in his Variations for Wind Band. Celestial parody illumines the profound counterpoise of verbal significances in *Moses and Aron*.

But a great, boyish belly-laugh of parody exploded in 1891, in the musical wilderness of American New England where no one observed it, when the seventeen-year-old Charles Ives composed (and may have played at a concert on July 4, 1891) his *Variations on "America"* for organ, giving warning, though none who heard could have interpreted the prophecy, that by these means, wrong notes, truncated passages, harmonic mixes and misses, tone reaching out to the dimensions of inchoate noise, a new era of music was opening.

One can classify the greater portion of Satie's art, verbal and musical, as parody. His parodies are often funny and for that reason put aside as jokes. Satie continually uses the wrong notes, like Mozart in *A Musical Joke,* to expand what would be otherwise a harmlessly flat measure or passage into a succession of not quite explicable tonal relationships, which he makes no effort to resolve or to explain. In the seemingly simple melodic contours of his early works he emphasized false relations no more than Debussy did. As Satie's style developed, it became thinner, more brittle, glittering with unexpected tones. One's first—and for most persons, final—reaction is that this music is without substance, trivial, colorless, bad musical joking puffed out with nonsensical nonsequiturs in words. The words may be read aloud before playing; the music plays with the scene, both description and action, in ways which are nonexplicit. For example, the words tell a day in the life of a bureaucratic clerk; one plays the *Bureaucratic Sonatina.* One is tempted to recite the words with the music, but Satie forbade this. So Satie's humor is usually put aside and no thought given to his art.

In fact, it is consummate musical criticism, accurate and uncommonly prophetic, composed as music and when heard in its parodic meaning devastatingly effective.

With his late *Nocturnes,* Satie showed that one aspect of his composition was of the same order as Stravinsky's, comparable to *Piano-Rag Music,* published in the same year, but Satie lacked, as he had always lacked, the energy. None of the other Parisians could match this harmonically free tonal nonchalance, though some tried to simulate it. One steps across to the discerning, would-be but not so nonchalant early work of Virgil Thomson. The pilgrim could admire but did not aspire to Satie's natural habitat; he could not so rapidly travel beyond it as Stravinsky.

Only the Parisian composers seem to have recognized Satie's merit, admiring it as the Parisian painters admired the painting of *douanier* Rousseau and writers admired the *Ubu Roi* of Alfred Jarry. It was an epoch of eccentrics, the first era of collage, Dada, surrealism, names still to be invented. The best painting, writing, architecture, music of this period has entered history, textbooks, museums; the creative example of the eccentrics has continued living, re-emerging with even greater force as one aspect of the American experimental tradition.

In this country much of the credit for such eccentricities has gone to the painter and exhibitor of objects Marcel Duchamp, who after an early career in Dada retired from art to chess. Duchamp, like Jean Cocteau, was the outsider looking in, whose considered eccentricities explain themselves without difficulty, so that the public feels safe with them. Duchamp's *Nude Descending a Staircase* is an explanatory reduction of movement. A propped-up urinal is to be viewed as sculpture.

Jarry, Rousseau, and Satie were the real thing lived from the inside, their products data of an imagination which does not explain itself. Satie's music anticipates surrealism, a real object in a real setting where it does not belong. Surrealism explores the fantastic elements of parody, the unconscious realities of nightmare and farce. Dada is the extreme of parody become irresponsible. Satie's art reports few nightmares; as he grew older his farce went over towards slapstick and Dada, by example of the cinema—an assemblage of the commonplace in events which occur as it were by accident rather than by dictation of the unconscious. The ballet *Parade,* for which Satie wrote the music, includes a motion picture, for which he also wrote music, in which he appears, bearded, bowler-hatted, in his fantastically formal dress, firing an artillery piece.

With the decline of neoclassicism, parody in music had become too well established to be discarded. It became confused with musical joking, with a sort of gutless triviality masking as comedy. In the work of the composers called "the Six"—in tribute to the St. Petersburg "Five"—who for a time regarded themselves as Satie's disciples, comedy, parody, triviality, lightness, offset by a belated, bloated polyglottery and Wagnerism, got thoroughly mixed up with musical skill. Two of "the Six," Durey and Tailleferre, came to nothing. Poulenc somewhat outgrew the mixture, to produce excellent songs, a Mass for voices *a capella,* and a virtuoso *Gloria* for soprano and orchestra.

Darius Milhaud, as if wearying of the youthful effort with which he had labored to compile his bulging pastiche opera *Christopher Columbus,* found a more comfortable path. Auric went aside into motion-picture composing. Honegger composed the powerful tone-poem *Rugby,* which was in advance of his time, and the cinema-musical locomotive, *Pacific 231*, which was not. Afterwards he ceased to recognize himself as a parodist and was neither properly amusing nor properly serious. One wonders what the composer of *Socrate*, the *Mass of the Poor*, and the *Bureaucratic Sonatina* would have made of *Jeanne d'Arc au Bûcher*—the principal figure chic but not peasant. The unceasing inventiveness of Satie's parodic skill dwindled in the work of his disciples to pretentiousness.

A developed sense of parody in the listener can betray drama that aspires to tragedy and is not tragic. In the last scene of Poulenc's opera of the French Revolution, *Dialogue of the Carmelites*, the repeated thud of the guillotine offstage distracts attention from the music—as the photograph of an execution strikes quite different emotion than the etched scenes of Goya's *Disasters of War*. A graveyard act in drama easily turns comic. Sentimental solemnity renders the emotion safe and painless for the ladies and gentlemen who have come from dinner dressed for the opera. Comedy can transform the appearance of reality into a dimension larger than life. In the motion picture which accompanies *Parade* a funeral procession gradually transforms itself crescendo into a transcendent silent movie chase.

To work with such means one cannot live outside them. They break down, as the motion picture does, the proscenium barrier between stage and audience. The actor is no longer set off objectively but like a man in the next seat rising to speak. The leader of that element of the American experimental tradition which looks back to Satie has been John Cage, whose art and whose philosophy force on us with shocking reality as esthetic events acts of daily living that we have not conceived to be esthetic. This contradiction provokes misunderstanding, and, because it is real, dramatizes Cage, when he appears in person before an audience, among the great comedians.

Satie's involvement with the detail of life was less conspicuous than Cage's: Satie dramatized himself as an eccentric; Cage does not. The involvement of each is typified by his place of living. Cage lives in the country, at Stony Point on the Hudson, in a small colony of varied artists, not closely related in their work; his home with two rooms, one glass wall opening to the woods, was until recently almost without furniture. Much of the time he is traveling as a lecturer and performer.

Satie's room during the last decades of his life was in the

Parisian suburb of Arcueil, a tiny room never entered by his friends until after his death. They found there two upright pianos, one on top of the other, without action or strings; eight new suits unpacked from their boxes; two hundred umbrellas; the floor strewn with shirts, which he had worn once and discarded. There was no running water and no heat. The bedsheets were black, because they had not been changed for twenty years. They were sewn together with the bedclothes in an intricate heating arrangement of wine bottles. On a cold night, Satie would go down for water, return and heat it over a primus flame, and pour the hot water into the bottles to warm him into the night. (I am indebted for this description to a broadcast talk by Virgil Thomson; he had it from Darius Milhaud, who saw Satie's room.) It is reported, too, that many times when Satie had walked from Paris to his suburb, he would arrive when the sun had risen and at once walk back.

The nightmare of the unconscious had been absorbed into an environment, which could be disregarded, discarded without laundering as easily as a used shirt. Sophisticated, isolated among friends, any one of whom he might put out of his life over a trifle, Satie created a small art that is completely joyous, not innocent but guiltless, without soil.

15

STEIN-THOMSON

Most incorrigibly American of the expatriates who centered their
lives on Paris during the first half of the twentieth century,
Gertrude Stein befriended and advised the painters, poets, and
eccentrics of her adopted environment, while sorting out and
mothering a continually evolving tourism of Americans who
looked to Paris for esthetic inspiration and to her for esthetic
wisdom. They looked to her as the characters in her *The Mother
of Us All* look to Susan B. Anthony for leadership, guidance, and
the last word. And she gave these.

The large, firm handwriting of her manuscripts proceeds without hesitation or revision, a few lines to each page of a French
student notebook, as one looks through these notebooks today in
the files of the Stein collection at Yale. Occasionally a word is
struck through in favor of another, and the line proceeds. It is a
complete esthetic consistency working immediately, with intense
self-concentration and criticism but no feeling of fear or need of
change, in the language of its own thought-patterns, vividly
aware of surrounding personalities, presences, voices, furniture,
landscape, and the reality of words as objects equivalent with
experience and interchangeable with things, communicative as a
telegram, a painting, music, an event, exceedingly conscious but
free of literary habit, ruminating on ideas like a cow on grass.

True poetry has nothing to do with conventional word-patterns, though it customarily relies on them for convenience; these merely assist the release of mind into words. Poetry should be the most extreme concentration of experience in words, not discursive but immediate. Therefore a long poem requires a consistency of concentrated acts, each not discursive but complete—quotable as units each conveying a longer teleological reach, not an observation but as if it were a whole person with a purpose. It was this concentration of the longer reach Gertrude Stein tried for but many times did not accomplish, the poem falling apart into successions of word-patterns like a collection of better and worse lyrics. But there was no denying her style, which overran all impediments.

Those who knew her compared her with a Buddha—she resembled one—remote, concerned with the disasters of the world around her but untroubled. Her prejudices were as decided as her monumental normality. She involved herself imperturbably in the emotions of bullfight, religion, war: though a Jew by race and name, she remained untouched in a French village during the German occupation of the Second World War. She became a figure for admiration in the minds of countless Americans who could not understand her writing but liked her for it and had no thought to read her. Rather than T. S. Eliot, she, Henry James, and Ezra Pound represent the real challenge of American literature during the first half of the twentieth century.

Gertrude Stein had slight interest in music but appreciated having her writing compared to the music of Bach; she admired Satie's *Socrate*. For the very American composer Virgil Thomson, who early in his career took up the cause of French music against "Mitteleuropa," his term for Germanic taste in music, Gertrude Stein wrote in her own style two opera librettos: *Four Saints in Three Acts*, a sort of oratorio in costume, to be performed rather like a ballet without dance; and *The Mother of Us All*, the story of Susan B. Anthony, crusader for women's rights, placed among such disparate historic figures as John Adams, Daniel Webster, Ulysses S. Grant, Anthony Comstock, Lillian Russell, and Donald Gallup; characters representative of the common people, Jo the Loiterer, Chris the Citizen; as well as several of her friends; and Gertrude S and Virgil T.

Virgil Thomson composed around these librettos operas somewhat after the example of Satie's later musical collages but without the cinematic technique, made up of simple and seemingly familiar tunes in common harmony, adapted in the style of French art-song to the natural flow and rhythm of the words. Because this speech is rhythmically American—Gertrude Stein explained that she lived in France to write like an American—the two operas are idiomatically American, not French. They are more American than any other operas, with the exception of the operas by Marc Blitzstein. But Blitzstein's operas, even the best, are derivative: *The Cradle Will Rock* after the manner of the Brecht-Weill politically oriented, deliberately vulgarized, hard, parodic drama; *Regina* the melodramatic setting of a stage play in grand-opera music.

The libretto of *Four Saints* is too large for the music and too long for the stage; words and music are best heard in the reduced, oratorio-like version prepared by the composer for phonograph recording.

The Mother of Us All is, to the present day, the most satisfactory and the most beautiful American opera, whimsical, full of laughter but without vulgarity or Germanic hardness, appealing in the musical realization of its characteristic personalities and their modes of speech, and in consummation deeply moving, when the heroic figure of Susan B. Anthony, growing in reality throughout the opera, sings from her monument the great aria, "We cannot retrace our steps," interspersed with long silences of meditation.

The Mother of Us All has not become a popular opera, not because the public dislikes it but because the public has seldom enjoyed the chance to hear it. Operatic impresarios in the United States recognize modern opera only in the grand melodramatic style, preferably *verismo* in staging, after Puccini or Strauss. Newly commissioned American operas are usually in this style; they are expensive to stage and to costume, and they generally fail; failure only persuades the impresarios that American audiences do not like opera by American composers.

The Stein-Thomson *Mother* is comic opera resembling in grace and elegance the operas of Rameau and Handel, though it is not at all like them. Alfred Frankenstein wrote: 'The music is Ives plus the deliberate, wicked perversity of using all the right notes." This is the right idea but the wrong idiom. Stein-Thomson is the style of two operas, an amusing but less successful cantata, *Capitals, Capitals,* and a few songs.

Satie and Gertrude Stein (with the musical help of Virgil

Thomson)—as much as the French painters and more than the French poets, the French composers, even Debussy and Ravel—carried forward the new French spirit deep into American esthetic thought, as counterpoise to the weightier influences of Stravinsky and the Germans, Hindemith and Schoenberg. It's a good question whether this French tradition may not prove to be, in the long view, the more creatively influential.

"I should be the last to know whether there is justice in the oft-drawn parallel between Satie and myself," Virgil Thomson wrote, reviewing Wilfrid Mellers's book, *Music in a New Found Land.* "Mellers says that 'both the technical methods and the cultivated naivety are the same.' But when he essays to identify the disciplines of spontaneity as 'inconsequential' and 'childish' regressions (in both my case and Gertrude Stein's) he misses the fact that simplifications, abstractions, radical compactions, and restored-to-beauty commonplaces, no less than Debussy's and Cage's 'liberation of the individual sound,' are inherent in all our century's radical art, and especially to that Paris-centered modernism which from Picasso in painting to Robbe-Grillet in writing has served as norm and mainstream for artists working West of the Rhine."[1]

One thinks of Satie, by comparison with Webern, as a small composer, but there is more music by Satie than by Webern. Thomson's operas expand on the public Satie of *Parade,* the artificial entertainer. Anyone who has studied the work of Satie is aware that his public habit covered a privacy at once reverent and tormented. The notion that because Satie could not be a serious big composer he chose to be a comic little one is untrue. The composer who began the *Mass of the Poor* and completed *Socrate* has absolute stature, no less than the master who summarized a lifetime of technical wisdom in the series of small pieces, *Sports et Divertissements.*

It is this technical wisdom Virgil Thomson emulates. Listen to the opening phrase of the *Kyrie eleison* of his *Missa pro Defunctis,* his undramatic but expressive overlapping entrances. John Cage, after analyzing Thomson's complete works to the length of half a book, dismissed that art as "entertainment." The Requiem does not entertain, it is not operatic, it strives for no great climaxes, it does not shed tears for the audience. But at the opening of the *Agnus Dei* and in the great cry at the end one hears all that has been held back, the mingled hope and grief.

So too with the *Sanctus;* beginning in its long, measured, divided, instrumental tread and the gathering repetition of the word, one meets again the composer who could create in full seriousness amid comedy the figure of Susan B. Anthony and release the culminating emotion of a long life in its reality with the final aria. And it is reasonable that, composing a Requiem for soldiers, he should break in with the *Reveille* for the *Tuba mirum.*

16

THE POPULAR ART OF MELODRAMA

Puccini to Britten

To recover the tastes and pleasures of the ordinary concertgoer fifty to a hundred years ago (1865–1915) is more difficult than the ordinary concertgoer today may be able to realize. The fact is that a large proportion of the audience for serious music today, at all levels of appreciation, knows by ear and is capable of enjoying almost absent-mindedly a larger literature of demanding music than so interested a connoisseur as Sacheverell Sitwell had at his disposal so recently as 1930. In the last chapter of his book *Mozart*, published 1932, Sitwell lists what seems to us an astonishing number of familiar works by Mozart under the chapter title "Some Little-Known Masterpieces." Though the opportunities provided by routine musical performance have enlarged, and recording has brought each of these "Little-Known Masterpieces" to common recognition, the conditions of routine performance fifty or more years ago and today are not markedly different.

In those days, musical taste was formed around opera, not around the symphony orchestra. Ability to enjoy large, abstract instrumental music, unguided by words or narrative, was the privilege of a restricted audience, similar to the audience for chamber music concerts today. Outside the cities, band, chorus, organ, and piano were the customary providers of music.

I myself grew up in such surroundings, although late enough to have possessed phonograph records from earliest boyhood, nearly all vocal, operatic, or popular music. My musical surroundings provided no distinction between Bispham singing "Danny Deever" and the Overture to *Semiramide*, reduced in length and played by Arthur Pryor's band. My criterion of musical genius was not a composer or a conductor but Enrico Caruso. At the local band concerts, played by a militia band in the city park, the feature of the performance might be an operatic excerpt, with a solo cornet giving out the vocal part, or a fantasy in operatic style. We were edified to hear the Overture to *William Tell* played by the local piano teacher and a pupil on two pianos. The teacher had been a pupil of Leschetizky, who had been once a pupil of Czerny, who was a pupil of Beethoven.

Preludes, fantasias, toccatas—and fugue—by J. S. Bach, read at the organ in pedantic stiffness, were my introduction to great music. At college I encountered Wagner by way of a few orchestral excerpts played on organ; at this time electrical recording made orchestral music at last satisfactorily available on records. (The German recording industry, more ambitious and perhaps less commercial than the American, had recorded by acoustical means in 1915 Beethoven's Fifth Symphony directed by Nikisch and in 1917 Mahler's Second Symphony for orchestra and chorus, complete, directed by Oscar Fried.) In 1928, at the age of eighteen, I heard for the first time a symphony orchestra in live performance and a symphony by Brahms. Soon afterwards the famous broadcasts of the New York Philharmonic-Symphony and the Philadelphia Symphony commenced bringing the symphonic repertory to a vast public audience previously unaware of such music.

The vogue of opera-house building in the United States during the later nineteenth century did not promote any large increase in operatic performance; the opera house was taken over by traveling troupes of every sort, musical and otherwise. Only in a few cities was a symphony orchestra or an opera company established; some of these original establishments survive to the present day, in New York, Boston, St. Louis. The opera house fell into disuse or became a movie house. Similar decline may befall a good share of our present-day music centers, if those who manage them continue dodging the greater responsibility of assembling around these buildings an active, communally creative musical life.

In Europe every major city had and has an opera house and a body of singers and instrumentalists able to perform the commoner operatic and symphonic repertory. In Italy and France the opera is controlled by a local functionary, who chooses what is to be performed and arranges for the conductor, stage direction, and principal soloists. In Germany the opera has been more frequently under the direction of a trained conductor, assisted by an administrative staff and stage director; the conductor, as musical director, is finally responsible for all details of administration and performance, including staging and acting. Under his baton the opera orchestra plays symphony concerts. "When I was a boy in Vienna," Arnold Schoenberg told us at the start of one of his last public lectures, "there were two opera houses, and the orchestra performed eight times in the season." This was the Vienna of Brahms, whom the young Schoenberg saw once in the opera-house lobby, and of Gustav Mahler and Richard Strauss.

Throughout Europe, responsibility and authority belong to the professionals, who either adjust their repertory and standards of performance to satisfy public taste or hold to their conviction and require the public to accept it. Taste may not be better or character more decisive, but the bureaucratic position focuses responsibility on the official, however pompous or evasive.

In the United States, responsibility for administration of symphony or opera is usually the job of an employee under the direction of a nonmusical committee which also hires conductor and musical director and has a say in all administrative and musical decisions by concealed interference, enabling the committee members to escape public responsibility. The solution of all problems is to discharge an employee, very often the conductor, seldom to grant full authority with responsibility to the musical director. The officials aim to please the committee, seldom to inform or lead it. The public remains apathetic. Even when aroused, the audience is seldom able to penetrate and change the closed inner circle of control which dictates musical policy. All interested groups exclude the composer, as an individual apart from the musical establishment: a wall of indifference he must try to breach by means having little to do with musical skill.

The requirement for membership in the inner circle is not musical taste, or knowledge, or experience, but money or the ability to raise it, plus an appetite for social power. When Gustav Mahler, who had presided in full authority over the great Vienna Opera and its orchestra, came to New York as musical director of the Metropolitan Opera and conductor of the Philharmonic Orchestra, he suffered a breakdown brought on in part as a result of the interference of the society women who regarded him as their employee.

These self-satisfied local cliques, whose in-group machinations have ruled the larger community musical activities in America since before the start of the century, are bound together by a small, tightly knit imperialism of professional New York management, which controls artists and conductors and decides musical destinies with complacent disregard of esthetic change or national or community musical advantage. This complacency (knowing "what the public wants"), coupled with a degree of active suppression difficult to expose, has nearly destroyed the national market for recitalists, except a relatively few "name" artists who appear too often; it blacklists and denies employment to any conductor who tries to educate his audience by performing "unwanted" music. One can list as conspicuous examples the broken or interrupted American careers of such important conductors as Nicolas Slonimsky, Otto Klemperer, Sir Thomas Beecham, and Leopold Stokowski. The same attitude helps not at all to increase the audience for chamber music and controls the permissible repertory in all media. This power too long exercised by faceless executives is gradually losing control of the national scene, its authority perishing in ignorance and inertia. The international traveling of composers and non-name performers, the steadily increasing repertory of newer and older music and non-European music, the dissemination of chamber music, and the encouragement and promotion of creative musical activity have been passing into the administrative grip of the universities, which today, part by necessity and part by inadvertence, provide a large share of the nationwide musical market. A few American communities have begun taking charge of their own musical affairs by means more open to community participation.

A popular theatrical art has existed since the sixteenth century, directed to the audience which likes the show as much as the music, which enjoys shedding tears and shuddering at sentimentally exaggerated horrors, while it dislikes being driven to the extremity of a more profound emotional experience; for this audience the proscenium barrier between actor and audience furnishes an existential safeguard. This audience wishes to feel but not to think.

The general type of such emotionally appealing art is melodrama, and as the name indicates it is a drama linked with music. The greater part of successful opera is outright melodrama: in historic setting or in the more homely style called *verismo* (true to life).

"Real life" in opera must be at once inflated to provide for the antirealism of dramatic song and reduced to dramatic essentials to eliminate verbal exposition and explanation, so that scene (atmosphere and action) plus musical elaboration take the place of words, which are often incomprehensible and may be in a foreign language. The resulting art wavers between sentimentality, conveying the feel of the emotion instead of the reality of character, and morbidity, the preference for extreme types and situations which offer a unified intensity or simplicity as substitute for a more adequate development of the characters as human beings. Each exaggerates an appearance of dramatic situation at the cost of dramatic and spiritual truth.

By contrast, Marc Blitzstein's *The Cradle Will Rock* has probably never again seemed so real as when it was first performed with, as the result of official interference, the composer sitting alone at a piano on the stage, accompanying the performers who sang from their places in the audience; the social actuality of the conditions melodramatically portrayed was increased by the lack of artificial representation.

So long as opera uses drama no more seriously than as a vehicle for song, there is no problem, and the music may be exalted. Such are the operas of Rameau and Handel. True dramatic opera with real characters in developed relationships has been always a rarity, attempted by Gluck and not quite confined to Mozart and later Verdi.

Of the hundreds of melodramatic operas which have been laboriously written, a small, well-worn but seemingly durable, middle-level group still holds a central place in the operatic repertory, its model Mozart, its master Verdi, its most popular exponent Giacomo Puccini.

Yet the first performance of Puccini's *Madame Butterfly*, at La Scala, Milan, complete with a "whole 'concert' of twittering birds," provided by the stage manager to "mark the break of dawn," was a disaster. "No doubt, as with *La Bohème*," Mosco Carner comments in his excellent *Puccini: A Critical Biography*, "the impressionist and fragmentary style of the work, combined with the novelty of its harmonic language, created obstacles for the ears of Puccini's older contemporaries who still regarded Debussy as an iconoclast."[1] In America, soon afterwards, during 1906 and 1907, *Madame Butterfly* toured the country for seven months.

Puccini's last operas retain melodramatic trappings but turn away from the commonplace pathos of *verismo* in hope of higher musical achievement. Though he wrote no music of consequence except opera, Puccini understood better than the majority of his contemporaries what was happening in music; he borrowed from Debussy, used the whole-tone scale, admired Schoenberg's *Pierrot Lunaire* and went on from the *chinoiseries* of *Butterfly* to a more substantial incorporation of Oriental melody in *Turandot*. But the last operas remain more pathetic than tragic, and *Turandot*, in subject and its central figure, peculiarly psychiatric.

The libretto, not the music, is the chief problem of anyone who would write an opera. In earlier times, when operatic music was a vehicle of song, almost any serious subject, well versified for music, stripped bare of explanatory text, sufficed to produce an evening of arias and concerted numbers, each a formally closed composition, plus some orchestral business, and a ballet. Gluck cracked this formal pattern by his determination to re-create in opera the musical declamation of Greek tragedy. Mozart shattered it by creating a dramatic reality as vital as the plays of Shakespeare and Molière, fusing the contrary modes of tragedy and comedy. Rossini struggled to achieve a similar formula; Verdi accomplished it with the literary help of Boïto in *Otello* and *Falstaff*. Strauss did as well with the assistance of Hofmannsthal. But the melodramatic type continued.

One reads in the correspondence of Puccini, Strauss, and Debussy the unceasing labor of the gifted composer to obtain from his poet a viable libretto. For without a satisfactory play, adapted in every detail to stage conditions which supply by atmosphere and action the lack of verbal exposition, without a decisive artificiality which supports the dramatic substitution of song for spoken dialogue, enabling every scene to reach dramatic concentration in at least one episode of extended song, no ordinary opera can achieve its musical objective or survive as drama.

A strong libretto can sustain inadequate music, but the best music, as beautiful as that of Mozart's *Idomeneo*, cannot sustain an inadequate libretto.

Wagnerian music-drama at once disregarded and transcended these requirements. The dramatic poem and its music were composed as one conception; the subject and plot are ideological instead of realistic; the body of song is an extended exposition; and the voice serves for a principal instrument of the orchestra. No succeeding composer was capable of mastering either the style or its music, except Schoenberg in his massive dramatic song cycle of the *Gurrelieder* and the solo opera of unprecedented musical concentration, *Erwartung*.

Richard Strauss compromised between the two extremes, emphasizing the dramatic effectiveness of the musical stage-play. His *Salome* and *Electra*, and Schoenberg's *Erwartung*, like Wagner's *Tristan and Isolde*, are at the same time dramatic exposition and erotic reaction to the crisis of events, following the example of Euripides' *Medea*. This aspect of serious opera revived that type of the Greek drama which survived by way of Seneca, Renaissance Italian drama, and the *opera seria*, a dramatic form which had been reconstituted by Corneille and Racine and later, as opera, by Gluck. Though the two Strauss operas seemed exceptional, they were in fact in the true classical tradition.

The melodramatic opera, intensified by Wagner, Strauss, and to a less extent by Mussorgsky, evolved into an erotic and even pathologic art-form, music and stage-setting carrying an ever heavier psychological burden, in several operas by Franz Schreker, little known outside Germany, by Leoš Janáček, by Paul Hindemith, who set to music one play, *Murderer, the Hope of Women*, and by Benjamin Britten. In Britten's *Peter Grimes* the orchestral interludes depict psychological development by means of sea sounds and the crying of gulls. Comic operas of similar psychological import were as a whole less successful; one might except Stravinsky's *Rake's Progress*, a tragicomedy, Schoenberg's one-act *Von Heute auf Morgen*, and Britten's *Albert Herring*.

Reduced to Broadway dimensions and plausibility, the several small melodramas by Gian-Carlo Menotti, especially *The Medium*, where the emotional inadequacy of the music is supplemented by outright screaming, *The Consul*, and the Christmas play with music, *Amahl and the Night Visitors*, written for television, prove the continuing popular effectiveness of the style. Psychodramatic opera culminated in the depth psychology of Béla Bartók's short opera *Bluebeard* and two operas by Alban Berg. *Wozzeck,* assembled from fragmentary scenes of Georg Büchner's century-old *Woyzeck,* remains an objective drama, with emotionally explicit music, in strict abstract formulas, sweeping the listener forward upon waves of climax. In *Lulu,* based on two plays by Frank Wedekind, Büchner's dramatic inheritor, the musical frenzy, composed around obsessively re-iterated tone-rows, a distinct row for each character, sustains the psychological unity and presumptive ethical purpose of what seems on the surface a demented nightmare. The plot is not in fact more irrational than that of Wagner's *Ring*—for example, Siegfried's fire-bowered dalliance with his aunt Brünnhilde.

Melodrama has also taken a generally less popular direction away from physical, emotional, and erotic violence, intended to stir up the audience, towards an objective contemplation of events which invites philosophic thought. I call this genre "oratorio opera"; it derives in part from the Germanic Passion settings and such oratorios as *Belshazzar* by Handel. Among such operas one might list: Mozart's *Magic Flute;* Beethoven's *Fidelio*—the genre gives a better appreciation of its form and content; Wagner's *Flying Dutchman, Tannhäuser, Lohengrin,* and *Parsifal;* Boïto's cosmic pageant, *Mefistofele;* Busoni's deeply meditated *Dr. Faustus;* the three interrelated works by Debussy, *The Blessed Damozel* and *The Martyrdom of Saint Sebastian,* both oratorios, and *Pelleas and Melisande,* a true tragic opera; and Schoenberg's *Moses and Aron.*

Distinction between the plot or libretto and the music is fundamental to melodrama. In cruder form, the plot is spoken and enacted, with interruptions for song. Gay's *Beggar's Opera,* Mozart's *Abduction from the Seraglio,* Beethoven's *Fidelio,* Strauss's *Ariadne,* and the Bertolt Brecht plays with interspersed dramatic songs and music by Kurt Weill, as well as his *Three-penny Opera,* a recasting of Gay's *Beggar's Opera,* show with what varied subtlety this type can be adapted; for one virtue, the plot can be understood. The Brecht-Weill *Mahagonny,* a deadly explosive comic *Singspiel,* should be ranked with the Plato-Satie *Socrate* and the Stein-Thomson *The Mother of Us All* among the absolutes of twentieth century dramatic art.

Modern composers have tried various methods of distinguishing important emotional or expository fragments of dialogue to give them the significance, if not the verbal comprehensibility, of language. The *leitmotif*, a musical figure signifying a character or a symbolic reference, is the most common type.

Schoenberg's *Moses and Aron* is, to the present day, the most consistent example of the oratorio opera. Schoenberg himself wrote the libretto. The plot begins and ends in dialogue between the two principal characters, concerning the nature of God and his promise to mankind. Moses, trying laboriously to express the reality of God and promise, speaks in *Sprechstimme:* "The tempo of Moses' speaking is governed by the music, the tone intervals should serve only for declamatory outline and characterization . . . the voice rising and falling relatively to the indicated intervals, and everything bound together to the time and rhythm of the music except where a Pause is indicated." (From Schoenberg's instructions for the speaking of Moses.) Aron persuasively sings in his high tenor the interpreting of God and promise to man's own advantage. The music of the closing dialogue, ending with Moses breaking the tablets of the Law, reverses that of the opening dialogue in which Moses invokes God.

The entire opera is composed around a single tone-row. The significant motives, instead of being symbolized by musical figures, consist of word-plays, ambiguities, syllabic assonances which stress by a common sound the tension of an opposed meaning. Allen Forte lists such opposed pairs as *einig* (joined) and *entzweit* (torn loose), *Moses-Aron, Gott-Pharao, Volk-Wort. Blut* (blood) re-echoes against the hard words *Gold, rot* (red), *Lust,* culminating in the cry *Blutopfer!* (blood offering). The ambiguity of *mit* (with, from) is caught up in varied accentual relationships, at once binding and dividing people and God. *Unvorstellbar* (inconceivable) is reiterated in varying contexts to emphasize its double meaning: inconceivable God and a God inconceivable by man; the word is thrown shockingly against *Vorstellung* (fantasy). These are not textual word-plays but the core of the vocal sound, signs intended to be heard.

The Voice from the Thornbush simultaneously speaks and sings, the background voices blending in slower melody, nearer voices singing the same words more emphatically and rapidly, while speaking voices in short, intense snatches which are almost shouts drive home the concentrated burden: the voice of God in the thought of his prophet formulating the ambiguous message of the promise. Throughout, the purpose of the music is to concentrate. Voices singing and speaking together in solo and in chorus at many levels of intensity, speed, contrast, counterpoint, pitch, are enabled by the music to offer conflicting statements simultaneously, to dramatize by immediate opposition contrasting aspects of the same thought. The meaning-sound relationships exist not only for themselves but as a viable addition to the music. Schoenberg has had in mind also the Straussian conception of the Greek drama.

Though the number of instruments is large, the use of the orchestra is extremely economical. Important passages are marked by instrumental underlining or by the breaking through of decisive figures or types of instrumental sound. With the start of the scenes around the Golden Calf the orchestra comes into the foreground, supplementing for the ear what the crowded stage action can never render with full satisfaction to the eye, the most comprehensive bacchanal in opera.

Some critics have identified Moses with Schoenberg and Aron with Hitler; this is incorrect, although the religious crisis of the opera reflects the moral crisis of Germany which brought Hitler to power. Nor does the defeat of Moses symbolize Schoenberg's feeling of defeat. At the time of writing the opera (1928–1932) he was happily remarried, he was winning recognition and performance, he held the Berlin professorship of composition previously occupied by Busoni. This good fortune ended in 1933 with Hitler's coming to power and Schoenberg's exile. But the two acts of the opera were complete; the third act or epilogue, though existing in libretto, never became music.

If one were to choose a single work to represent the pre-eminent achievement of twentieth century music until the present day, that work would be *Moses and Aron*.

17

THE DICTATORSHIP OF POPULARITY

One eminent editor-critic writes of "Masscult" and "Midcult," declaring that "Midcult" is the more dangerous; another distinguishes "Highbrows," "Middlebrows," and "Lowbrows," favoring the preferred level of his readers with the sly pretentiousness of the fellow who, without insisting on his personal status, can have his aristocratic fun both ways.

It is flattering to one's complacency when, standing on a mountaintop or flying much higher and peering from a window in the side of a jet transport, one sees the world below spread out as a plane surface, the larger dimensions no more hidden by trees, buildings, and surface undulations. A book such as I am writing, designed to survey a broad historical area from a visually restricting distance, must necessarily reduce the greater part of the ground-level critical detail to a single indifferentiation. Though by this circumstance of writing I may seem to present myself as technically exalted, I must take care to remind myself and my readers that the few larger masses, lakes, mountains, stretches of apparent flatness, are by no means so simple or without complexity as they show themselves from this distance. If for the moment I fly comfortably at a great height, the wings I fly with are not mine; they are lent by the occasion, and I make the best use I can of them, knowing that, although my prospect is wide, the accuracy and fineness of my vision are by so much reduced. From this height there are no people on the ground, no automobiles on the roads or in the streets. The highways of communication are no wider than directional lines.

It is too easy to compress all human distinctions and discrimination into a few flat areas of difference. The critic, when he does this, should try to make clear that no single human response can be compressed into any one of a few broadly distinguishable attitudes. People are in continual movement back and forth and up and down. Views from the ground are narrower, but the person who walks along a street sees in knowledge and imagination beyond the narrowness of the street. The listener who sheds tears over *Madame Butterfly* is not for that reason incapable of responding with fervor and insight to Bach's *Art of Fugue*.

But we can narrow our own prospects; in knowledge and imagination we can too easily deny that there is more to be learned, to be imagined, than we presently comprehend. Looking from a great height we make out the larger outlines that distinguish the aerial view of the continents we inhabit and the seas between them. The opportunity should add not to our complacency but to our wish for knowledge. In going up and coming down we can learn to appreciate the infinite variety of differential detail which makes up the human prospect. In the variety of human prospects we are all highbrows, middlebrows, and lowbrows, and the more dangerously limited when we believe that we are not.

The threat of very large discriminative categories becomes seriously real when anyone who believes in such categories has the power to enforce them: when such a person is able to run down (as critic), or exclude (as impresario, editor, concert director, maker of programs), or punish (as exponent of official policy) whatever he believes, for whatever reason, to be good or bad. If Schoenberg's Orchestra Variations or Ravel's *Bolero* or Gershwin's *Rhapsody in Blue,* or current or historic popular music of any sort pleases an audience, nobody should forbid that pleasure. This is, in the longest view, the only discrimination which can be depended on to separate the temporary in art from the enduring, to provide the continual adjustments of taste that make possible the enjoyment and recognition of great art and the creation and appreciation of new art.

If music of temporary worth, making less demand on audience perception, always commands a seemingly disproportionate amount of performance opportunity, we should remember that nothing so rapidly destroys the spiritual individuality of the more demanding and enduring works than to hear them too often. What is commonly available is soon commonplace, even if no living artist is thought able to produce art of equal value. The phonograph record has enormously increased our acquaintance with the literature of music; it has also depreciated our enthusiasm for the small group of masterpieces which until recently bounded the horizon of musicians and their audience. It would be impossible now to reproduce the worldwide excitement of the expanding audience for music during the decades of the 1930s and 1940s, to a less extent the 1950s, when month by month new record issues brought for the first time opportunity to hear as often as we pleased still another work we had not known or had scarcely known, opening up new vistas of style and period, new instrumental combinations, new aspects of performance—and, above and beyond all, knowledge of the complete works of masters whom we had recognized by a few admitted masterpieces, which as we now learned were not always their best work. With the help of the long-playing record the public has long since come to accept its Beethoven and Brahms as readily as its Tchaikovsky and is now domesticating the more than heavenly lengths of Bruckner and Mahler.

The reaction occurred during the later decades of the 1950s with the increasingly rapid spread of "festivals" of new, unknown, and less-known music, where the discovery of fresh musical vistas seems more worthwhile than the cold appreciation of such music on phonograph records.

Throughout the world the spiritually emancipating music of the illiterate American Negro crying to the Lord out of his environment or dancing in forgetfulness or sorrowing in the private language of the "blues" has become symbolic of individual emancipation. In those countries where "degenerate jazz" has been forbidden, jazz has come to represent the comparative freedom of the land where it originated, though the originators of jazz were by no means so free as their music. In a mass environment the jazz symbol has often been accompanied by cruder symbols of nonconformity, liquor, drugs, violent and antisocial acts, sexual confusion; so jazz shows itself "degenerate." Among the Negroes, jazz and religion were the outlets to freedom, and a feeling of that religion enters into true jazz. So, in the nations where jazz was suppressed, jazz became a nearly religious symbol of personal ecstasy and freedom.

A great part of the most popular music at any period symbolizes in the mind of the listener his own would-be heroism, religiosity, pathos, melodrama, his yea-saying and nay-saying, apart from any action, so that the music is not only symbolic of but identified with the emotion. The music, as many say, "communicates." By middle life or after a few years of listening, this circle of symbolic identification seems complete; there can be no other heroism, no other religious utterance, though one usually finds space for a little more pathos and a considerably larger mix of melodrama. This closed circle, shared in common by a majority of individual listeners, includes what is thought to be, for that time, popular; it includes great music, bad music, and dull music. It becomes a stockade behind which the acculturated defend themselves against the assaults of new experience. The standards of "Value" fly over the stockade.

Several quotations from an article by Susanne K. Langer, "The Social Influence of Design," exemplify a higher level of sensibility and judgement.

"Only one function belongs to good art alone, and is what makes it good: the objective presentation of feeling to a beholder's direct perception. This is something quite different from 'expression of feeling' in the usual sense, which is the exhibition of emotions the artist is undergoing. . . ." (The notion that art is the external record of an artist expressing his feelings, emotion, mental disease, latest love affair, is and always has been a pathetic fiction, encouraged by a few successful instances where artists actually did do so, or claimed to do so.) Miss Langer then glosses the word: ". . . 'feeling' . . . comprising sensibility as well as emotion. The word is often used in narrower senses. . . . I am using it in the widest sense, as we popularly use it, including all its accepted meanings. Our peripheral sense organs feel the impingements of the external world; we call this our perception of objective reality. Inwardly, we feel the rise and pulse and cadence of emotions, the strains of concerted thinking, and the more or less voluntary evocation of images from some unknown deep sources of memory and fantasy. . . .

"Our imaginative conception, or humanized envisagement of things, places, acts and facts, is guided by the steady development of our feeling toward the world around us. Feeling is native, spontaneous, instinctive; but feeling is also developed, formed, and learned. . . .

"[Feelings] are formed as our ideas of the world are formed: by the influence of images which articulate them and exhibit them for our contemplation, so that their rhythms become clear and familiar. . . . Moreover, we *learn* feeling from seeing it expressed in art, because that expression makes it conceivable. A work of art is a logical projection in which feeling appears as a quality of the created object, the work. That quality is what good art has and bad art lacks; it is the artist's idea, inexpressible in verbal propositions, but clearly perceptible as the import of his presentation. To distinguish this sort of emotive expression from what is usually intended, we might call this *expressiveness*."[1]

But feeling and sensibility together, plus the other elements of Miss Langer's exemplary conglomerate, do not add up to the whole of what she means by "our feeling toward the world around us." "Feeling and sensibility" in her use of them, and as exemplified, are *reactions* to stimuli. Nothing is included to provide for the deliberative significance of meanings. Miss Langer's audience *responds to* music, but there is also what the individual listener, in his own individual collaboration of traditions, inferences, verbalized influences, criticism and esthetics, personal and public references, and susceptibility to outside external opinion or authoritarian rule, *thinks about* a work of art. Some writers about art are so dominated by these accumulated abstractions, which *think for* them, that they seem scarcely able to have encountered the "feeling and sensibility," in Miss Langer's terms, of the art about which they write.

Habituation is a powerful factor in every reaction and response to art. Habituation is related to accepted images and forms; when the work of art presents itself in new images and new form, or without recognizable image or schematic form, the listener must deliberately direct his attention, unassisted by these helps, to the event that is offered as work of art. His habituated response to form and image will conflict with that feeling which "appears as a quality of the created object"—the "work of art" as "logical projection." To say "that quality is what good art has and bad art lacks" is to justify the opinion of the critic who rejects a new work as "bad art" because, through the screen of his habituated sense of form and image, he is incapable of discerning the "logical projection," if one wishes to call it that, that the new work is.

"Value judgement" has often little or nothing to do with the sensible reactions and responses stimulated by a work of art, or with its distinctive character or shape; "value judgement" may be no more than a statement of unwillingness to react in sensibility or imagination to these responses. Musicologists, estheticians, historians, critics, and daily reviewers too, often find it easier to react to their own incapacity to receive the unexpected, as if the report of their failure had something to do with the work of art they have *sat in the sound of* but have not perceived.

Some persons are willing to condone failure of this sort by claiming that the imperceptive opinion is at least "honest." Stravinsky replies: "I find this illogical as a defense and alarming as an indication of the state of ethics. I am not concerned with the honesty of an opinion but with its worth. And what a condition we have come to that honesty is so exceptional as to deserve citation. . . . I might also add that I have grown quite a garden with the flowers that reviewers have thrown at the supposed graves of works of mine over the past fifty years."[2]

Defenders of the popular audience and its—and their—incapacities spring up on every side. The popular audience needs no defending; it exists by the very action of human nature. Every generation starts once more at the beginning, but a different beginning. More important to awaken this audience to awareness of and desire for some of the opportunities it misses.

It is part of the game that a critic shall perversely distort the audible evidence and humorously lie about the facts concerning any composer whose work exceeds the critic's grasp. This malicious cruelty often masking as humor is unpleasant enough when directed against a composer so well known as Stravinsky but foul and cowardly when the critic seeks to persuade readers to laugh and pass by the work of one less firmly established.

In America, the dictatorship of popularity has not lost its Russianizing trend. The official governors of American musical habit—it is not a fashion which changes with each season, though fashion temporarily espouses some new works and new composers, but a slowly evolving habituation—decry and refuse to encourage when they do not outright deny performance to works and composers they hold to be unpopular—that is, contrary to the prevailing habit and expectation. The attitude is anesthetic rather than esthetic, and its exponents, whenever pricked in conscience, insist that they must "give" their audiences "what the public wants"—which is, by habituation, what it gets. So the defenses they and their critical spokesmen offer as "value judgements" are no more than statements in favor of the prevailing habituation and against change. When popular opinion goes beyond them, as it will, such persons follow after and adopt the new habituation. But they are often as incapable as before of distinguishing the "logical projection in which feeling appears as a quality," and therefore of discerning whether the "quality" is "what good art has and bad art lacks" and of discovering its "expressiveness."

It is not the mass audience, or "Midcult," or the "far-out" small audience we need to fear, but the persons who, basing their presumptions on the habituated "good" or "bad" of any group, limit or dictate the musical opportunities of the public by the rule of these presumptions. If purveyors to the mass audience exert a dictatorship of popularity, and "Midcult" a smaller dictatorship where they can exploit their influence as snobs, there are also exponents of the "far-out" who impose their authority in favor of some one new compositional technique or attitude or group. The effect shows in bad or restricted programming, critical infighting, esthetic gobbledegook, and googols of inept effort.

In Russia, and to an even more restrictive extent in Nazi Germany, the dictatorship of popularity was made official policy. The Soviet government forbade performance of the music of the two great Russian exiles Serge Rachmaninoff and Igor Stravinsky. Theories of "music for the worker" were expounded with the prejudice of unenlightened moral law, the conventional imitation being preferred to the real achievement. In America the same prejudice expounds a good taste defined as "the best works by the best performers," meaning the established repertory done yet again by performers of established name.

Two great Russian composers in particular suffered. Dmitri Shostakovitch, whose splendid First Symphony seemed to have opened Russian music for the first time to the full resources of Germanic idiom, especially from Mahler, was crushed to conformity by the suppression of his Second, Third, and Fourth Symphonies and the opera *Lady Macbeth of Mzensk;* he has never resumed the great promise of his First Symphony. Serge Prokofiev, who traveled freely in America and Europe without relinquishing his loyalty to the new Soviet government, was put down but did not conform. At a disciplinary meeting in 1948, the war hero A. A. Zhdanov, who before the war had crushed the young Shostakovitch, lectured the Soviet composers for three days on the requirements of "Soviet art" and the errors of "capitalist" music and "formalist" style. Prokofiev, then at the summit of his reputation, sat with his back turned to the speaker. Nevertheless, having in mind the fate of his friends, Meyerhold, the theatrical director, who disappeared and whose wife was murdered, and the poet Mayakovsky, who committed suicide, Prokofiev officially apologized. He did not alter his composing; in 1951 he was awarded the Stalin Prize for his cantata *Stand Up for Peace*.

We should keep in mind that in Soviet Russia the composer is subsidized, given great privileges, ranked with the upper class of public officials and administrators, segregated from the working class for whom he is supposed to write, and his work performed by authority of the government. This system holds the artist in line more efficiently than any Czarist persecution. (To learn what happens when the system breaks down, one need only read that chapter in the *Memoirs 1921–1941* by Ilya Ehrenburg, one who survived.) During the Second World War all the remaining Soviet artists were assembled and sent by special train—as the other European governments hid the contents of museums—to continue their work far from the fighting front.

In Russia an accredited composer can subsist comfortably for a lifetime by the product of a talent not even mediocre, and he is not required to teach. In Soviet terms, the state supports the artist in the understanding that the artist will conform with public policy, including restrictions concerning the subject matter and the style of art.

In America a professor of composition, equally talentless and conformist, can hold permanent tenure in a university until retirement, but he must teach. The one danger in either case is the accident of real talent, the uncompromising directional authority of genius, rising to disturb policy. A few American universities have lately recognized this possibility and are attempting some creative outlet for it. American governmental policy seldom interferes with art and then but slightly.

Unique artists, like unique saints—the blessed reality comes but seldom and one of a kind—are not happily welcomed by the hierarchy who control the status quo. Their virtue discredits compromise; their vision disrupts conformity; they topple tradition by their personal authority; and to deny them confirms their example. Their sometimes hapless presence among men seems to reassure us of immortality, because death does not end it. So they are at last called blessed, saint, or genius, and their example perverted. No one can rise to their unique state by imitation; each must discover and pursue his unique virtue to its consequence.

In America, the concentration camp for the nonconforming artist has been silence, a polite exclusion, no jobs, no grants, no performance, no publication, no distribution, therefore no reputation and no income, modified by the saving intervention of a minority who provide occasional jobs, occasional grants or gifts, occasional performance, but cannot overcome the largest problem, distribution. Harry Partch, one of the most distinguished of American composers and an important musical theorist, hoboed for eight years and has subsisted throughout the remainder of his career on occasional grants, gifts, and a trickle of earnings from the sale of records of the few performances of his compositions, which he himself pays to have made and personally distributes by mail.

So long as the officially endorsed attitude, that music is a commercial product sold for entertainment, persists in America, we have no better cause than the Russians to boast of "freedom of the arts."

SCRIABIN, RACHMANINOFF, PROKOFIEV

To the gift of a master every work is relevant. This is as true of Satie as of Stravinsky. It is almost true of Scriabin. It is not true of Rachmaninoff or Prokofiev. Major works stand out, but the lesser do not carry the same blessing. Prokofiev seems a master, therefore the aphorism should be questioned.

We are always in danger of condescending to that music in Russian idiom of which we know in fact so little, though major examples of it cling in the repertory as our American music does not yet. Russian music uses the same notational and harmonic systems as Western European music, and its grammar and syntax through the eighteenth century to the present day derive from the Italianate tradition. Yet the indigenous Russian music is as unlike the Germanic or the Parisian, or the French or Italian, in spite of two centuries of exchanged influences, as our own music.

Indeed, this may be the cause of our incomplete ability to comprehend Russian music: American composing has been rather sharply divided between a traditionally rootless academic polyglot, almost entirely borrowed out of Europe, and a strongly experimental native growth; in Russia, the majority of composers, however pedantically academic, have written within the scope of a native idiom that came into use during the nineteenth century. By comparison with the progressing evolution of European music, this Russian style was, with a few exceptions, provincial from the start. Despite its quantity, modern Russian music is a backward province of European music; except the occasionally performed choral works by Alexander Gretchaninov, it has not recovered the authority of the older Russian and Byzantine liturgical music, nor has it become Asiatic, though several recent composers have explored Asiatic folk idioms.

The claim that this is a more popular music, written for the people, cannot be taken seriously; these dozens of Russian symphonies are not popular like Gershwin's music or even the music of Ravel. Band-concert music is not more popular than symphonic music; if it were, we should have more records and broadcasts of band music and fewer of symphonic music. Band music is easier to play and to hear than symphonic music and therefore thrives where musical skill and appreciation are relatively simple. In America, bands and band concerts now emulate the variety and character of symphonic music, rather than the other way round. Tchaikovsky's most popular music is his least simple. Worldwide experience has proved that audiences can rise to Beethoven's Fifth Symphony and then to his Ninth, that music at this highest level is and has been the most enduringly popular music, though it certainly does not become so at once. Audiences rise to these masterpieces by familiarity, not by any reduction of the music, and this has been as true in Russia.

The simplistic criterion of popularity is that a piece of music should carry and be composed around at least one recognizable tune. This criterion does not in fact apply to the composition but to the audience: to the kind of tune the audience is accustomed to expect; to the listener's ability to distinguish the idiomatic character of a melody and what is done with it. Gershwin's "Bess, you is my woman now" is note for note the same as part of the principal melody of the slow movement of Schoenberg's First Quartet, but the handling of it is entirely different (see pages 28–29). Few listeners are able to distinguish Schoenberg's continually varied melody as a single unit and recognize that it is the same as Gershwin's. Gershwin's song harmonizes the fine melody as if it were a tune.

The simplistic development of Russian music began in the nature of nineteenth century Russian society at every level, the entertainment-seeking lethargy which the farther-seeing Russian novelists and dramatists abused and satirized. Words provide a more immediate weapon of dissent than music; Pushkin was more potent and officially dangerous than Glinka. It began, too, in the reforming belief of Mily Balakirev that Russian music should speak to the Russian people, that it should put aside its European formulas and learn to speak its native language. Instead of the increasing technical and chromatic complexity of Germanic music, the Russians preferred tune, color, simple design, and narrative content, a plain harmonic statement capable of being tricked out with the appearances of folksong but unaffected by any genuine understanding of the harmonic self-sufficiency of folk melody.

Debussy wrote: "The young Russian school has endeavored to give new life to the symphony by borrowing ideas from popular melodies; it has succeeded in cutting brilliant gems; but are not the themes entirely disproportionate to the developments into which they have been forced? . . . This gives them an appearance of pathetic discomfort, but a lordly counterpoint ordains that they shall forget their peaceful origin."[1]

It is as if American composers had followed Dvořák in using for themes the simplified shapes of Negro spiritual reduced to a bare tune. From Stephen Foster to George Gershwin, a few American composers have seemed to do this, but a symphonic literature in this style has not developed, and Gershwin's melodies are of far more complex origin. An American musical literature growing out of the real character of Negro spiritual would have been as unlike polyglot music of the European tradition as the music of Béla Bartók or Charles Ives, both of whom understood this difference.

From our divided academic-experimental attitude we see the Russian composers as academically well schooled (like the composers produced by the eighteenth century Italian schools) and provincial (as this Italian style soon came to be) and superficially, if on occasion sumptuously, barbaric, with a tendency to harmonic noise.

☘ Diatonic harmony in equal temperament without chromaticism exaggerates the conflict between theoretical consonance and actual discordance, the more so as the vertical relationships are thickened. Melody and accompaniment avoids this clashing; the trouble appears when a composer in this style tries to compete with the Germanic complexity. Chromaticism diffuses the acoustical prominence of key and so dissipates the increment of discordance, as in Schoenberg's First Quartet and much music by Strauss. It was this problem, both esthetic and acoustic, how to deal properly with discord (unwanted harmonic noise), which was causing the more adventurous composers throughout Europe and already in America to seek new solutions: the key-rejecting, individually contrived, vertical sonorities of Debussy; Scriabin's labor to create a new harmony of superposed fourths; the dependence of Wagner and Strauss on polyphonic orchestration; Schoenberg's emancipation of the dissonance; Ives's untheoretical realization that he must violate not only "nice" harmony but all harmony, using in multivoiced plasticity the entire medium of sound.

So we can recognize Rimsky-Korsakov, instead of the several composers whose music now seems more meaningful to us, as the characteristic figure of Russian idiom: academic, well schooled, provincial, a disciple of Balakirev, on occasion sumptuously barbaric, and harmonically noisy. With the emphasis on "academic" and "provincial," this characterization applies as well to other prolific Russian composers, only a small part of whose work is known outside Russia: Nikolai Medtner, Reinhold Glière, Alexander Glazunov, Nikolai Miaskovsky, as well as their younger counterparts, Dmitri Kabalevsky, Aram Khatchaturian, Dmitri Shostakovitch (except his great First Symphony). (Although Stravinsky calls Glazunov's orchestral music "German-academic," it is essentially Russian.) With emphasis on "well schooled" and "sumptuously," this description provides for Serge Rachmaninoff and the mature Prokofiev. "Provincial" seems to explain why both Scriabin and Prokofiev, who traveled widely and made their own selections from the polyglot and Parisian idioms, remained in comparison with Stravinsky quite restrictedly Russian. Of all the great flowering of Russian composers during the nineteenth century and so far into the twentieth century, only Stravinsky has been able to transplant his mind and art, complete from the idiomatic roots, to a central place in the Western European tradition. His ballet *The Fairy's Kiss*, orchestrating tunes and small compositions by Tchaikovsky, indicates, for all its sophistication, what might have happened if Stravinsky's nostalgia for Russia had caused him to remain within the Russian provincial orbit.

The Soviet rule of popularity, with its rejection of "formalism," did not alter the character of Russian music, but it prevented any growth of Russian composing beyond the limits of the established, habitual, and well-rewarded provincialism. If American composers, putting aside their Germanic training and European polyglot preferences, had united behind the leadership of a fanatical Louis Gottschalk and a firmly authoritarian Edward MacDowell, a similar American provincialism of independent styles might have occurred.

✿ *Formalism*, like all Soviet officialese, means the exact opposite of what it says, a common result of propaganda by contradiction. In ordinary usage, *formalism* signifies the primacy of accustomed formal method, at the cost of intrinsic structural and melodic growth. In Soviet parlance, "formalism" signifies intrinsic structural and melodic growth, at the cost of expected formalistic method.

We might have had imposed on us in America an idiom of Jazz as the jazz formalists understand it, in their critical language which is more like that used for the compiling of baseball statistics and players' biographies than for music. Our composers, fortunately, knew jazz too well to be deceived in this way; after a few tentative ventures they drew back.

The Soviet rule merely continued the forms of Russian academic tradition, as practised by the inheritors of Tchaikovsky, Taneyev, and Glière at the Moscow Conservatory, and by the inheritors of Balakirev, Rimsky-Korsakov, and Glazunov at the St. Petersburg Conservatory. That the art of Mussorgsky was exceptional in this tradition is proved by the care with which Rimsky-Korsakov trimmed the difference. The recent Soviet edition of Mussorgsky's complete music as he wrote it has not altered the Russian attitude towards any living composer who might claim equal freedom.

Since Tchaikovsky, Mussorgsky, and Rimsky-Korsakov, three Russian composers have won a major place in Western music without escaping the consequences of their provincialism: Scriabin, Rachmaninoff, and Prokofiev. To appreciate the difference, listen to any piano concerto by Rachmaninoff in comparison with either piano concerto by Brahms; or any orchestral or piano composition by Scriabin in comparison with a similar work by Debussy; or any mature instrumental work, or opera or ballet, by Prokofiev in comparison with a similar work by Stravinsky. It will be evident that in each case the difference is not just a matter of individual talent. Prokofiev's concertos for both piano and violin are more widely played than Stravinsky's. Rachmaninoff's Second and Third Piano Concertos are heard, in America, scarcely less often than the Brahms piano concertos. The difference lies in what each composer expects of his composing in conscience and his relation with his audience; in the common idiom he works with or within; and in the esthetic consistency of the culture that has contributed to the formation of his own esthetic consistency, his content, and therefore his style. The first is in some degree but not entirely a result of conscious thought and decision; the second, a consequence of education and habituation; the third operates below the level of deliberative consciousness.

❀ The influence of his audience in the large on a creative artist is difficult to estimate. Many successful artists conform to a creative pattern which successfully represents them as individuals before "their" audience. Other artists appear to do so but insist that they do not. The carefully managed platform appearance, some exhibition of hair, the artfully disheveled photograph, represent the self or the *persona,* according to the artist's attitude. One can often hear Beethoven's anticipation in his music of the audience response he aims at, and be amused with him when he willfully violates that expectation. One wonders what he would think of the Beethovenian scowl that has become his trademark. John Cage, like any great comedian, is at once quite natural and at ease before his audience and therefore aware of the responses he creates; a commonplace action in stage forms can be upsetting, disturbing, hilarious. The good showman is one for whom the present occasion is the *real* performance, no matter what happens, not an idealized perfect performance. Any first-rate creative mind resents being patterned for the trade; the extent of the patterning an artist permits, disregarding his extenuation, gives one clue to an estimate of his worth. But no artist of distinction can escape the public effect of being what he is, and the influence on himself of his own abstract *persona:* his image as the public sees him, his myth as the public believes whatever it believes it knows about him, the critical and biographical explanations of his art and life. An unpremeditated action, a quoted statement, a clever critical invention, may devastate like a tornado an area of his created work. An artist who openly flouts the public merely adds this flouting to the public picture of himself. Except in complete privacy, having no audience, there is no way out of it. How could Charles Ives, one might ask, be influenced by an audience which did not exist until at least thirty or forty years after he wrote? Listen to his music. A great artist, in the long view, creates his audience.

One must presume that Stravinsky, for all his "genius"—a word he disowns—would have remained, like Prokofiev, within the Russian provincial orbit if he had not rapidly and decisively broken with the Russian tradition at a time when the circumstances of political change prevented him from turning back. When Prokofiev at last went abroad, the First World War had ended; he traveled on a Soviet passport personally authorized by the Soviet Commissar for Education, Lunacharsky; and he never ceased to be, unqualifiedly, a citizen of the USSR. All of Prokofiev's later travel in Europe and America was approved by his government; he was never anti-Soviet, nor did he suffer any government interference with his work until after Stalin had closed the borders against international travel. He was out of Russia during the disciplinary action of 1936 which crushed Shostakovitch.

But it is more significant that Prokofiev was a prodigy, who presented to his examiners for admission to the St. Petersburg Conservatory (among them Glazunov and Rimsky-Korsakov) two large portfolios of his own compositions: four operas, from the latest of which he read and sang at the piano, two sonatas, a symphony, and a large number of piano pieces—the operas and symphony fully scored for orchestra. He was thirteen years old, and his principal teacher, after his mother, had been Reinhold Glière. His habitual style was already formed before entering the Conservatory, and though his radical harmonic usage, at the ages of fifteen and sixteen, confounded his professors, and at seventeen he composed and played his *Diabolic Suggestions,* and at twenty, before completing his final examinations, won a prize for piano playing (over Glazunov's objection) by performing his

own Second Piano Concerto, his stylistic deviations had been
established within his native tradition.

Stravinsky, the son of an eminent professional singer, did not
turn from law to music until he was eighteen or become a
radically independent composer until he had left the country to
join Diaghilev in Paris soon after completing his formal training
under Rimsky-Korsakov. During the First World War and after
the Revolution he remained abroad, an exile, who did not return
until invited by the Soviet government to visit the USSR and
perform his music there in 1963.

In 1941 Prokofiev began writing an *Autobiography,* which he
did not complete. At the end of the first chapter he analyzes the
"basic lines along which my work had developed up to this point."
At first thought, "this point" would seem to be the previously
mentioned date, May 1914, when he played his First Piano Concerto at the graduation exercises from the Conservatory. But the
analysis refers to, among other works, his ballet *Le Pas d'acier*
(1926) and the Fifth Piano Concerto (1932). We may presume
therefore that Prokofiev is reviewing his five "basic lines" of development from the viewpoint of 1941.

"The first was the classical line, which could be traced back to
my early childhood and the Beethoven sonatas I heard my mother
play. This line takes sometimes a neo-classical form (sonatas,
concertos), sometimes imitates the eighteenth century classics (ga-
vottes, the *Classical Symphony,* partly the *Sinfonietta*). The second
line, the modern trend, begins with the meeting with Tanayev
when he reproached me for the 'crudeness' of my harmonies. At
first this took the form of a search for my own harmonic language,
developing later into a search for a language in which to express
powerful emotions (*The Phantom, Despair, Diabolical Suggestions, Sarcasms, Scythian Suite,* a few of the songs, Op. 23,
The Gambler, Seven, They Were Seven, the Quintet and the
Second Symphony). Although this line covers harmonic language
mainly, it also includes new departures in melody, orchestration
and drama. The third line is the *toccata,* or the 'motor,' line
traceable perhaps to Schumann's *Toccata* which made such a
powerful impression on me when I first heard it (*Etudes,* Op. 2,
Toccata, Op. 11, *Scherzo,* Op. 12, the *Scherzo* of the Second Concerto, the *Toccata* in the Fifth Concerto, and also the repetitive
intensity of the melodic figures in the *Scythian Suite, Pas d'acier,*
or passages in the Third Concerto). This line is perhaps the least

important. The fourth line is lyrical: it appears first as a thought-ful and meditative mood, not always associated with the melody, or, at any rate, with the long melody (*The Fairy-tale,* Op. 3, *Dreams, Autumnal Sketch, Songs,* Op. 9, *The Legend,* Op. 12) . . . This line was not noticed until much later. For a long time I was given no credit for any lyrical gift whatever, and for want of encouragement it developed slowly. But as time went on I gave more and more attention to this aspect of my work."[2] (I have been quoting from S. *Prokofiev, Autobiography, Articles, Reminiscences,* the English translation published in Moscow. Lawrence and Elisabeth Hanson, translating the same passage, give this stronger statement: "This direction of mine was not allowed any serious existence until much later and developed slowly because I was set down everywhere as a modernist pure and simple who for some extraordinary reason is not permitted the luxury of expressing or indeed of possessing feelings."[3]

Prokofiev concludes his statement: "I should like to limit my-self to these four 'lines,' and to regard the fifth, 'grotesque' line which some wish to ascribe to me, as simply a deviation from the other lines. In any case I strenuously object to the very word 'grotesque' which has become hackneyed to the point of nausea. As a matter of fact the use of the French word 'gro-tesque' in this sense is a distortion of the meaning. I would prefer my music to be described as 'Scherzo-ish' in quality, or else by three words describing the various degrees of the Scherzo—whimsicality, laughter, mockery."[4]

This "analysis" seems to be a reaction against the popular opin-ion in Europe and America that Prokofiev was a follower of Stra-vinsky. At the time of writing this statement Prokofiev had already withdrawn again into the Russian orbit. It signifies less that to have mentioned the influence of Stravinsky might have been politically inadvisable. Nobody has questioned Prokofiev's cour-age or his willingness, in or out of Russia, to speak and praise as he pleased. As with Schoenberg's similar testimonial to the wholly Germanic sources of his music, the *truth* of the statement, how-ever politically dictated, did not seem to the composer to be false. In the same first chapter of his *Autobiography,* Prokofiev twice mentions Schoenberg and claims to have been the first to play his music in Russia.

Yet to assert that the Toccata, or "motor" line was the least im-portant, while mentioning so many examples, including such major work as the *Scythian Suite, Le Pas d'acier,* and the concerto movements, seems ambiguous, as if directed to two groups of readers: officially, to those who would expect his disclaimer, and by the examples to those who would recognize that he could not disclaim such examples of his best work.

Prokofiev was not required to be a modernist; his youthful compositions had outraged his professors at the Conservatory, including Rimsky-Korsakof, at about the same time that Stravinsky, nine years older, was peacefully completing his private study with the same master. Prokofiev continued the same direction abroad, responding to Stravinsky's rapidly matured art, *The Firebird, Petrouchka,* and *Rite of Spring,* though he found them "lacking in real thematic material" and professes not to have understood them. Soon after meeting Stravinsky, Prokofiev recomposed an earlier composition as the *Scythian Suite.*

Prokofiev wrote that, of all the Futurists, the radical Marinetti most impressed him.

Afterwards, like Stravinsky himself, Prokofiev reacted against this style and experimented with composing in a more simple manner. When Russia was again his principal scene of action, and particularly after the Soviet esthetic terrorism of 1936 and the following purge years, he stressed, in place of his "motor" modernism, the melodic Russian aspect of his art. "In my childhood in Sontsovka I had often heard the village girls singing in chorus . . . but their performance had not impressed me with the beauty of Russian folk music and I did not remember a single tune. It is possible, of course, that subconsciously I was affected by the village songs, for now the Russian national idiom came quite easily to me. It was as if I had stumbled upon an unsuspected store of wealth, or as if I had planted seeds in virgin soil that were now bearing rich fruit."[5]

But Prokofiev never succeeded in becoming a highly developed melodist. Sergei Eisenstein, the great motion picture director, tells of Prokofiev's habit of remembering telephone numbers by their intonation. "And intonation is the foundation of melody. Prokofiev uses the same 'intonational' method when he scans a sequence of film. For intonation, i.e., the 'melody' of speech, is the foundation of music."[6] And it is true that Prokofiev's vocal music, like that of Mussorgsky, grows from and requires the sound of Russian speech. His melodic writing is angular and figurative, ornamented, coloristic, and sometimes tuneful. He labored to achieve transparency in orchestration and to reduce the number of instruments. His abandoning of all international bad influences was not a retreat but a final step upward to maturity, by acceptance of the Russian tradition he had not abandoned. His "grotesque" style, which has charmed generations of children with *Peter and the Wolf*, never grew in the direction of Mussorgsky's *Nursery* or the *Songs and Dances of Death*. One of his most splendid achievements was a film score, now heard as the orchestral suite from *Alexander Nevsky*. At least four of his operas, several ballets, symphonies, and piano concertos, his two violin concertos, and the brilliant flute sonata, all expert but hinting few hidden resources not evident at first or second hearing, hold or deserve place in the repertory.

Prokofiev expanded like a virtuoso upon a limited fund of ideas, but it is to be remarked that in performing his music at the piano his playing was not virtuoso. Though his playing was admired, he did not wish to spend time working at it; he played with natural ease and great competence. This unwillingness to develop his skill as a performer preserved him from the blighting dual existence of those great aristocrats of the piano in his generation and the generation before him, who aspired to be known as composers but instead made their careers playing other men's music. Rachmaninoff, Busoni, and Bartók accomplished both. Prokofiev for the most part played his own music. He performed it simply and plainly and not at all as if to supplant by an appearance of virtuosity what was not there, though his Second Piano Concerto has what is perhaps the largest and thickest cadenza in the repertory. Others have played virtuoso for him, and the music to a degree sustains them but does not gain by it; the effort exposes the impoverishment.

At his death some called him the greatest composer of his lifetime. Across the board from piano solo and instrumental duo to symphony, ballet, and opera, he was certainly one of the most fertile and accomplished, a courageous artist who kept his spiritual freedom with stubborn integrity. This stubborn spirit held him throughout life within a range of style which came to him too early.

Though Serge Rachmaninoff traveled abroad as a composer and virtuoso pianist, he did not go abroad to live until he fled after the revolution. An aristocrat, an isolate, and a mind of narrow appreciation, desiring a creative freedom he did not know how to possess, he remained a Russian in his songs and works for piano solo; his symphonies improve on Borodin without the strength of Prokofiev or the masterly directness of Tchaikovsky. He wrote at his best in the four symphonic piano concertos, the first rewritten late in his career, and the *Rhapsody on a Theme of Paganini* for piano and orchestra, yet he could not sustain a melody like Brahms but fell into sentimental repetition, and when his harmonic assemblage became large it became noisy. Because he was unable to comprehend what was happening in music during his lifetime, he did not let his concertos stiffen into neoclassic patterns or struggle in experimentation. These temptations seem not to have occurred to him; he composed always at the height of his old-fashioned style and performed with the seeming reluctance of an aristocrat forced to exhibit himself in public, a noble serenity of style that no other pianist has equaled in exhibiting his music.

Alexander Scriabin was, like Prokofiev, a prodigious child, trained to music by his mother. He fed like Debussy on the polyglot, but he carried in him the Russian tradition and adapted whatever he learned to that style. As a pianist he was the sole, but weaker, inheritor from Chopin. The discovery of Wagner possessed him, and that, too, he tried to gather into the Russian tradition which opposed it; his *Poem of Ecstasy* and *Prometheus, Poem of Fire* erupt in a frenzy of orchestration, which he supported by pantheistic explanations. He could no longer be at ease in the Russian tradition or, as Debussy did, put aside the Germanic urge to theorizing. He tried to create a new harmony, without the consequent vision of Schoenberg to recognize that no harmonic substitute could survive the emancipation of the dissonance: both composers made chords of superposed fourths, but Scriabin's use of his new harmony was esoteric, limited by the innate expectations of his training. Emotional excitement tried to do the work of structural coherence.

❀ The medieval tradition of harmony was built around the concordant octave and concordant fifth; the Renaissance tradition was built around the total concordance of the scale with mutable intervals (the twenty-two-tone Hindu scale in just intonation solves the same problem by supplying alternative notes instead of mutable intervals). For reasons deserving study the continuation in England of a harmony built around the correct fifth (in tempered Pythagorean tuning) was gradually displaced by the European harmony built around the correct third (meantone), with a very narrow fifth and a very wide third. In equal temperament, with a much widened or sharpened major third and a more nearly correct fifth, the composer had his choice of a more nearly concordant but slightly flattened harmony built around the fifth, or a strongly discordant (though theoretically still concordant), sharpened and more brilliant harmony built around the third.

The other alternative was to build a harmony around the nearly correct but wide, or sharpened, fourth, which was now in equal temperament less wide, sharp, and discordant than the major third. But chords of superposed fourths become, by addition of the extra width in each interval, progressively more discordant, with the result that the increasing microtonal divergence begins to encroach on the interval of the minor second. Increasing use of these extremely nonconcordant intervals, and the increasing presence of unadmitted microtones in the steadily enlarging vertical harmony hastened the disintegration of the simple chromatic scale into a more complex microtonal usage not provided by Western European formal theory.

We should realize that harmony is in fact not the relationships the notes theoretically provide but the auditory consequence of these relationships: the interval relationships that for acoustical reasons our ears learn unconsciously to expect. The new extreme of hearing transmitted by a radical composer to his listeners soon outmodes theory, but it may continue to progress beyond the mode the composer is himself aware of, and another composer, learning to hear music at that point, carries the progression farther, the audience for the same reason but very belatedly coming along with him. Trying to evade this state of affairs, for which theory has no language and the keyboard no provision, the composer is compelled either to atonality or to some temporarily satisfactory tonal compromise. For this theoretical muddle, underlying all composition and theory during the last century, a complete reconstitution of musical relationships in terms of the entire field of sound offers the only practical solution.

Scriabin contributed more than the majority of his contemporaries to the rise and acceptance of atonality, but he did not himself recognize or enter into this new musical conception.

Having no solution for the problem he had raised, Scriabin's art grew steadily towards the ecstatic: *this is how it feels to me* rather than *this I think.* Lacking the profound formal concentration for which Stravinsky's preferred ballet term, *ordonnance,* is more precise, Scriabin tried to escape through ecstasy beyond form, offering in the manner of some other Russian artists a mystical explanation: in this his mood resembles the ecstatic mood of Schoenberg but without the transforming inner discipline. Under the ecstatic surface he retained a scaffolding of formalism. Lou Harrison wrote in the margin of this manuscript: "Scriabin's 'ecstasy' is always 'Spanish'—i.e. 'impassioned geometry.' "

Scriabin's esoteric attitude affected even such nonmystical artists as the pianist Josef Hofmann, who during the year after the composer's death toured Russia playing only his compositions, and Prokofiev, who rapidly recovered from it. Outside Russia, Scriabin's esoteric music was much talked about but seldom played, and it has had no strong continuing influence. His last two piano sonatas, the Ninth and Tenth, and the last Preludes, opus 74, stop just short of discovering atonality. The interest of the music is great, yet compared with the mature contemporary keyboard works by Debussy, or the *Six Little Piano Pieces* by Schoenberg in which the atonal answer is admitted, Scriabin's forcing of the emotion and lack of economy are evident. Some result of Scriabin's style appears in the powerful single piano sonata by the American composer Charles Griffes.

19

USEFUL OR PRACTICAL MUSIC

Hindemith's COMPLAINT AND
Copland's ENTERPRISE

"A quarter of a century ago, in a discussion with German choral conductors, I pointed out the danger of an esoteric isolationism in music by using the term *Gebrauchsmusik*. Apart from the ugliness of the word—in German it is as hideous as its English equivalents workaday music, music for use, utility music, and similar verbal beauties—nobody found anything remarkable in it, since quite obviously music for which no use can be found, that is to say, useless music, is not entitled to public consideration anyway and consequently the *Gebrauch* is taken for granted. . . . Some busybody had written a report on that totally unimportant discussion, and when, years after, I first came to this country, I felt like the sorcerer's apprentice who had become the victim of his own conjurations: the slogan *Gebrauchsmusik* hit me wherever I went. . . . Apparently it met perfectly the common desire for a verbal label which classifies objects, persons, and problems, thus exempting anyone from opinions based on knowledge. Up to this time it has been impossible to kill the silly term and the unscrupulous classification that goes with it."[1]

In this passage of his Preface to *A Composer's World*, the Charles Eliot Norton Lectures which Hindemith delivered at Harvard during the winter 1949–1950, the composer dissembles. He does not admit that, in an effort to supplant an "esoteric

isolationism in music," he and several other German composers
advocated and wrote examples of music for practical use.

Hindemith, a gifted performer on string, wind, and keyboard
instruments, and a revealing conductor particularly of choral
music, set about to enlarge the repertory by writing useful
sonatas with piano accompaniment for nearly every instrument.
The idea caught on, and in spite of the fact that few of Hindemith's compositions of this type could be thought *easy* and
several are difficult enough to exercise virtuoso skill, the name
Gebrauchsmusik became peculiarly but not exclusively attached
to these compositions. Hindemith did not always wait on inspiration and, as Cecil Gray has commented, "his numerous works are
apt to give the impression of being lengths of the same material
cut off according to the requirements of the moment," but the
compositions were received with gratitude and have been widely
used for study and recital.

Hindemith's best gift to music may be this repertory of useful
compositions, as Bartók's best gift may be his no less practical
repertory of piano pieces; to say this does not invalidate their
larger compositions for instruments, orchestra, solo voice, and
chorus, their operas and ballets. Chopin in a letter put the case
the other way around: "They plague me to death urging me to
write symphonies and operas, and they want me to be all in one,
a Polish Rossini and Mozart and Beethoven. But I just laugh
under my breath and think to myself that one must start from
small things. I'm only a pianist, and if I'm worth anything this is
good, too."

One may sympathize with Hindemith's feelings but not with
his argument. Few would think the less of his evidently practical
compositions, his admired sonatas and chamber concertos, because the term *Gebrauchsmusik* can be applied to them. The
content, the musical substance, is the point at issue; the term can
be applied as well to Beethoven's crudely fabricated *Battle of
Vittoria*, the elegant dance music by Haydn, and the two profound and tragic fantasies by Mozart, all composed to be played
by a musical clockwork.

One can sympathize, too, concerning the misuse of terminology. Webern's practice of passing the melody by one or two notes
apiece among a group of disparate instruments receives the
monstrous title *Klangfarbenmelodie*, more suitable to Wagner;
the correct English term would be *timbre-melody*, but in view of

what has developed in this style *clangor-music* would more adequately cover the area and distinguish the type. Then there is John Cage's "composition using chance operations" that he later called *indeterminacy*, both terms borrowed from a conjunction of ancient Chinese religious-oracular practice (*I Ching*) and a philosophical attitude in present-day science and mathematics; this was internationalized by the vaguer term *aleatory*, from the Latin word for dice. The English *chancy music* would be more accurate and appropriate. The habit is to invent a term of portentous vagueness and then flourish it like a constable's cudgel or a mouth-filling legalism to intimidate the laity. English-speaking experts prefer a foreign incomprehensibility; Germans invent words to the same purpose.

Nothing is wrong in meaning with the term *Gebrauchsmusik* nor with the two plainest equivalents in English, *useful music* or *practical music*. The term may be redundant and unnecessary, but it had meaning in its time. The word came probably from the idea of the dramatist Bertolt Brecht that a work of art should communicate directly with the popular audience at their own level by artifice without illusion, that it should make vivid a comprehensible interpretation of human affairs rather than aim at popular or esoteric entertainment or esthetically pleasing abstraction. It is the opposite of *surrealism*, yet the savage mutual incomprehension of human beings going about their affairs in Brecht's dramas or Strindberg's surrealist dream plays contributes equally to the *drama of the absurd*. An idea fully realized bursts its categories; other art merely follows along the same line. Brecht's *Threepenny Opera* and *Mahagonny*, set to music by Kurt Weill, Ernest Krenek's *Jonny spielt auf*, Blitzstein's *The Cradle Will Rock*, Hindemith's own *Neues vom Tage* were written in this practical spirit. Stravinsky in the same manner composed his very unlike *Duo Concertant* for violin and piano each accompanying the other and Concerto for two solo pianos, obviously a practical device, and such practical oddities as a *Polka* for circus elephants, which he does not disown.

American composers followed the same line. It gave excuse for empty cleverness and academic joking. But Virgil Thomson's score for a motion picture, *The River*, and Aaron Copland's for *Quiet City* and his ballet *Appalachian Spring* head a group of practical masterpieces, which soon came to take the small place in the repertory awarded to American music.

Copland did not dissemble his purpose. In his Norton Lectures at Harvard (1951–1952) Copland wrote: "The conviction grew inside me that the two things that seemed always to have been so separate in America—music and the life about me—must be made to touch. This desire to make the music I wanted to write come out of the life I had lived in America became a preoccupation of mine in the twenties. . . . in greater or lesser degree all of us [American composers who had gone to live abroad] discovered America in Europe."[2]

Observe that this is practical music for a different purpose than practical use: the audience for music in America, a continent without musical tradition, had grown to vast size, but there was no recognizable American musical idiom. The notion that jazz might be such an idiom had not taken hold, and experienced composers knew it in any case to be erroneous. Copland had tried it. Copland wrote: "One of the crucial questions of our time was injected: how are we to make contact with this enormously enlarged potential audience without sacrificing in any way the highest musical standards?"[3]

One way, of course, would have been to forget about the "highest musical standards" and go to work as Charles Ives did. But Copland wished his music to be practical in both senses: to be immediately acceptable by those whose opinion approves acceptability and to be at once performed; in both ways his practical music was successful.

Copland continues: "I was simply pointing out that certain modes of expression may not need the full gamut of post-tonal implications, and that certain expressive purposes can be appropriately carried out only by a simple texture in a basically tonal scheme. As I see it, music that is born complex is not inherently better or worse than music that is born simple. . . . The inference is sometimes drawn that I have consciously abandoned my earlier dissonant manner in order to popularize my style—and this notion is applauded enthusiastically; while those of a different persuasion are convinced that only my so-called 'severe' style is really serious."[4]

In saying this Copland also dissembles a little; he *did* wish to compose in a popular style but on his own terms. He agreed with the belief that music should speak an idiom understood by the people, but not that it should have to. This was also in a way the corrective, corrosive critical purpose of Erik Satie and Dada.

Such an attitude offers a necessary antidote to the belief that great music appears only on a mountaintop to which the ordinary listener must struggle, that it is written in an abstract language, like that of higher mathematics or philosophy, which can be interpreted only by professionals, that the expressive emotions of music are not and indeed should not be within ordinary reach, that whatever is not so exalted should be rejected. These consequences of Germanic nineteenth century philosophizing are still firmly established among us, expounded by musicians, musicologists, and estheticians, exhorted upon one another by advocates of musical professionalism. It is a tissue of fallacies, as Copland was aware in striking at it.

But Hindemith, one of the original leaders who had acted within Germanic music to overcome these esthetic fallacies, fell back when he heard himself named as a leader of the revolt and tried to dissemble his leadership. Against the "dangers of esoteric isolationism" he had urged the need for a practical music, setting aside the fetish of difficulty, music to be generally understood and for all types of instruments. Now he denied what he had intended; more seriously, he deceived himself. His statement is the complaint of a great artist who has lost integrity, who has become dishonest with himself and concerning the purpose of his work. After Hindemith's lectures were published I wrote an article, saying more briefly what I have written here; the article came to Stravinsky, not by my doing, and he spoke of it. He said to me then about Hindemith, "He has gone sour—German sour."

The aforetime radical, who had suffered the interdict of Hitler as a *Kulturbolschewist,* who during years of exile in Turkey had established there a modern system of musical education, became in his later years a rallying figure of musical reactionaries and the Germanic type of musicologists who will not admit the relevance of any fact they do not have in print or any score they cannot analyze, who *explain* music by inventing fantasies of interpretation. Hindemith himself, in attacking atonality and by implication Schoenberg, fell into such methods.

In the first chapter of *A Composer's World,* Hindemith summarizes the six phases of musical perception and understanding, a thoroughly modern inventory, as set forth by Saint Augustine in the sixth book *On Music:* (1) the physical fact of sound; (2) the physiological faculty of hearing; (3) the ability to imagine music without hearing it; (4) musical memory; (5) thoughtful perception; (6) musical order as the image of a higher order "that tends towards the order of the heavens and towards the unification of our soul with the divine principle."

"The order of the heavens" is Pythagorean, Ptolemaic, an astronomic projection of abstract mathematical order, of which music is another projection. For Augustine, memory, intelligence, and will are not powers, properties, or faculties, but each is the one soul, which perceives by sensation but is not acted upon by what it perceives.

"The tenor of that doctrine is," Hindemith declares: "music has to be converted into moral power. We receive its sounds and forms, but they remain meaningless unless we include them in our own mental activity and use their fermenting quality to turn our soul towards everything noble, superhuman, and ideal. . . . The betterment of our soul must be our own achievement, although music is one of those factors which, like religious belief, creates in us most easily a state of willingness towards this betterment. . . . Composers, performers, teachers, listeners— they all must outgrow the mere registration of musical impressions, the superficial and sentimental attachment to sound."[5]

Hindemith then proceeds to Boethius, *De Institutione Musica:* "Music is a part of our human nature; it has the power either to improve or to debase our character." Here it is no longer the soul which is active but unmoved; it is sensation which acts for good or evil on the soul.

"Extremes they really are!" Hindemith concludes. And aiming at Augustine he rationalizes after Boethius: "The Augustinian precept, in which our mind absorbs music and transforms it into moral strength; and the Boethian precept, in which the power of music, its ethos, is brought into action upon our mind. . . . Augustine's musical philosophy, with its decided renunciation of external effects, its inclination towards superhumanity, is never threatened by the danger of degeneration. . . . Boethius' musical philosophy, however, demanding a submission to the ethic power of music (hence implicitly to its sensual allurements as well) easily becomes the subject of degeneration. Its strongly intellectual trend may produce music that in its utter aridity is unpalatable; it may transform the listener into the frequently occurring snob. The emphasis on all facts technical may end in meaningless sound . . . without moving the listener's soul. The stress laid upon the outward qualities of the musical material—on sound and form—may in megalomaniacal hypertrophy explode into unartistic noise. The essentially active function of music may force the listener into such a state of passivity that his faculty of musical perception will crave only pieces which offer no resistance . . . a cheap and trashy amenity, an opiate always and everywhere available. Our present era, in which the majority of listeners is constantly subject to this kind of music, has, in my opinion, reached a point below which a further degeneration of the Boethian attitude is impossible."[6]

But by now the clamoring composer has brought down his argument to the same level of esthetic complaint with which he turned against those who in his belief misrepresented him by speaking of *Gebrauchsmusik*.

Augustine, in his majestic examination of Memory—"Certainly, O Lord, I am working hard at it, and my work is being done on myself; I have become to myself a soil of difficulty and of too much sweat"—approaches every possibility, even to deception: "They love truth when it enlightens; they hate it when it reproves. Since they do not wish to be deceived, and they do not wish to deceive, they love (truth) when it reveals its own self, and they hate it when it reveals themselves. Its retribution upon them stems from this: those who do not wish to be revealed by it, it both reveals against their will and is not itself revealed to them."[7]

The idea of a nonesoteric, practical music took still other form. "We wanted," Aaron Copland explains, "to find a music that would speak of universal things in a vernacular of American speech rhythms. We wanted to write music on a level that left popular music far behind—music with a largeness of utterance wholly representative of the country that Whitman had envisaged.

"Through a curious quirk of musical history the man who was writing such a music—a music that came close to approximating our needs—was entirely unknown to us. I sometimes wonder whether the story of American music might have been different if Charles Ives [had been known] and his work had been played at the time he was composing most of it—roughly the twenty years from 1900–1920. . . ."[8]

There is the more than probability that if a mature Copland had known Ives during this period, he might have offered Ives this advice: "What seems to me a waste of time is the self-deceiving 'major' effort on the part of many composers who might better serve the community by the writing of a good piece for high school band."[9]

If high schools had bands in those days and one of them had asked him for a composition, Ives undoubtedly would have supplied it, as many good composers have done in more recent years. It is doubtful whether the high school band would have played it. Few high school orchestras have attempted Schoenberg's Suite for String Orchestra, written for such educational performance.

Ives wrote much practical music, for church use, and *play* music and parody. In *Hallowe'en,* for string quartet and piano, the instruments read the same material in pairs and then together in accelerating dynamics, the work to be played, Ives suggests, around a campfire. The campfire setting, for those instruments, is unlikely, but no more so than Mahler's great outdoor setting for his Eighth Symphony or Ives's for his unfinished *Universe Symphony,* a symphony intended never to be finished. So that, in full circle, practical music joins hands with the impractical. Ives's "campfire" was more likely the visual image he meant his music to convey.

The nonliterary mingling of words, visual images, natural sounds, and musical correspondences in Ives's imagination creates a richness of texture and allusion difficult for the critical listener to assimilate. For this reason Copland speaks of Ives's "inability to be self-critical." The violinist whom Ives hired to read his violin sonatas looked at them, took his money, and called Ives a fool.

"Don't think for an instant," Copland admonishes, "that he was a mere provincial with a happy knack for incorporating indigenous material into his many scores. No, Ives was an intellectual, and what is most impressive is not his evocation of a local landscape but the over-all range and comprehensiveness of his musical mind."[10]

It is only by unceasing, unrelenting, merciless, and withal good-humored self-criticism—without good humor he could not preserve himself in patience—that a composer can create a musical continent of unprecedented content and idiom requiring generations to explore it before it is known. Such a composer has self-critically removed exactly those handles of obvious and common style which his less self-critical fellow composers have learned to grasp. If Beethoven or Ives had been incapable of the self-vision that provokes great comedy and great laughter, and therefore the ability to penetrate to what is most serious, they could not have endured the pressure of self-criticism they imposed on themselves: the hearing of both grew distorted; Ives's health broke; though he lived for another thirty-five years he lost the ability to write consecutive music.

During the work day Ives totally immersed himself in the insurance business, to which he contributed a fundamentally new conception of salesmanship, out of Emerson, Alcott, and Thoreau, that the salesman is responsible for the correct guidance and protection of his customer. In the off-hours Ives immersed himself in music. It is all part of the legend, but he lived it. In later life he could have afforded to buy performance and propagandize his music, if he had wished to. Instead, he contributed a large part of the cost of publishing the quarterly *New Music,* edited at different periods by Henry Cowell and Gerald Strang, a magazine which contained nothing but the scores of new compositions by living composers; Lou Harrison has called it "the *Fitzwilliam Virginal Book* of the twentieth century." Most of the scores were by relatively unknown American or Latin American composers. This is practical music at the highest level of philanthropy.

The awareness of fundamental individuality in music is blocked for many by the need to hitch their imagination to a referrable process. This seems to have been Hindemith's block. Though he wrote, "The emphasis on all facts technical may end in meaningless sound . . . without moving the listener's soul," he said elsewhere that, when one loses "this firm stand on solid ground," the music is deprived of its esthetic character and becomes an "individualistic vagary," having no validity except for the composer and his "bewitched devotees." This criticism, directed from both angles against Schoenberg, would apply as well to late Beethoven, to Bartók, or to Ives. Taste expanding with opportunity has brought out of obscurity the music of Machaut, Bach's *Art of Fugue* and *Musical Offering,* each first performed in 1927, Beethoven's *Diabelli Variations,* and may revive Kaikhosru Sorabji's *Opus Clavicembalisticum* (a piano composition of 250 pages, on several staves without key-signatures, in twelve movements, including one theme with 49 variations and another with 81 variations, fugues and canons of every type, and filling two hours in performance) or the several giant compositions by Nikos Skalkottas.

It is precisely such "individualistic vagary" which periodically creates new musical understanding, new content and style, a new musical era. Bach's *Art of Fugue* stands behind Schoenberg's method of the tone-row. Hindemith wrote: "There is, however, one work which is the *pièce de résistance* of the more art-conscious set of arrangers: the *Art of Fugue*. . . . The ideal behavior is to enjoy it in the same spirit of nonsounding abstraction as the composer did when he wrote it." (Bach composed it in open score, not indicating what instruments should play it.) The *Art of Fugue* is a practical treatise in notation on the art of writing fugues and canons. Is it therefore *esoteric* by Hindemith's description, or *Gebrauchsmusik* in the way Hindemith disliked? Does Hindemith's "art-conscious" mean "long-haired" in the sense of the popular reviewers, or *esthetically aware?*

If Bach had preferred the sort of esoteric music in the head that one practises by looking at the notes without performing them, he would not have spent so much of his busy life writing and rewriting his own and other men's music for practical use. He would not have set the pattern for one pair of future arrangers of the *Art of Fugue* (the version for two pianos by Richard Buhlig and Wesley Kuhnle) by rewriting the most abstract portion of his most abstract composition, the glistening pair of mirror fugues, to be played by two keyboard instruments. The supreme arbiters of Bach scholarship, Spitta, Schweitzer, Tovey, ruled against the structural coherence of the *Art of Fugue* in the form in which it survives: every hearing overrules their decision.

❀ It is probable, however, that the succession of fugues and canons in the *Art of Fugue,* as it has been published, is incorrect. Eric Vaughn has worked out, by comparison of many internal factors, a successive ordering of the fugues and canons which, though it cannot be proved to be Bach's intention, seems as a whole more reasonable in progression than the published order. This new version was first performed by Margaret Fabrizio in San Francisco (see page 6).

Hindemith published a new harmonic method, challenging atonality and the tone-row, and with curious pedantry insisted on rewriting, to conform with his new method, some of his best-loved works, in particular the song cycle *Das Marienleben*, a setting of poems by Rainer Maria Rilke, a vagary as curious as if Schoenberg had rewritten his song cycle, *The Hanging Gardens*, on poems by Stefan George, to conform with the Method of Composing with Twelve Tones. There is, of course, the possibility that Hindemith may have done this, as Stravinsky has recomposed several of his popular early works, to establish a new copyright. War and change of nationality play havoc with a composer's ownership of his creations. So too, I might add, does the still unreformed American law of copyright.

In his *Unterweisung im Tonsatz*, Hindemith developed a theory of musical structure and analysis from the acoustical relations of tones, but he did not abandon equal temperament, and his method, designed to contradict the resolution of atonality by the tone-row, does not solve but adds still another to previous rationalizations of the problem.

It is hard to imagine Hindemith writing a piece like Schoenberg's little cantata, *The Lover's Wish*. The piece lasts three and a half minutes; at first hearing, it seems almost impossibly complex and indirect. Four or five hearings only intensify the inwardness of this tiny orient of music, poised and at its center serene. Hearing it almost apart from emotional dynamics, one is more aware of the musical involvement, the multiplied counteracting and crossing rhythms and tones, their connotation as sound, not by analysis or by any verbal or ideistic reference, but in the way sound grows melodic by extension and harmonic by vertical implication. In Hindemith's compositions one is conscious of formally designed musical ideas going well-marked musical roads. A comparable piece by Hindemith would be *Serenades* for soprano voice, oboe, viola, and cello, a wonderfully witty, delightfully calculated lyricism of unaccompanied solos, duos, and asides, a masterpiece of craftsmanship with every idea exposed. For all that, Hindemith must be ranked among the few great song-writers of the century, and the *Marienleben* cycle one of its outstanding achievements.

In Hindemith's music the rhythm changes but is seldom varied from within. Dryness and uniform tone-color prevail through large areas of his later music. The inflexible melodic-thematic patterns do not sing as melodies or transform themselves by flowering into memorable themes. The earnest counterpoint fears foreshortening, as the movement fears rest. The statement is often powerful, but the development relatively unrevealing. The symphony derived from his opera *Mathis der Mahler*, one of his best scores, lacks the nightmare and transfiguration of its painterly original. Hindemith's ballet of Saint Francis, *Nobilissima Visione*, is among the most fully realized of his larger compositions. But the great opportunity afforded by his setting of Whitman's *When Lilacs Last in the Door-yard Bloom'd* as an elegiac cantata, *For Those We Loved*, was dissipated in the unstable realization.

Hindemith, like Prokofiev, had the courage to resist tyranny; his opera *Mathis der Mahler*, written under Hitler, reflects by its setting in the Thirty Years War the outrage of Nazi rule. Yet the real subject is the painter-hero's self-questioning whether being an artist he should involve himself in these political disasters. At the end he withdraws defeated to his studio.

In his art, by comparison with his great contemporaries, Debussy, Schoenberg, Satie, Stravinsky, Bartók, Ives, who went their own way in defiance of popularity and tradition, Hindemith lacked the ultimate courage to remain beyond and outside that security. His consuming desire to refer everything to controlled tonal process tells us less than Schoenberg's mystical pride when he speaks of "the miraculous contributions of the unconscious . . . the power behind the human mind, which produces miracles for which we do not deserve credit . . . the intoxicating recollection of the inspiration that enforced production."

Hindemith wished the credit; his fate is one of the lessons to be learned from twentieth century music. Instead of cultivating the integrity of compromise which he had in fact practised, he deceived himself and spoiled his integrity.

THE INTEGRITY OF COMPROMISE

*Nielsen, Falla, Vaughan Williams,
Sibelius, Bloch*

Critical and popular opinion attacks more often the authority of uncompromising genius, while respecting the integrity of compromise. In longer retrospect, the same opinion founds its critical assurance, with too little discriminative justice, on the uncompromising authority of genius, while running down the integrity of compromise.

I do not mean by "compromise" the limitation of a composer by his tradition, as with the Russian composers except Stravinsky. Nor do I mean the limitation of a composer by his talent; there was no compromise in the laserlike minuscule of Anton Webern. I mean by compromise the limitations a thinking artist imposes on his talent by his effort to create an individual style, an individual content or esthetic consistency, by means of his own gift, apart from the help of a tradition or the authority of uncompromising genius.

Max Reger was a talented composer, so habituated to the Germanic tradition that he could not alter or advance it. Paul Hindemith was a man of genius, in the Germanic tradition, gifted with the authority of an individual style, who by self-deception impaired his integrity. Béla Bartók was a composer of uncompromising genius, who created for himself an individual content and style reinforced by his integrity. Carl Nielsen, a composer of less talent than Prokofiev or Ravel, made himself by integrity of purpose the musical spokesman of Denmark and a composer to be respected, something much more than we mean when we speak of a respectable composer. One might say the same in honor of Smetana or Janáček, who were nationalist composers.

The distinction between *national* and *nationalist* is hard to define and may be unreal. Janáček's brilliant *Glagolitic Mass*, honoring the tenth anniversary of the founding of the Republic of Czechoslovakia, draws color and character from *Boris Godunov*. Was Janáček more nationalist than Vaughan Williams, who was unquestionably *national?* Is nationalism in a composer determined by his intention, by the idiomatic sources of his content, by localization, by provincialism? Need it imply chauvinism? The answer is, in each case, no. Going abroad changed Dürer from a medieval to a modern artist; Dante, Shakespeare, Blake did not need to travel far to inhabit the world. The much traveled, cosmopolitan artist is too often esthetically glib. *Nationalist* is an applied description, inadequate to the composer's purpose, like the presumptive "Jewishness" ascribed to Ernest Bloch. A self-proclaimed "nationalist" composer is more likely to be a patriotic polyglot.

Sibelius was not a nationalist composer in the origins of his style or in the development of a music of national character; like Nielsen he was a polyglot by taste, as his smaller music indicates, whose symphonies speak for his nation as his tone poems dwell upon the *Kalevala*, the Finnish national epic, compiled of traditional material during the nineteenth century.

You are cutting it too fine, some reader may admonish me: Janáček was an obvious polyglot, who turned towards Mussorgsky, and his music was welcomed in Germany. True. But his temperament like his music came out of the long-established, submerged Moravian tradition, which in his use proved inadequate for his purpose.

Manuel de Falla was educated in the modern Spanish style—it was not yet a tradition—revived by his teacher, the Spanish composer Felipe Pedrell; behind them lay not a tradition but centuries of Spanish music. If Falla had stayed in Spain, he might have been, like Pedrell, a national composer, his work scarcely known outside his native country. But after winning a prize for the best Spanish opera with *La Vida Breve*, Falla went to Paris, where his friends included such disparate composers as Paul

Dukas, Debussy, Stravinsky, and Ravel, and he wrote for the Diaghilev ballet one of his better-known works, *The Three-Cornered Hat.* Like Bartók, he developed a style combining the deliberate Parisian artificiality of Debussy and Ravel with the authority of his own study of folk music, for example, in his chamber concerto for harpsichord; this mingling made him something more than a national composer. Portions of *El Amor Brujo* show an awareness of *Firebird* and *Petrouchka,* well embedded in native Spanish idiom. The *hard* element of his piano fantasy, *Fantasía Bética,* comes directly out of the Spanish guitar tradition.

Ralph Vaughan Williams, the most British of composers, studied in Germany with Max Bruch and, informally, with Ravel. He possessed to an extreme that integrity of compromise which enabled him to create for himself work of the quality of the earlier great period of English music that he cherished and from which he enthusiastically "cribbed." He became one of the conservatives of twentieth century music, yet he was also for a while one of its more substantial radicals; he lacked that authority of uncompromising genius which would have driven through to create music his countrymen might have rejected.

"The mixture of integrity and respect for what is practicable shows itself throughout his music, with few exceptions. . . . He never thought of music apart from performance and frequently . . . said so; he was, of all twentieth-century composers, the *Gebrauchsmusiker par excellence.*" (That typically English-speaking pedantic cliché of mixed metaphor in mixed foreign language means that Vaughan Williams was a great writer of practical music for immediate use.) "Amateurs, professionals, children and adults, the orthodox and the strange—all found him ready and willing to write for them. . . . Unlike many modern composers, he was willing to go much more than half way to meet his audience and did so without sacrificing his artistic integrity."[1]

Instead, he dissipated his powers in writing music of convenience, sacred and choral works suitable for immediate performance. The British choral festivals provide a good market for strong but compromising art, as the best British choral music from Elgar's *Dream of Gerontius* to Michael Tippett's *A Child of Our Time* and Britten's *War Requiem* demonstrates.

The so-called impressionist character of Vaughan Williams's

early *Sea Symphony* with chorus, his *London Symphony,* his *Pastoral Symphony,* was put aside in writing his abstract and powerful Fourth Symphony in F minor. Rather than *impressionist,* his most naïve music might be better called *pictorial;* he seems to have thought on the whole more comfortably outside abstract music. His *Concerto Accademico* for violin and orchestra seems dry and stiffly formal. His ballet *Job* is in the same way more laborious than impressive. Yet it is the abstract strength, instead of the pictorial element, that most convinces in his best symphonies, notably the Fourth and Fifth, scarcely less in the *London* and *Pastoral.* His later symphonic writing gradually fell away from this height. He is at his most agreeable in compositions that almost visually realize his awareness of English scene and character—among the best the song cycle, *On Wenlock Edge.*

Vaughan Williams believed that composers should write music in their native surroundings. "If I might give a word of advice to young composers," he said in 1957, talking about his teachers, the composers Hubert Parry and Charles Stanford, "I would say 'learn the elements of your art at home; then, only then, when you feel sure of what you want to do, and feel the ability to do it, go and rub noses with the composers of other lands and see what you can learn from them. You may say that you do not want to be national, but that you want to be international. You will not achieve this by denying your own country from the start. If you subscribe to that extremely foolish description of music as a universal language, you will find that you have achieved nothing better than a standardized and emasculated cosmopolitanism which will mean nothing to you nor to those whose mannerisms you have been aping.' "[2]

It is excellent advice and should be set over the doors of every foundation or agency which gives young composers money to go abroad and study while they are young. The givers of the money do not always enter their offices by these same doors; if they did, the advice might provoke them to thinking. Should not a composer start by learning his native language? For his native musical language Vaughan Williams studied with two masters of that language, Parry and Stanford, whom at the end of his life he still believed to be great composers. "What about Parry as a composer? Potentially, I believe, he was among the greatest. But something stood in the way of complete realization. . . ."[3]

This "something" that stands in the way needs also to be examined. The student, if he is to master what is taught him, must at the same time challenge it: the tradition, the accustomed esthetics, above all the habit of practising what others preach. A school of composers is a body of common habituation, but it can spread so wide as to produce a group of masters, a succession of genius, using a common language each with creative individuality, like the Viennese school from Haydn to Webern, like the Tudor and Jacobean composers, among whom Vaughan Williams preferred Weelkes to Byrd. "Weelkes is the true English artist. . . . There is nothing to suggest that Weelkes hated conventionality. It simply did not exist for him. When his treatment of a subject happened to coincide with the convention of the day, it just coincided, and there is only the superb craftsmanship to show us which is his work."[4] Vaughan Williams's characterization of Weelkes is an outward-looking reflection of himself.

A composer should listen to the music that is going on about him, to the sounds of the world he lives in, to popular and folk music, to the speech of his countrymen with attention to its subtle deviations, which are idiomatically expressive, necessary to comprehend in accent and rhythm if one sets them to music, but above all because they are one's countrymen thinking in a manner that belongs to one's country. A composer's countrymen are his natural audience, though they may reject him. He need not cater to them or condescend, but he must understand them; and if he understands them well, he will not cater or desire to condescend. (By understanding, I do not mean reckoning with their box-office prejudices.) He will be among them what in the long view we expect a great artist to be, though we always deceive ourselves by looking first for other and more common qualities, an artist prophetically speaking native idiom.

I believe that I have by now made evident that my business here is not to survey the works of a number of composers point by point, telling good and bad, nor to paraphrase their biographies, but to see them as unitary figures in a larger scene, conformations in a landscape, makers, exchangers, continuators, and sometimes perpetuators of creative thought for others to experience. Parry, Stanford, Edward Elgar, Gustav Holst, Frederick Delius, Ralph Vaughan- Williams re-created music in a country which had so nearly lost it that Samuel Wesley, a century before, and Arthur Sullivan were their only significant predecessors.

To this new British music Benjamin Britten and the composers of his generation have made great contribution. Their art has been a compromise of varying integrity, yet as a whole of such integrity that it has re-established British music after nearly two centuries of foreign domination. No one of them has possessed the uncompromising authority of genius; their gift has been compromised in every instance by "something that stood in the way of complete realization," yet as a group they have raised British music to a level equal to that of any national music in the twentieth century. Ralph Vaughan Williams stood at the head of them.

Jan Sibelius would have been among the minor composers of a great period, if he had not composed symphonic music. The Sibelius symphonic works, including the one symphonic String Quartet, stand as a unit, as the symphonies by Vaughan Williams and the symphonies and concertos by Prokofiev do not. These are both larger composers, yet they lack the symphonic individuality of Sibelius.

With infinite labor the authority of genius seems to move determinately to the right solution, not the merely satisfactory, pathetic, pleasing, or arousing; while the artist of integrity, with perhaps as much labor, achieves precisely those satisfactory, pathetic, pleasing and arousing effects, interspersed with areas of compromise, or indecision, or routine, which enable his music to be more immediately apprehended and less finally authoritative. The listener, becoming acquainted with this great art of compromise, finding reassurance in the conventional or routine elements to which his thought consciously gives slight notice, grasps with more confidence what seems to be original.

Yet the symphonies, a few of the tone poems, the Violin Concerto, and the one symphonic String Quartet by Sibelius offer no handle of conventional or routine passages, though the style as a whole is as popularly convincing as that of Tchaikovsky. It is this lack of customary handles, combined with the plain statement and popular effect, which the unconvinced critic boggles at. The man is a bad composer; he does nothing as he should; he is nonetheless popular; and this can be only by the error or bad taste of those who like him. It is not true. Sibelius is the complete symphonist, and his talent in that line is as impossible to define usefully by analysis as the gift of a more complete composer across the entire field. His symphonies are of a piece, and nothing he wrote that is not symphonic in style is worth bothering with.

He is to the symphony what Puccini is to opera, and being in that one way so complete his art enjoys in retrospect the popularity it deserves. The ability to write greatly acceptable popular music at a consistently high level, however restricted the field of accomplishment, is an exceptional gift; whoever has it will seem to possess the uncompromising authority of genius, but that exactly is what he does not have. He is like Blondel who could walk a tightrope over the gorge at Niagara Falls and do so repeatedly with a daring increase of impediments, pushing a man before him on a wheelbarrow, sitting on a chair at midpoint, or carrying a man on his back, but he cannot perform miracles. We are at fault when we try to prove that Tchaikovsky or Sibelius is a good or bad composer. Say rather, each walked strictly the tightrope of his style and did not fall off, in such circumstances that he was more than a stylistic acrobat.

A quarter-century before his death, Sibelius, in good health, ceased composing. His long-promised Eighth Symphony—some believed it was to be published after his death—has not appeared. No one can tell whether creative exhaustion or an increasingly severe self-criticism stopped him. The Eighth Symphony would have been looked to as something like an epochal event, and he must have known it could not be that.

The influence of Sibelius has hung like an oppressive darkness over two generations of Finnish composers, who could find in his work nothing to go on with and, outside his influence, no acceptable music to combat it. In England, where Sibelius was greatly admired, composers who took him for a model perished of it. In America, the better composers, angered by the long vogue of his orchestral music, which displaced their own, criticized and did not follow him.

Ernest Bloch is another example of that integrity of compromise which does not seek popularity but establishes a man as artist by the consistency of his best work. Fashion may toss him as high as Sibelius or make a mock of what in him is most genuine. Bloch, a Jew born in Switzerland but a European by residence in Belgium, Germany, and France, wrote an opera, *Macbeth*, while still quite young, had it performed in Paris, where it was thought radical, and conducted orchestral concerts of his music. The American dancer Maud Allan, more firmly established in England, though less notorious, than Isadora Duncan on the Continent, invited the rising young conductor to direct the orchestra which accompanied her American tour. Afterwards Bloch stayed in America, to become the principal teacher after Horatio Parker of the rising generation of American composers. Roger Sessions, who had studied also with Parker, and Elliott Carter were among his students. Bloch's composing followed an independent course apart from every fashion of his time, with a strong tendency to melodies resembling Jewish cantillation that do not easily combine with a similar tendency to abstract formalism; the resulting compositions are heavy and powerful; they soon began to seem old-fashioned in comparison with the prevailing trend of thin, slick neoclassicism in the manner of the Parisian "Six" and the new *practical* music of the 1930s.

Bloch's passionately expressive music is divided between the tone poem of emotional but rather abstract style, for example his popular *Schelomo* for cello and orchestra, and the stoutly neoclassical *Concerto Grosso* and Piano Quintet, the latter exploring some use of quarter-tones. Horatio Parker before him had won two contests for new operas with works which reached the stage but did not stay there; Bloch won a contest with his symphony *America*, concluding in a proposed new American national anthem. The anthem had no appeal because it had no relationship with the idiomatic music Americans think natural to sing. Bloch gradually withdrew into a solitary life outside the trend of musical fashion and devoted his last years to writing string quartets in the full refinement of his art. Like Bartók, he wrote best for strings, notably his Violin Sonata and Violin Concerto.

By a quirk of taste which exaggerated one aspect of his music, Bloch has been typed as a "Jewish" composer, as if this assumed typicality were a limitation. His principal work, the *Sacred Service* for chorus and orchestra, is Jewish in the largest sense. Schoenberg, too, honored the great tradition of Jewish faith with his *Kol Nidre* and *A Survivor from Warsaw;* neither composer was accepted as a spokesman by the Jewish community either in America, Europe, or Israel. It is strange that during a century of unprecedented activity by Jewish composers and musicians, no composer from Meyerbeer and Mendelssohn to the present day, whether or not he wished such recognition, has seemed to the Jews in any country to be the musical voice of their tradition.

THE ISOLATED ARISTOCRATIC COMPOSER IN A COMMERCIALIZED ENVIRONMENT

Mahler, Busoni

Any major artist stands apart from his environment, as creator and critic. In a temporal community of artists, as in a henyard, the local pecking order takes on an exaggerated importance. The cocks crowing from one yard to another seem to be passing along significant messages. To be "in" is to know the henyard gossip; within a few years henyard and gossip are a byplay of reminiscence. The artist of fundamental individuality stands apart from his contemporaries. The popularity of his art, or popular neglect of it, does not define the long-range achievement. At the present time the formerly neglected music of the Vienna school—Schoenberg, Berg, Webern, and their posthumous followers—has been in the ascendant fifteen years, while the string quartets by Bloch are neglected. The snob believes in his critical acumen that the fate of the Bloch quartets is just. Does the enthusiast of the recent Vivaldi revival temper his enthusiasm with the reflection that this is not Bach? At the very start of Handel's career, age twenty-two, he composed in Italy his mighty Psalm 110: *Dixit Dominus,* the powerful, classic rectangularity of defined levels and verticals controlling all melodious ornament. Handel never gave up this Renaissance formality, however the baroque elaboration might play over it. Should the Italianate Handel have given more thought to the melodious, emotional working of his inner voices after the Germanic, provincial habit of J. S. Bach? At that time, a sound critic would have esteemed the bourgeois Handel's Palladian classic formality more aristocratic than his native baroque idiom.

The distinction can be summarized in this sentence from a chapter on architecture by Heinrich Wölfflin: "The elementary phenomenon is this—that two wholly different architectural effects are produced according to whether we are obliged to perceive the architectural form as something definite, solid, enduring, or as something over which, for all its stability, there plays an apparent, constant movement, that is, change."[1] Handel's classical formality inspired in turn some of the most beloved pages of Mozart's *Magic Flute* and Beethoven's Ninth Symphony; Bach's melodious emotionality reaches its extreme in Beethoven's last quartets. In each at all times there is an awareness of the other. During the nineteenth century the Germanic emotional severity was sweetened and became less drastic, the Italianate classical formality softened to the stuffiness and pomposity of French opera. The Germanic style which has governed our most serious, twentieth century musical responses grew from the rediscovered inspiration of the Beethoven symphonies and quartets. We now respond once more with equal seriousness to the classic Italianate formality of Handel. Taste has no absolute; it is a constant discovery and rediscovery of content.

Some great musical figures of Europe before the First World War lived and thought like barons and princes. These baronial figures cultivated a manner of life more fantasy-feudal than romantic; they were not romantic bohemians. Wagner's patron, the "mad" King Ludwig, and Napoleon III invented a stuffy, ornamental, bourgeois imitation royalty, its social pretensions perpetuated even today by opera houses. Wagner added the stuffy, imitation ritual of Bayreuth. This was not true of all; Schumann, Bruckner, Brahms, and Reger were distinctly unpretentious middle-class.

In feudal style, the great nobles took on the training of their squires. At Mannheim, Bülow brought forward Richard Strauss to be his squire and successor; at Hamburg he brought forward Gustav Mahler. Mahler at Vienna counted among his squires Bruno Walter and Otto Klemperer. After the First World War, these aristocratic conditions, in France already sunk to a bourgeois indifference, could not be resumed. The attitude of middle-class privacy typified by Brahms replaced that of the aristocrats.

Economic and political disorder and the increasing rapidity and ease of travel broke up the principalities and patronage; musical ability became a commodity for sale. Society no longer took for granted the aristocracy of a great artist; he might live like an aristocrat in private, as Rachmaninoff did, but in public he was an entertainer, subservient to the public audience and its spokesmen and managers.

Worse still, he became, himself, manager and symbol—the impersonal "personality" of public print and photograph—self-publicized by choice: von Karajan and low-slung sportcar, excitingly bouncing among responsibilities in Berlin, Salzburg, Vienna, London; Bernstein on television; Stockhausen sounding Germanic profundities on platform or in print—marvelously talented in an illusory world, where reputation does the work of contemplation.

Though the great opera houses and musical capitals stayed active, the luxurious, pseudo-spiritual concept of the music festival, initiated at Bayreuth and by the choral festivals in England, was taken over now by businessmen for tourism: reputations, labeled by name value, offering the currently fashionable classic and contemporary music to a styleless gathering of tourists.

After the First World War and increasingly after the Second World War, the festival idea, while encompassing ever more impersonal exhibitions in the larger centers, has spread to smaller communities, for more special purposes, following the example of the Haslemere Festivals in England, where for many years Arnold Dolmetsch and his versatile family propagated the revival of older European music, its instruments and performance practices. The Glyndebourne Festival of opera and more recently the Aldeburgh Festivals, directed by composer Benjamin Britten, have set the example of a consistently high quality of program and performance, free of commercialism. Community-sponsored festivals of genuinely independent music, from Warsaw, Poland, and Darmstadt and Donaueschingen in Germany to Ojai and Aptos in California, and Japan, emphasize program rather than performer; although many are subverted by concealed box-office attitudes, not all succumb to the facile temptation. The intent of these festivals, to revive lost classics and make new works known, reflects a desire not only for new musical experience but for a renewed experience of live music, apart from the routine schedules of the cities and the recorded repertory.

In Berlin and Vienna, Richard Strauss upheld lifelong the rights of the composer and the authority of the music director against social and political interference, arguing his cause in person with Hitler as he had argued it with the Kaiser. In New York the transition from aristocratic to what one might uneasily speak of as "democratic" music-making came suddenly to Gustav Mahler, his reputation honored, his own music nearly incomprehensible to a public amid which, for the next thirty years, the Bruckner Society would strive to win occasional performances of the Bruckner and Mahler symphonies. With the arrival in America of Bruno Walter, Otto Klemperer, and Dimitri Mitropoulos, and the impetus given by the congeniality of these immense works to the new long-playing phonograph and records, the symphonies of Bruckner and Mahler were at last domesticated here. The careers of these conductors, as of Willem Mengelberg, Sir Thomas Beecham, and Artur Rodzinski, who tried by firmness under pressure and sometimes by personal arrogance to maintain the aristocratic isolation of the traditional music director in opera and symphony, show the steady shifting of authority from the individual to the box office and its representatives. Only the idolized Arturo Toscanini was able to play the game through to the end without concessions.

The tone poems and narrative symphonies by Strauss quickly won place in the repertory, but the ten long and relatively abstract symphonic compositions by Mahler were seldom performed during his short lifetime. Mahler's early death and the change from gigantic to soloistic orchestral composition after the First World War made these symphonies seem historic rather than contemporary. Entering the repertory so late, Mahler's symphonies had little influence on the work of subsequent composers. Some critics and historians hint the influence of the Mahler symphonies on early works by Schoenberg. Schoenberg himself, while reaffirming his reverence for Mahler—"It always becomes very quiet after one of these great men has spoken"—denied any influence of Mahler on his music; consideration of dates and works affirms his denial. Schoenberg had already written the *Gurrelieder* in 1901—the orchestration was delayed several years—before Mahler had composed the majority of his symphonies. Schoenberg's reverence for Mahler began after hearing a performance of the Seventh Symphony. There had been before that a period when he held Mahler's work in disregard. In public Mahler firmly upheld the music of his young contemporary against criticism; in private he confessed that often he did not understand it. The young Shostakovitch was the principal inheritor from Mahler.

Mahler's First Symphony includes a funeral march; his Second, with vocal soloists and chorus, is entitled *The Resurrection;* his Third is a gigantic religio-descriptive apparatus with vocal soloist and two choirs; his Fourth, a completely satisfying, radiant work of reasonable length with one voice singing the happy finale in a rustic heaven. The Fifth, Sixth, and Seventh Symphonies are dark and obscure instrumental meditations at great length interrupted by an occasional lighter movement. The Eighth Symphony, a vast two-movement cantata, has been nicknamed "The Symphony of a Thousand" because of the unprecedented number of participants; the second movement dramatizes in concert form the last scene of Goethe's second *Faust*. It is this symphonic-emotional abstract dramaturgy, such music as Wagner might have written if he had composed mature symphonies, which Thomas Mann's novel *Dr. Faustus* envisions as the native work, in twelve-tone style, of its composer hero, the result of his temptation by the devil. Schoenberg angrily rejected the unwarranted attribution. Only Schoenberg's unfinished oratorio, *The Jacob's Ladder,* in any way fulfills these cloudy descriptions. In composition and conception Schoenberg's discipline was, with few exceptions, more precise, concentrated, and economical than Mahler's.

Partly to delay the dread necessity of composing a Ninth Symphony, Mahler wrote his *Song of Earth,* commencing the long succession of farewells to man and invocations of eternity with which he ended in evident despair his sadly short career. When Mahler did at last compose a Ninth, the scherzo movement, *Burleske,* seems to represent a tearing down of the symphonic edifice erected a century before by Beethoven. Mahler's finale is another agonized farewell. And the agony and farewell continue into the unfinished Tenth Symphony—less unfinished than was supposed and already re-created by scholars as a complete work—any doubt of Mahler's personal identification with his music dispelled by the marginal comments he wrote on his manuscripts. Though other symphonies by other composers would still appear, the great sierra of the Germanic symphony ended with Mahler. Its high point, in Germanic spiritual aspiration though not as music, was the unfinished Ninth Symphony by Bruckner. "Those who have written a Ninth," Schoenberg wrote, in Germanic hyperbole, "stood too near to the hereafter."

More than any other composer who had not known Liszt, Ferruccio Busoni carried forward that aristocratic inheritance, as pianist, composer, conductor, scholar. He was the son of an Italian clarinet soloist in the older virtuoso manner which Busoni memorialized in his *Concertino* for solo clarinet. Busoni made his home among the great capitals of Europe, eventually settling in Berlin, where his apartment became the educational center for a group of distinguished young composers and pianists. In formal capacity as a professor of piano or composition, Busoni taught at several conservatories; privately, in the tradition of Liszt, he did not teach. One went to him during the afternoon when he received visitors and, winning his interest, withdrew from the gathering to another room, where a problem was discussed and possible solutions were explored; master and pupil than rejoined the company. Busoni's extraordinary gifts as a pianist, his ability to refer to a vast repertory of musical and esthetic knowledge, his generosity, and the power of his personality have been described to me by several musicians once of this group, even to his last days when he would rise from bed, against his doctor's orders, to demonstrate a point at the piano.

As lately as 1963 the pianist Artur Rubinstein said in an interview: "We pianists, young and old, were always sitting spellbound by Busoni. Unfortunately, the rest of the public often asked—'Where is his magic, where is that greatness?' He was above them. He was a man ahead of his time, one of our time. Today, he would beat us all."[2]

My friend the pianist Richard Buhlig went while still a boy from Leschetizky in Vienna to join the Berlin group around Busoni; his young comrade, Artur Schnabel, followed in the next year. Buhlig would describe how when Busoni played, the sound seemed to float above the instrument, to come from beneath the floor, as if detached from its source. At dinner many years ago with the dancer Maud Allan, who went from Los Angeles to make a great career in England, where she was an intimate friend of Busoni—"He was an Archangel!" Maud Allan uttered in hushed exclamation. "Archangel and Archdemon!" Buhlig growlingly replied.

Before settling in Berlin, Busoni taught at the conservatory in Helsingfors, Finland; Sibelius was among his pupils. Later at an Italian conservatory Busoni tried to awaken the students to the great Italian tradition of instrumental music and to contemporary and Germanic music; the effort ended in defeat. A few years afterwards the Italian composer Alfredo Casella, returning to Italy from a long stay abroad, repeated the same effort, eventually with more success. Casella's slow progress swung from contemporary Germanism through a brittle Italian neoclassicism, until he found for himself the materials of a native style. His colleague in this educational program, the composer Francesco Malipiero, edited the complete works of Monteverdi. Italian musicians were rediscovering their tradition.

Not many years ago Riccardo Malipiero complained to me: "La Scala in Milan will perform any opera I write, but there is no place in Italy where I can hear my chamber music." But conditions of musical performance in Italy have been changing. Luigi Dallapiccola has blended knowledge of the tone-row with a marvelously refined vocal art, enabling Italian nonoperatic song to share on equal terms with the best music of contemporary Europe; at festivals of twentieth century music, Bruno Maderna, Luigi Nono, and Luciano Berio now share authority as composers with their best contemporaries from other nations.

A period of nearly forty years intervened between the ending of the aristocratic tradition of European music at the start of the First World War and the democratic assembling of composers and performers in the new society of music festivals following the end of the Second World War. This period lies between 1912, the year of *Rite of Spring* and *Pierrot Lunaire,* and the death of Schoenberg in 1951. It is the final period of theoretical tonality, under the ascendancy of Igor Stravinsky, and its length measures the time-lag in public acceptance of *Pierrot Lunaire.*

During this period the creative musician, as composer and performer, tried to carry forward in isolation his aristocratic heritage against the growing demands of commercialized music-making. One watches in memory Serge Rachmaninoff making his way to the piano as reluctantly as a caged performing lion to its stool; Artur Schnabel bitterly complaining, "Have I learned everything I know to go on performing in public like a child!" Schnabel, who had spent his earlier years playing chamber music in Berlin, altered his course to solo playing in time to reap the suddenly growing enthusiasm for more serious music with his recorded cycle of the Beethoven sonatas; a pianist by inclination, he was a composer by preference.

In speaking of composition or performance one must take into consideration many unlike factors—not merely better or worse. The member of the audience who believes that he is at one with Beethoven is more likely to be responding to the performance style and mannerisms of a period. Artur Nikisch in 1915 recorded the opening of Beethoven's Fifth Symphony as a relatively slow melodic figure of four distinct notes; Toscanini struck it out as a dynamic unity, in one pulse.

In Europe between the wars there were still audiences seeking and capable of the severest musical challenge. The European radio networks were beginning their practice of presenting contemporary composers performing or directing their own works. American commercial radio broadcasts during the 1930s presented an amount of "live" performance of classic repertory unequaled since that time but gave few opportunities to living composers. The isolation of the composer-performer on both continents did not start with audience rejection but with the unwillingness of the purveyors of music to encourage him in performing his own works.

One must not forget, too, that the expanding mass audience, still making its first encounter with the classic repertory, cherished this new cultural experience and, in the aura of Tchaikovsky, Beethoven, and Mozart, disdained the comparably exacting music of its own time. For this audience Hindemith, Stravinsky, Prokofiev, Casella, Falla, and Ravel composed in a prevailingly neoclassic style. A much smaller audience, localized in a few cities, reached out to the new art of the more experimental composers, enabling them to survive and continue working; with the start of the worldwide economic depression of the 1930s this audience and its patronage almost disappeared. The vogue of modern ballet, initiated by Diaghilev, elevated the ballet suite, assembled by the composer from his less unified original for dance, to equality with the tone poem and the symphony. Composers who had turned to practical music (*Gebrauchsmusik*) as an offset to more esoteric composition now clung to it for a living.

Busoni, traveling in isolation through the earlier period of this transition, began his career as an aristocratic virtuoso in the older style; like some other composers of this transitional era, he abandoned his earlier composition and began over, at once a radical and a neoclassicist. His radical compositions continued the art of scholarly difficulty initiated by Liszt. But Liszt had written and performed on two distinct levels: an entertainer for the mass audience; for the smaller, sophisticated audience, a master. Busoni disdained to perform for the mass audience and would not write for it. He believed that great music should be performed, after the example of Wagner's *Parsifal* at Bayreuth, only on particular occasions and in special surroundings, where the audience must seek it. The unfamiliar Bach-Busoni transcriptions he imposed on his audience were unwelcome. His programs avoided the popular nineteenth century repertory except for the more rigorous Chopin. In his last years he taught composition at the Prussian Academy of the Arts in Berlin; his successor was Schoenberg.

Busoni disowned all of his compositions before the Second Sonata for violin and piano. His later works include the enlarged versions of his *Fantasia Contrappuntistica*, for piano and for two pianos, his Piano Concerto with men's chorus in the last movement, and his *Indian Fantasy* upon American Indian themes for piano and orchestra, experiments outside of and away from the evolution of music. The *Elegies*, the sonatinas, and the *Toccata*, for piano solo, and especially the seldom heard but revered symbolic opera, *Dr. Faustus*, hold a prestige today like that accorded Erik Satie. Despite their very distinct personalities, Satie and Busoni are alike in the prestige they have not lost among the small, skilled audience which knows their work, and in the authority of their continuing message to composers.

Busoni's message is the short, rhapsodic prophecy of his *Sketch of a New Esthetic of Music*. The message was as vital to Edgard Varèse during the 1920s as, later, to John Cage; each has accomplished in his own idiom what Busoni prophesied.

"Notation, the writing out of compositions, is primarily an ingenious expedient for catching an inspiration, with the purpose of exploiting it later. But notation is to improvisation as the portrait to the living model. It is for the interpreter to *resolve the rigidity of the signs* into the primitive emotion. . . .

"So narrow has our tonal range become, so stereotyped its form of expression, that nowadays there is not one familiar motive that cannot be fitted with some other familiar motive so that the two may be played simultaneously. . . .

"What we now call our Tonal System is nothing more than a set of 'signs'; an ingenious device to grasp somewhat of that eternal harmony; a meagre pocket-edition of that encyclopedic work; artificial light instead of the sun. . . . And so, in music, the signs have assumed greater consequence than that which they ought to stand for, and can only suggest. . . .

"That some few have already felt how the intervals . . . might be differently arranged (graduated) is manifested in isolated passages by Liszt, and recently by Debussy and his following, and even by Richard Strauss. . . .

"I have made an attempt to exhaust the possibilities of the arrangement of degrees within the seven-tone scale; and succeeded, by raising and lowering the intervals, in establishing *one hundred and thirteen different scales.* These 113 scales (within the octave C–C) comprise the greater part of our familiar twenty-four keys, and, furthermore, a series of new keys of peculiar character. But with these the mine is not exhausted, for we are at liberty to *transpose* each one of these 113, besides the blending of two such keys in harmony and melody. . . ." (And he proceeds to demonstrate.)

"With this presentation, the unity of all keys may be considered as finally pronounced and justified. A kaleidoscopic blending and interchanging of twelve semitones within the three-mirror tube of Taste, Emotion, and Intention—the essential feature of the harmony of to-day. . . .

"The question of notation seems to me subordinate. On the other hand, the question is important and imperious, how and on what these tones are to be produced. Fortunately, while busied with this essay, I received from America direct and authentic intelligence which solves the problem in a simple manner. . . . Dr. Thaddeus Cahill . . . has constructed a comprehensive apparatus which makes it possible to transform an electric current into a fixed and mathematically exact number of vibrations. . . . Only a long and careful series of experiments, and a continued training of the ear, can render this unfamiliar material approachable and plastic for the coming generation, and for Art."[3]

Thus Busoni prophesied in 1907 not only a music of many scales, and of increasing numbers of microtonal divisions of the octave, but a music which disregards these fixed divisions, a music of sound and also an electronic music.

AN INTRODUCTION TO
BÉLA BARTÓK

Béla Bartók was one of the last and most uncompromising of the multiskilled, self-made musical aristocrats. These musicians were aristocrats not by birth but by assumption. In a time of strong class demarcation their claims to aristocratic privilege were not denied; the prestige included no guarantee of financial security. Living with the air of princes, they never ceased hard work. The majority achieved their careers by compromise, with greater or less integrity. Bartók never wavered. His music had been successful in Germany; after the Nazis had revealed their destructive policies he refused to allow performance of his compositions where they might be heard on German soil.

In New York at the end of his career, an impoverished exile, unable to support himself as a pianist because he would not compromise pride or purpose or seek favor of the audience, his health gradually failing, he refused any offer of help which did not involve employment; his friends and publishers had to devise roundabout means to preserve him and his wife from destitution. He did receive from ASCAP (American Society of Composers, Authors, and Publishers) free medical care and hospitalization, which he could not otherwise afford. To his last days he worked at the compositions several admiring musicians paid him to write: for the Koussevitzky Foundation the Concerto for Orchestra, for

Yehudi Menuhin the Sonata for Solo Violin, for William Primrose the Viola Concerto he did not live to finish. Before his death his music was winning renewed recognition; three years later public enthusiasm broke in a flood of demand on his publishers. Like Mozart he was of his time and apart from it, his first reputation obscured but not eclipsed by the new art which came after him.

At Berlin in 1908 the young Béla Bartók played the first performance of his *14 Bagatelles* for piano to the members of Busoni's piano class. Busoni sent him to the music publishers Breitkopf and Härtel with a letter recommending publication; they refused—"your little pieces are too difficult and too modern for the public." The pieces were printed the next year in Budapest. Busoni also obtained for Bartók an invitation from the Berlin Philharmonic Society to conduct the Scherzo of his Second Suite; he asked Bartók's collaboration in editing the complete works by Liszt, a project unfortunately not continued.

Busoni, Debussy, and Ravel carried ahead, each in his own manner, the inheritance from Liszt; Bartók explored Liszt's music with the fresh understanding of a twentieth century composer. Putting aside the decoration and the bravura, Bartók found in Liszt's B minor Piano Sonata material fundamental to his own idiom, the strong-rhythmed clashing of close intervals. Following up Liszt's studies of Hungarian folk music, Bartók rejected the popular gypsy style Liszt called Hungarian and discovered instead his native musical speech. For several years he and his young fellow composer, Zoltán Kodály, went into the villages of Hungary, recording on wax cylinders thousands of Hungarian and Rumanian folksongs, afterwards editing some of them for publication. Bartók's later researches took him to North Africa and Turkey.

Bartók did not distort these indigenous melodies by forcing them into the arbitrary relationships of Western European harmonization; instead he derived his harmonization from the melody, in simple arrangements or composed settings which do not violate their melodic consistency. Thus his vertical harmony, as well as the entire movement or composition, is in relation to a tone but not in or on a key. We are inclined to think of such harmony as "Oriental," but it is also the harmony of the bagpipe and of the more primitive combination in which one player blows the chanter, performing melody and embellishment, while the other player monotonously reiterates the drone; one finds the same practice in the organ accompaniment of fourteenth century vocal music by Machaut.

Bartók sometimes retains the drone, in native style or as an ostinato, or uses the single tone in extension for a melody, or conceals the root tone among more complex relationships with elaborate digressions, as in his larger music. Bartók's ostinato is therefore tonal although not in a key, whereas Schoenberg's ostinato, or the repetition of a single tone in tone-row composition, merely underlines that tone as a sustained element or rhythmic plateau apart from tonality or key.

These differentia need not confuse the listener; the musical events are there to guide his ear, and if he listens without presuppositions he will hear them. Music is not the explanation how a thing is done but the result as sound and silence. Our listening to the music of a repertory confined within the last two hundred years has taught us to expect certain harmonic relationships which emphasize a few particular intervals producing the satisfaction of music in a key; from this expectation Bartók's music, in simple as well as complex forms, diverges no less perceptibly than Schoenberg's but by different means. For this reason practitioners of Schoenberg's tone-row method, the more specialized techniques of Berg and Webern, and the consequent habit of atonal composition now called *serial* are inclined to misunderstand and underestimate the divergent and quite distinct keyless tonality of Bartók. Listeners should accustom themselves to hearing the work of each composer in his own speech, his idiom and syntax, without concerning themselves too much to explain it. An artist's art is about what he does with it and no more than incidentally about extraneous matters, unless such matter becomes central to what he does. Schoenberg held Bartók's work in high esteem.

It is true that the composers of our classical period— J. S. Bach as far as Schubert—shared a common language. This was the common gossip of improvisation, which a musician learned then as another today learns the improvisational commonplace of jazz. Listeners a generation ago were more aware of this eighteenth century common talk than we are today; they accused Mozart of too great reliance on the Alberti bass. Such criticism came out of the individualist nineteenth century romantic reaction against the improvisational substratum of these classics. The reaction brought about a century of linguistic experimentation, during which the older stock of improvisational commonplace gave way to many different varieties of technical dialect, mingled with new idiomatic derivations from traditional and folk music. The consequence has been a total reconsideration of music as a means of communication, of expression, of abstract experience for itself, in terms of form and pattern recognition, and so on, composers at one time anxiously preserving the recognizable linkage with the musical past, at another as anxiously denying it. Tradition and a common understanding connect the generations of Newton and of Einstein, but the larger part of the questions which preoccupied the intelligence of Newton's contemporaries are of no creative value today, except to historians. While the Germanic composers were still extending the nineteenth century grand tradition which runs from Beethoven's Ninth Symphony to Mahler's Ninth, Bartók in his First Quartet and again three decades later in the first movement of his *Music for Strings, Percussion, and Celesta,* took off in twentieth century style from the opening of Beethoven's C sharp minor Quartet. (The same source is evident in the opening of the Second Quartet by Roger Sessions.) I once heard Schoenberg lecture enthusiastically about Verdi's opera *Otello,* drawing truths of serialist usage from the growth of the first motif of the murder scene.

At the Budapest Conservatory Bartók taught piano. He refused always to teach composition, perhaps because he recognized early the uniqueness of his compositional devices. Schoenberg for the same reason would not teach his method of composing with twelve tones and discouraged his pupils from attempting it, believing that each composer should discover his own way forward from the traditional techniques.

Besides teaching piano, Bartók produced new editions of the keyboard music by Chopin, Schubert, Beethoven, Haydn, Mozart, Domenico Scarlatti, and François Couperin, and of Bach's *Well-Tempered Clavier.* The sensitivity of his ear for the coloration of Eastern European melody, for the rich overtones of harpsichord and the Hungarian *cembalom,* for the characteristic voices of the string instruments and the native pipes, is evident in the distinctive sound-patterns of his compositions, in the small teaching pieces for children and the 153 progressive piano studies of his *Mikrokosmos,* in the 44 short study pieces for two violins as well as in his largest works. He tried to increase the listener's capacity for musical difference, apart from the Western European convention. His deep understanding of the intervallic structures of non-Western melody enabled him to incorporate these relationships in fresh structural and melodic combinations, to which he added an unusually thorough knowledge of embellishment and ornament, derived from Couperin and Scarlatti as well as from folk music. Heard played on a piano in equal temperament, Couperin's *Les Fauvétes Plaintives* from the *Fourteenth Order* might well be mistaken for a piece by Bartók.

With the *14 Bagatelles* Bartók removed from his idiom the earlier influences of Brahms and Richard Strauss; his transcription of *A Hero's Life* by Strauss had been one of his early pianistic display pieces. One might guess that he learned more from Strauss's chittering music to describe the critics than from his lush melodies. The music of Liszt and Debussy taught him their freedom from traditional harmonic rule; he did not succumb to their impressionism or exoticism. He broke with the Germanic art practised by his friend Ernst von Dohnányi, the common idiom in which Hungarian musicians were then educated, as decisively but more vigorously and using a greater range of devices than Anton Webern in Vienna, and from that time he was his own man. He did not, like Webern and Berg and at a later date Stravinsky, accept the new discipline of Schoenberg's method of composing with twelve tones, though some portions of his music prove that he examined it. Antiserialists argue that this refusal demonstrates a contempt for Schoenberg's method; it should be evident that Schoenberg's melodic style was no more adaptable than that of Schubert to Bartók's independently derived idiom and syntax.

"In many ways . . . he was ahead of his contemporaries," Halsey Stevens wrote in his splendid study of Bartók. "The piano music of 1908 shows experimentation with bitonality, dissonant counterpoint, chords in intervals other than thirds, somewhat before the works of Stravinsky and Schoenberg in which these devices first came to general notice. But, important as these procedures were in the formation of Bartók's language, all other considerations are relatively insignificant in relation to the influ-

ence of the peasant music of Hungary. This music being monodic, it became necessary to derive harmonic materials from it,
rather than superimpose harmonies of the Western type upon
melodic materials of Eastern European origin. . . . There is
never a question, even in the setting of a folktune, of modal
harmonization; the supra-diatonic tones are used freely, chords
support melody notes which do not form a part of them, and a
system of functional harmony—so important to a Hindemith—
never makes its appearance." Bartók and his friend Kodály
accepted dissonant major seconds and perfect fourths as consonant, assigning them "unhesitatingly to points of repose—even to
final cadences."[1]

As the American composer Lou Harrison has done more recently, Bartók and Kodály made much use of pentatonic scales, a
practice Western European musicians are inclined to dismiss as if
it were a retrogression to the music of more primitive peoples;
there is of course no scale, no melody or mode, no interval, no
harmony or combination of tones, which the creative imagination
of a composer may not use to advantage. Theoretical inhibitions
against such usages are a weakness not of composers but of
theorists; a theoretically inhibited composer will seldom be a
great one.

Although he was as positive a melodist as Schoenberg or
Stravinsky, Bartók's melody does not stem from Germanic song or
the polyglot romantics. He did not need the exigencies of Schoenberg's method to resolve the long Germanic wrestle of counterpoint and song. The melodies of his larger works, put together of
intervallic fragments derived from folk music and from his close
editorial study of the Western European classical composers,
reawakened the analytic subjects and variational procedures of
Haydn and Beethoven. But he was not a neoclassicist. His themes
are extended, contracted and so intricately varied that Stevens
comments: ". . . many of Bartók's motives have generic resem-
blances of such strength that one hesitates to insist that *this* was
derived from *that*. They may both be coincidental manifestations
of entirely separate impulses: to make a decision on this point is
quite unnecessary." The procedures are "both variational and
developmental."[2] Bartók believed, like Schoenberg, that each
composer should seek and devise his independent means.

In his use of embellishment, clashing intervals, the extension of
such intervals by the invention of new chords, and the elabora-

tion of his melodically derived analytic counterpoint, Bartók seems to have been aware of the microtonal consequences implicit in his music. The sound of his music began with the piano— I do not mean necessarily *at* the piano—by a complete acceptance of the equally tempered interval as the basis of harmony. Though he collected, studied, and steeped his thought in folk music, he did not, any more than Kodály, Falla, or Alois Hába, deviate from the equal-tempered misplacement of the leading tone. (Hába told Adriaan Fokker how in one village he was warned not to return unless he had learned to perform the leading note correctly, as the folk of the village sang it. He did return and played it correctly. But Hába's reduction of equal temperament to a scale of quarter-tones [twenty-four-note scale] did not resolve that error, merely narrowing the difference. Bartók also, but seldom, wrote quarter-notes, for example in the Violin Concerto and in the original score of his Sonata for Solo Violin, though it was printed without them; the effect in such usage is coloristic rather than idiomatic.)

Stevens writes of the Fifth Quartet: "The first and last movements center around B♭, which may be taken as the key of the quartet. So long as no attempt is made to identify the mode (major, minor, or any other), the analysis is valid, but it must be understood that the tonality is extremely free. On the first page, for example, the key of B♭ contains both D and D♭, both E and E♭; this is not unusual in certain Asiatic scales, which, while not completely chromatic, contain more notes to the octave than Western heptatonic scales. Bartók's Second Violin Sonata (1922) and other works show the use of augmented scales, in which what might casually be considered chromatic inflections are actually an integral part of the mode."[3]

In other words, Bartók is employing, by notation and implication, a scale he does not define which includes more than twelve notes. Thus Bartók returned roundabout to the condition of a note in meantone tuning, which changed its intervallic relationship within the unequal-intervalled scale each time the music modulated from one key to another, becoming, as if by microtonal displacement, another note. Stevens says again of the Fifth Quartet: "The device which begins in bar 183 is characteristically Bartókian: a minor second is progressively enclosed within a minor third, a perfect fourth, and a perfect fifth, and changing to a major sixth, encloses the whole complex."[4] The microtonal coloration produced by the overtones of such an acoustical complex should be self-evident. In his several *Night Music* movements for piano and for instrumental groups these complex overtone mixtures seem to be consciously created. Bartók supplemented his unusual harmonic coloration by glissandos, by the indefinite raps and clangors of nontonal percussion and his device of snapping the strings against the fingerboard, and by a foundation of instrumental cluster-chords. Noise for its own sake, however, is a very minor part of Bartók's art. He enlarged the domain of tonality but was conservative in adhering to it.

A large portion of his music is for his own instrument, the piano. His powerful Piano Sonata, the Suite *Out of Doors,* and the First Piano Concerto make emphatic use of the tone-clusters, which, with aristocratic courtesy, he formally requested permission to borrow from Henry Cowell, in whose youthful compositions Bartók had first encountered them. Afterwards he preferred to stretch such clusters sideways into tight, close-intervalled, scalewise figures accumulating to long, close-ordered melodies, amplified again into scalewise passages of chords. Bartók did not always treat the piano, as some have claimed, as if it were a percussive instrument; he seems to have developed the percussive aspect of piano sound, the tone-clusters and close-intervalled scalewise figures, to counter the songlike interweaving of Germanic music after Beethoven.

Though he wrote much for the piano, he composed more amply for strings. He never wrote a symphony; the early symphonic poem, *Kossuth,* and his Concerto for Orchestra could each serve for one. None of his compositions in larger form could be easily mistaken for the work of another composer. The six string quartets define the stages of his growth. The First Quartet, romantic and densely packed (like Schoenberg's First Quartet), refers in the same manner to the nineteenth century from Brahms back to Beethoven. It is in other respects a twentieth century composition, horizontally and melodically oriented, with regenerative motives which evolve into melodies, showing already the effect of his studies in folk music and his awareness of Debussy. With the Second Quartet he has largely removed external influences and discovered the full significance of his own idiom and style; there is a powerful, bare, folklike middle movement in the idiom he was developing at the piano, including the dronelike repetitions of single tones. The writing is less packed, more open, more free of Brahms, like Schoenberg's translucent Second Quartet. The final movement introduces what would be his characteristic mood of deep contemplation, in the style of progressive, sectional growth that would spread through many of his later compositions. The treatment of the material is now analytical, in the classical tradition, put together of short figures which are continually varied and reassembled. The two classical types of fantasy, a continuing development resembling free improvisation and a severely formal arch with the opening and closing sections sharing material, become more evident in the Third Quartet, where the third section recapitulates the first and the fourth section is a coda referring to the materials of the second section. This three-movement pattern recurs in the Second Piano Concerto and the Violin Concerto. In the Fourth and Fifth Quartets the arch extends to become an interlocking structure of five movements, the first and fifth and the second and fourth movements motivally and rhythmically related and balanced around the central movement. The elegiac Sixth Quartet, written as if in premonition of his permanent exile from his homeland, abandons the arch-form for a progressive development in four movements, each preceded by the same introductory subject in enlarging combinations, which itself becomes the final movement.

Many persons believe that the six Bartók string quartets are the best since those of Beethoven. I would say instead that these quartets, with the four string quartets and the one string trio by Schoenberg, the Debussy quartet, and the Second Quartet by Ives, are a cordillera—the mountain axis of a continent—thrust up by the seismic awakening of twentieth century composers to the last quartets by Beethoven. Schubert, Wagner, Liszt, Brahms, Debussy himself, can be detected among the tossed strata of their slopes. Fundamental to their structures are the analytical shapes and variational procedures, rather than the strict sonata-form movements, of Haydn, Mozart, and Beethoven. The new peaks have been thrust upward by the creative pressures generated by the effort of composers to resolve in styles as unduplicated as those of Beethoven's later quartets the contrapuntal conflict between polyphony and harmony, which in greater extension but less concentration produced the range of the Germanic symphonies from Beethoven through Mahler. It is a phenomenon almost exclusively of the Germanic tradition, standing above and apart from the wide plains, both barren and fertile, of the Italianate tradition and melody and accompaniment.

We are right and wise to lament the passing of this creative era, which may be thought to have ended with the death of Schoenberg; its disintegrative tendencies, its revolutionary fire at the core, the heritage from J. S. Bach, enter deeply into the creative impulses and strains, at once destructive and prophetic, of the newer musical actions we try today to comprehend.

With Bartók's string quartets one may include as no less meaningful achievements his two Violin Sonatas, *Music for Strings, Percussion, and Celesta,* the Sonata for Two Pianos and Percussion, *Mikrokosmos, Contrasts* for clarinet, violin, and piano, the Violin Concerto, the Concerto for Orchestra, the *Cantata Profana* for double chorus, soloists, and orchestra, and the Sonata for Solo Violin, each a unique form, result of the unending struggle between Bartók's intense individuality and the increase of his personal classicism, his aristocratic formality, the careful balancing of motival orientation in movements and parts of movements, his need of structural unity.

The clashing harmonies—*harmony* in the most inclusive meaning—of Bartók's most characteristic music have remained "too difficult and too modern for the public." Slick virtuoso performance vitiates or avoids the challenge of the inherent difficulties by concealing them; the effect may be showy and pleasant but it is not Bartók. The authority of his larger mature compositions has won them a firm place in the repertory. Because he did not borrow from, compromise with, or steal from his contemporaries, Bartók's art remains an island bounded by his isolating genius, an example but not a model for other composers.

In perhaps fifty or a hundred years composers of a new order may return to him for renewal, as he himself and Schoenberg and Charles Ives did not imitate Beethoven but renewed their art in his.

23

THE MORPHOGENESIS OF IDEAS

Webern, Berg, Messiaen, Villa-Lobos

Morphogenesis is a biological term for the production and evolution of the features, collectively rather than in detail, comprised in the form and structure of an organism and its parts.

What is the *organism* of a work of art? does it grow by itself or is it mechanical? "In comparison with all our developments in mechanics," Schoenberg wrote, "a tool like a pair of pliers might seem simple. . . . The idea of fixing the crosspoint of the two crooked arms so that the two smaller segments in front would move in the opposite direction to the larger segments at the back, thus multiplying the power of the man who squeezed them . . . can only have been conceived by a genius. . . . The tool itself may fall into disuse, but the idea behind it can never become obsolete. And therein lies the difference between a mere style and a real idea.

"An idea can never perish." (Schoenberg's italics)[1]

The morphogenesis of small tweezers or tongs, with the pressure applied in front of the pivot, into large tweezers or long-handled tongs, with the pressure applied to multiple advantage behind the pivot, and of these into cutters, clamps, pliers, shears, scissors, surgical devices, and so on, demonstrates how an idea can proliferate in form and use without ever losing its original existence. The crookedness of the pliers is accommodated to the shape of another gripping instrument, the hand, while the shape of the head adapts to many uses; the head twisted sideways and a vise replacing one grip while the other straightens to a lever gives the wrench. One can see how such an idea grows of itself, though it is mechanical. Human imagination creates and implements the growth.

"My secret desire of enchanted gorgeousness in harmony has pushed me toward those swords of fire, those sudden stars, those flows of blue-orange lavas, those planets of turquoise, those violet shades, those garnets of long-haired arborescence, those wheelings of sounds and colors in a jumble of rainbows of which I have spoken with love in the Preface of my *Quartet for the End of Time;* such a gushing out of chords should necessarily be filtered; it is the sacred instinct of the natural and true harmony which, alone, can so change itself."[2]

This example of prose-poetry by Olivier Messiaen, a power applied this side the pivot by twin grips reaching back to Wagner and to Baudelaire, represents a valid musical idea. The resilient idea proved itself under the duress of imprisonment in a German prisoner-of-war camp during the Second World War; in those surroundings Messiaen conceived it as a *Quartet for the End of Time*—transcendental-ironic ambiguity!—which was played with satisfaction by four captive musicians to their fellow prisoners. When I first presented this Quartet to an audience, the illumined faces of those who had been listening astonished me. Yet the means of illumination, of emotion, seem external to the music: the music does not live by them; they attempt their own life—in the same way that the "desire of enchanted gorgeousness in harmony" seems external to the words which convey it.

Schoenberg wrote: "Every tone which is added to a beginning tone makes the meaning of that tone doubtful. If, for instance, G follows after C, the ear may not be sure whether this expresses C major or G major, or even F major or E minor. . . . In this manner there is produced a state of unrest, of imbalance which grows throughout most of the piece, and is enforced further by similar functions of the rhythm. The method by which balance is restored seems to me the real *idea* of the composition."[3]

Messiaen embellishes the same idea: "Dissonances or foreign notes, they are all the same. With our complicated chords, is a dissonance possible? And, in this multitude of added notes, what becomes of the old foreign notes: pedal, passing note, embellishment, appoggiatura? They are indispensable to the expressive and contrapuntal life of music; let us preserve them by enlarging them. The pedal will become the pedal group; the passing note, the passing group; the embellishment, the embellishment group. Each of these groups will contain several foreign notes, forming a complete 'whole music' (rhythm, harmony, melody) and being analyzed as: a single pedal, a single passing note, a single embellishment. . . ."[4]

Messiaen first cancels Schoenberg's idea as no longer pertinent in the present condition of music; he then restates the idea as a particular case; finally he restates the particular case in the form of the original idea, as a more advanced substitute for it. Theoretically the procedure seems reasonable enough, but as sound heard by ears the first and last forms of the idea are not the same at all. This is not to say that Messiaen's method will produce bad music, only different music. Because the procedure of identification and variation involves not single notes but groups, the means by which progress, variety, and movement are achieved will seem audibly more limited; the listener will identify at best but a few of them. The composition will seem elaborately colorful but static and dramatically limited for lack of identifiable variety; dramatic events will require larger contrasts because they will not clearly register in detail. "Color, like light and shadow in the physical world," Schoenberg believed, "expresses and limits the forms and sizes of objects. Sometimes these elements serve as a camouflage. In general, lucidity is the first purpose of color in music. . . ."[5]

It is not against Messiaen's practice to say that it embodies a type of orientalization: a group of tones embellishing the substance of one tone. Someone may remind me that the common improvisational or embellishing figure in Western European music elaborates the tone similarly. But harmony and rhythm still direct notice to the individual tone, the *good* note instead of the *bad* note, as eighteenth century musicians thought it; whereas in the groups of notes serving for a tone that Messiaen advocates no individual tone is brought to notice; rather, this is avoided. The tools are different, if not entirely distinct; the idea has taken a new form.

"Instead of one sustained note, foreign to the chords which surround it, we shall have a repeated music (repetition and sustaining are equivalent), foreign to another music situated above or below it; each of these musics will have its own rhythm, melody, harmony. . . ."[6]

Listeners may well question Messiaen's parenthetic assumption, that repetition and sustaining are equivalent: theoretically perhaps, audibly not; a sustained tone is rhythmically different from a repeated tone, as the usages of Bartók and Schoenberg demonstrate. Every rhythmic gradation, from a single tone sustained without vibrato, or one with vibrato, or the quick repetitions of the Italian *trillo*, to the same note repeated by successive notations or each repetition divided by rests, is audible and should be regarded as a distinct idiomatic device.

One must beware the tendency of an artist to justify what he has done new by pretending that it is different but the same, as one must beware the claim of an artist that he has done new what is in audible reality the same. Among creative persons a degree of insistence too often indicates an equivalent misrepresentation. One should beware also the tendency of some artists to substitute their explanation of what is being heard for the actual conveyance of the music. A motif does not *mean* the label the composer has attached to it. This becomes a fault in the composer only when he wishes or expects the listener to hear his explanation, either literary or theoretical, as the cause, significance, or justification of his art, regardless of what the music conveys, substituting verbal for musical expressiveness. The marginal comments Mahler appended to his manuscripts may indicate his intention; they do not explain his practice. The hyperbole of his emotion tells much about his state of mind when writing, but we assemble to hear what has come through as music. Mahler ordered for one of his symphonies the building of an unusually large bass drum to increase the emotional dynamics of one passage, but the giant drum wouldn't boom. The title of Messiaen's *Sept Visions de l'Amen* does not spiritualize these seven compositions.

Explaining a notated example Messiaen writes: "Course of anguish, of desire, of horror; in A panting upbeat; at B, accent; in C, termination." Or, "The direct movement and the cruelty of the chords give to this example a great expressive strength. The accent B is lacerating. . . ."[7] This is the literary-descriptive language of the program note. Messiaen's own program notes are works of verbal art comparable with and often more explicit than the music, which seems to have been created as ritual and monstrance for the verbally conceived idea.

Messiaen's art, rooted in religious mysticism, first Christian, then Oriental, led him, as it has since led other composers, to study Oriental music, especially the Indian, in which melody and rhythm are related to extramusical considerations, such as the season and the time of day, the desired mood or excitation of feeling, and correspondences with zodiacal signs, colors, and birdsong. Upon this tendency to a pantheistic inclusiveness of musical significance he imposed a post-Schoenberg urge to total serialization, both rhythmic and melodic. In America, Milton Babbitt, developing to complete serialization the implications of the tone-row, had already done the same. Messiaen found a particular inspiration in birdsong; one might characterize his technical problem as an attempt to mingle the free singing of birds, carefully imitated, with the strictness of completely rationalized form.

Eric Salzman, writing of Messiaen's *Chronochromie*, gives a vivid word-picture of the result. "Messiaen's music is built, like that of Varèse, in densities and in static volumes of revolving (not evolving) sound; within these outlines, the somewhat arbitrary system of duration is imposed along with densities, textures, and colors of great fantasy. *Chronochromie*, written in 1960, is a kind of grand (twenty-two minute) optimum synthesis of all this: rushing water and wind (transcribed we are told in the French Alps); massive cluster chords (rocks); Japanese, Swedish, Mexican, and French birds in long, free, random, forest-noise simultaneity (or heterophony; polyphony and counterpoint are misleading words in this context); exotic timbres on the Oriental-percussion side and (as in much of Messiaen's music) highly concentrated in the upper registers; a scale or series of thirty-two different durational values (from the thirty-second note to the whole note which is the sum of thirty-two thirty-seconds); an arrangement in a fairly primitive, alternating form of implacable, static blocks and levels of sound within which the time-duration series are 'colored' by the imaginative range of sonorities—hence *Chronochromie* or 'Time-Color.' The whole . . . has a rather timeless, ecstatic, boring, Oriental, ritualistic, even visionary quality which is certainly, in its dogged, transcendental way, rather remarkable."[8]

Messiaen plainly does not wish to create an indeterminate music; every interaction of the notated material is intended to be felt, to be if possible brought into awareness. His use of birdsong may be compared with the multitude of ornamental refinements the Indian musicians use to embellish and elaborate melody.

John Cage, by the opposite means, using indeterminacy, tries to bring the present moment to awareness. The goal seems similar, but Cage has leaped the structural barrier of causality: that there is a necessary succession or interaction of events. Therefore the disciple of Messiaen, recognizing Cage's authority, insists that Cage's compositions, however interesting, are no longer music.

❀ During the eighteenth century, the most learned Italian composers, led by Padre Martini, cultivated and taught a formalized music, derived from historical theory reaching back to whatever they believed they knew of classical Greek theory. But they ranked performers according to their ability to ornament and embellish freely, "in the best style," whatever music they performed. The French composers preferred to write out their music, with ornament and embellishment notated, leaving a modicum of decisions to be made according to taste. The convention that the French did not play their music as they wrote it applied principally to their temporal alteration of the notated rhythms. German composers turned, as J. S. Bach did, from the Italian free embellishment to the French notated governance. Many works by Bach and Handel are compendious records of the Italian free embellishment at its best, but written out in nearly full notation as a guide to players relatively unskilled in the Italian practice. The musician who had learned this practice was expected to improvise and embellish as freely as he wished, but only "in the best taste." Thus an important skill in playing, from Bach through Beethoven, is to distinguish rhythmically but not by accent between the principal note and its embellishment. Taste became form but not rule, and Germanic music grew freely in the works of C. P. E. Bach, Haydn, and Mozart, until the foliage covered the trellis. In Italian and French music the tradition of embellishment gradually disappeared, though the habit survived as late as Gottschalk and still longer in Italian opera. Taste became rule instead of form and inhibited free growth; the still-living trunk and branches, close-pruned, did not conceal the trellis. The romantic composers trampled all rules, at once impulsively disowning and compulsively obeying them, until the resulting confusion of theories initiated a new body of theoretical rationalizations by which we are still troubled.

Schoenberg, Berg, Webern, Debussy—and Cage, until towards 1960—wrote for the ear, although the justification of their art, as art, was directed to the theoretical intelligence. The seduction of their theory produced in each case a contrary music still directed, in positive or negative response, to the theoretical intelligence. The positive response brought about a music of theory, like that of Milton Babbitt, which sought to make its points by sound. The negative response produced a music of sound, which tried to strip itself of theory. Cage's practice shifted gradually from sound to action. But the exponents of positive theoretical intelligence had learned from Cage that the free combining of sounds, and sometimes actions, gives advantage beyond the governance of theory; therefore they superimposed on their strict theories the more or less arbitrary rearranging of composed pages or parts, after Cage's guidance, and gave openings for improvisation or directed it relatively by graphic means: a method they called *aleatory*.

Thus the old Italian practice of formality plus embellishment was revived with new rules of taste. Cage, increasingly concerned with the extension of his practice, went on from music as "indeterminacy" or by "chance operations" to music as "theater" and then to music as "celebration," a "purposeful purposelessness," in which whatever occurs as a result of the preconceived nature of the event suffices for the event. Several of the composers who had worked with Cage or learned from him, Lou Harrison earlier, Morton Feldman later, and more recently LaMonte Young, turned in the other direction, to a primary concern with controlled sound.

But the real difficulty of art does not change, however one alter or deny its governance. Whatever is to be done is to be done in this manner and not that, accordingly as the composer directs; and whatever he offers as direction is his art.

The disciples of Messiaen use many notes and many words; if the effect of words and notes together is their purpose, that is their tool, their version of the idea. Their practice, not anyone's approving of it, is the work of art. The same is true of Cage's compositions.

Entire books have been written to qualify such differences: if a discussion of facts glossed by theory, all right; if a discussion of theory glossed by fact, more likely all wrong. The idea becomes the tool, it is not the theory of the tool; the idea of any theory is theory.

Schoenberg wrote: "In a manifold sense, music uses time. It uses my time, it uses your time, it uses its own time. It would be most annoying if it did not aim to say the most important things in the most concentrated manner in every fraction of this time. This is why, when composers have acquired the technique of filling one direction with content to the utmost capacity, they must do the same in the next direction, and finally in all the directions in which music expands. Such progress can occur only step-wise. The necessity of compromising with comprehensibility forbids jumping into a style which is often overcrowded with content, a style in which facts are too often juxtaposed without connectives, and which leaps to conclusions before proper maturation."[9]

This is what happened during the parallel maturation of Mahler and Schoenberg. Schoenberg's music increased in concentration more rapidly than Mahler's; Schoenberg seemed to be "compromising with comprehensibility," to be leaping to conclusions without connectives, while Mahler carefully and at length avoided these apparent faults. But a still more decisive example would be to compare a contemporary short work, *The New River*, for chorus and orchestra by Charles Ives, which lasts one and a half minutes, with any passage from a symphony by Mahler, or Ives's Fourth Symphony with Mahler's Ninth; the Ives works, even more than those of the same period by Schoenberg, compromise with comprehensibility, juxtapose facts without connectives, leap to conclusions before proper maturation. The concentration, as in a madrigal, is not by length. Only forty years later are listeners becoming able to recognize the immense concentration of a major work by Ives, to juxtapose the facts, to leap to the conclusions as promptly as he wished, so that we are able to go with him the farther distance he demanded of us. In his art the idea becomes a tool still unreckoned with.

During the first part of the century the idea of the symphony was enlarged in three ways: by increasing length, by increasing massiveness, and by increasing concentration. In the creative reaction after the First World War the idea of the symphony dispensed with length and mass, and composers turned instead to sharply defined musical shapes and to developing the contrasting voices of the solo instruments. The tendency of the young composer to dream in vast textures performed by banks of strings, horns, trombones, and thunderous drums, amplifying the Wagnerian example, was supplanted by a new interest, awakened by the example of Stravinsky in his three ballets, composed before the First World War, *The Firebird, Petrouchka,* and *Rite of Spring,* to persuade the solo instruments to sing with fresh melodic voices. Stravinsky's melodic skill was convincing; too often his imitators failed, and the result was neoclassic dryness.

Robert Craft wrote: [Stravinsky] "enriched both his art and his own era by restoring intellectual prestige to bel canto. . . . Bel canto led Stravinsky to a full-blown vocal line, compelling him to set it off with a more complex variant of Italianate instrumentation. . . . Like most of the pieces in *Pulcinella* and the variations in the *Octuor* [*Octet*], [the duet for trombones and contrabass in *Pulcinella*] at once displays the virtues of the form and mocks, while observing, the time-worn conventions. Only a few notes imitating the old Italian: *She*—I love you, *He*— I love you, are played by the ridiculous combination . . . The first alteration of the theme of the *Octuor's* slow movement is also a hilarious satire, this time on the very nature of variations with their bewildering spray of notes; and yet it is a real variation."[10] Real song, real parody, real wit and satire enlivened a style which, imitated by other composers, remained concerned with the formalistic interplay, in response to an externally applied idea, of instruments and notes. For Stravinsky, the purpose, the play, the wit were in the notes, not applied.

The great Germanic orchestral orations, enforcing their eloquence with substantial modulation and cannonades across the valley between tonic and dominant, gave way to comparatively bare, sometimes acridly harmonized and often polytonal compositions. The discursive subtlety of Debussy yielded to the sharply defined rhythms and rhythmic contrasts of Stravinsky. When one asks why Stravinsky's art so dominated the musical imagination during forty years, the answer may be given simply: Stravinsky defined the new orchestral idea and its terms. That he wrote more ballets and works of a special character than symphonies does not alter the fact of his supreme influence as an orchestra composer. For string quartet he wrote only three short pieces, which he later orchestrated.

Stravinsky preserved and renewed the traditional symphony orchestra in its established instrumental groupings, the appearance of unbroken continuity masking for the audience the extreme changes that were occurring behind the façade of the neoclassic instrument. Schoenberg, having mastered the enlarged orchestra with the *Gurrelieder,* explored with *Pierrot Lunaire* the most extreme capacities of the solo instruments. Stravinsky, in relative austerity, investigated the orchestral choirs and their component voices. Austerity and reduction have been his natural mode. Schoenberg weaves instrumental voices to mutual enlargement; Stravinsky pits them against one another like fighting cocks.

Stravinsky did not confine himself to orchestra when other means were more practical. In Switzerland during the First World War he composed *The Soldier's Tale* with an orchestra of seven solo instruments. After experimenting with different combinations, he composed *The Wedding* with an orchestra of four pianos, kettledrums, bells, and xylophones, "none of which instruments," he remarks, "gives a precise note."

While orchestral music was returning to neoclassic brevity and sharp definition, chamber music turned back to the unfinished business of the late Beethoven quartets. The era of Schoenberg and Bartók, obscured by the continuing predominance of the traditional symphonic apparatus, is the first great period of chamber music since the last quartets by Beethoven and Schubert. One may give all credit to Brahms for clinging to the idea of Beethoven in chamber music, but these trios and quartets no longer have the classic openness; they are dense and heavy like the symphony. The G minor Piano Quartet is a more satisfactory composition when heard as a symphony in Schoenberg's arrangement. Brahms's two-piano composition which became his Piano Quintet is in the original already a potential symphony. The real revival of chamber music did not begin until composers turned from massive to soloistic orchestration, from the chord to the composite sound, expanding on these discoveries in chamber works composed only for solo instruments, a musical development which has not ceased. One might say that Brahms initiated the new soloistic mode in his last quintets, especially the Clarinet Quintet; passages of the instrumentation of the earlier Piano Quintet attempt to re-create the extreme separation of voices characteristic of Beethoven's later compositions. But the true innovator was Debussy, with his String Quartet. And the message reached Schoenberg, as one perceives in comparing his densely Brahmsian First Quartet with the translucent Second Quartet. Chamber music became as complex as symphony had been, but it was in effect a new art, no longer restrained within the symphony-sonata shape but exploring every variety of new combinations and new types of instrumental individuality within the more traditional boundaries. Stravinsky's *Symphonies for Wind Instruments in Memory of Claude Debussy,* which is in fact an orchestral chamber music, and more immediately and particularly his Octet for Winds, directed a new attention to these instruments. Mozart's wind-oriented Divertimentos and Serenades emerged after long obscurity.

Stravinsky's Octet for Winds (1923) articulates sharply defined timbres in rhythmically distinguished vertical and horizontal figures. Schoenberg's Wind Quintet (1924) winds together in intricate distinctions five almost completely independent solo voices of equal prominence playing variations of a single tone-row melody of twelve notes. Each movement in both works is designed upon a neoclassical matrix. (Critics and composers in recent years have made much of Schoenberg's failure to dissolve the neoclassic formal matrix in the same works with which he was realizing the new classicism of the tone-row. The problem was formidable enough without that change. Ives, by contrast, dissolved the formal matrix but attempted no new classical formality.) These two compositions and their nearly concurrent dates mark the Continental Divide where the prevailing idea of the Harmonic Era becomes the new idea of the approaching Era of Sound. Stravinsky's Octet lies upon the up-slope looking backward, Schoenberg's Quintet on the down-slope looking forward. One can say that in the Octet the polyglot Parisian idiom of melody and accompaniment attains a final definition and balance, while in the Quintet the Wagnerian orchestral polyphony achieves a final and, in traditional terms, an almost incomprehensible statement; in the common critical opinion, looking from the past, the Octet is of course the more acceptable work. Seen from the future both have helped create, both works are prophetic. But the Quintet commands a totality of atonal organization beyond the reach of the Octet. With Schoenberg's Wind Quintet the new art of sound is already in existence.

This new art stems from Schoenberg's *Pierrot Lunaire,* not

solely but as the central work. The American critic James Gibbons Huneker was among the first to recognize the significance of this new, intensified, formally strict but audibly unpredictable music; quotation from his far-seeing, sensitive comments unfortunately seldom goes beyond the one famous passage of sardonic-humorous descriptive parody which has been too often reproduced. The example of *Pierrot Lunaire* has influenced composers around the world, especially the young European composers of the 1950s; the Wind Quintet, like the work of Ives, has yet to exert its full influence.

The older idea of the long symphonic work did not completely disappear but took a new turn in the larger compositions by the Brazilian composer Heitor Villa-Lobos. Villa-Lobos strung together symphonic movements in loose European polyglot idiom interspersed with passages of highly colored birdsong and vividly tangled sound suggesting the Amazonian arboreal florescence. A series of *Bachianas Brasileiras* for a variety of instruments from solo piano to orchestra imitate in decorative color the contrapuntal texture and the concerto-grosso style of J. S. Bach. Two of these, one for eight cellos, the other for eight cellos with soprano voice, have become widely popular. A series of *Chôros* in a more freely developed Brazilian style includes a gamut of forms, from a short, powerful duo for violin and cello to a piano concerto and a work for mixed chorus and orchestra. Uninhibited and prolific, Villa-Lobos brightened the contemporary musical literature with a great quantity of brilliantly woven smaller compositions, melodically commonplace but seldom lacking the popular excitement of a decidedly individual imagination. He is at his best in smaller and medium-size compositions, as attractive as Guatemalan textiles, but weak in larger constructions, which lack structural and emotional unity.

Olivier Messiaen admits Villa-Lobos to the pantheon of those from whom he has learned: Berlioz, "the greatest French composer"; Debussy; Paul Dukas—"the scene of the precious stones in *Ariane et Barbe-bleu.*" Messiaen's immense and disarticulate *Turangalila Symphony,* expressing "the sublime love ending with death" of Wagner's *Tristan and Isolde,* carries to an exotic superlative the connection between sounds and colors that has been "the obsession of a lifetime." "I hear certain colors when I hear certain sounds . . . extremely complex combinations of colors." (From a recorded radio interview) His favorite colors are violet, red, purple, and orange.

The tendency to equate tones and colors reached a peak during the first half of the twentieth century. Scriabin's *Poem of Ecstasy* is scored to include a *keyboard of light,* throwing colors on a screen. Schoenberg composed a color score to accompany his short, allegorical music drama, *Die glückliche Hand.* Edward MacDowell heard a particular color for each key; Rimsky-Korsakov and Scriabin drew up key-color charts, agreeing that D major is yellow and E major blue, sapphire, or bluish-white, disagreeing sharply over C major, which Rimsky-Korsakov heard as white and Scriabin as red, and F major, which Scriabin also thought of as red, while Rimsky-Korsakov called it green.

Esthetic inventors have designed and built color organs to project symphonies of light. In my experience, moving light or color detracts from attention to music, since we are more habituated to sustained looking than to sustained hearing, but sound or music can increase our responsiveness to color. The dramatic effectiveness of music accompanying a motion picture seems to be greatest when one is aware of the music but not separately listening to it, as in the skillful use of banalities by theater pianists to accompany silent movies. But Prokofiev, Copland, Thomson, the longtime professional cinema composer David Raksin, and Hanns Eisler, who wrote a book on motion-picture composing, have composed scores which both serve the motion picture and achieve individual existence as orchestral suites.

Schoenberg and Webern created the new idea of *Klangfarbenmelodie,* first appearing in Schoenberg's *Five Orchestra Pieces* (1909). *Klangfarbe,* meaning sound-color, is the German word for timbre. Thus the idea of sound-color, in some relation to visual color, achieved a formal synthesis: the melody, instead of being played by one instrument and then another or the two in counterpoint, is passed in groups of tones or single tones from instrument to instrument or among unexpected simultaneous combinations of instruments through continually changing timbres—as one hears in Webern's arrangement of J. S. Bach's *Ricercar* from the *Musical Offering* or the *Polyphony X* for 18 solo instruments by the French composer Pierre Boulez. In such music each instrument is given an almost equal value and opportunity, dispensing with solo and accompaniment. Theoretically, the timbres will be heard in succession, like a melody, but the accentuation of discordance as an extension of dissonance nowadays very often deprives the timbres of sonority. Performance, difficult for routined instrumentalists, becomes like a game for players who accustom themselves to its challenges.

In the mid-1950s, Robert Craft, encouraged by Stravinsky, recorded on three discs the *Complete Music of Anton Webern*. For the young composers who accepted the example of *Pierrot Lunaire* the almost diagrammatic precision of Webern's minute genius seemed for a time to exclude all other music. The brief orchestral and instrumental movements, the jewellike songs and compositions for voice and mixed instruments (several performed for the first time at these recording sessions), and even more the multidimensional abstractions Webern could achieve with a handful of notes in expanded tone-row (now called serial) composition attracted especially composers who had accepted the teachings of Messiaen, among them Boulez and Stockhausen. (Though his own compositions have had no important imitators, Messiaen's teaching has entered deeply into subsequent styles.)

The thirty-one opus numbers of Webern's progress can be heard as if they were a single work. To comprehend the miracle of Webern, to have the whole of it in miraculous completeness, perhaps somewhat enhanced by the chronological succession of the works on the records, one need only put on the first record of the *Complete Music* and play through to the first work on the last side. Though breaks of years intervene between one work or group of works and the next, there is no break in continuity, no change in style so radical that it cannot be accommodated as if it were the change between two movements. Then, after the Second Cantata, the transcription of Bach's *Ricercar* will enter like a fitting conclusion to a triumph, linking the miniature universe of Webern to the cosmos of our musical tradition. Now play the final work of the last side, the early Piano Quintet without opus number, hearing how the nodes of pure Webern stand apart from the idiom of diminished Brahms.

Almost from the start Webern thought of music as continuous or total variation. Schoenberg would say that this principle is more fundamental to music than the tone-row. Webern refined this principle so closely that it became an art of the variation of each tone, the individual timbre being as significant as the pitch. So that each tone might impinge separately on the hearer as a distinct moment of design (rather than *in* the design), Webern brought in silence as the texture against which the individual moments of controlled vocal and instrumental timbre should be heard. The search for this control was his first period: in five works he shook off the entire past of music to emerge in the *Six Pieces for Orchestra* as free of the medium as a hummingbird in air; these and the *Five Bagatelles* for string quartet are already established in the popular repertory. The revelation of his control may be called his second period. From this time on he never left in any composition a superfluous note or one that altered the function of another without having its own function. He wrote more music with fewer notes in less space than any other composer.

Schoenberg preceded Webern in every idea used by both composers. Suggestions of *Pierrot Lunaire,* not as origin but as a companion work of the same period, begin to turn up in Webern's compositions for voice and several instruments, with increase of a complex, archaic polyphony; in the works between opus 17 and the String Trio, opus 20, Webern takes up and resolves his own formality of the tone-row. After that a peculiar thing happened: Webern resumed the vestments of theory he had written about in his doctoral dissertation on fifteenth century polyphony, borrowing the most learned polyphonic rhetoric. In this style he wrote the masterpieces of his last period, a Symphony and Variations for an orchestra of solo instruments, a String Quartet, Piano Variations, and two Cantatas on mystical religious texts, as indeed nearly all his texts are mystical or religious. The simplicity of these last works consumes, as it subsumes, all technical complexity.

Webern has no gesture to the audience; even less than Satie's is his rhetoric for admiration. The listener should accept his music simply, not out of a great knowledge of technical procedures, which may be necessary to perform his music, but with an innocence like his own that does not hesitate to identify the sound of cowbells and of church bells as what they are, signs of normal country living, of distance, and of reverence, hints of landscape and mountain as the real presences of a visionary experience. But the musician who would play this music must be a master of his instrument: every note is a decision and exposed.

In 1945 Webern was shot, in tragic error, by an American soldier. Living he might have restrained the excesses of his enthusiasts. A horde of posthumous Webern connoisseurs and experts appeared, who had often known little or nothing of his music before the issue of these records. He who had set Schoenberg foremost, his most intimate creative companion, was now called greater than Schoenberg; in the practice of these enthusiasts, the formal organization of notes his few examples so exquisitely deprecated supplanted his refined balancing of the claims of intellect and ear. For his single notes the Messiaen disciples substituted the doctrine of multiple notes heard as if they were single notes. The formal practices which Messiaen had invented to define, not always audibly, the structure of his compositions were applied to a music not made for them.

For the Webern enthusiasts the notated diagram proved more exciting than the musical result; they missed Webern's genuine simplicity—they could not comprehend the humility of his profound pride—expounding and expanding instead the notated complications of his art. They resemble the multifarious exegetes who cluster around the writings of William Blake. Instead of Webern's sense of form, which completes itself precisely to the note, their compositions drag on by extensible devices which seldom clearly end.

This new, intensified, eclectic polyglot, totally organized by formalistic criteria the listener can seldom recognize, shows itself most completely in the two books of *Structures* for two pianos by Pierre Boulez. Here the claims of a determinate structural order do no more than assert the necessity of causal sequence, unrelated to tonality, though still confined within the gamut of twelve notes. The conflicting-combining opposites of a determinate yet indeterminate music moved another long step forward.

In search of justification for the increasing enlargement of their determinate procedures, some of these composers went entirely outside music, to James Joyce's *Ulysses* and *Finnegans Wake*. Others accepted indeterminacy as a supplementary or complementary means. The old idiom and the new, no longer necessarily in conflict, the preparation being always *in the sense of a game* determinate and the reception, even with a score to guide, still indeterminate, were together opening the way for the determinate-indeterminate elaborations possible with the new medium of electronic and computer music.

Debussy, Busoni, Scriabin, Ives, Bartók, Prokofiev, and

Hindemith were the last to compose large bodies of music for the solo instruments; among the newer generation a composer might offer an occasional sonata or a set of variations, but his idea of music expressed itself most naturally by combining several instruments in new styles and forms. The great art of the solo recital became historical and gradually receded from the stage.

At the same time a new idea was appearing, an art of sound, by nontonal percussion, by noise, by extratonal means, and eventually by electronic generation, predicted by Busoni and in more extreme terms by the Italian Futurist Marinetti, "an absolutely free expression of the universe beyond the limits of prosody and syntax—a new way of feeling and seeing—a measuring of the universe as the sum of forces in movement," an orchestration of "colors, noises, sounds . . . words distorted and invented, the cries of animals and the roar of motors," disregarding proportion and the restrictions of good taste. Such a music, but positive instead of negative, already existed in the unknown works by Ives: for a good example, *From the Steeples and the Mountains,* for bells, trumpet, and trombone, composed in 1901. Marinetti accomplished in art little more than the excitement of his manifesto, but an American boy, Henry Cowell, fulfilled the conditions more simply, composing piano pieces to be played with fists and forearms on the keyboard, to be strummed, brushed, and plucked on the strings and rapped on the wood of the piano case. Edgard Varèse, a pupil of Busoni, created during the 1920s a succession of compositions for instruments, percussion, and noisemakers in unprecedented numbers, sirens, and other sound-producers. For two decades after 1931 Varèse withdrew from creative leadership, and the new idea was given fresh creative impetus by John Cage. Here again the indeterminate sound had encroached on the determinate note; fixed pitch, precise notation were no longer necessary.

During the nineteenth century the human voice had continued in the traditional paths of song, chorus, and opera, where the demand was now for endurance and volume rather than flexibility and skill. Schoenberg added a new vocal technique, which he called *Sprechstimme* (speech-song, the voice speaking to approximate intervals a notation not intended to be sung); in *Moses and Aron* (see pages 117–18) and the cantata *De Profundis,* Schoenberg composed speech and song in direct contrast, combining them in simultaneously speaking and singing choral mixtures, an example Stravinsky admired and followed in several of his later works. "I like very well the speaking-singing of Schoenberg in his last cantatas," Stravinsky told me. Harry Partch composed melodies for speaking voice in the fine intervals of his forty-three-tone scale. Other composers preferred to distort the natural singing or speaking of the voice, on tape or by carefully notating the desired effects, so that voice followed instruments into the new idea of sound.

Amid these developments the two operas by Alban Berg at once furthered the interest in total organization and maintained the traditional care for the melodic profile, so that while every note in *Wozzeck* or *Lulu* can be theoretically placed and justified in terms both of abstract form and of emotional-dramatic purpose, the melodic presence is not diffused. Thus the motival usage of Wagner continued into a period and an art which had otherwise discarded Wagnerism.

The total organization of the two operas is made up of equally significant, successive, neoclassical forms (sonata, fugue, theme and variations, and so on), after the example of *Pierrot Lunaire*. (I might point out here, to set straight some misunderstanding, that *Pierrot Lunaire* and *Wozzeck* are not tone-row or serial compositions; they were conceived and completed before the advent of the method of composing with twelve tones.)

Berg's *Lulu* is composed around a set of independent motival twelve-tone rows, each related to a leading personality of the drama. In spite of Berg's explanations, afterwards published by Willi Reich and several times reprinted by authors writing about Berg, that these rows are each derived from a single source, I have it on the authority of George Perle, a close student of Berg's operas, that the motival rows are each separately conceived. The total form of Schoenberg's *Moses and Aron,* which is contemporary with *Lulu,* is derived from a single row, dispensing with the subordinate neoclassic formal sections. But the neoclassic formal matrix survived until this time in Schoenberg's chamber music.

Schoenberg's total forms, each growing from a single row of the twelve tones, expose by comparison the lesser satisfactions of works derived by serial manipulation of more than one row, which some composers commingle with devices contrived after the theories of Messiaen. Few composers to the present day have succeeded in following Schoenberg beyond *Pierrot Lunaire* into the more largely contrived concentration and expressiveness of his later art. Nor have the successors of Berg and Webern achieved a comparably unique expression.

In the new idea of commingled determinate-indeterminate composition each of the preceding methods has its place. Only the one fundamental conception of music has been irretrievably altered, that composed music, by the fact that it is composed must be determinate. Thus music has arrived at the "New Esthetic" prophesied by Ferruccio Busoni. In the new idea any sound may do the work of a note, any random assemblage may be musical, because the composer has created it for that purpose.

24

AN INTRODUCTION TO
IGOR STRAVINSKY

During this first part of our book we have been looking backward down the vista of a hundred years. In so doing we suffer the common illusion that the lives of composers are separated by their dates of death; we see them end as individuals, as nearer or farther sources of influence in relation to ourselves, instead of recognizing by birth a common generation. We think of living composers, old and young, as contemporary, and of their music, written over a period of five to fifty years, as "contemporary music"; thus the time-lag between the so-called "classic" and the presumptive "contemporary" is exaggerated.

We are now in the first centennial decade of that generation of composers who created twentieth century music. Igor Stravinsky is still actively composing, heroically traveling about the world conducting his oldest as well as his newest compositions. If we reckon a generation as twenty years, Stravinsky, born in 1882, is the last of that great generation which began with Debussy (1862) and includes Strauss (1864), Satie and Busoni (1866), Scriabin (1871), Vaughan Williams (1872), Schoenberg and Ives (1874), Ravel (1875), Ruggles (1876), and Bartók (1881). Mahler, who remained independent of these others, was born in 1860.

Wherever we look throughout the history of the arts, we observe that one generation has been creatively gifted to bring about change and the intervening two or three generations to rock more gently between the swells of change. The creative generation after Beethoven is that of Berlioz (born 1803), Chopin (1810), Liszt (1811), and Wagner (1813), who dominated the romantic reaction of the mid-nineteenth century. But what of Brahms, who was born (1833) a generation after Wagner? The composers of a median period may seem the more distinguished because they share what has become for that time a relatively common usage. A Haydn, coming late in a median period, seems to gather in himself the inertia of many static energies and to release their power like a fertilizing thunderstorm, its worth not dependent on the accompanying rumblings and lightnings, upon the parched land.

Stravinsky's art sustains itself upon equal arches like a Roman viaduct, a conduit of water, an enduring static presentness, across a wide, flat median valley. His presence dominates each vista in which it participates; he takes shape to his purpose not from any aspect of the valley, which seems instead to move together in its many shapes always in relation to him. These are the most fortunate composers, whose art, containing seed of the future, is at once rejoiced in by the present.

One can reckon by other measures. Anton Webern (born, a year late, in 1883) could well be included in the generation Debussy-Stravinsky. Yet he belongs not so much to this generation of Schoenberg, nor to the median generation of Prokofiev (1891) and Hindemith (1895), as among those composers to whom his previously almost unknown music gave a new vision in the 1950s. Or, by the circular measure of renewal, we see Haydn's gift renewed through knowledge of Mozart, and Stravinsky's gift renewed in later life through knowledge of Schoenberg and Webern.

Igor Stravinsky came to music late, at the age of eighteen, after matriculating as a student of law at the university. Because of his age he did not attend the Conservatory but studied for three years as a personal pupil of Rimsky-Korsakov, under whose guidance he grew rapidly as a composer. In this still formative condition he was invited to compose for the Diaghilev Ballet and then go to Paris, with the result that he did not mature like Scriabin, Rachmaninoff, and Prokofiev, in the Russian tradition. His first great ballet, *The Firebird,* is still predominantly Russian, gleanings from the art of his master and his contemporaries, for example from Scriabin's *Poem of Ecstasy* and Ninth Sonata (the

latter quotation more evident in Stravinsky's piano-roll performance, recorded in 1928, than in the orchestral version), plus the
same radical, powerfully rhythmic impulse which had already
appeared in Prokofiev's adolescent music. (William Malloch has
pointed out to me that the rhythmic figuration of certain passages
in the earlier version of *The Firebird* closely resembles that of
passages in Balakirev's once famous tone poem for piano,
Islamey. In the later version of *Firebird*, Stravinsky has simplified the passage to accentuate the melody by removing most of
the figuration.)

Prokofiev gave as the origin of this rhythmic impulse the
Schumann *Toccata* for piano and in later years denied, against
the evidence, its large place in his music (see pages 135–36).
Stravinsky tells nothing at all about the sources of this *motor*
rhythm, to use the other and more contemporary name Prokofiev
gave it. A similar rhythmic impetus drives the finale of Ravel's
Daphnis and Chloe—"one of his finest scores," Stravinsky says of
it—performed the year before *Rite of Spring*, though that work
was already written. No rhythm of such character or sustained
power had occurred in European music since Beethoven; *Islamey*
and the Schumann *Toccata* are by comparison frail and over-
wrought; a common source may be Beethoven's Seventh Symphony, the *Great Fugue,* and the finale of the C sharp minor
Quartet. This was the first generation of composers for whom
orchestral performance of the Beethoven symphonies, instead of
reading them at the piano, was a familiar experience, the first
able to hear played in public the late Beethoven quartets.

One must presume that the new rhythmic impulse appeared,
like certain famous scientific discoveries, in several minds from
similar sources at approximately the same time. Ravel did not
return to it after the one sophisticated example. Prokofiev
strengthened and varied but did not refine his adolescent invention. Stravinsky alone developed and refined it in many aspects,
from *Rite of Spring* to *The Soldier's Tale, The Wedding,
Oedipus,* and the powerfully concentrated *Symphony of Psalms,*
until it became in general recognition the most characteristic
aspect of his music.

Yet it is not this rhythmic growth but his gift of instrumental
melody that was the rootwork of Stravinsky's art: not melody in
abstract as *absolute music* in the Germanic term, whether in
tonality or polytonality, but melody discovered in the timbres of

each solo instrument, often by giving to a melody lying conveniently for one instrument the voice of another instrument of unlike registration.

I described the effect of such procedure in reviewing the first performance of Stravinsky's *Agon*, Los Angeles, 1957. " 'Instruments are nothing in themselves; the literature they play creates them. The mandolin and guitar did not exist until Schoenberg imagined them in an entirely new way in his *Serenade*.' So Stravinsky tells us; the demonstration is a dance contest, a ballet of instruments. Schoenberg's mandolin tenderly bubbles spring-like through one movement but only after she has put on a mask and pretended to be a harpsichord playing a melody of wide Schoenbergian intervals. Cellos bray; tucket flourishes on virginal shakes are tossed off by all instruments; the piano clumps in the part usually assigned to the bassoon; tenderness passes, in dissonant tonal rows; the solo violin takes her turn of partners and like a fine lady at a village wedding steps to the center of the circle with three gawkish-handsome trombones. To the slow metallic beat of a simulated castanet the instruments throw off harmonic and rhythmic decency, until, just as the shock of this sophisticated Saturnalia has begun to register in the bewildered mind, we are off in fine garments to a fling of counterpoint. And as in *Così fan tutte* all the marriage pairings turn out wrong before they come out right, so in *Agon* every instrument has been irreverently coupled before it is harmoniously joined." For fifty years critics had been instructing Stravinsky to compose another *Petrouchka;* in *Agon* they did not recognize it.

Credit for Stravinsky's instrumental awareness must go first to his master, Rimsky-Korsakov. Hindemith, who performed with skill on many instruments, wrote for the most part with a drab unawareness of the peculiar individuality of their sound. Stravinsky, a composer by his own admission totally dependent on the piano—"I do not hear a new composition until I have sounded it at the piano," he said to me—created a twentieth century language of the instruments.

"In the course of a talk about *Oedipus Rex*," Walter Piston has written, ". . . an observation that he made threw a bright light on a most important aspect of his artistic ideals. He said, 'How happy I was when I discovered that chord!' Some of us were puzzled, because the chord, known in common harmonic terms as a D-major triad, appeared neither new nor complex. But it became evident that Stravinsky regarded every chord as an individual sonority, having many attributes above and beyond the tones selected from a scale or altered this way or that. The particular and marvelous combination of tones in question owed its unique character to the exact distribution of the tones in relation to the spaces between them, to the exact placing of the instrumental voices in reference to the special sound of a given note on a given instrument, to the dynamic level indicated, and to the precise moment of sounding of the chord."[1]

Stravinsky's opera *The Nightingale* commences in Russian style but was resumed after several years in the new, dry (*sec,* as one says of a wine) melodic idiom he had developed by creative adaptation from the musical art of Paris. *Petrouchka* had its origin, in the Russian tradition, as a concert piece for piano and orchestra in the style of Weber's *Konzertstück;* when Diaghilev invited Stravinsky to recompose the music as a ballet he once again made the creative transition from Petersburg to Paris. From this time forward, although he might return in poetic nostalgia to the memory of his Russian homeland, Stravinsky has never been diverted from his true course as a creator independent of both idioms.

The radical break in Stravinsky's early life could have destroyed him, as separation from homeland and tradition has destroyed many artists, but Diaghilev's request that he should write music for immediate production nerved him to a concentration into which he assimilated not only all he had known but the newer music he was discovering. He became himself apart from any tradition, a heroic action, but he was from that time a creative artist without a tradition, concentrating to assimilate into form one new thing at a time. He learned to know himself, but there was for a long time much music that he did not know. This wide, progressive ranging of a mind freed from its tradition made him the creative opposite of Schoenberg—as either was incapable of the total plunge past theory of Ives.

In Berlin during the winter of 1912–1913 Stravinsky first met Schoenberg, at an audition of the newly written *Pierrot Lunaire.* His own *Rite of Spring,* already composed, would have its famous first performance at Paris the following spring. In his *Autobiography,* written in 1935, Stravinsky commented that he felt not the slightest enthusiasm for Schoenberg's work, but "the merits of the instrumentation are beyond dispute." His disdain for—and one should fairly add, misunderstanding of—Schoenberg's esthetic attitude, and Schoenberg's reciprocal disdain, did not end during Schoenberg's lifetime.

During the 1930s and 1940s they lived seventeen years in the same city, Los Angeles, without meeting, while the quarreling of their intolerant partisans divided taste and exacerbated criticism. Stravinsky was often seen at concerts and traveled widely; Schoenberg traveled little and was seldom at concerts. Schoenberg came to the first program Evenings on the Roof gave of his music, at my home; he did not attend the concerts Evenings on the Roof gave in honor of his seventieth and seventy-fifth birthdays or the concert at the end of the tenth season of Evenings on the Roof, which included the first Western performance of his String Trio. Stravinsky came to these concerts occasionally during the later 1940s and continually during the 1950s.

In the year of Schoenberg's death (1951), Stravinsky began studying the little known and generally unappreciated compositions Schoenberg had written during the forty years since *Pierrot Lunaire,* especially the *Serenade* for seven instruments and voice and the Suite for Seven Instruments, both of which Stravinsky's young colleague, Robert Craft, directed for a series of Schoenberg retrospective concerts presented in the autumn of that year by Evenings on the Roof. Soon afterwards Stravinsky composed his own Septet, using for each movement a notated row; in the first two movements the treatment of the thematic material is, in his idiom, conventional; in the two final movements the row consists of sixteen instead of twelve notes, only eight of these different notes, and the treatment includes tone-row procedures.

The evening before Stravinsky was to go to the hospital for an operation, a group of instrumentalists assembled at my home to play for him the first reading of his Septet. At the end, springing to his feet, he exclaimed, "It is tonal—strictly tonal!" His ear had heard what his intelligence was not yet ready to admit, that in his music he had gone beyond the rule of the Harmonic Era. Tonality, which he had retained, was no longer the point in question. At a later time I asked him why he had used a trio of wind instruments instead of the three clarinets in different keys of Schoenberg's Suite. He replied, "I do not like the sound of the other clarinets." The Septet is his first acknowledgement of Schoenberg.

In the next year, as the result of a similar program of Webern's music, and subsequently while Craft was preparing his recorded album of Webern's *Complete Music*, Stravinsky adapted this material also to his own use, dedicating his first work in this style, his *Three Songs by William Shakespeare*, to Evenings on the Roof. During the next decade, although he did not alter in admiration of the art of Webern, his enthusiasm for the later music of Schoenberg steadily increased. His followers throughout the world at first denied and then loudly decried this "borrowing" from the work of two masters of the rival school they had so long criticized and abused, but Stravinsky was no more deterred by this outcry of his partisans, and of others who had seen in him their champion against change, than he had been deterred by earlier criticism, including Schoenberg's, of his neoclassical derivations. At an age above seventy he could continue adjusting his musical prosody to new methods, without changing his esthetic consistency and distinctive idiom.

Firm as he is in his convictions, Stravinsky has never hesitated to reverse his prejudices, keeping his mind open to discovery even in matters about which an earlier critical statement would seem to have been final: for example, his low opinion of Verdi's "music-dramas," *Otello* and *Falstaff*—an opinion he afterwards dismissed to me with a wave of the hand.

At Weimar in 1923 Stravinsky met Busoni, who had been described to him as "an irreconcilable opponent of my music." Sitting together at a performance of *The Soldier's Tale* Stravinsky was "very much impressed by the sincere emotion that I saw he was feeling while my music was being played, which was confirmed by him that same evening. I was all the more touched by this appreciation, since it came from a very great musician, whose work and mentality were fundamentally opposed to the spirit of my art."[2]

Busoni believed that "all arts, resources and forms ever aim at the one end, namely, the imitation of nature and the interpretation of human feelings." "The audible presentation, the 'performance,' of music, its emotional interpretation, derives from those free heights whence descended the Art itself. . . . Great artists play their own works differently at each repetition, remodel them on the spur of the moment, accelerate and retard, in a way which they could not indicate by signs—and always according to the conditions of that 'eternal harmony.'"[3]

Stravinsky has always disagreed with this opinion: "For, as

have already said, music should be transmitted and not interpreted, because interpretation reveals the personality of the interpreter rather than that of the author, and who can guarantee
that such an executant will reflect the author's vision without
distortion?"[4]

Both Stravinsky and Schoenberg opposed expressive interpretation of music. Schoenberg praised Mahler as a conductor for "the
precision of his performances as well as their tonal beauty and
clarity," with this qualification: ". . . the rubato corresponded to
his youth, the steadiness to his maturity." Reacting against the
virtuosity typical of performing artists in their generation, each
wrote, by notation as precise as possible, exactly how his music
should be played. In his later years Schoenberg became still more
severe in this belief. I stood beside him one afternoon following
with him the score of his Suite for Seven Instruments, while we
listened to the record from his private library of a performance he
had directed many years before in Paris, probably in 1927. He
deplored the deviations from tempo, the rubatos, he had permitted.

Stravinsky recorded his own compositions on piano rolls and
records, because by this means "I was able to express all my
intentions with real exactitude." His piano-roll reading of the
complete *Firebird* is strict as a diagram or a dance-rehearsal
accompaniment, the tempos much slower than those of his later
orchestral performances on records. The records "have the importance of documents which can serve as guides to all executants
of my music." Musicians generally assert that he has not been the
best conductor of his music; this is debatable, since few do better.
In recent years his willingness to let the play of melody as he
hears it in performance divert the strict flowing of the composition has been more evident.

In point of fact, there is no solution to the problem, and the
argument is unreal. Only the performer, to the extent of his
comprehension and musical capacity, can release the composer's
notation into sound. Stravinsky's own recorded performance at
the keyboard is inimitable. A note-perfect, brilliant performance
may be empty; another player, charging the music with personality, may convey a unique drama. Any great performance is
unique, any routine performance imitation. Performing taste and
audience expectation are not constants. Stravinsky's recorded
reading of *The Soldier's Tale* with musicians of the Northwest

German Radio Orchestra shows the strictness of Germanic orchestral discipline, the players coming together exactly for each chord. His later performance of the same work recorded in Los Angeles reflects the greater independence of part-playing practised by these musicians, the individual voices flowing through the chord never quite together. No conductor, without very long preparation, could effect a change in these habitual methods.

The alternative is to compose music by such means as punching slots, after careful measurement, in piano rolls, in the manner of the American composer Conlon Nancarrow's rhythm studies, or to record the music directly on a disc or tape without the intervention of performers. Even so, speed and pitch will be at the mercy of the reproducing instrument.

Writing to Alban Berg about the *Gurrelieder*, Schoenberg said, in part: "The whole composition was thus finished, I should say, in April or May 1901. . . . Indications of the orchestration were, in the original composition, not very numerous. . . . one must see that the part orchestrated in 1910–11 is quite different in style from the first and second parts. I had no intention of concealing the fact; on the contrary it is self-evident that my orchestration of ten years later would be different."[5]

Stravinsky writes to the same purpose: ". . . I received from the newly founded Théâtre Libre of Moscow a request to complete the composition of my opera, Le Rossignol [The Nightingale]. I hesitated. Only the Prologue—that is to say, Act I—was in existence. It had been written four years earlier, and my musical language had been appreciably modified since then. I feared that in view of my new manner the subsequent scenes would clash with that Prologue. . . ."[6]

Neither composer believed that he could, as one might say, *fake* his own style of a few years earlier. Each held that style is innate and changes with the man. It would seem inevitable that this would be true also of the performer, even of a composer repeating his own work in performance.

Before the vogue of practical music (*Gebrauchsmusik*) Stravinsky was already a practical composer. As he explained in his *Autobiography*, the composer of ballet music had been looked down on in Russia, until Tchaikovsky proved with his famous ballets that music for the dance could be of equal value with abstract music. The greater part of Stravinsky's music was composed with practical intent for a particular purpose and immediate use. Composition, he has said, begins for him at the keyboard with the feeling of the intervals in his fingers, and the resulting work is played first with two or four hands at the piano. Schoenberg, in the tradition of J. S. Bach, composed apart from any instrument. He wrote rapidly but seldom for an immediate occasion; only a few of his compositions can be called practical music.

There is no doubt that Stravinsky wished to be and set out to be a popular artist; it testifies to his strength of musical purpose that he became a popular artist without sacrifice. A great showman, conscious of his audience, he never deviated from his chosen direction when each new work was received with critical displeasure or when, every few years, the audience seemed to be turning away from him. The audience, recognizing in him this great force of character, has never for any long period ceased to cherish him; it runs down his new work not by comparison with that of others but in comparison with his well-beloved and familiar early compositions. He did not try to be the profound thinker Schoenberg was by nature. His religious music remains, in the Catholic tradition, objective—celebration, ritual, lamentation, narrative; it does not question in Germanic style, like Schoenberg's, the religious ultimates or the nature and relationship of man and God.

Preparing to write his Piano Sonata, Stravinsky began playing the sonatas of Beethoven, from whose music he tells us he had been alienated for many years because of the habitual language and mannerisms of Beethoven's interpreters. "Cured and matured by age, I could now approach him objectively. . . . It is in the quality of his musical material and not in the nature of his ideas that his true greatness lies. . . . As for those who attach no importance to Beethoven's instrumentation, but ascribe the whole of his greatness to his 'ideas' " . . . they make the "fundamental error of regarding instrumentation as something extrinsic from the music for which it exists."[7] (This could certainly not be said of Schoenberg, and "ideas" in this context does not mean the same as "the idea" of Schoenberg in the previous chapter.)

Schoenberg drew a sharp distinction between genius and talent, writing in 1911: "Genius . . . learns only from itself; talent chiefly from others. Genius learns from nature, from its own nature; talent learns from art"; and again, in his tribute to Gustav Mahler: "Talent is the capacity to learn, genius the capacity to develop oneself."

Schoenberg believed firmly in the role of genius; Stravinsky feels no need of the distinctive implication.

In the Germanic tradition the artist *expresses* himself and his ideas by esthetic means which arise out of or reflect his inner, or subjective, emotions and sensations. In Schopenhauer's words: "The composer reveals the innermost being of the world and expresses the deepest wisdom in a language which his own reason does not understand: like a somnambulist, who tells of things of which he has no clear knowledge in his waking state. This is the reason why, in a composer more than in any other artist, man and artist are quite separate and distinct."[8] Or as Schoenberg says: "But, above all, the artist *must*. He cannot influence what he produces; it depends not on his own will. But since necessity drives him, he can produce. He can even acquire what is not innate—manual skill, mastery of form, virtuosity. But such qualities are his own, not those of others."

The opposite of this is, in one aspect, the French term *impressionism:* rendering objectively the immediate sense-impression of the artist as he receives it with a minimum of infused thought or emotion; therefore the play of light on an object or through a landscape requires no other sign, significance, or meaning. But the succeeding developments of French painting, poetry, or music show the instability of impressionism in practice. The received impression was soon translated into the represented impression: the painter, seeing through his eyes *red* where his mind knows *green,* paints the *red* he sees; Matisse translated this optical reality into the represented impression of a room entirely red, with factual discrimination of objects only by shape, not color—as the hand feels for the mind the shape of objects in a pocket or purse. Or the received impression became the symbolically infused impression: in Debussy's music the audible sign symbolically re-creates the experience.

Debussy wrote of Carl Maria von Weber: "His work had a sort of dreamy melancholy, characteristic of his time, though never marred by the crude German moonshine in which nearly all his contemporaries were bathed. He was perhaps the first to face the problem of establishing the due relationship of the infinite spirit of nature to the finite spirit of the individual."[9]

Stravinsky saw no value in such language. "*Expression* has never been an inherent property of music. . . . If, as is nearly always the case, music appears to express something, this is only an illusion and not a reality. . . . Music is the sole domain in which man realizes the present. By the imperfection of his nature, man is doomed to submit to the passage of time—to its categories of past and future—without ever being able to give substance, and therefore stability, to the category of the present.

"The phenomenon of music is given us with the sole purpose of establishing an order in things, including, and particularly, the coordination between *man* and *time*. To be put into practice, its indispensable and single requirement is construction. Construction once completed, this order has been attained, and there is nothing more to be said. . . . It is precisely this construction, this achieved order, which produces in us a unique emotion having nothing in common with our ordinary sensations and our responses to the impressions of daily life."[10]

Schoenberg wrote in his tribute to George Gershwin that an artist is like an apple tree: when his time comes he has apples. He wrote similarly in "Criteria for the Evaluation of Music": "Creation to an artist should be as natural and inescapable as the growth of apples to an apple tree. Even if it tried to produce apples in response to the demands of a fashion or of the market, it could not. Thus artists who want to 'go back to a period,' who try to obey the laws of an obsolete esthetic or of a novel one, who enjoy themselves in eclecticism or in the imitation of a style, alienate themselves from nature."[11]

Schoenberg believed in art as an organic experience, through which the entire being of the composer will express or, in a sense, expose itself. His art will be more than he can know or consciously create. The *necessary* means and connections will be therefore unavoidably indeterminate, however foreseen and disciplined the consequence: the artist cannot produce a true work of art when it pleases him to do so; he must wait until his art works. When the artist's content, his esthetic consistency, falls into certain order, it creates. The unconscious decision precedes the conscious, deliberate, and for Schoenberg the rapid writing out.

Stravinsky believes in an art as objective to the senses as the *ordonnance*, the formally prepared and rehearsed order of a ballet, a combining and succession of individually prepared acts, from which one receives through eyes and ears at the same time a subjectively ordered experience. The material of ballet is conventional; only the assembly and structuring of the material in each work must be fresh. Music in the same way can take its material from any source; the composer can "steal" as he pleases; the work of art results from what is then done with the material. One realizes that from this it is only an imaginative step to assert that *any material* in *any objective assemblage* may be received as a subjectively ordered experience.

Some hold with the American composer Carl Ruggles that every note of a composition must be creatively generated by the composer; few composers practise this extreme, and perhaps severely inhibiting, experience as he has done it.

A well-conceived conventional theme plus some related episodic material can suffice for a large fugue. It is not the subject but what happens along the way that makes the difference between talent and art. Not the melody of a tone-row but its organic shape in consideration of all that can grow from it is important. Texture and structure, encountered in time and space, are equally significant.

Neither was consistent in his doctrine. In 1926 Schoenberg satirized the neoclassical composers, aiming his criticism at Stravinsky, although not by name, for his compositions ending in C major. "The shoe of his satire on C-major endings fits five of my works at that time and perhaps twenty since," Stravinsky commented in his review of Schoenberg's *Letters,* written in 1964. Schoenberg wished to show up the mere talent of the neoclassical composers: "talent learns from art." Yet the apple tree has no apples but its own; an artist who feels in himself or his material the innate necessity of a C major ending is as right as Schoenberg was when in his later career he composed again in tonality.

In "Composition with Twelve Tones" Schoenberg wrote: *"the unity of musical space demands an absolute and unitary perception.* In this space . . . there is no absolute down, no right or left, forward or backward. Every musical configuration, every movement of tones has to be comprehended primarily as a mutual relation of sounds, of oscillatory vibrations, appearing at different places and times. To the imaginative and creative faculty, relations in the material sphere are as independent from directions or planes as material objects are, in their sphere, to our perceptive faculties."[12]

If "so-called atonal music . . . cannot satisfy our desire for gravitational attraction," as Hindemith declared, this is only because we have been too long habituated to the play of tonal relationships which gives us, with the supreme authority of Beethoven, a feeling of controlled spatial tensions within three-dimensional space—as vivid to some listeners as the emotional tension of his modulatory drama is for others. When one feels esthetically that the music of Beethoven is the central structural achievement of music as an art, one cannot help but suffer dizziness, loss of spatial orientation, and perhaps even nausea, on first entering the multidimensional, seemingly uncontrolled, chaotic spatial unity of Schoenberg. It will be like first encountering the weightlessness of space beyond our gravitational sphere.

Schoenberg himself put it more simply: "Just as our mind always recognizes, for instance, a knife, a bottle or a watch, regardless of its position, and can reproduce it in the imagination in every possible position"—and one might add, as the hand feels an object in the pocket and knows it for what it is—"even so a musical creator's mind can operate subconsciously with a row of tones, regardless of their direction, regardless of the way in which a mirror might show the mutual relations, which remain a given quantity."[13]

Of course the introduction of the mirror does confuse things a bit, as anyone has experienced when trying to perform a manual operation, like knotting a necktie, while watching the optical inversion of movements in a mirror; there is a similar mental-spatial confusion in playing cross-hands at the piano. For this reason Schoenberg wrote out for each composition in a little notebook the row in each of its forty-eight primary positions, the row and its retrograde, and their mirror inversions.

Instead of the harmonic spatial box within which the post-Beethoven mannerist could walk always upright, every gesture accentuated by a common sense of spatial limits, Schoenberg revived the spatial conception of J. S. Bach, in which a theme, like a rococo angel or a cherub, can occupy real space or spin visually in any direction, up or down, in imaginary space on a two-dimensional or a curving surface. This spatial universe, in which the one-directional pull of gravity (thoroughbass) operates with diminishing force, is quite familiar today in our new scientific comprehension of space.

Stravinsky had composed within the harmonic spatial box as

naturally as he conceived music in terms of ballet movement on a stage, where a dancer may leap but cannot fly, the head is usually upright, and movement of the hands is normally above and of a different order than movement of the feet. All is *natural*, to a scale governed by the dimensions of the human body.

He has, like Tchaikovsky, a remarkable ability to present his composition in clear profile. Since the content is far richer than that of Tchaikovsky's music, Stravinsky's compositions have often the classical definition (security within projected shape) of major works by Haydn and Mozart. He avoids the entangling of songlike melodies which leads by way of Schubert and Wagner to Bruckner, Mahler, Pfitzner, Strauss, and Schoenberg; he is not involved in the Brahmsian effort to achieve a balance between melodic freedom and contrapuntal weight. Like the painters of clear profile, he loses in spaciousness and depth what he has gained in definition. Seldom in his compositions are more than two things happening together at the same time. One might suspect that he overcompensated for Germanic expressiveness; it would be at least equally true to presume that his experience in writing for ballet accustomed him to a linear simplicity which could be visualized like dance.

In *Oedipus* the scale becomes monumental, made more than normally decisive by starkly contoured melodies moving in shallow depth across chorded vertical columns, realizing in one medium the two-dimensional character of the Greek drama on its native stage. The vocal method is musical oratory, directed to the gods and to the audience, in Latin and musically syllabified, not as one would speak it. "I have always considered that a special language, and not that of current converse," Stravinsky explained, "was required for subjects touching on the sublime. That is why . . . I finally selected Latin. The choice had the great advantage of giving me a medium not dead, but turned to stone and so monumentalized. . . ."[14] (For a directly contrary method, in the work of Harry Partch, see pages 200, 298–99.)

From *The Firebird* as far as *The Wedding* Stravinsky is thinking in three dimensions, yet already in *Rite of Spring*, "I had imagined the spectacular part of the performance as a series of rhythmic mass movements of the greatest simplicity . . . with no superfluous details or complications such as would suggest effort." In what one may call for convenience his middle-period compositions, Stravinsky reduced the scale very nearly to the two dimensions of a plane surface, resembling the two-dimensional conceptions of his friend Pablo Picasso, in which the vestigial third dimension plays with the mind and sometimes enrages it, like the movements of a matador's cape. So whether in the witty crossplay of Stravinsky's *Pulcinella,* the unceasingly beautiful *pas de deux* for two instruments of *Duo Concertant,* the two-dimensional parody of the *Grande Sonate* that is the Concerto for Two Solo Pianos, as far as the paper-thin, virtuoso, musical game of *Jeu de Cartes* (*Card Game*), every movement of the design, each gesture of the individual instrument is as visible as the cakewalk—on a shallow stage, before a bare curtain, of vaudeville—of the *Dumbarton Oaks Concerto.* It was for this reason and by such means that Stravinsky had developed his stamping motor rhythms and refined them to utmost nicety.

Those who had called neoclassicism "back to Bach" were incorrect; only now, with *Orpheus,* did Stravinsky enter the multidimensional baroque through the monodic and dissonant special door of Monteverdi. It was inevitable that his eye would follow painting, his sense of style would comport with the dance discoveries of his friend the choreographer George Balanchine, and his ear would penetrate into the multidimensionality of a new scheme of composition which had commenced learning from Schoenberg, as from Kandinsky, an art abstract and representative in and of itself, where the scale is neither human nor infinite and space no longer gravitationally oriented but conceptual.

Stravinsky at first still rejected the discontinuity—the implied circularity, without necessary succession or real beginning or real end—of the *Polyphony X* by Pierre Boulez, but the logic of the new composition, argued with the sophisticated persuasiveness of its composer, afterwards convinced him. For all these technical excitements in which Stravinsky still participates with ever youthful eagerness, almost glee, his thought turned more often to Schoenberg, looking backward across their common lifetime, "a time that," in Stravinsky's far-seeing reconsideration, "Schoenberg lived and formed and that now to some extent—for centripetal as he was, other developments were and are possible—lives and finds its form in him."[15]

Yet the time was also, and in immediate possession even more, Stravinsky's. What other composer of his rank could have been rhymed so alertly and so casually with "Minsky"—the burlesque show—knowing that a large share of the audience of *Guys and*

Dolls would catch it in the mitt. During the forty-year time-lag after 1912, from which Schoenberg's later masterpieces are still gradually emerging to assume the stature that will make their content, as esthetic consistency, part of common knowledge, Stravinsky's successive creations had oriented the successive decades. Yet critics writing in honor of his eightieth birthday were still deploring his gradual decline as a composer since *Rite of Spring*. He too had suffered in depth, and in old age and illness, amid the travel and adventure his unceasing energy and curiosity and creativeness still commanded, the shamefulness of uncomprehending criticism, replying to it now with a perfect marksmanship and wit, wasted on these bedraggled reviewers; he too, throughout their mutual lifetime, had not comprehended the necessity of Schoenberg.

One can pay to Stravinsky the final homely honor that in his own words he at last paid Schoenberg: ". . . there is something triumphant in the old man."

They will not be forgotten; the future will match them, as the two chief masters in their generation, who divided the creative world between them. Only Bartók, who stood alone, and Charles Ives, scarcely known in that creative generation, were their creative equals.

PART II

"Mr. Price. Please don't try to make things nice.
All the wrong notes are right."

—MARGINAL NOTE ON THE
MANUSCRIPT OF *The Fourth of July*

THE PROOF OF THE NOTATION

Until now we have been looking at music as history, in retrospect; now we shall see it, in prospect, as a great wave rising.

What is a wave good for? It can only break on the beach. But much may happen while it is passing across the ocean surface. Most waves are similar, formed to a common pattern of place and time. Yes, but no two waves are the same, and the pattern changes constantly, influenced by time, tide, wind, a distant storm at sea, a seismic convulsion. A tidal wave, carrying its burden of potential destruction thousands of miles across the ocean surface, may be no more than a few feet high; such is the music of Erik Satie, of Anton Webern.

Is there esthetic worth in a destructive force? The art of tragedy affirms it. Nature and need do not value our categories of form and permanence. The oldest surviving creatures are not the powerful predators. Wind and water erode rock, shape cliff and desert; fire, storm, nature, and human nature destroy habitations and cathedrals; evolution involves constant destruction and replacement, not the survival of the fittest by overt competition but continual adaptation of that which survives to changing circumstance. No music of another period is heard today in the style or sound in which it was conceived.

"Compare a concept with a style of painting," Ludwig Wittgenstein proposes, almost at the end of his *Philosophical*

Investigations. "For is even our style of painting arbitrary? Can we choose one at pleasure? (The Egyptian, for instance.) Is it a mere question of pleasing and ugly?

"What is most difficult here is to put this indefiniteness, correctly and unfalsified, into words.

"We find certain things about seeing puzzling, because we do not find the whole business of seeing puzzling enough." (Gertrude Stein wrote: 'What is strange is this.')

". . . It is the field of force of a word that is decisive."[1]

Substitute a musical note: it is the field of force of a musical note that is decisive. What is a musical note?

Notation is the skill of expressing musical ideas in writing—or, as Busoni put it, "an ingenious expedient for catching an inspiration." Stravinsky speaks of the *Danse sacrale,* which, while composing *Rite of Spring,* "I could play but did not know how to write."

Most notational systems are imperfect, like systems of spelling and pronunciation. They may change decisively, bringing us unexpected and unprecedented knowledge and ability to think and say new things; this has happened during the past century to our long-established mathematical systems. A notational system implies a corresponding system of interpretation, according to a traditional usage which is at once acquired by habituation and learned by rote (repetition of forms or phrases—and the dictionary adds, "often without attention to meaning"). Challenging our established system of musical notation we direct fresh thought to its substance, its significance as a language of signs; and, as it has happened in mathematics, we gain unexpected and unprecedented knowledge and the ability to think and say new things.

In the eighteenth century, musicianship was the ability to read notes, not simply as written but often by embellishing them with ornaments, by the addition of other notes, and by alteration of the notated rhythm, according to principles of learning and good taste: musicianship focused on the skill of the performer. During the nineteenth century, with the establishing of large orchestras, musicianship was divided between two contrary skills: the ability of any group of orchestral musicians to play the same written notes almost exactly alike under the direction of a conductor; and the ability of the conductor or solo player to interpret the notation in his own way, which resulted in excesses of applied demonstrative rhetoric. The conflict has not ended. Conductors still mime a ritualistic interpretation between orchestra and public—they are admired either because they do this or because they do not—to which the players give no notice, watching only for the downbeat. Soloists prove their expertise with note-perfect, mechanically expert renderings, which by their impersonal efficiency cease to be musical. "The young pianists all play exceedingly well," Virgil Thomson said to me, "and they are nearly all equally uninteresting."

By the early twentieth century, Arnold Schoenberg could write to a singer: "I am anxious to explain to you why I cannot allow any will but mine to prevail in realizing the musical thoughts that I have recorded on paper, and why realizing them must be done in such deadly earnest, with such inexorable severity, because the composing was done just that way. I should very much like to do some thorough rehearsing with you, so that you should get to know the way to solve the musical picture-puzzles that my works constitute. . . ."[2]

Can a "musical picture-puzzle" be "in deadly earnest"? The answer is, yes, of course—with some allowance for Schoenberg's humor. Stravinsky, at a later time, would be complaining that conductors failed to study his phonograph records to learn how they should prepare his compositions for performance.

Schoenberg wrote that the effect of a musical composition changes with each hearing, therefore one must study it in score. Today, a composer can write out his exact instructions on a worksheet in the language read by a computer, have these instructions fed on punch-cards into the electronic machine, which does none of his composing for him but works out his instructions in the sequence he has indicated; converter and tape recorder translate the numerical output into an analogous magnetic trace on tape, which can be translated into audible vibrations (music) when played anywhere by means of tape player, amplifier, and loudspeaker to an audience of any size. Where is the score? It is not the composer's worksheet; any musical "secrets" hidden there which are not audible on the recorded tape as the composer desired them reveal technological failure but no fresh understanding of the music. The musical thoughts have been realized "with inexorable severity," and the puzzles have been solved in the making of them, "because the composing was done just that way." The composer has decided the interpretation while composing it.

Schoenberg was aware of this possibility, which he did not live to see realized.

Schoenberg repeatedly refused invitations to direct his music when ample time for rehearsal had not been guaranteed. Writing to Edgard Varèse in 1922 he was holding up the example of "something like 100 rehearsals" for *Pierrot Lunaire* in Vienna, "with everyone shivering and starving." About twenty years after this, when I brought a group of Los Angeles musicians to Schoenberg's home to discuss performing *Pierrot Lunaire* under his direction at Stanford University, he was still asking between sixty and a hundred rehearsals; the musicians gave up the project. At a later time, for a program of Schoenberg's music in honor of his seventieth birthday, we prepared the same work with no more than the usual number of rehearsals expected in this country; when Schoenberg heard a broadcast of the performance, directed by Ingolf Dahl, he praised it.

In today's economic conditions it is probably not possible anywhere in the world to afford rehearsal time for a performance on Schoenberg's terms. Preparation of the first performance of Ives's Fourth Symphony, a superlatively demanding, very large score, though scarcely more than a half-hour in playing time, needed eleven rehearsals—and a grant of money from the Rockefeller Foundation to pay for part of them.

Today, musicians who would play any but routined music must learn to read difficult compositions accurately at sight and work them out for performance with a minimum of rehearsal. The proliferation of chamber compositions for groups of solo instrumentalists encourages individual musicians to make this effort, and reflects their willingness to do so. One of the most admired, and the prime model of such compositions, is *Pierrot Lunaire*.

We may say that music consists of: (1) notation; (2) the score, the entire ensemble of notes, plus expressive indications; (3) a more or less exact translation of the notation into sounds; and (4) what the listener hears. Each of these, however anyone may insist otherwise, is a variable. Notation may be by other means than musical notes; a score may not exist. Even a performance by electronic means will vary with the equipment and acoustics.

The odd fact is that while most composers and lovers of music at the present time continue to believe that a notated composition should be performed exactly to the composer's notation and instructions, they question the musical worth of an electronic composition which dispenses with a live performer's interpretation. Is the beauty of a musical performance to be scored negatively, like that of a diving or gymnastic contest, according to the performer's errors?

Composers have written puzzle-canons in musical notation without consideration of the sound as music, because they did not intend that the canons should be performed. Schoenberg wrote a number of these; some are in performance "interesting" and some very beautiful. Notation as an art can exist without sound, as handwriting can be an art apart from its message, or a graphic musical score may be exhibited as a visual work of art. Music as an art exists to be realized in sound and silence.

Silence can be musical. Silence plus one note can be musical, but one note is not music. The most primitive music consists of at least two sounds in rhythmic relationship. Notation thus implies rhythm, and rhythm depends on dynamics (relative volume and timbre), which notation can but approximately indicate. A new notation to provide for these is possible. In a score for computer the composer must control each of these variables by writing out exact instructions. Even "indeterminacy" must be programmed in advance. The machine will not think for him like a musician; it will do only what he tells it to do. Is it desirable that an orchestra or a soloist should reproduce a score with a computer's exactness?

A note is, by contemporary agreement, the sign for a particular sound. With the continual rising of musical pitch during the nineteenth and twentieth centuries, a note written by Mozart will be played and heard today at a pitch perhaps a half-step higher than Mozart intended: in Mozart's ears it would be another note, the wrong one. The disparity is enough to intensify the brilliance of the note when played by a string instrument or sung, because the string will be more taut and the voice strained to rise higher, and the sonority will be correspondingly lessened. We give no thought to such disparity, which would assuredly have brought sharp protest from Mozart.

We perform today in equal temperament music meant to be heard with different pitch relationships in just intonation, or meantone or well-tempered tuning, and give no thought to the distinct changes in intervallic relationships and consequently in harmony which result. It is as if we played these compositions on a mistuned instrument. An eighteenth century musician hearing such performance would be convinced that we think music only in terms of notation regardless of its sound. (We may soon be able to record and perform Bach fugues and Beethoven sonatas by computer, adjusting the intervals to acoustically correct relationships not obtainable with a twelve-note keyboard. Some string quartets claim to do this at the present time. Would Bach and Beethoven prefer it?)

Even when playing older music on the correct archaic instruments, as many now do, we customarily tune these instruments to our higher concert pitch and equal temperament, so that the instruments no longer sound with their natural voices. The vocal *tessitura* of Beethoven's *Ode to Joy* is as high as Beethoven could risk; we force it still higher. Because we pay no attention to the rhythmic conventions, the eighteenth century musician would be doubly convinced that we think music only in terms of its exact notation, with no sense of the correct rhythm. (The same thing is already happening in our "musicological jazz.")

We accept as consonances or permissible dissonances such discords as the eighteenth century musician took care to avoid, calling them "the Wolf." Indeed, many composers seem to have lost understanding of the difference between dissonance and discord. Our extreme inconsistency of intonation leaves many notes and intervals in doubt. A great composer and a great instrumentalist have each complained to me: "Our orchestras today sound like mud." For an ear sharpened by the microtonal distinctions of electronic and noise music the confused spread of intonation in ordinary orchestral playing can be distressing.

A note is consequently, at the present time, the sign for an arbitrary pitch, generally agreed to be correct when produced by a well-tuned piano (unless originally for harpsichord, in which case a majority of the overtones will have been lost), less accurate when produced by a string instrument, and no more than approximate when produced by the thick, heavily wound lower bass strings of a piano, or a string bass or a tuba. A note differs also according to the timbre or overtone pattern, attack, decay, etc. (the *sound envelope*) of the instrument which sounds it.

Correct pitch or intonation is not the ultimate consideration. To play a melody as they believe it should be heard, musicians deviate above or below the correct pitches, if the instrument permits, with the result that voice or violin often do not sound the same pitches as an accompanying piano; the player alters the exact fall of the notes to shape a melodic rhythm by degrees which our notation cannot indicate. The rhythm of a melodic passage played on organ or harpsichord will need to be articulated by a more decided differentiation in the time-span of intervals notated as alike than when the same passage is played on a piano, because the organ and harpsichord cannot provide the dynamic shaping of piano tone. That is why the altered rhythm of eighteenth century organ and harpsichord music changed to the dynamically shaped rhythm of nineteenth century piano music, revising completely the fundamentals of musical interpretation.

Stravinsky wrote the keyboard obbligato of his opera *The Rake's Progress* to be played on a harpsichord, because of his pleasure in the sound of that instrument, but in piano style. He told me that he had at last solved the problem of balance by doubling the keyboard parts at the octave—thus creating in effect an instrumental quality which belongs neither to harpsichord nor to piano. Several composers, among them Frank Martin and Elliott Carter, have written concerto-type compositions for contrasting solo harpsichord and solo piano, after the example of C. P. E. Bach's concertos for the two instruments. Bach's harpsichord and piano sounded very nearly in the same volume and register, focusing the stylistic differences between the two instruments, which shape and color every phrase. In the works by Martin and Carter the disparity in volume and register between a large modern harpsichord and a large modern piano are very great, but the stylistic distinction has been lost; the contrasting sound of the two instruments, however well managed, is too often obscured—certainly in a large concert hall—by the lack of balance. Amplifying a harpsichord by electronic means to increase the volume distorts the tone quality. We are so accustomed to amplifying records of harpsichord music beyond the normal sounding of the instrument that many do not recognize the distinction, but a good harpsichordist knows it: a strident brilliance replaces the natural coloring of the intonation. The question arises: Does the modern composer of an ensemble work including harpsichord intend that the harpsichord tone should be amplified, and that the consequent brilliance, unnatural to the instrument but not to our contemporary hearing, should be its *correct* intonation for his composition?

Ivor Darreg in Los Angeles has built a steel-strung clavichord, with iron and steel tangents, and electronic pickup at three different sounding-points on each string, like the different pluck-ing-points of a harpsichord. These give a timbre resembling that of a clavichord, a second timbre approximating that of an early piano, and a third related to the timbre of a clarinet. The instrument retains useful characteristics of the clavichord, for example the vibrato; it permits a variety of coloration and control of individual tones which, if developed, could make it an ade-quate foil for a concert grand piano, whereas a true clavichord would be inaudible. Lou Harrison has adapted the so-called *tack piano,* having thumbtacks in its hammers, used sometimes as a homemade substitute for a harpsichord, to furnish a new quality of pitched percussive tone which he has used with notable effectiveness in several compositions.

In the music of Webern and much of Stravinsky the field of force of a single note in relation to the other notes around it may be decisive. In Schoenberg's music and in Alban Berg's a note is usually decisive not for itself alone but because of its place within a larger melodic pattern of intervals; the field, as in J. S. Bach's music, is that of the entire melody, the melodic consistency remaining coherent, with a unified texture of continual melodic, not analytic, variation. (Compare Webern's little pieces for violin and for cello with piano and Berg's pieces for clarinet and piano or Schoenberg's piano pieces, opus 19.) With Bartók, the field of force of the single note diminishes as the melody enlarges, but Bartók will often contrast this melodic tonal expansion against a single tone constantly reiterated; analytic variation of the melody by the addition of new notes and percussive sounds embroiders the contrast. In Messiaen's music a group of notes does the work of a note, the field of force of the single note being so much the less decisive. In several of Henry Cowell's youthful compositions and some of Bartók's middle period, as well as in earlier instances by Ives, a *tone-cluster* (an extraharmonic clump of notes sounded by fingers, fists, or forearm, or in the *Hawthorne* movement of the Ives *Concord Sonata* by a fourteen-inch rule) may do the work of a note; the harmonic field of force will be increased, but not the fineness of discrimination.

John Cage demonstrated with his compositions for *prepared piano* (screws, bolts, nuts, rubber strips, or other objects placed at measured points between the strings sounded by some keys of a piano, altering the pitch and timbre) that a note (as written) may be read as instruction to strike a certain key of the piano keyboard, the sign having no other relation to the quite unexpected tone (pitch and type of sound) the instrument may produce, transforming the piano into a percussive instrument of microtonal variability. Lou Harrison in one work indicates by notation the identity of the note and by a mathematical figure above it the exact pitch frequency he wishes. Partch frequently notates in this manner.

A note intended to be played by a percussive sound-producer of indefinite pitch may have a distinct timbre like a snare drum, or an indeterminate clangor like a cowbell, a thump or thud like a bass drum, or a knock. The snare drum functions as a solo instrument in Ives's *Putnam's Camp* for orchestra and Lou Harrison's *Song of Queztecoatl* for percussion group. Cage and Ben Johnston have composed interesting works made of the various timbres to be obtained by knocking on the piano frame or strings.

Stravinsky employed a battery of indeterminate sound-producers with the four pianos in *The Wedding;* the rich spread of imprecisely focused pitches accentuates the polytonal motor of the pianos, creating by simple means a consistency of sound-atmosphere which colors the dramatic variety of vocal styles. The great tapestries of abstract instrumental and percussive sound which Edgard Varèse created divorced still farther the expected sound from the notated sign. Cowell, Milhaud, Gerald Strang, Carlos Chávez, and other composers explored in various ways the tonal freedom of such percussive media, with and without instruments of determinate pitch.

In the later 1930s, John Cage, with Lou Harrison and William Russell, created a new extratonal percussion orchestra and a percussion literature, strongly influenced at the start by the Indonesian *gamelan* orchestra and by the melodic-rhythmic proportions (*raga* and *tala*) of Indian music. Harrison composed a large number of percussion pieces in an increasingly melodic and polyphonic style, the intervals relative to the arbitrary pitches and timbres of the sound-producers. Among these are a Concerto for violin and a wide range of percussion including flowerpots, one-pound coffee cans, and metal bucket, and *Concerto in Slendro* (a five-note scale) for violin with two tack pianos, celesta, tympani, and two garbage pails. The seemingly arbitrary and unmusical sound-producing objects become, in these settings, distinctly musical, each unusual timbre exerting a distinguishable field of force. Percussion groups playing the percussion literature now exist in several universities and cities; and composers are steadily adding new compositions.

After these developments, it is only going a step farther to substitute for the twelve–note scale any microtonal scale or pattern of intervals, or any note or tone-cluster selected by chance means (as in Cage's *Music of Changes* for piano—the name and the idea are from the Chinese *Book of Changes, I Ching*), or indeed any sound or noise, however indeterminately arrived at or produced, for an instrumental tone. Substitute words for notes, and there is a lecture; substitute actions, and the result is *theatrical-performance music*.

Nothing is wrong with these substitutions, except the temporary incapacity or unwillingness of the audience to accept them.

The consequences of these logical decisions, resulting from no arbitrary waywardness but inherent in the current evolution of music, as I have tried to demonstrate, are rapidly changing our conception of music as an art, while increasing our skill to use sound musically and our knowledge of its creative potentialities.

During the present century, musical notation, as a result of the composers' efforts to adapt it to a continually changing and enlarging scope and opportunity of music, has been constantly adopting more refined and elaborate and also cruder means, depending on what the composer expects of the performer. If the composer looks to the performer for an exact reproduction of his notated message—the notated composition is not in reality the music but an instructive message to the performer telling him what to do—the composer is hampered by the inadequacy of any notational convention to convey his message in sufficient detail. Paraphrasing a statement by Roger Reynolds: Interest in the independence of sounds (their right to a full life and freedom of individual movement) is the cause of many notational problems: free pitch-alteration in time; differing and changing tempo references for each voice; decay times of sounding units made up of instruments having different modes and periods of attack and decay (this is most crucial and difficult). The effort to resolve these problems is clearly evident in Reynolds's beautifully notated scores, each desired effect carefully but economically described.

Some composers (among them Morton Feldman, Christian Wolff, Karlheinz Stockhausen, Earle Brown, Bo Nilsson, Sylvano

Bussotti, Morton Subotnick), but not in all compositions, provide merely a rough chart of their intentions, leaving it to the performer to decide the specific interpretation, or the assembling of parts, or the order and grouping of the notes, or the types and kinds of sounds. The resulting composition is both new and old, since it revives for example the Italian white-note convention or the jazz convention, where the notation serves for the basis of an improvisation, the player supplying by choice out of an agreed idiom the notes or sounds he performs. In such case, notation will be diagrammatic or graphic; a large quantity of such music, substituting actual graphs or diagrams for much or all of the notation, is already in existence. The permanent value of such music, as much as survives, will be comparable with that of a white-note keyboard composition by Alessandro Scarlatti (which scarcely anyone at present can perform correctly), or a written composition by one of the already historic jazz composers who didn't expect his music to be played like it looks, or of any ensemble music requiring realization of the continuo accompaniment (for which players today substitute common chords and passing notes).

J. S. Bach and Schoenberg held in disdain any "keyboard-rider" who composed at the piano. Wagner's Bechstein piano held a writing desk, and Stravinsky unabashedly composes at the keyboard. L. M. Gottschalk admired Beethoven's orchestral compositions but not his piano sonatas, which in Gottschalk's opinion lacked the modern refinements of piano playing added by Liszt, Thalberg, and himself. Gottschalk held in low esteem any mere performer of other men's music, if he did not also improvise, compose, and vary his compositions in performance. As to that opinion, J. S. Bach, Mozart, and Beethoven would have agreed with him. But Mozart despised in Clementi the type of piano playing which became the virtuosity of Liszt, Thalberg, and Gottschalk, while Chopin, who admired Liszt's piano playing, thought poorly of his compositions. David Tudor, the pianist whose creative skills and ingenuity have contributed largely to realizing the more oddly notated and unpredictable piano compositions of the last fifteen years, is a collector and profound admirer of the piano works by Gottschalk.

It is possible that generations of pianists will follow David Tudor in inventing, to the composer's indications, their own performing versions of such music by indicia as John Cage's

Winter Music, for which any sound obtainable on, in, or by means of any part of a piano is valid, the notation consisting of isolated clusters of notes in irregular location on a page; or Stockhausen's composition by assembling pages of separately notated parts; or a wide variety of compositions written out as graphs or by graphic or pictorial devices. Students may begin exploring, with a new sort of musical pleasure, combinations of game and dramatic action with musical performance, such as Robert Ashley's *Maneuvers for Small Hands* in notes, graphic indicia, and brief verbal instructions on one hundred separate cards. Roger Reynolds's *The Emperor of Ice Cream* dramatizes a choral and instrumental performance of Wallace Stevens's poem with pistol shot, bursting paper bag, graphic indicia, and variously written sizes of verbal text, as well as notes. Malcolm Goldstein graphs a vocal score by the rise and fall, size, and visible convolutions of the handwritten text, the vocal pitches rising and falling indeterminately with the graphic line within the normal vocal span.

The argument does not by any means all run in one direction. The goal is not total or anarchic freedom. Earle Brown came to music through the mobiles of Alexander Calder, the later paintings of Jackson Pollock, and the writings of Gertrude Stein. Brown writes: "The greatest single misinterpretation of our time is the general feeling that my kind of work is intended to be 'free' of art, choice, responsibility, beauty, form, content, or *anything*. From the very beginning I have been attempting to intensify and expand the composition-performance potential of responsible, sensitive, contextual, human-artistic *choice*, choosing within an intentionally ambiguous environment of generalized potential, on the basis of the given 'programme' and the 'feed-back' effect inherent in human awareness, spontaneity, memory, accepting, rejecting, liking, disliking, and just plain activity in relation to the particular materials I have given and the alternatives I have permitted in each composition.

". . . One does not diminish the amount of 'meaningful' control within a work but seeks to create the work as an entity, a quasi-organism, and to 'programme' a life for it within which it comes to find its shape, extensions of meaningfulness, and its multiple formal identities of its basic nature [composed] through its programme of process potential."[3]

Is the performer, after he has assembled and completed his

performing version, or worked out the graphic instructions, the real composer? If so, David Tudor is one of the most potent composers of the new era of sound. One man serving many different composers, he asserted and reiterated the new possibility, transforming the perishable nature of incompletely specified musical intention to give it validity. But Tudor, like most of those who perform this music, still credits the composition as the work of the composer. Say rather that the composer creates new opportunities for the performer, instead of the customary final statement of his idea completely predetermined in notation, and the performer in turn shares what he has accomplished with his audience. This is the significance of Cage's spontaneous reply, "Composing's one thing, performing's another, listening's a third. What can they have to do with one another?" The creative-imaginative opportunity is distributed among all participants.

Composers, that is to say, are breaking down the three components of the esthetic experience as we have known it, composition, performance, audience reception, into an indefinite number of distinct experiences. Instead of the notated composition as a completed structure or texture, there may be a succession of individual or composite sounds heard each for itself. Cage writes of his audibly radical String Quartet: "The composition, a melodic line without accompaniment, employs single tones, intervals, triads, and aggregates requiring one or more of the instruments for their production. These constitute a gamut of sounds." An earlier example is Cage's *Suite for Toy Piano,* using a gamut of nine somewhat arbitrarily pitched tones. The melodic consistency of the tone-row, which Cage had rejected, is replaced by an indeterminate consistency of notated tones. When the line ceases to be melodic, does it cease to be a consistency? At what extreme does this occur?

Cage tells us: "A sound does not view itself as thought, as ought, as needing another sound for its elucidation, as etc.; it has no time for any consideration—it is occupied with the performance of its characteristics: before it has died away it must have made perfectly exact its frequency, its loudness, its length, its overtone structure, the precise morphology of these and of itself."[4] A sound therefore need not be melodic; it may be still a note or a combination of notes; it may be, instead, a sound which is not a note: a noise, a scrape, a spoken word, an electronically generated or altered pitch or noise, anything indeed which can be heard, or a silence which not being heard is musically resonant or filled with chance sound-events.

On one occasion when I was listening to such a composed, prepared, enacted silence, during a concert given in a small church, the silence was filled from outside the hall, too eloquently, with the songs of mockingbirds.

Cage's *Concert for Piano and Orchestra* consists of: a piano composition of separate sheets to be assembled by the pianist, which may be heard alone; an orchestral composition of instrumental parts (nonconsecutive figures on separate sheets, to be played in any order), which is to be performed according to predetermined rules by an indeterminate number of musicians, preferably at least twelve or as many as a full orchestra; an aria for vocal soloist (a variety of voice techniques in five languages and eleven styles from coloratura song to barking dog) which may be performed separately accompanied by the taped composition, *Fontana Mix,* both or either of which may be included in the *Concert:* the length of the performance is indeterminate, to be decided in advance of the occasions. One sees that the work when fully assembled is indeed more like a concert than a concerto.

The resulting auditory complex is no more complicated, if listened to quietly and without dismay, than traffic at a busy street corner, where more different things may be expected to be going on at one time than at another; where the volume and direction of the sound alter with each change of traffic lights (marking chronological time, as in Cage's *Concert,* instead of metrical time as in Beethoven); where all events are indeterminate in arrangement but determined by the shape of traffic flow; and the cop at the corner knows the score but does not direct the play.

Such a composition is a rational extension of Schoenberg's "picture-puzzle" . . . in "deadly earnest." However elaborate the choices he provides, Cage, like Schoenberg, "cannot allow any will but mine to prevail . . . because the composing was done just that way." The *Concert* is a completely ordered and structured formal composition, the ordering and structure determined in detail by indeterminate means. Cage knows when the musicians play wrong notes or disobey his instructions; he knows when the composition has been well or incompetently played.

Oh but! one may exclaim, this is farce, satire, parody, not

music, antimusic! Pierre Boulez said to me that after the pieces for prepared piano Cage went "outside the musical continuum." (Stravinsky had said, apropos of Boulez's discontinuous *Polyphony X*, that music cannot exist without continuity.) Boulez's criticism resembles Hindemith's complaint that the tone-row destroys the sense of musical space by denying the gravitational uprightness of harmony. Quite true, one might reply. That's what it does. To emphasize his point, Boulez rapped on the wood frame of the piano. Cage wrote his *Wonderful Widow of Eighteen Springs* (text from James Joyce's *Finnegans Wake*) with accompaniment of knocking by fingers and knuckles on the piano frame, a highly sophisticated primitive music.

"Is it," in Wittgenstein's words, "a mere question of pleasing and ugly?" That is an argument the critic by polemic seldom wins. (Such criticism exposes the inadequacy of the critic but not the inadequacy of the work which is his subject.) Though the intrusion of indeterminacy in both composition and performance may seem to deny the facts of order and structure, it does not really do so, since the resulting performance, however different on each occasion, will be ordered by the rules of the game—as gamblers play by strict rules—, the composite structure is clearly stated, and the composition presents itself in terms subject to exact description, as much as a game of chess or football or a yacht race.

Cage's descriptions of his works, in the catalogue published by C. F. Peters, are, in each instance, or unexceptionable lucidity, overcoming the difficulty of putting "indefiniteness, correctly and unfalsified, into words." The compositions, so stated, are not indefinite, not haphazard, not nonsense, and therefore, unavoidably, compositions. Anyone may concede that much, as of Beethoven's *Great Fugue*, and still dislike the music. But it is very unwise if, disliking the music, one explains that Beethoven could do no better because he was deaf.

A haphazard noncomposition may exist; musical literature is crowded with haphazard compositions in traditional idiom and formal layout, which have no validity except habitual practice. A *happening* is one name for a haphazard noncomposition; happenings are, generally, inadequate noncompositions seeking a false justification in disorder, though some may be amusing. Anarchy, however plausible in generalities, fails too often in the instance.

How to distinguish the one from the other? How distinguish a good from a bad fugue? Creative activity does not offer its products for the purpose of enabling critics to sort them into good, mediocre, or bad. The generation of composers from Debussy to Stravinsky—except Ives—believed in the created composition as an absolute and labored to make it so; the present generation has been much influenced by the improvisatory practice of jazz, in which the performance is relative to the occasion and to the skills of the participants. In this way perhaps more than any other, true jazz has influenced the most seriously composed music. Between, there is a broad area of fully composed music which seeks to convey, with more determinate order, the freedom of jazz improvisation—for an example, *All Set* by Milton Babbitt.

The determinate-indeterminate composition, determinate in conception but indeterminate in execution, or designed to impede or distract the audience from grasping it as a unit, has come into full existence. Causality has not been excluded but made indefinite in time-sequence. A computer can carry such invention much farther, but the broad band of causality in time-sequence has not been done away with; it still begins with the composer and proceeds to the performance.

The proof of the notation is in the reading. Most of the notational systems which are being devised and experimentally tried today are too complex to be practical, too individual or specialized to be of general application, and inadequate to serve the composer's needs. Abundant performance has proved that Cage's notational systems, though specialized each to its occasion, do not impede performance and may present modifiable types, capable of wider application; these have been widely and variously imitated.

The established system of twelve notes in the octave is being pulled out of orbit by the new potentiality of sound. (It is still of course perfectly reasonable to compose twelve-note music with a twelve-note octave in any appropriate style.) The technical inconvenience of the established body of instruments (a much smaller number than the thirty-five families of instruments which were counted during the fourteenth century in the music room of Rheims Cathedral), to which a musician may devote a life's labor yet never graduate from a back seat in the orchestra, is already resulting in a scarcity of professional string players, with a corresponding increase in the number of amateur orchestras across the American continent. The instrumentalist does not cease to be a lover of music or wish, any more than in the past, to cease playing his instrument; he chooses to play for pleasure, according to the degree of skill he can maintain without great effort, and has no desire to make his living by this means. The symphony orchestra as we have known it, in which a few musicians play all the solos while the remainder drudge through season after season of unenlightening routine, may give way to amateur orchestras, in which the back-seat player can take part to the best of his ability, and to smaller groups in which all the players are skilled soloists. (One amateur orchestra, the St. Louis Philharmonic, has been in existence since 1860; the members pay a small fee for the privilege of playing and give four concerts a year.)

At this point music-lovers become frightened: What shall we do to preserve our high standards of performance, our Beethoven, our Brahms, our Berlioz, our operas, our ballets, our beloved symphonic and solo repertory? Are our standards really so high, or are they merely rigid? Do players in large orchestras play at all times to the best of their ability, right through to the back seats, or as slackly as they can get away with? In updating our repertory, as we do in any case periodically, do we lose more than we gain?

The change will be gradual, and our ears and minds will make it by necessity—no use worrying about it. The symphony orchestra will not disappear tomorrow; the opera will be around for quite a while. Only a small part of the audience has learned to appreciate the higher skills and standards of soloistic playing in chamber music. But the change is occurring. The ballet is changing already under the influence of contemporary dance, the new dance art created in this century by American women from Isadora Duncan and Maud Allan to Martha Graham, influenced again from abroad by Mary Wigman and combining with the more traditional European dance from Pavlova to George Balanchine. It is an art not of soloists and a great, static *corps de ballet* but of individual dancers in well-led cooperative groups, a model of what is also happening around us in music. Connoisseurs and dilettantes are always afraid of what they may be losing, devoting themselves to perpetuating the past instead of looking about to discover what is coming to pass.

Temporary certainties vanish. Medieval and Renaissance music, using a notation we read but do not correctly interpret, is

being rediscovered, widening and increasing our musical awareness, contributing to the fresh creative synthesis that is already
occurring, not a Hegelian but a revolutionary synthesis. Oriental,
Indian, Indonesian, African music, of many periods and kinds;
the cumulative influence of our recent perception of the true
nature of folk music; the new experimental music of Europe
which responds to the American experimental tradition; the
music now coming out of Central and South America and from
the Caribbean countries: all these contributions to fresh modes of
conceiving and of hearing music are coming together like a great
wave gathering, urging music forward.

Technical problems, notation among them, will solve themselves as the new musical period we have entered, like it or not,
gains impetus. We are at the inception of a new musical orientation, like the change from polyphony to harmony at the start of
the seventeenth century, with new content, new idioms, new
styles, new instruments, and new routines, combined with new
experiences that will sharpen and increase our musical perception. Amateur musicians may again become as skilled as the
amateur singers and instrumentalists of the madrigal period. Our
pleasure in music is our ability to share in it; skills of performance
follow the composer but often begin with the rise to prominence
of a new instrument: the organ, the violin, the computer. Comprehension follows listening. This is an extraordinary time in an
art which by custom and habituation clings to its traditions.
Today as never before, certainly not since the later sixteenth
century, tradition is being reassessed and much of it rejected.
Composers are trying out new, expedient means to catch an
inspiration. And in some cases, to judge by the technical literature, the importance of the means seems to be greater than that
of the inspiration. In Charles Ives's words, "manner breeds a
cussed cleverness."

26

"EVERYTHING IS ADMISSIBLE"

"It appears, then, finally, that the actual basis of harmonic music is extremely limited, consisting of concords and their inversions, and at best not more than a few minor sevenths and major and minor ninths; and on this basis the art of modern music is constructed by devices and principles which are either intellectually conceived or are the fruit of highly developed musical instinct, which is, according to vulgar phrase, 'inspired,' and thereby discovers truths at a single leap which the rest of the world recognise as evidently the result of so complex a generalisation that they are unable to imagine how it was done, and therefore apply to it the useful term 'inspiration.' But in every case, if a novelty is well based, it must answer to verification, and the verification is to be obtained only by intellectual analysis, which in fact may not at first be able to cope with it. Finally, everything is admissible which is intellectually verifiable, and what is inadmissible is so relatively only.

". . . The history of harmony is the history of ever-increasing richness of combination, from the use, first, of simple consonances, then of consonances superimposed on one another, which we call common chords, and of a few discords simply contrived; then of a system of classification of these concords and discords by key-relationship, which enables some of them to be used with greater freedom than formerly; then of the use of combinations which were especially familiar as analogues to essential chords; then of enlargement of the bounds of the keys, so that a greater number and variety of chords could be used in relation to one another; and finally of the recognition of the principle that harmony is the result of combined melodies, through the treatment of the progressions of which the limits of combination become practically co-extensive with the number of notes in the musical system."

If musicians had thoroughly understood this statement by C. H. H. Parry in the article "Harmony" of the 1906 edition of *Grove's Dictionary*, Debussy's dismissal of customary harmonic practice would have caused no serious confusion, Scriabin's harmonic premise would have seemed a slight matter, and Schoenberg would not have needed to proclaim the emancipation of the dissonance. There would have been no despairing, ignorant cries that Schoenberg or some other composer was "destroying music," there would be little of the argumentative critical nonsense about such details that appears in reviews and criticisms even today, but instead an awareness that music for a long time has been building a larger commonwealth around the no longer restrictive boundaries of the harmonic system.

Furthermore, if "the limits of combination become practically co-extensive with the number of notes in the musical system," it follows that these limits are able to be expanded by the addition of notes in an increasingly microtonal system, whether quarter-tones (twenty-four-note scale) or fifth-tones (thirty-one-note scale) or any other subdivision of intervals within the octave; and by notes of indeterminate pitch, and consequently by any sounds or noises, as well as actions.

The entire field of sound is thus accessible as a musical system, and Charles Ives was the first composer to grasp that fact. I doubt that he had it in mind as a technical premise.

"In many of the medieval ecclesiastical scales," Parry explained in the article "Leading Note," in the same edition of *Grove's Dictionary*, ". . . the note immediately below the tonic was separated from it by the interval of a whole tone, and therefore had none of the character of a leading note; but as the feeling for tonality gained ground in the Middle Ages . . . the use of the leading note, which is so vital to its comprehension, became more common. Ecclesiastics looked upon this tampering with the august scales of antiquity with disfavor, and Pope John XXII passed an edict against it in 1322; consequently the accidental which indicated it was omitted in the written music; but the feeling of musicians was in many cases too strong to be suppressed, and the performers habitually sang it, wherever the sense of the context demanded it. . . ."

So that, as W. S. Rockstro proceeds in the article "Tetrachord": "The natural craving of the refined musical ear for a leading note led, first, to the general employment of a recognized system of accidental sounds; and in process of time to the unrestricted use of the Aeolian and Ionian modes—the prototypes of our major and minor scales. These changes naturally prepared the way for the unprepared dissonances of Monteverde; and, with the introduction of these, the old system was suddenly brought to an end, and our present tonality firmly established upon its ruins."

Today, a still larger commonwealth of music, as we see it in course of formulation and construction, is rising upon the ruins of the harmonic system.

The "natural craving of the refined ear for a leading note" had driven musicians to the practice of *musica ficta*, the insertion of the leading note at the correct pitch by the performer—to avoid writing it in defiance of the papal edict—, a habit taken for granted by true folksong. When the leading note came at last to be written, composers had no alternative but to write it either a half-step or a whole-step below the final note, this being seldom the correct pitch at which it should be sounded. Folksingers could carry on their uninhibited natural habit, players of flexibly pitched instruments might still correct the difference, but keyboard players could not; when the keyboard replaced the voice as the arbiter of musical sound, the notated pitch replaced the correct acoustical pitch. As a result, the leading note became a dissonance intellectually implying close, while ceasing to lead by natural melodic sequence to that conclusion. The now invariably discordant leading tone was accepted as a dissonance, which, when heard, implies resolution. For this reason much music by Anton Webern sounds to an innocent ear more consonant than music by other composers which is actually less dissonant; the innocent ear *hears* a resolution which does not occur and by habit, unconsciously, resolves it.

But in some musicians, the "natural craving of the refined ear" is not satisfied when it encounters a wrong note (by notation or intonation) leading to a right conclusion. The desire for a correct intonation, in this as in other instances, brought about a long search for a temperament which would most nearly give what was missing: for two hundred years the meantone temperament, and for a short while the well-tempered modification of meantone, came nearest to supplying it.

The change to equal temperament supplanted a partially correct scale (in acoustical relationship) with a totally incorrect one, except the just interval of the octave. To be musical meant now, in Schoenberg's concise statement, "to have an ear in the *musical* sense, not in the *natural* sense. A musical ear must have assimilated the tempered scale. And a singer who produces natural pitches is unmusical." As Schoenberg meant it, the statement is correct: music had become an art of arbitrarily pitched tones with certain definite consequences; the acoustical relationship of tones and even the previously accepted key-relationships had been replaced by a system of tones "related only to one another."

Schoenberg did not disregard the acoustical problem; indeed, as I learned in conversation with him, he was fully aware of it. Mahler had spoken to him, he told me, of the great loss music had sustained by the change from meantone to equal temperament. Schoenberg's correspondence includes several letters written in reply to challenges by advocates of just intonation, who believed, like Lou Harrison, that with all harmony reduced to a single key of the twelve tones one should go farther and retune the intervals to their correct acoustical relationships. Schoenberg denied this, pointing to his statement in the *Harmonielehre* that dissonances are "those relations which are more remote" and that dissonance is today as comprehensible as consonance. Schoenberg's dissonance in its melodic context, unlike Webern's, seldom implies resolution.

The broader the texture of melodic consistency from simple to extremely complex relationship, the more easily the music will assimilate the acoustical extremes, from octaves (just intonation), fifths and triads (relatively concordant or consonant harmonies), to unprepared dissonances, discords, and noise. By eliminating the more simply consonant relationships Webern narrowed the texture of melodic consistency, so that his music could not sustain itself at any length. The serial composers of the 1950s and 1960s, following this pattern, tried to support at greater length larger consistencies made up almost entirely of dissonance and discord. The lack of simpler, or sweeter, relationships to balance these sour extremes forced them to the use of such sweet-sounding instruments as the vibraphone, an inadequate solution.

Working from the other extreme, the acoustical richness of noise provides a broad, indeterminate band of textural consistency which easily assimilates discord, as some composers have been discovering by exploration and experiment.

To comprehend what is happening in music today, one must give equal attention to every area of the field of sound. Composers can no longer rely on thinking the notation or reading the score but must recapture the exact experience of sound across the entire field. But the fact that an exceptional imagination can anticipate previously untried and exceedingly complex mixtures is proved by the repeated effectiveness of large and small works by Ives when these have come eventually to performance. Critical listeners will usually agree: We don't know how he does it, but the music sounds.

With the score a skilled musician thinks the notation, not as a substitute for musical sound but as the self-existent, fully conceived composition. As Schoenberg wrote: "A real composer conceives his ideas, his entire music, in his mind, in his imagination, and he does not need an instrument." In composing by computer such knowledge of the exact significance of the sign as it will be realized in sound is still important, but the sign is changed; a great amount of exploration throughout the field of sound will be necessary before the potentialities of the new instrument can be adequately realized by the composer's ability to imagine the immense variety and variability of sounds able to be invented.

Schoenberg saw no need for any series of intervals smaller than those of "our own scale." Reading his several letters on the subject of justly tuned, microtonal, or other alternative scales, one might think him as intractable as Pope John XXII. In reality he was conversant with other possibilities and willing to discuss them; he simply did not agree that they were needed. At our last meeting I asked him about his disciples and students. In reply, he spoke only of John Cage, without any prompting and indeed to my astonishment, since Cage had ceased studying with him rather abruptly and had strongly and publicly criticized the twelve-tone method. Schoenberg said of Cage: "He is not a composer, but an inventor—of genius." The statement summarizes in few words Schoenberg's awareness of what had been happening in and to music during the last decade of his life.

Anyone who has heard music sung in just intonation will be inclined to question that the production of natural pitches is unmusical. But Aafje Heynis, a Netherlands singer who performs with great beauty in just intonation, singing when I heard her Hebridean folksongs and Psalms especially written to be sung unaccompanied in just intonation, was careful to qualify my praise for her accomplishment: "When I sing Schubert, I sing like the piano." That is correct, too, and the skill to do both doubly to be admired.

Some theorists from Helmholtz to the present day have argued that just intonation is the natural manner in which intervals are heard, and I have been given experienced assurance that one can produce these intervals accurately with comparative ease, whereas it is difficult to sing accurately the intervals of equal temperament. Today a number of composers are experimenting with the revival of just intonation.

The three most satisfactory systems are, on the evidence: twelve-tone just intonation—or on fixed-pitch instruments, just temperament—(with a great literature from the polyphonic period, as well as an increasing amount by present-day composers); the thirty-one-tone equal temperament of Huyghens, revived by Adriaan Fokker (for which several Dutch composers, notably Henk Badings, have created a small literature); and the forty-three-tone unequal-intervalled just intonation of Harry Partch (with the rich panoply of instruments and compositions he has created in total independence of habituation and convention). By tuning a piano to correct twelve-tone intonation choral conductors could easily re-create the early choral polyphony in its true sonority and coloration; recognizing and adjusting the mutable intervals, to avoid discords, would not require great musicianship. The medieval Pythagorean intonation, with correct fifths and wide thirds, is easier to tune on an instrument and not more difficult to sing than equal temperament; correct intonation would brighten the presently drab sound of medieval music.

It is reasonable to predict that the current extension of music beyond the extremes of dissonance into discord, arbitrary pitches, and noise will before long be offset by a corresponding revival of just intonation and simple consonance, bringing into use the entire field of sound.

Many musicians discount the significance of the history of tuning, in both Western and Asiatic music, as a guide to what is happening in music today; their foresight in this respect is as short as their hindsight, since it should be obvious that nearly all the world's melody until the present time has originated in one or another scale of unequal intervals or some recognized series of arbitrarily related extratonal pitches. A scale or mode of unequal intervals exists as a melodic form. An equal tempered scale is not in itself melodic, all intervals being the same, though melody can be made of its harmonic components, as Western musicians have been doing for 150 years, and the scale can be twisted to provide motival rows, as in twelve-tone and serial composition.

With the ending of the period of harmony, composers are exploring three principal types of melody: the atonal row figure, of any number of notes, replacing the conventional harmonic figure; the purely melodic mode (after medieval or Oriental practice, or in twelve-tone or microtonal just intonation) harmonized only by its own melodic consistency; and the melody of unequal intervals or of arbitrary, indeterminate, or unpredictable intervals between arbitrary and unpredictable sounds. One may question whether, if the sounds and intervals are consistently unpredictable, the resulting succession of events can be melodic, yet an increasing number of composers believe that listeners are capable of recognizing such melody in considerable extension, with or without repetition. The melodic effectiveness of this method of composing, in more extreme examples, has yet to be proved to general satisfaction. Certainly few listeners today, however willing, are capable of it.

Many composers at present actively reject any type of approximately fixed or determinable rhythm. The negative term *arhythmic* has taken on a positive character, as the term *atonal* did fifty years earlier; it is a convenience designating a new state of affairs. *Atonality* did not deny that a tone has certain fixed characteristics but indicated that these characteristics belong to the tone itself, apart from any harmonic or enharmonic relations. Schoenberg, although he had precipitated the musical conditions which gave meaning to the term, never accepted "so-called atonality" but insisted, with a slightly different emphasis than Stravinsky (see page 207) that any music in tones is tonal.

In the same way it is possible to claim that where a melody can be discerned rhythm must be present. One can claim, too, as a point of style, that a music without detectable rhythm would be merely spastic or inert, resembling the condition of certain types of "officialese," a deliberately formalized style meant to be scanned quickly but not read; the lumps and gobbets of accustomed terminology disappear into a kind of mental *potage du jour* of insignificant flavor, in which float the few items of particularizing information which the mind therefore immediately discerns. For the ordinary reader of prose, even journalese, which at its worst retains some effect of verbal rhythm and is translated by thought into a simulacrum of audible speech, officialese will be almost impossible to read, deadly and opaque; a skilled official can scan it at high speed, extracting the particularized matter, unimpeded by the mental need to translate terminology into sound. A greatly gifted mental eye, like that of the late Chief Justice Hughes, is able to leaf through a hundred pages of such matter and discern and retain all essentials, without the effort of reading. This explains the meticulously formalized composition of legal briefs.

Couperin, Schoenberg, and Ives deliberately wrote what they called musical "prose": nonmetrical melody interwoven in relatively free temporal relationships more complex than the nonmeter of operatic recitative. For a long time many persons claimed, as did John Cage (see page 304), that Schoenberg's music lacked rhythm, defining rhythm by the changing signatures and strongly metrical cross-rhythms of Stravinsky. Cage later reverted to the opposite extreme, advocating *arhythmic* composition as an advance over rhythmic composition. The position is not really well taken: it is like saying that prose is better than poetry. Scanning is a method of mental rejection of unnecessary matter. Since all matter in a work of art should be of significance, the mind does not expect to scan a work of art. And the mere statement that one's composition "rejects art" does not alter the conditions: the receiving mind will strain nonetheless to formalize all matter offered it, in the same way that it struggles melodically with the sound of dripping water or automatically phrases the ticking of a clock. The phrasing imparts a seeming temporal inequality to the equal tick. The mind will therefore try to hear or impose rhythm insofar as the composition does not actively reject rhythm; a truly arhythmic music will resemble officialese in being less comprehensible the more one tries to hear it. One can only sit back passively and let the successive sounds occur as they please. Even then the mind will be trying unconsciously to detect or impose some rhythmic order to overcome the otherwise spastic effect.

In fact, arhythmic music, like prose, accomplishes no more than the elimination of *metrical beat,* a quite acceptable condition, since beat is not a necessity of rhythm. Instead of beat, the mind will discern some sort of periodic relationship, by length, by accent, by pause, by emphasis, even by occasional silence, and the sense of *fall* determined by such means will determine the interplay of phrases. A great part of Ives's music requires such oblique cross-play of unexpected against expectable relationships. Henry Brant has composed obliquely related harmony.

To compose a music which rejects any possibility of fall or phrase is as pointless as writing bad or unreadable prose or officialese. I have watched a composer unconsciously tapping his foot in time to the seemingly arhythmic fall of Cage's *Fontana Mix.* Experiments in mathematically exact placement of sounds or tones demonstrate that the ear cannot hear unphrased sound relationships so accurately as phrased relationships.

It is always dangerous to claim that any seemingly unacceptable music is bad music or any unreadable prose bad prose; the capacity of the mind to adapt itself to new means requiring new receptive arrangements is very great. Nevertheless, melody, in however extreme form, seems to be a condition of good music as of good prose; rhythm is a determinant of melody, itself imposed by phrasing, which is, whether or not marked by beat, a division of the audible material into lengths having to do with the normal—or a well-trained—span of attention. When the presentation of material exceeds the span of attention, the mind ceases to attend actively. If the result is not inattention and consequently indifference, the effect may be either soporific and lulling or contemplative and ritualistic: in other words, to some degree *anesthetic.*

In one of LaMonte Young's "Dream Tortoises" in just intonation, one musician plays a viola that has been modified to allow the production of sound from three strings at once with equal intensity, another plays double-stops on a violin reinforced by a resonating string, while Young and his wife vocally produce other tones, in equally strict just intonation, so accurately that the resulting accumulation of tones in correct acoustical relationship gives a play of overtones and difference tones which, via loudspeaker, sounds almost orchestral. The harmonies are selected from a gamut of twenty or more tones in the octave. The over-tones and especially the difference tones must be kept in tune as accurately as the fundamentals, while being sounded loudly enough to be heard, no slight task of concentration. Nothing else happens, except the moment of impact when Young from time to time enters vocally with the lowest tone of the ensemble, having the effect of the long *Om* of Hindu ritual. On the occasion when I observed this, the small audience sat without shuffling its feet or coughing, seemingly quite relaxed. My two hours of listening paid tribute to a unique musical experience. The ritualistic self-sufficiency of such exactly produced just intonation must be heard to be believed. In sound at least, Young has got very close to a psychological nerve of ritual. Even in that case, the recurrence of the relatively short vocal intonations, however deliberately un-metrical or out of phase, does relieve attention by an intimation of phrasing.

To listen with predetermined criteria to any music which does not accept such criteria ensures esthetic defeat. But it is not true by corollary, as some wish to believe, that any rejection of any criteria will produce substantial work of art. The examples of Cage and Young show quite the contrary.

Beat is a condition not of rhythm but of performance accuracy, a point from which and a point to which rhythmic relationships can be directed, a coordinating device for group performance and, in many musical traditions, for dance. Musicians playing in the new large orchestras of Haydn, Mozart, Beethoven, and Berlioz needed a marked beat to keep them together. Harry Partch must write decided metric accents into his forty-three-tone compositions, for the convenience of musicians and vocalists, who in most cases have had no previous experience of his notation, intervallic system, or instruments; without metric accent, re-hearsal would be almost impossibly time-consuming. To complain of the beat, as some do, misses the point. Partch believes, too, that beat, however complex, is an ineradicable human and dra-matic element of music.

Ives had broken the tone-row even before it was invented by showing to what extent melodic consistency can be expanded both horizontally and vertically. The authority of Schoenberg does not depend on the tone-row but on composition, as he insisted. The search for new degrees of consistency and coherence continues on a larger scale.

Music is not the written score, nor even the sound of what is performed; music is what the mind makes by studying the notation or by the simultaneity and time-sequence of sounds while creating or while hearing them. A musical composition is what the mind immediately reconstructs of the experience from the score or while listening, and by memory the whole effect of the experience, an intellectually reconstituted esthetic consistency, which may differ in almost every way from the composer's intentions, and which may be supplemented by related and in many cases unrelated events that occur externally to the reading or performance, or by imagination or reverie. One should not critically discount or dismiss the esthetic response of the listener's imagination or reverie while listening or while remembering. In this abstract *theater of the unconscious,* with its acoustics of emotion, the mind shifting imaginatively between reaction and deliberation, between observation and dream, the final response which stands for the work is shaped. The composer's name becomes a sign for the consistency of his music, and therefore for the consistency of the musical response. Each listener will discover his own Mozart, his own Beethoven. He may also, though less easily, discover his own Byrd, his personal Alkan, the Berg or Janáček of his emotion. The adventures of a listener's progress may be as singular, as primitive, as colorful, as filled with meaning, as endearing or as vulgar as those of Alice—or of Dorothy, the Tin Woodman, the Cowardly Lion, *et al.* in the many books of Oz. And in the spiritual awakening, when that occurs, may be something of *The Pilgrim's Progress.*

The listener is the last in a series of composers, in a creative process which never ends, since the listener may be also the composer or another composer, the performer or another performer; and the music, so heard and reconstituted in his mind, re-enters the creative process.

Wagner's Symphony in C is a composite of idiomatic borrowings from composers such as Dussek and Meyerbeer, plus some noticeable thieving from Beethoven's Second Symphony. A similar composite, already recognizable in Wagner's Symphony, though formless as an abstract composition (the substance of Stravinsky's objection to the music-drama), became with the addition of text, narrative, and voices *The Flying Dutchman.* Wagner had found in his disorganized materials both the esthetic consistency of a major opera and the substance of his mature style.

For these reasons forms and styles have only a temporary

validity, and a Bach fugue, a Beethoven sonata, or a composition by Tchaikovsky, Stravinsky, or Schoenberg will have as many potentialities of form and style as there are creative listeners. In this way the revival of previously unknown older music and the discovery of music of other traditions create new music. The art of the composer is to hear and enable others to hear.

That is why composers, performers, and many listeners question what Stravinsky has called the "musical deception" of a recorded performance. Two factors are involved: the lack of effort required to hear it, and the invariability of what one hears. The recorded performance becomes in its invariable recurrence a substitute for musical thought. This is not to deny the enormous importance of recorded music as an audible library, a means of hearing music which would otherwise be out of reach.

Many devoted collectors of the old 78 rpm records, which had to be turned and restarted every four minutes, began losing interest in music with the appearance of the automatic record-turner and gave up their passionate hobby with the advent of long-playing records. The removal of effort had dissipated attention to the music. More subtly, the listener's response to the music had become one with the particular performance he owned and constantly replayed, even to the extreme of hearing the breaks between record sides as a sort of musical periodicity, each record side a distinguishable fragment of the composition. Confronted with the relatively inexpensive choice of several no longer fragmented long-playing performances of the same work, the listener returned by preference to his venerated album; knowing well that the album was *not* the composition, he was yet unable to adapt his thought of the music to another manner of performance. The same work in a live performance might still challenge his attention—though I have known a few listeners so addicted to their records that they avoided the distraction of any live performance—but the reiterative influence of the recorded album continued its destructive effect. The recorded album had become the matrix—as knowledge of the score is for some musicians—with which any new reading would be compared, almost invariably to its detriment.

Such musical possessiveness, which scarcely existed when nearly all music heard was new music but grew rapidly with the nineteenth century rediscovery of the musical "classics," is a major cause of the resistance of audiences to unknown and especially to contemporary music.

The routine concertgoer identifies his taste and musical interest, his value judgements and esthetic standards, to a degree he is usually not able to admit, with the accustomed repertory of his earlier enthusiasm and the idiosyncratic habits of certain performers. (This is probably the reason why male concert artists publicly labor and sweat encased in a formal dress scarcely less archaic than wig and knee-breeches—as if female athletes still swam in skirted bathing dresses and sprinted in bloomers.)

The audience resists particularly the unaccustomed demand which any new work of idiomatic independence makes upon its sensibilities. Each listener rationalizes his incomprehension by defending with prejudiced arguments the reasonableness of his dislike. The biography and letters of any composer resound with his denunciations of such prejudice, which denies him recognition and delays the acceptance of his work.

AN INTRODUCTION TO CHARLES IVES

"If an interest in, and a sympathy for, the thought-visions of men like Charles Kingsley, Marcus Aurelius, Whittier, Montaigne, Paul of Tarsus, Robert Browning, Pythagoras, Channing, Milton, Sophocles, Swedenborg, Thoreau, Francis of Assisi, Wordsworth, Voltaire, Garrison, Plutarch, Ruskin, Ariosto, and all kindred spirits and souls of great measure, from David down to Rupert Brooke,—if a study of the thought of such men creates a sympathy, even a love for them and their ideal-part, it is certain that this, however inadequately expressed, is nearer to what music is given a man for, than a devotion to 'Tristan's sensual love of Isolde,' to the 'Tragic Murder of a Drunken Duke,' or to the sad thoughts of a bathtub when the water is being let out. It matters little here whether a man who paints a picture of a useless beautiful landscape *imperfectly* is a greater genius than the man who paints a useful bad smell *perfectly*.

"It is not intended in this suggestion that inspirations coming from the higher planes should be limited to any particular thought or work, as the mind receives it. The plan rather embraces all that should go with an expression of the composite-value. It is of the underlying spirit, the direct unrestricted imprint of one soul on another, a portrait, not a photograph of the personality—it is the ideal part that would be caught on this canvas. It is a sympathy for 'substance'—the over-value together with a consciousness that there must be a lower value—. . . the sublimity, against the vileness of Rousseau's *Confessions*."[1]

This is not one of the more engaging passages from Charles Ives's belatedly reprinted *Essays Before a Sonata*, privately printed by the author in 1920 after the end of his active musical career. It is the declaration of a representative of the New England culture preaching against *art*—a rebellious reaction, the start of a creative revolution.

It is not at all what an artist of today would write: the names of Kingsley, Whittier, Swedenborg, Channing, Ruskin, Ariosto, and Rupert Brooke would not occur to him. Charles Ives did not think himself an "artist," did not live like one; yet he is today, fifty years after he ceased composing and more than a decade since his death, one of the most active participants in the rapidly altering conception of the art of music: what it is, what it's good for, how it should be made. Though the surface and references are unlike, the substance of Ives's statement is very near what many twentieth century artists, today more than ever, have been thinking and are trying to create.

In his music, and in the texts he wrote or borrowed for hymns, songs, choruses, and in the laborious and inspired Essays and other writings that followed his breakdown in 1918—"I did almost no composing after 1918"—Ives re-created the spiritual image of a suddenly vanished era, the Puritan-Transcendentalist civilization of New England.

This civilization produced such difficult, withdrawn, cantankerous men as Emerson, Henry James, Sr., and C. S. Peirce; from this panathenaic, enclosed culture, like a voltaic jar having its opposite poles at Boston and New York, the several Jameses periodically fled to Europe, as Thoreau before them had fled to the nearby solitude of Walden Pond. The intellectual strictness of Nonconformist Puritanism, released by the intellectual liberation of Unitarian noncommitment, stirred by industrialism and the Civil War, brought forth two generations of New England genius, conscience rubbing like a hairshirt against the inclination of their taste. From this conflict emerged Hawthorne's and Melville's images of evil, the destroying visions which pursued Henry, Sr., and William and Henry, Jr., and Alice, and the other Jameses, and the Adams brothers, Brooks and Henry; a polished, self-contained, and superficially limited society which took all the world for its province and all ideas for its unending ruminations;

a wonderfully complete and homely rural community running on like a river, threatened and already befouled by the encroaching, raucous city.

Ives's music contains all this, except the images of evil. Until the First World War the problem of evil seems to have been the one large thought which did not concern him. The Hawthorne images in that movement of the *Concord Sonata* are more playful than serious. I believe it was the war, the collapse of all he had believed in, rather than worry about nonreception of his music, which precipitated his breakdown, though it is true that during the twenty years before then he had lived two lives in the space of one.

After the defeat of the League of Nations in the 1920 presidential election, Ives wrote his song *An Election* to his own angry words, with a *Note:* "The assumption, in the text, that the result of our national election in 1920 was a definite indication, that the country, (at least, the majority-minded) turned its back on high purpose is not conclusive . . . The voice of the people sounding through the mouth of the parties, becomes somewhat emasculated." Ives sent me the sheets of this song in an earlier printed version, probably a proof sheet, with a shorter version of the *Note,* both corrected in his own hand. This version of the *Note* concludes: "It is not inconceivable that practical ways may be found for more accurately registering and expressing popular thought [corrected to: "the thought of the people"]."

With this he sent three carbon-copied sheets from "a rather long article, papers, etc. written for the most part during the First World War," giving his plan for a "constitutional amendment" together with an article discussing the plan in some detail. In the angry voice of earlier New England transcendentalists and abolitionists Ives challenges "MEN with the strength and courage of most of our Forefathers . . . to do a bigger job than one which just has to do with our national defense:—to help defend Humanity from having to live or die in a world too much disgraced by mediaeval slavery, dark age bossing by 'half-wit' bosses, a world of too much animal-like weak suspicion also disgraced by too much pragmatism, materialism, greed and thievery —thievery between countries enslaving the minds and souls as well as the bodies of mankind. A Peoples World Nation in which every honest country will be free to live its own native life with

the help of its World Army Police will bring the greatest hope of
the world today to its realization; a world where men can stand
up as men and friends, and 'do unto others as they would be done
by' . . . And some morning glorious (but not quite tomorrow)
the trend up the mountain resounding around the world will
bring a new and radiant horizon to all."

The "trend up the mountain" refers to the final movement of
Ives's Second String Quartet. The accompanying "written during
the First World War" proves that, in spite of the Second World
War, Ives still held to his conviction.

The music of Ives conveys with sufficient completeness a way
of life as remote from ours, and suddenly lost, as that of the city-
state of Athens—pervaded as are his occasional writings by the
native Transcendentalism: idealism in isolation empowered by
a passionate curiosity and distaste, "a responsibility transcending
nations, which has the world for its field, humanity for its object, and the inner light to guide it accepting no restraints." (The
quoted passage is from my description of Ezra Pound; the spirit
of the New England culture had spread into many sections of
the continent, its spiritual anger, resistance, and unease strength-
ening the Abolitionists and permeating the vulgar slogans of the
Populists. Ives, unlike Pound, was neither esthete nor expatriate;
he had disciplined himself in business and in his attitude to
money; his later political writings still aimed at a united world.)

At the height of European colonial, cultural, moral, and intellectual imperialism the revolutionary minds clustered around four
distinct communities were corroding the self-confident nineteenth
century mechanistic materialism with the product of their spiritual dissatisfactions, in Vienna, Paris, London, and New England.
From where we are, looking backward, the insecurity of the
mechanistic materialism seems self-evident, as evanescent as the
vanished empires. Take any small roster of names: in Vienna,
Freud, Schoenberg, Kafka, Hitler; in Paris, the artists of the
period 1885 to 1914; in London, Marx, Lenin, Rutherford, White-
head, Russell, Wittgenstein; in New England, Peirce, the
Adamses, the Jameses, the Holmeses. The Viennese and the New
Englanders were natives, the Parisians and Londoners more often
transients or expatriates. One realizes that the New Englanders
were not the more provincial.

Ives—in business as in music he signed himself, American

fashion, with the middle initial, Charles E. Ives—was during his lifetime a successful self-made businessman. Starting with a small office and a single partner he created an insurance agency doing a business of millions. His partner, Julian S. Myrick, was still an active officer of the Mutual Insurance Company of New York (MONY), in the Empire State Building, when I called on him in March 1965, the morning after his eighty-fifth birthday, which had been celebrated the evening before with a closed-circuit broadcast of the New York Philharmonic Orchestra, directed by Leonard Bernstein, performing *The Fourth of July*, dedicated by Ives to Myrick. At a time of moving to a larger office, Myrick had discovered the manuscript, left behind in a corner of the office safe. "My God!" Ives shouted, "that's the best thing I've done yet!"

If Ives's spiritual education grew from the glacial moraine of Connecticut, rooting in a compost of Thoreau and Emerson, his musical and moral education came from his father, George Ives, a Yankee bandmaster with a mind as inquiring as that of the senior Henry James. George Ives was a man who would try to reproduce at the piano the sound of the off–pitch ringing of the church bell. He experimented with quarter-tones and tried to persuade his family to sing them. He would stretch twenty-four or more violin strings and tune them various ways to satisfy his curiosity. He experimented with glasses and bells. Ives wrote that "after getting used to hearing a piano piece when the upper melody, runs, etc., were filled out with quarter-tone notes (as a kind of ornamentation), when the piece was played on the piano alone there was a very keen sense of dissatisfaction—of something wanted but missing."[2] Ives himself composed quarter-tone pieces for strings and for two pianos tuned a quarter-tone apart.

Henry and Sidney Cowell, in their great and fascinating book about Ives, describe other experiments by his father. ". . . he tuned a piano in actual partials, to match the sounds of the overtone series, and he devised and tried out, again with tuned glasses, some new scales without octaves. He was interested in echoes and played his instruments one at a time over Danbury Pond, which amplified the echo that came back to him. He made endless attempts to imitate the sound of the echo itself, which he recognized as being different in quality—in tone color as well as in volume—from the initial tone."[3] He divided his band or several bands, placing them at several distances and at different heights, to play variations on some common hymn, so that he could compare the musical results. From this came Charles Ives's idea of the divided orchestra, in such works as *The Unanswered Question* and the Fourth Symphony, a practice carried forward in later years by Henry Brant, and tried again still later, with evident unawareness of these previous accomplishments, by the German composer Karlheinz Stockhausen.

Ives as a boy learned music from his father's band; from dance fiddlers, for example the movement *In the Barn* from the Second Violin Sonata; from psalms and hymns, formal and church style and revivalistic; from popular songs, including those of his father's friend Stephen Foster; from minstrel tunes, sentimental parlor piano pieces, chamber music, and ragtime. Ragtime came to him more naturally than jazz to his successors. He preferred Bach, Handel, Beethoven, and Mendelssohn, called Haydn and Mozart "pretty," had no liking for Wagner.

His ear and mind distinguished between natural and artificial sounds, as between substance and manner. "We would be inclined to say that Thoreau leaned towards substance and Debussy towards manner." "Or we might say that [Debussy's] substance would have been worthier, if his adoration or contemplation of Nature, which is often a part of it, and which rises to great heights, as is felt for example, in *La Mer,* had been more the quality of Thoreau's."[4] Debussy's impressionist responsiveness to natural beauty appealed to Ives, though he compared it to that of the "city-man with his week-end flights into country-aesthetics." Ives was a country man in the city, as one becomes aware through the stillness of meditative sound that is the substance of his orchestral tone poem, *Central Park in the Dark,* broken through by the raucous city noises and a ragtime piano. That stillness of sound, a mingling of dissonance and consonance, seeming to go nowhere, is the inward field of Ives's spiritual vision, recurring through many of his compositions, a sound for which I can think of no precedent, across which move the dramatic reminiscences of memory and vision.

"At the outdoor camp-meeting services," Ives wrote, ". . . I remember how the great waves of sound used to come through the trees . . . sung by thousands of 'let-out' souls. The music notes and words on paper are about as much like what they were at those moments as the monogram on a man's necktie may be like his face."[5]   Cowell Charles Ives p. 23-24

So George and Charles Ives, quite unaware that they were in the lead of the new generation of composers (Debussy to Stravinsky), began the American experimental tradition. The consequences of their work did not become evident until the 1940s, two decades after Ives had ceased composing, and are still becoming known. In the meantime, during the 1920s and 1930s, other American composers, Leo Ornstein (for a short while), Henry Cowell, Carl Ruggles, Edgard Varèse, Harry Partch, John Cage, Henry Brant, Lou Harrison, commenced finding their ways, by individual experiment, in the same direction.

When the boy tried experimenting on his own at the piano: "It's all right to do that," his father told him," *if* you know what you're doing."[6] The young Ives, age thirteen, heard an orchestra publicly perform his *Holiday Quickstep;* at fifteen he played a Bach toccata and a Mendelssohn sonata for an evening concert— "The greatest artistic success of the season"—on the organ at the Baptist church. In 1891 he wrote and performed his *Variations on "America"* for organ, containing both the formal precocity of canon in two and three keys and a rocky individualism of parody, melodic truncation, and sheer musical cussedness—"nice" was Ives's adjective of detestation for any music that did what the books said it should—which placed him outside and beyond his creative generation. When he wrote a fugue in four keys, his father warned him: "Charlie, it will be time enough to write an improper fugue and do it well when you can write a *proper* fugue and do *that* well."

Then Ives entered Yale, and in the next month his father died. Ives went on doing a job as church organist while he studied four years with the man who was probably the best academic composer in America, Horatio Parker. Ives respected Parker, but said his father was the greater man. Ives was still composing improper fugues. "So if the first statement of the theme is in a certain key, and the second statement is in a key a fifth higher, why cannot (musically speaking) the third entrance sometimes go another fifth higher? And the fourth entrance another fifth higher? And if it must hold to the nice old key system, why can't these themes come back in the same way? . . .

"One Mus. Doc. says: 'Because it destroys tonality.' Now having four different men playing tennis together does not always destroy personality."[7]

This seeming nonsequitur is a clue to Ives's feeling about

music, and an example of his compositional shortcuts. The four parts, like those of his Second String Quartet, are in his thought of them four personalities, each going its own way through its own episodes but sharing and participating in a common effort, seldom tragic, often robust or comic, very often transcendental, with "the world for its field, humanity for its object, and the inner light to guide it accepting no restraints." These fictional personalities may perform their parts separately or join together for a hymn; during the first two movements of the Second Quartet they converse and argue—the movement titles are: (1) *Discussions;* (2) *Arguments*—and in the third they walk up the mountain with a subtle reasoning of reconciliation which is also an Ivesian chorale fantasia on the hymn "Nearer, My God, to Thee." The subject of their discussion and argument reveals itself in fragments of Civil War tunes, Northern and Southern; the talk ranges more widely and Tchaikovsky and Beethoven appear. The use of the Tchaikovsky quotation is as idiomatically Ivesian as the growth of the "Beethoven Fifth" motive of the *Concord Sonata.* At another level of byplay the second violin becomes "Little Rollo," who gives up for a while because the music is too hard. One does not know which came first, the musical event as a focus of its context or the parodic jesting explained only in marginal comment on the manuscript. "For example, this: ". . . as a Cadenza to play or not to play! if played, to be played as not a nice one—but evenly, precisely unmusical as possible!" The Cowells observe that Ives's music resembles a partially assembled diary.

Ives liberated his technique from harmony, freeing dissonance and consonance impartially; he gave to each voice an individual melodic freedom of movement adding up vertically to unexpected harmonic events, often overlaying them so that several different things were happening together; all of it, so the ear tells the mind, requiring no theoretic justifying. Instead of dwelling on the chords or separate lines, he brings out the melodic interplay, very often obliquely, the continual shifting of melodic leadership among voices, the melodious and dissonant cross-chiming of tones and chordal groups. Working over his music Ives would substitute more *wrong* notes for the *right* notes, defeating harmonic expectation by the melodic intuition growing out of his boyhood experience. An impressionist of visual and sound images, he wound the melodic cross-play through the brightness and shade of specifically recalled experience, trying to preserve in music the immediacy of a countryside and a communal culture he saw vanishing.

Two notes by Ives on the manuscript of his First Piano Sonata reveal the intermediate thought process in words of ungrammatic verbal reverie already on the way to becoming music: "what is it all about—Dan S asks. Mostly about the outdoor life in Conn. villages in '80s & 90s   Impressions, Remembrances, & Reflections, of Country Farmers in Conn Farmland   On pg 14 back Fred's Daddy got so excited that he shouted when Fred hit a Home Run & the school won the baseball game but Aunt Sarah was always humming—Where is my wandering Boy—after Fred an John left for a job in Bridgeport—there was usually a sadness—but not at the Barn Dances with its jigs foot jumping & reels mostly on winter nights   In the Summer times, the Hymns were sung outdoors, Folks sang—as ole Black Joe—& the Bethel Band—Quickstep Street Marches, & The people like things as they wanted to say and to do things as they wanted to in their own way—and many old times . . . there were feelings, and of spiritual Fervency!"

A few pages later: "L.H. a little louder than R.H as a kind of the nature sounds which like a tree toad etc sometimes is heard in the woods a chronic beat & over the outdoor singing. Hawks or crickets!"[8]

He refused to stop with the impression. The flowing shadow-play of trees and river in *The Housatonic at Stockbridge* rivals the best of Debussy;[9] *Over the Pavements* (composed in 1906, the year of Debussy's *Images*) goes far beyond. The orchestral water-rhythms of *The New River* combine with voice parts packed as a psalm of David with reference and symbol, in the duration of a short madrigal. The music describes and dramatizes river pollution, urban spread, the appearance and movement of the river and broken rhythms where the industrial flume pours into it, by every means from gently flowing tonality to raucous noise, all in one and a half minutes.

An early offering of faith, written for his church choir, divides the chorus in two parts, each singing triads in one key, which by rhythmically displaced vertical relationship give the effect of polyharmony (*Psalm 67*). A similar study in arpeggios (*Psalm 24*) even more drastically translates simple displaced harmony into emotional power. Like young Bach at Arnstadt, Ives at the organ expanded to his own taste the plain harmony of the congregational hymn-singing; his rector, instead of reprimanding him, agreed that God, having heard the same harmonies so often, might welcome dissonance.

Going to New York, Ives entered the insurance business as an actuarial clerk. This balancing of the universal and the individual, reminding him of Emerson, started him writing tracts for insurance salesmen which helped to alter the nature of the insurance business from a hard-nosed concentration on sales to an inquiring concern for the customer's real needs. He invented the idea of estate planning. For good reason, business increased. With the same attitude Ives limited the earnings he took from the business to a modest estimate of his domestic needs. He was generous but not lavish in helping others and preferred no public acknowledgement. Downright and outspoken, he was, by expert testimony, a purple master of cussing.

While working at the insurance business, Ives continued serving as organist and choirmaster and, as always during these hardworking early years, composing. He seldom had time or felt the inclination to attend concerts; he had his piano, knew the classics, and heard in himself a music none of his contemporaries could match. He did not respect their art-conscious craft. Until 1931 he had heard nothing by Stravinsky except *The Firebird* and *The Nightingale*. The former "reminded me of something I had heard of Ravel, whose music is of a kind I cannot stand: weak, morbid and monotonous; pleasing enough, if you want to be pleased." He knew no music by Hindemith or Schoenberg. It is doubtful that he heard much or any music of these composers after that date.

✺ In September and October 1944, Evenings on the Roof celebrated the successive seventieth birthdays of Schoenberg and Ives by concerts entirely of their music. Schoenberg told me then with evident pleasure that, soon after their arrival in New York during 1933, Ives had come in spite of illness to a reception for him. Schoenberg clearly recalled his appearance. Carl Ruggles told me, in 1964, that he had sat with Schoenberg at a performance including Ives's *Unanswered Question,* presumably in 1933. The Cowells question both stories, and I have no other evidence that Schoenberg ever met Ives or heard any of his compositions. Yet in 1944, presumably following the two seventieth-birthday programs, Schoenberg wrote the tribute to Ives that Mrs. Schoenberg found among her husband's papers after his death and sent to Mrs. Ives.

> There is a great Man living in this country—a composer.
> He has solved the problem how to preserve one's self
>   and to learn.
> He responds to negligence by contempt.
> He is not forced to accept praise or blame.
> His name is Ives.[10]

However they might have responded to each other's music, the tribute speaks a common language.

Ives's conception of "what music is given man for," instead of "Tristan's sensual love," Verdi's "Tragic Murder of a Drunken Duke," or Strauss's domestic bathtub, alienated him from the contemporary European composers. Bach and Beethoven were his guides but not his models, though he used, like Bartók, the analytic expansion of a theme. I have told so much of the Ives story to emphasize the fact that his theoretical innovations, the *anticipations* of subsequent developments in twentieth century music for which he has become too famous, were not theoretical but experimental and concerned themselves with the music at hand. When an interviewer mentioned to him how many innovations by subsequent composers he had anticipated, Ives replied, "That's not my fault." (See Appendix A.)

Ives's anticipations are not ideas which someone has since used to better advantage; they are uses equal to and as good as any use which has been made of similar ideas until the present time. One might as well speak of Beethoven's, or Palestrina's, or Gesualdo's, or Machaut's "anticipations." These are of importance not because they anticipate what may be done adequately sometime but because the composer has done with them what—if not all that—these permit doing. It is not a degree but a finality of accomplishment. Ives was as aware as Schoenberg of his accomplishment; unlike Schoenberg, he had no opportunity to hear his instrumental compositions in performance. His orchestration is the work of silent knowledge, his most remarkable anticipation, which our experience validates.

Ives did not compose for the future; he composed in the present. He composed in fragments or patches, which he joined with others, and these to other combinations and patches of compositions, in such a way that the sequence of completed works, instead of representing graduated steps of progress or a gradual transformation of means, seems to be all of a heap. Only with the invaluable *Catalogue* of Ives's manuscripts prepared by John Kirkpatrick, which shows in great detail the vinelike interweaving of these compositions, can one trace his musical development.

During the organist years he was most free in shorter compositions, among them the two *Psalms* for unaccompanied chorus and the *Harvest Home Chorales* for voices, organ, brass ensemble, and string bass, composed and recomposed from 1898 until 1912. Much of the early choral and organ music was lost after Ives left it in the church where he had been organist. One feels that with his First and Second Symphonies and the First String Quartet he tried to bend his skill to the convention; his art gave some but could not bend. Many performers of his music, and the critics who accord his symphonies a type of response more suitable to an unrecognized Dvořák, fail to recognize the incommensurability of his music with other works by later nineteenth and early twentieth century composers. Ives's anticipations are the very stuff and substance of his music.

As a result of Ives's peculiar methods, some of the fragmentary pieces kept on growing larger and still intertwining. The form, like that of Shakespeare's more popular plays, presents an entanglement of contradictions drawn together through rewriting at different times; the unconscious reality and contradiction of content showing more clearly than in uniformly defined and finished compositions.

The *Concord Sonata*, as it is familiarly called (Second Pianoforte Sonata: "Concord, Mass., 1840–1860"), originated as a piano concerto and exists, in part, in several forms; it was published privately in 1921 and republished in 1947, after much editing and changing of *right* notes to *wrong* notes by the composer. Ives knew what he wanted but was seldom content with just that. If asked how to play a passage, he would reply, "Play it as you see it."

✿ John Kirkpatrick, whose performance of the complete *Concord Sonata* in January 1939 set off the first nationwide recognition of Ives as a major composer, recorded the work for Columbia Records in 1940, but the album was not re-leased until 1948. Columbia is now recording the complete works by Ives, as they have been recording the complete works by Stravinsky and Schoenberg and have already a complete Webern. Frances Mullen Yates performed the first movement (Emerson) of the *Concord Sonata* in the presence of Otto Klemperer at an Evenings on the Roof concert en-tirely of Ives's music in Los Angeles during 1939 and the complete Sonata at another Ives concert in 1940. In 1910 Gustav Mahler took the score of the Third Symphony with him on his return to Europe but died soon afterwards with-out performing it. Klemperer showed a similar interest in 1939, taking with him the score of *Three Places in New England*, but he has never played it. During the 1930s Nicolas Slonimsky directed a number of Ives performances, Columbia Broadcasting presented several broadcast pro-grams of Ives directed by Bernard Herrmann, and Webern directed one performance in Vienna. Playing an Ives work does not prove an understanding of it, as some recorded performances clearly demonstrate.

I corresponded with Charles and Harmony Ives from 1939 but was never able to meet him. He did not speak of tech-nicalities. Once Mrs. Ives sent a photograph: "This is the little white church where Mr. Ives and I worship every Sunday."

Portions of the *Hawthorne* movement from the *Concord Sonata* are heard in the second movement of the Fourth Sym-phony; this is only one of the more noticeable of such instances. Familiar patriotic tunes—a favorite, "Columbia, the Gem of the Ocean"—and hymn tunes too many to mention show in one texture, then another, and reappear often in variation somewhere else, seeming in every instance a necessary focus or derivative of the surrounding music. Multiple overlays of familiar tunes turn up in fragment and at length. The composition does not usually start with or require the tune; the tunes emerge as resultants of the more abstract motives, consisting of a few notes, continually varied by both analytic and melodic means, each reappearance as familiar yet individual in its setting as Cézanne's Mont Sainte-Victoire or Marsden Hartley's Mount Katahdin in their several landscapes.

The songs are from all periods. Ives assembled and rewrote many of them during 1920 and 1921 for the privately printed collection (*114 Songs*) he issued at that time, reducing a number of brief choral and instrumental compositions to solo voice and piano accompaniment. There are very simple songs, lyrical songs, dramatic and action songs, popular ballad types, and extremely difficult and complex songs, some quite short, including those reduced from larger media. The idiom is consistent, but the form and manner of presentation radical to the subject. Performance of Ives's vocal music is still too much influenced by song-recital formalities. One must recognize also a dangerously emotive approach: the song not the sign for the event but the event itself, as in evangelical hymn-singing; the affect of an emotionally uncontrolled performance may resemble that of a more cheaply dramatized music. The technical sophistication of Ives's songwriting should never be lost in an effort to make the song go. Radiana Pazmor gave a model of great Ives song in a record of "General William Booth Enters Heaven," very imperfectly recorded in 1935: the fervor of belief, the liberation of jazz, and the control of a Purcell solo cantata or a Mozart aria.

"If a fiddler or poet does nothing all day long but enjoy the luxury and drudgery of fiddling or dreaming," Ives asked, ". . . does he or does he not have anything valuable to express?" Many have claimed that Ives's compositions suffered because he could not hear his music in performance. Ives contradicts this opinion: "I seem to have worked with more natural freedom when I knew that the music was not going to be played, at least publicly. . . . One has a different feeling in playing his music before an audience or a public that cannot help itself. . . ."[1] Keep in mind that he was a performer, with a church audience, for some fifteen of his twenty-six composing years. Many of his ideas were tried at the organ before being composed by other means; a sense of organ improvisation explains certain of his musical habits. Success might have persuaded him to caution or to compromise; it might, beneficially, have caused him to simplify problems of notation.

Ives did not think his music difficult. Since he had no respect for the conventional formalities, his use of them was generally parodic. He shows his feeling about musical commonplace in such a movement as the fugue on "From Greenland's Icy Mountains" of the Fourth Symphony, parodying the cramped style of the organist and the happenstance freedoms of the congregational singing, with the rousing emotional inspiration of unrefined fugal form, like a Billings anthem, organ and voices making a holy sound at the expense of musical niceties. The idea is, in fact, more complex. Ives wrote in a program note for the symphony: "The Fugue is an expression of the reaction of life into formalism and ritualism." He meant it with humor.

Nothing that could be tried in music was alien to him. In the first of the three *Harvest Home Chorales,* as Henry Cowell describes them, "the singers chant without specified rhythm on the same dissonance with which the brasses opened, and the trumpets and trombones are set in counterpoint against each other in a series of perfect fifths which sound a magnificent fortissimo, making a triumphant climax against the monotony of the choir."[12] The last chord of the third *Chorale* "contains simultaneously the tonic, dominant, and subdominant chords of the key of C major—a symbol of universal praise." Again, "the song *Soliloquy,* one page long . . . is an extremely condensed exploration of the possibilities of building chords on intervals and in ways that produce startling new chord types, without ever deviating more than a little at any point from the usual."[13]

Rudolph Reti points to Ives's use of a twelve-note theme in the third of the compositions by coincidental prophecy called *Tone Roads* (composed 1915); the piece is remarkable not so much for its opening and repeated tone-row as for what happens afterwards; it is not an anticipation of Schoenberg's procedure, developed nearly ten years later, but a distinct conclusion from a similar premise. Musical analysts look for what they know, not for what they do not know. It is not extraordinary that Ives, in a period of chromatic writing, used a tone-row; Bartók in early years did the same. But where Schoenberg created a new harmonic grammar and syntax of the row consistency, Ives opened all doors, as if foreseeing Schoenberg's definition, that the twelve tones are "related only to one another." Schoenberg explored new devices, by preference, in setting verbal texts, the words requiring the devices to express them; Ives may have found a like emotional direction and reassurance in the unsung words of the familiar tunes and hymns.

Ives did not usually repeat his experiments. ". . . The true importance of his achievement," Reti continues, "and the potentialities it holds for the future are still far from being fully comprehended. . . . The polyphony of Schoenberg and his followers, for instance, much as it may surpass previous ways of formation . . . still remains a polyphony of single lines, even if of diversified, melodically autonomous lines. So also is Stravinsky's polyphonic web. . . . But Ives for the first time in history establishes, or at least tries to establish, in quite a number of his compositions *a polyphony of groups.* . . . In fact, almost all the other characteristic features of his style: his much discussed polyrhythm, his entirely free way of phrasing and grouping, even his frequent blending of outspokenly tonal and outspokenly atonal elements, and sometimes even his peculiar notation, are often but consequences of his concept of group polyphony. . . . Indeed, in such designs the essential problem, of which recent imitators of Ives often seem to be little aware, is whether such divergent groups can be unified in one artistic organization. . . . And this diversity can only be—and is often by Ives—reconciled through those very cross-relations of 'tonalities of a higher order.' . . ."[14] Reti calls these *pantonality.*

The criticism of "recent imitators" would apply as well to the more aimless extremes of tone-row composing and the amorphous consequences so often resulting from *Klangfarbenmelodie.*

The music of Ives runs a gamut from utmost simplicity to utmost complexity. *Psalm 90,* composed 1898–1901 and reworked probably in 1924 for mixed chorus, organ, bells, and gong, shows Ives's extraordinary ability to write music of utmost originality exactly to the purpose of the text. The harmony reaches from simple chords through a gradual expansion of dissonance into outright discordance, culminating in chords of 18, 20, and 22 separate tones for the words "in Thy wrath." Yet the power of the music is conveyed as fervently by the most simple as by the most complex tonal relationships.

Ives's written comments on the score are of great interest. The opening chord, for organ, is marked "God's Eternities"; it modulates to the second chord, marked "Creation," and then to the third, marked "God's wrath against sin (Flood etc.)." Above the fourth chord—"Prayer and Humility." Then, after another brief modulation, a passage for organ or bells is marked "Rejoicing in Beauty and Work!" Farther down the page, the passage "from one generation to another, to another, to another" is given the indication: "(As evolution, quiet, unseen, and unheeded, but strong fundamentally)." One sees how the *substance* of the Psalm enters into every thought of the music, as idea, as sound, and as manner of expression.

The entire forty-five-minute structure of the *Concord Sonata*

—as large as Beethoven's *Hammerklavier Sonata*, opus 106—is derived from the opening four-note figure of Beethoven's Fifth Symphony and melodic permutations of that figure. At the opposite extreme, Henry Cowell points to a measure in the last movement of the Fourth Symphony, "which, nominally in 3/2 meter, proves to have twenty different simultaneous rhythmic figures, with three, four, five, and six notes of equal value filling the measure in different voices, the rest of the figures being made up of notes of unequal value."[15] Much vaunted "daring innovation" by other composers since Ives is by comparison weak and sterile.

It is for these reasons that Ives, though his life ran concurrently with that of Schoenberg, and his creative career ended before the period of Schoenberg's full maturity, opens the door to experience of all that is happening in the present evolution of music.

Stravinsky by the decade but Schoenberg by the half-century transformed the past of music in the direction of its present. Stravinsky from decade to decade preserved his lead, his independence, free of tradition, transforming and endorsing the new proposals of music as he understood them, the master, like Picasso, towards whom all fashion turned, himself always ahead of and the maker of that fashion; and in the end he accepted what seemed to be the ultimate product of that half-century, transforming and endorsing it again to his own purpose.

That product was, as contemporary opinion now holds it to be, that portion of Schoenberg's music which led to the tone-row from the emancipation of the dissonance. Beyond this Stravinsky would not go, into the regions of the Wind Quintet, the Suite for Seven Instruments to which in his own style he paid the deference of his own Septet. It is not a mere question of pleasing or ugly. Stravinsky could admire the multifarious scope of such achievement, taking from it the guitar and mandolin, the later speaking-singing, adapting these and the row principle to his own clarity and conciseness. He had turned aside after his first discovery of Schoenberg to the manageable sufficiency of Webern but again looked back. In the glory of his long creative twilight he could take and use what he pleased, could end as he began, apart from a tradition.

During the half-century the older competing traditions had been broken off. A new prevailing and better-informed polyglot, product of new habituation, incorporating ideas from earlier styles, had merged all traditions, until even the Germanic had absorbed it and grown indifferent. Only this can explain popular enthusiasm for the music of Carl Orff. The Brahmsian compromise had reached an end, through Reger, in Hindemith. Bartók, strongest of the nationalists, had created his remarkable island, as the British nationalists shared theirs—not in either case because they were nationalists but because what they chose to do diverged from the central movement. Schoenberg's unyielding determination and perseverance had established his unique authority in a new era of music all other music must begin with. Composers coming to it first through Berg, then Webern, must at last reckon with the source.

In contrast to this suddenly world-recognized authority, however abused by the excesses of the tone-row addicts upon whose earlier stirrings Schoenberg so often pronounced his interdict, there were only what appeared to be the first flutterings of a new way of thinking in America, which I have called *the American experimental tradition:* the almost forgotten work of Varèse, the implementation of Henry Cowell, the inexplicable oddities of Cage.

Then Cowell, by long propaganda, and a few musicians in performance began bringing forward the music of Ives. And the younger American experimentalists, still isolated, found in these so-called *anticipations* proof that an entire field of music could exist which was not obedient to the nineteenth century, to the French, to the current polyglot, or to the Germanic tradition of Hindemith, and did not stand on the authority of Schoenberg. Music which their more formally minded elders called "primitive" or imperfectly composed sounded to these younger ears and minds a natural idiom. In music now contemporary with their own, Ives had proved, a half-century earlier, the substance and worth of their experiments. Through him they found a foothold in their own tradition.

Schoenberg had emancipated the dissonance and given a new classic formal coherence to the art of the twelve notes. Ives had emancipated music, both consonance and dissonance, from the necessity and rule of the Western European tradition. The result was difficult to grasp, but they grasped at it. Long before Schoenberg had commenced debating whether or not the octave could be used in atonal or tone-row music, because of the danger of establishing unwanted key-relationships—an American composer, George Tremblay, who was closely associated with Schoenberg in Los Angeles, claims to have persuaded him that it could and has himself in one symphony brilliantly demonstrated the effect—Ives was using octaves, consecutive fifths, and triads (just intonation and simple consonance) as a concordant offset to dissonance and flaring discord, at the same time emphasizing the opposite extreme boundary of the field of sound by noise. Yet the Fourth Symphony, which seems to include all extremes, contains only one use of noise, the soft solo entry of the snare drum in the last movement. While Schoenberg's music remained within the field consonance-dissonance-discord, Ives had reinstated the two extreme boundaries of the field. He had shown how much could be done with this new music, made up equally of tonality, atonality, and deliberate noise. He had already entered and justified, as music by music, the new field of sound.

THE AMERICAN EXPERIMENTAL TRADITION I

Seeger, Cowell, Varèse, Ruggles, and Others

The American experimental tradition, portent of new music in the world today, enters musical history with the circular twist of a tornado. The tradition begins not at the beginning, in the work of Charles Ives, but during the early 1920s in the unprecedented workmanship of Carl Ruggles, a self-taught composer, of Edgard Varèse, a French-educated composer who became a disciple of Busoni, and of Henry Cowell, pupil of the remarkable composer become musicologist, Charles Seeger, with whom Cowell came to study at the age of eleven.

At the time of this writing, Charles Seeger, husband and father of distinguished musicians, is still actively engaged in music at the University of California, Los Angeles. An authority on sound and on folk and primitive music, he has had built to his design an electronic device, the *melograph*, enabling him to show by mensurally exact lines on a graph the real melodic outline, every fluctuation and embellishment of the fundamental tone and selected overtones, with the exact volume and rhythm, of primitive song and instrumental music from a recording of the original on tape. Thus he dispenses with the need to transcribe music of traditions unlike ours by falsely adapting it to the notational system of our own tradition, in which the original pitches and their microtonal deviations, the timbres and the rhythms can seldom be accurately reported. Here again, the new electronic medium and a system of graphic notation replace the previously conventional means, in musicology as already in composition.

Seeger's career spans almost the entire development of American experimental music, to which he and his late wife, the composer Ruth Crawford, have made important contributions. His career demonstrates that the growth of the American tradition of musical experiment is not the result of inadequate musical education but of a greatly expanding knowledge of other musical traditions reacting formatively within a still undecided musical content and its diverse idioms.

In America the orientation of musical learning had been Germanic until well into the twentieth century, but public taste followed far behind, veering from occasional Beethoven and Mendelssohn to popular airs and harmonized folksong, from occasional Wagner to Italian opera, preferring above all the more superficial virtues of the polyglot. Horatio Parker's oratorio *Hora Novissima* composed in 1893, refers in every measure to European antecedents. His pupil Charles Ives transformed the references, mingling Beethoven with Stephen Foster, abstract formality with ragtime, symphony with band, the abstract motive with its unexpected momentary resolution into a hymn or patriotic tune.

During the 1920s the rebellion of French composers against Germanic authority, belatedly influencing American expatriate composers in Paris, split serious responses between the familiar Germanic classics, now offset by the popular Russian classics, and the flow of fashionable novelties from Paris. Italian opera and the suddenly too familiar staples of the nineteenth century polyglot receded from view. A young composer could no longer expect to receive the single-minded, pedantic grounding in stylistic fundamentals which had formerly been thought necessary for a musical education. Schoenberg, when he began teaching in America, complained of this inadequate training, at the same time admitting, "There are great talents among them, and they learn fast. They learn more from theories and lectures than from master models."

The musical thinking behind these theoretical rationalizations and increasingly indeterminate harmonic habits was no more securely established in the new experience of the teachers than among their pupils. Fannie Dillon, the first teacher of Roy Harris and John Cage, showing her own new piano sonata, explained that she had "written in" as much dissonance as she thought necessary. Tentative theorizing and lectures which, however analytical, went not far beyond the scope of musical appreciation, describing rather than distinguishing the contradictory approaches, at once liberated musical thinking from traditional authority and guided it into new channels of technical adventure, where the young composer, almost from the start of his education, must make his own decisions. One decision might be in practical usage as good as another.

The American experimental tradition is not, therefore, a concentrated tradition like the Germanic but a widely dispersed and weedlike growth of fresh ideas in new soil. One country's weeds may become in another country hothouse or ornamental plants, being cultivated there to greater or more prolific beauty, though they are not natural to the climate. British horticulturists favor California native plants; these do not thrive under cultivation in California, where instead South African plants are favored.

The fundamental direction of the American experimental tradition lies in a radical departure from accepted European antecedents and a radical incorporation of new means from the traditions of other cultures. It reaches back with fresh awareness, as Webern did, to the practices of earlier European composers during the Renaissance and medieval periods. A lecturer on fourteenth century isorhythm is said to have ended his talk: "If you still don't understand what I mean, listen to the music of Charles Ives and you will hear it."[1] Ives would undoubtedly have been astonished, but putting aside the exact principles of fourteenth century practice, it is true. Melody and rhythm, in independent, distinct patterns, continually form new patterns.

The American experimental tradition is not chauvinistic; it is rather continental than national. It includes Mexican, Caribbean, and Canadian composers. Despite the increasing number of American composers and the scarcity of opportunities to hear their work in any major performance, more European, Latin American, and Asiatic composers visit this country, teach, lecture, and have their works performed here than at any time before now. American composers attend and participate in European music festivals, but their names, reputations, and accomplishments are, with a few exceptions, less known in Europe than the work of their European fellows is known here. Western European and Russian classics still dominate the public concert; to include major work by American composers is a dangerous virtue that has cost more than one orchestral conductor his position. Among American composers only Aaron Copland seems to have found a secure place in the public repertory. Yet there is reason to believe that the American experimental idea is the most influential in the developing musical evolution, worldwide, today.

No composer of serious intent has come near equaling the success and the continuing popularity of George Gershwin. His native musical ability was greater than his courage or willingness to release it. His concertos and *Porgy and Bess* give no clue to what he might have done, if he had written like Ives to the full of his capacity. He lived the successful career of a popular tune-smith whose orchestration is no more than a stringing together of tunes. Unlike Ernest Bloch's proposed new national anthem in his symphony *America,* these tunes spoke and in a sense created common idiom. Ives incorporated in his music the similar common idiom of the immediately preceding period. This is not folk music. In twentieth century America, *popular music*—correctly so called—took the place of folk music. Jazz became erudite. The revival of what is now called "folk music" occurred by way of popular music.

Gershwin as an artist was more desperately trapped by his success than Schoenberg or Ives by seeming failure. The *Gershwin concert,* as a popular seasonal item, aimed to draw crowds not addicted to the classics, ranks him with the musical entertainers, Johann Strauss, Offenbach, and the successful tunesmiths of light opera and musical comedy. *Porgy and Bess,* though the tunes are memorable, is in every way a less well achieved opera than Blitzstein's *The Cradle Will Rock.*

In mid-adolescence Henry Cowell composed a succession of technically unprecedented, though musically undemanding, piano pieces, some with tone-clusters played by fists and forearms, some with the damper pedal depressed while the player's hands sweep or pluck the piano strings, and some in which one hand depresses the keys while the other hand, reaching over, performs directly on the strings. These boyhood *jeux d'esprit* have not lost flavor; they have brought about a new art of the piano, which disregards its ordinary character. The string-enclosing casket behind the traditional keyboard was discovered to be a Pandora's box of unexpected sounds. Such music has become today a part of the musical scene; in my experience only Bartók and Cage have improved on Cowell's original usage.

The verve and wit of the young Cowell and the attractive novelty of his radical compositions brought him a hearing, if not outright admiration. "Before 1920," he wrote in a letter, "there were just five composers in the United States who did not resolve dissonances—chronologically: Ives, Cowell, Seeger, Ornstein, Ruggles." His taste for Oriental and primitive instruments introduced new timbres and theoretical borrowings which have spread widely through American composing. As a salesman for the unusual in new music he soon made himself heard in New York and in Europe; returning to America he became a fertile propagandist of fresh idiomatic possibilities and new instruments— among them the *Theremin,* an electronic instrument better adapted to sliding than to fixed pitches. As a teacher of younger composers and as editor of *New Music Quarterly,* a magazine containing nothing but the scores of new compositions, for the most part by composers of the United States and Latin America, he made himself a central figure of the radical art he was helping to create and implement. His book *American Composers on American Music,* published in 1933, a collection of articles by almost unknown young composers about the work of other composers equally unknown, proclaimed the creative independence of American music. His critical writings over many years brought to attention what was happening in the invention of new music and new musical means. His constant traveling and lecturing on this continent linked together and educated the composers of his own and succeeding generations, until exhaustion and the constantly widening spread of new musical activity which he had helped to inspire forced him to curtail his labors. He has been one in the succession of great teachers, among them Horatio Parker, Ernest Bloch, Nadia Boulanger (at the American Conservatory, Fontainebleau), Arnold Schoenberg, Walter Piston, Paul Hindemith, and Roger Sessions, who have decisively influenced the growth of American musical thought.

Cowell was also the first to discover and bring to public notice the music of Ives, which until that time had been unknown. With his wife, Sidney Cowell, he wrote the biography of Ives; he became, after the death of Ives, the editor of his unpublished scores.

Through all this Henry Cowell continued producing his own

compositions, including some twenty symphonies and many more orchestral pieces and a great variety of chamber and solo music, in such quantity that he is among the most prolific of twentieth century composers. Learning from Sidney Cowell, who had been a researcher in American folk idioms, about the primitive music which had grown up on this continent by adaptation from the Western European tradition, he re-created this indigenous art in hymns and fuguing-tunes for several media. Some of his compositions make use in the same way of Oriental idioms and instruments.

In spite of the wide range of his compositions, Cowell was always a practical composer; his music, however unusual, is seldom problematic and has been widely played. He traveled around the world, finding that some portion of his work was known in many countries. At the time of his death, in December 1965, he was still actively composing. Whatever the ultimate worth of his total composition, which few at the present time know well enough to appraise, he achieved something larger and beyond it, the establishing of the American experimental tradition as an independent and viable field of musical art.

Edgard Varèse, born in 1885, barely missed being one of the creative generation, Debussy–Stravinsky. (He died, November 1965, while this book was being written.) Formally educated in the conservative French polyglot tradition under d'Indy, Roussel, and the organist Widor, he was perhaps the first European composer to break completely with that tradition and seek the new creative horizon dreamed of by his beloved master, Busoni. He was influenced, too, by the abortive Futurist Manifesto of Marinetti, that music should break away from notes to noise.

He did not take, like the young American George Antheil, in *Ballet mécanique*, what then seemed the obvious course of using noise without exploring it. Antheil's explanations after the event tried to rationalize a successful headline-seeking stunt into a considered esthetic achievement. In fact, it was most successful in its headlines. The sound lacks variety; the typewriters used for instruments do not compete effectively with the several pianos; the pianos are borrowed from Stravinsky's far more successful use of them in *The Wedding*; the airplane propeller is no more than Strauss's wind-machine in *Don Quixote*; and the rattling and banging of the percussive elements do not combine to produce musical substance. Similar faults are evident in much of the noise-music which has been composed since that time. Antheil's super-ficiality became more evident in later compositions, imitating the surfaces of more competent composers.

After two brief ventures in establishing musical organizations to perform contemporary music, Varèse joined with the composer-harpist Carlos Salzedo to found the Pan-American Association of Composers, one of the first of several large cooperative ventures among American composers. At the same time he began the series of sound-tapestries by the overlaying of instrumental timbres which helped make possible the future development of a sound-music freed of the chords and counterpoint of the Western European tradition. He investigated the overtone combinations of arbitrarily pitched tones and the effect of large bodies of in-determinately pitched percussion instruments. Such music is neither dissonant nor discordant, because it does not need to avoid the establishing of a tonality. It is an art of sonority, of sound for its own sake, stopping short of outright noise and of formally concordant harmony. Rhythmic variety and contrasting sonorous means give shape and articulation to what would be otherwise an indistinguishable body of rich sound.

It is interesting to observe that the four composers whose music first gave a modern meaning to sonority instead of line as a principal mode of Western musical expression—Indonesian *gamelan* music is as much an art of sonority as a Bruckner symphony—were either organists, Bruckner, Ives, and Messiaen, or in the case of Varèse, the pupil of an eminent organist-composer, C. M. Widor. Widor's organ symphonies fail not in virtuosity but by the incapacity of an organ to furnish an orches-tral diversity of timbres; all organ tone, being produced by wind from a pipe, is alike in quality and attack. But there are virtues in the organist's knowledge, if he uses it correctly for orchestral music. The freedom of improvisation with quasi-orchestral means available to an organist, the distinction between organ and orchestra in obtaining the effects of timbre by the deliberate addition of particular overtones instead of combining the discrete timbres of instruments, enabled these four composers to calculate more shrewdly the sonorities they desired. Thus their orchestra-tion is very unlike the linear-melodic orchestration of Wagner, Schoenberg, or Stravinsky. Varèse composes as if on an organ of innumerable registers and no fixed keyboard. Schoenberg said, by contrast, that the organ of the future would require not sixty or seventy different colors, as on the large modern concert instrument, but perhaps two to six colors only, capable of an expressive range, on each separate note, from the softest pianissimo to the strongest forte. "The purpose of the colors is to make the individual lines clearer." Varèse and Messiaen expand color at the expense of line. Bruckner balanced the two elements; his richest sonority is the multiplied octave, outlining the necessarily more dissonant melody.

In three major works of the 1920s, *Hyperprism*, *Octandre*, and *Intégrales*, Varèse combined wind instruments with large bodies of percussion. For *Arcana* he employed an orchestra of 112 musicians performing on conventional instruments, plus eight percussionists playing at one time or another on forty percussive sound-producers. *Ionisation*, from 1931, reduced the number of players to thirteen with a total of thirty-seven instruments: two fire sirens, hand-wound and able to produce controlled crescendo and diminuendo; two tam-tams; gong; crash cymbals; three bass drums of different sizes; bongo drums; snare drums; *guiro* (which Robert Craft, from whose record note I borrow these statistics, describes as "a desiccated Cuban gourd, serrated on the surface to be scratched with a wooden stick"); slapsticks; Chinese blocks in three registers; Cuban *claves* (short round hardwood sticks, struck lightly together); triangle; Cuban maracas (gourd rattles); sleigh bells; castanets; tambourine; two anvils; chimes; celesta; piano. "Only the last three items," Craft observes, "are able to produce notes of equal-tempered pitch, and Varèse saves all three for a final apotheosis that is a true glorification of sound." Of these earlier works, *Ionisation* has been, for practical reasons, the most often performed.

After *Ionisation*, Varèse disappeared from musical activity. Between 1931 and 1954 he wrote only a piece for unaccompanied flute, *Density 21.5*, so individual in melodic flow that it stands apart from all other Western music for the instrument. Of similar nature is the idiomatic melody which winds through his variously composed sonorous patterns.

In 1954 he reappeared, almost from musical oblivion, with a symphonic work, *Deserts*, divided alternately between four sections of instrumental sound and three sections of electronically produced sound, the first large orchestral composition in which electronically generated music is opposed to instrumental music. *Deserts* has been widely performed and presents no real difficulties for the listener. Since then, the reputation of Varèse has grown great in Europe and America; his music of the 1920s has been revived as it deserves; his example, however variously understood, has influenced all subsequent sound-music.

Varèse has issued for public performance since that time only one more composition. For the Philips Radio Corporation pavilion, a building resembling a circus tent with three poles somewhat inaccurately pitched, designed by Le Corbusier for the Brussels Exposition, the architect invited Varèse to compose his *Electronic Poem.* Four hundred loudspeakers projected the sound-composition from every point inside the continually curving structure; the music consists of natural sound, electronically altered, and electronically generated sound.

Varèse makes a valuable distinction in the use of the word *experimental* when applied to art. "My experimenting is done before I make the music. Afterwards, it is the listener who must experiment."

Carl Ruggles, the oldest living major American composer—at the time of writing, in his ninetieth year—had composed all but three of his few works by 1932, the year when the largest of them, *Sun-Treader,* had its first performance in Paris. The first American performance of *Sun-Treader* and the first recording both occurred in January 1966. His music still provokes many listeners to outright resistance. The works are short but immensely powerful; *Angels,* for muted brass, lasts two and a half minutes, *Portals,* for string orchestra, four and a half minutes. (The *Complete Webern* fills both sides of three records; a complete Ruggles would occupy less space.)

Ruggles is to Ives as Webern to Schoenberg, the mighty miniature, a close friend and devoted admirer. Webern occasionally stole from Schoenberg; Ruggles disdains in forceful language any use of another man's material. He has been described as a tone-row composer, who adapted the row to his own practice; this is incorrect—though his admiration for Schoenberg is only less than his devotion to Ives. Self-trained, Ruggles arrived at his compositional methods by his own choice of means: to repeat no tone or its octave until after the tenth progression. His scale comprises twenty-one tones, a sharp and a flat for each "white" note, the accidentals freely notated, easy to read but confusing for the analyst. He writes a polyphony with little repetition or embellishment in which every vertical relationship has been considered as a distinct complex of sound, a melodically fluctuating, oblique sound-texture, polyphonically striated. So delicately are these strong relationships balanced in his hearing that he is constantly reordering the composition to obtain even more exactly the vertical, oblique, and horizontal totality of unified effect he aims at.

His *Men and Mountains,* for chamber orchestra, is a miniature symphony as beautiful in brilliant force as a volcanic eruption. *Portals* resembles a few lines by Whitman. In 1945 he wrote a slightly larger and less concentrated work for orchestra, *Organum. Evocations,* for piano solo, consists of four brief movements in arpeggiated sonorities, dedicated to his wife and to three friends, one of them Ives. He has composed another piano work, *Flowers,* he told me in 1964, but it is not yet published. In the new era of sound-composition this small body of music, like the larger work of Ives, becomes more meaningful.

Unlike the orchestral works by Ives, the music of Ruggles contains no nostalgically familiar tunes to warm the atmosphere, and no similarity to any other music that the listening mind can grasp. Unlike the tone-row, which developed out of Germanic counterpoint and can be regularized in accustomed vertical and horizontal relationships, the intuitively self-enforced discipline of Ruggles does away with chord and linearity. The melody is there, a jagged figuration, always striving to rise, to achieve sublimity, twisted and thrown back. The harmony results from the vertical simultaneity of disparate effects. Gaps open in the firmament, and sounds break through them; the musical design is continually exfoliating outward. Heights and deeps respond; one recognizes the determining presence of the melody, in broad-reaching curves upward and downward, interwoven with brief periods of softly twisting lyricism. The sound does not metrically move forward but is continually broken, too ruggedly rhythmical to be called "prose," too wide-ranging for declamation. It is a continual upheaval but not, as one gets into it, disordered, an isorhythmic disproportion of melody and rhythm resulting in continually changing patterns. The movement is that of water boiling in a pot—an expanding universe which is at the same time necessarily contracting, a motion without external limit, quite unlike the static metrical reiteration of figures which gives compressed power to Stravinsky's *Rite of Spring*.

In what is still the best description of the man and his work, Charles Seeger wrote in 1932: "If the materials of the art of music are ever assembled into a new style comparable to that of the great styles of the past . . . Ruggles will be among the men who will have contributed to its making."[2]

Unlike Ives, Ruggles, or Varèse, Wallingford Riegger began as a romantic composer and became an experimentalist; he then adapted these contradictory directions to the tone-row. An inspired craftsman, honored by his fellow composers for that reason, he made up in workmanship what he lacked in melody, fabricating his compositions as earlier Americans built good furniture, as plain as honest.

When in a later year my wife played the piano sonata by Roy Harris for Fannie Dillon, his first composition teacher, she who had not heard it before exclaimed, "Why, that is the material he brought to his first lesson!" The powerful, naive, crude surfaces of his early compositions, the Variations for Orchestra on "When Johnny Comes Marching Home" and Symphony for Voices on texts from Walt Whitman, hacked from the block, brought him rapidly to fame as a so-called spokesman of the American West. Coming late to music at the age of twenty-seven, Harris seemed in a fair way to go straight through to the top. He was perhaps the first to make the general listener recognize, with whatever condescension, that a genuinely American idiomatic spirit in serious music could exist. His powerful native talent was blunted and diverted by an increasing dependence on formalism. He suffered the fate Ives also might have suffered, if he had been able to hear his music performed in an admiring atmosphere full of good advice. Instead of riding his native genius to a gallop or a fall, Harris accepted for his own use a neo–Bach-Busoni polyphony, with which he achieved the triumph of his Third Symphony, the first large American composition to be conducted by Arturo Toscanini, and his Piano Quintet. During the many subsequent years of composing and teaching he has not succeeded in re-establishing himself at the creative center.

Aaron Copland, less gifted with powerful crude talent than Harris, made up the difference by the sophistication which led Harris astray. His career has been marked by acute observation

of contemporary musical interests, reflected in a variety of successful styles and forms. He has a skill in borrowing or inventing
folkish melodies, rhythms, idiomatic fragments, and setting them
into an appealing context while retaining the admiration of
professional compeers by an obvious technical command. He has
not let the popularity won by these means divert him from
serious designs in abstract form. Each of his successive major
works has established him more firmly in reputation, if not in
authority. His Piano Variations, the ballet *Appalachian Spring,*
the Piano Sonata, the Violin Sonata, and a cycle of songs on texts
by Emily Dickinson are among the masterpieces of American
music. His content reveals itself in a relatively consistent idiom
but a widely fluctuating uncertainty of form. His later effort to
adapt the tone-row principle to his idiom, as Stravinsky did, has
been relatively unsuccessful, though there are many who admire
the glacial outlines of his Piano Fantasy.

Ingolf Dahl, a younger composer, succeeded at the point where
Copland failed. His early Quintet for Brass Instruments, his Trio
for Violin, Clarinet, and Piano, and works for viola and for cello
with piano reflect some influence of Hindemith and Copland, less
noticeable in later revision. His Piano Quartet successfully amal-
gamated the tone-row with his personal idiom, as Copland's
Piano Quartet of the same period did not. Dahl's two Piano
Sonatas and in particular his Piano Trio commingle a more free
atonality with a growing awareness of the larger harmony of
Ives.

The broadening American interest in the arts which began
during the later 1920s spread rapidly during the 1930s, bringing
about an accelerating increase in the number of university schools
and departments for the arts. The flight to America of European
composers and musical scholars improved the training of American composers and musicologists. A vast wave of musical academicism swept the nation, almost halting and then obscuring the
rise of the native experimental tradition. To be original was, and
in many circles still is, to write in an established or momentarily
fashionable contemporary European style. The presence in
America of such European composers of the first rank as Ernest
Bloch, Igor Stravinsky, Arnold Schoenberg, Kurt Weill, and soon
afterwards Ernst Toch, Paul Hindemith, Ernst Krenek, and
Stefan Wolpe, stimulated a new experimental mixture of native
and individual European idioms and styles, strong in theory and

weaker in content. American composers in large numbers went abroad, to study in particular with Nadia Boulanger at the American Conservatory at Fontainebleau. Probably never in the history of music were traditions, idioms, and styles so thoroughly confused. At the same time, the first great flood of the recorded musical classics swept the American continent, supplemented by broadcasts of symphonic and even chamber music. Famous string quartets, subsidized by Elizabeth Sprague Coolidge, performed cycles of chamber music at many universities throughout the country. Among the millions who accepted the opportunity to hear great music by no more effort than buying a collection of records or turning on the radio, the majority decisively preferred the classic composers but with a wider choice of their music than had ever before been available. A minority accepted some contemporary music with the classic.

In the midst of this unprecedented discovery of the musical classics by a nationwide audience previously almost unaware of them, the work of a few composers still asserted the presence of an American music. The vogue was towards a more practical and popular music, yet the chief composers, Henry Cowell, Aaron Copland, Ruth Crawford, Walter Piston, Howard Hanson, Marc Blitzstein, Virgil Thomson, Roger Sessions, maintained a firm balance between the practical and the difficult, between the popular and the creatively erudite. At the end of this period composers in America began aggressively challenging the classics. Virgil Thomson wrote a large body of music, both slight and serious, including a *Requiem*, which even today has not come to appraisal or recognition. Roger Sessions diverted to his own purposes the tone-row principle to create laboriously a small body of large compositions for piano, string quartet, and symphony, and two operas, *The Trial of Lucullus*, on a one-act play by Bertolt Brecht, and *Montezuma*, first performed by the Berlin Opera in 1964 with an American soprano from New Orleans singing the lead female part. It is worth remarking that American singers nowadays crowd the European opera houses, for lack of adequate opportunity on this vast, wealthy continent.

Howard Hanson, John Alden Carpenter, Deems Taylor, William Schuman, and Leonard Bernstein typify the mixed roles of numerous composers, executives, administrators, educators, who continue a creative career in spite of heavy extramusical responsibility. Hanson, for forty years head of the Eastman

School of Music at the University of Rochester, has launched into music as many educator-composers as compositions, exercising by both means a prevailingly conservative, romantic influence over the growth of American musical styles. Less rigid than Hinde-mith, whose American influence, seemingly more advanced, has been in the outcome more Germanically restrictive, Hanson opened a broad middle path between academicism and experimentalism. By performance and recording he has propagated American music of all types and schools. Carpenter, a business-man like Ives, cultivated music as a skilled amateur. Deems Taylor, a professional music critic, wrote operas which were performed by the Metropolitan Opera in New York but did not survive. Schuman, a pupil of Roy Harris, became director of the Juilliard School of Music in New York and then of the New York performing-arts complex, Lincoln Center. He has turned out a considerable body of music in a heavy contrapuntal style, incorporating many American references, from William Billings to jazz. Leonard Bernstein has successfully written ballet, musical comedy, chamber music, and three rhetorical symphonies, while rising as a conductor to become the musical director of the New York Philharmonic Orchestra.

Ingolf Dahl, Lukas Foss, and Gunther Schuller combine a thorough academicism with a radical willingness to experiment; they are also skilled conductors and performers, who give prefer-ence in their programming to contemporary European and American music.

The long, obscure maturing of Elliott Carter came to climax in a First String Quartet composed not at the median but at the extreme of his style, a work of superb rhetoric and, when well played, almost visible action. His Second Quartet carried forward the rhythmic experimentation and the dramatic distinction of performing styles among the four instruments, in the spirit of Ives's Second Quartet. One can hear Ives in Carter's ostinato basses and furious polyphony, as one hears the tone-row behind his melodic method, but his well-worked and deeply woven style has a more cautious, theoretically formalistic technique. Carter said to me that after studying Ives's scores he had decided that Ives was an imperfect orchestrator; Dahl, meditating on his discovery of these seeming faults, decided that Ives knew exactly the orchestral effect he wanted.

Since this chapter deals with the American experimental tradition and not with the history of American music, I mention only a few names from among the thousands of American composers who have created an enormous, little known, seldom performed, and for the most part almost unexplored music. Apart from a few scattered magazine articles and one book of useful history, *America's Music* by Gilbert Chase, this music has almost no critical literature. Much of it was written in styles immediately contemporary and almost immediately outdated; the contemporaneity of style does not decide the worth of what has been composed. From the honorable conservatism of Walter Piston and Harold Shapero to the equally honorable but cautious radicalism of Elliott Carter and the theoretical deviations of Milton Babbitt, the American academic composers have incorporated dissonant counterpoint, the twelve-tone technique in many individual adaptations, atonality to extremes, the new sounds of extratonal percussion, rhythmic innovation in great variety, and types of the determinate-indeterminate and aleatory styles; yet they remain as a group apart from the American experimental tradition, from which they have learned and to which they have contributed.

Three Latin-American composers should also be mentioned. Carlos Chávez, for many years the most important Mexican orchestral conductor, won quick recognition with two dynamic short symphonies, *Sinfonía de Antígona* and *Sinfonía India*. His Sonatina for violin and piano and a group of preludes for piano have a similar dynamic strength. He has written two important works for percussion, the most recent, *Tambuco,* an exciting display piece in successive groups of timbres (scraping sounds, knocking sounds, chiming sounds, drums). Silvestre Revueltas, a more prolific, colorful, and wayward composer, wrote a variety of orchestral and instrumental pieces, notably his *Homage to Garcia Lorca* with the bugle calls and dusty atmosphere of a Mexican bullfight, and a symphonic poem, *Sensemaya,* based on native sounds and rhythms. Both composers—Revueltas especially—borrowed the traditional music of the Mexican Indians, melodies and instrumental types which can be traced back as far as the Aztec and Mayan cultures. Revueltas died relatively young, leaving a body of music which deserves more notice than it has received.

Alberto Ginastera, from Argentina, is widely regarded as the most exciting South American composer of the present day. He has learned virtuosity from Bartók but without the radical substance which makes Bartók's music difficult. Latin American composing, after a sudden rise to wide recognition during the 1930s, seems to have slumped into a continuing cultural lethargy.

29

THE AMERICAN EXPERIMENTAL
TRADITION II

McPhee, Harrison, Hovhaness, Partch, Brant

The American composer Edward MacDowell wrote: "It is the Chinese conception of music that *the texture of a sound is to be valued;* the long, trembling tone-tint of a bronze gong, or the high, thin streams of sound from the pipes are enjoyed for their ear-filling qualities. . . ." MacDowell, in the romantic tradition, distinguished the thought pattern of music from the texture of its sounds. Exotic sound seemed to him unnecessary, yet his language sings with the responses of his sensibility to the Oriental sounds. Music, he believed, should aim at "causing the hearer to go beyond the actual sounds heard, in pursuance of a train of thought primarily suggested by this music." A composer in the polyglot succession from Liszt to Grieg, MacDowell romanticized his style to convey the idea which produced it. He could evoke in notes a water-lily, the heroism of Norse or Celtic legend, or the dirge of an Indian mother lamenting the death of her son.

His younger and unknown contemporary Charles Ives, holding a similar conviction that the substance of music weighs more than its manner, employed to idiomatic advantage every means of sound he believed natural to himself. He disapproved of the exotic for its own sake. ". . . if a man finds that the cadences of an Apache war-dance come nearest to his soul, provided he has taken pains to know enough other cadences—for eclecticism is part of his duty—let him assimilate whatever he finds highest of the Indian ideal, so that he can use it with the cadences, fervently, transcendentally, inevitably, furiously, in his symphonies, in his operas, in his whistlings on the way to work, so that he can paint his house with them—make them a part of his prayer-book—this is all possible and necessary, if he is confident that they have a part in his spiritual consciousness."[1]

The American experimental tradition has followed the direction of MacDowell's sensibilities and Ives's practice. Carl Ruggles, Edgard Varèse, each in his own way, created a new music of sound, going beyond the formerly permissible limits of the Western European tradition. With this breakthrough, American music began reaching towards the Orient.

Among the early orientalizing American composers were Henry Eichheim and Dane Rudhyar. But the chief influence of the Orient in American music came through Henry Cowell. As a boy in California he became acquainted with Japanese and Chinese music as it was performed on the West Coast; throughout his life he has retained close friendship with musicians of Oriental cultures. Among his last works is a Concerto for Koto (the Japanese psaltery) and orchestra. He has studied the music of many peoples, collected their instruments, particularly flutes, and incorporated both the musical idioms and the instruments in a variety of unusual compositions, among them his *Persian Set*, a symphony with Indian as well as Western instruments, and *Ongaku*, in a style reflecting the classical idiom of the Japanese court orchestra.

One of Cowell's early compositions was for strings with bull-roarer obbligato. In a New York performance the vibrating disk, whirling at the end of a thong, broke loose and lit on the stage apron, just short of the head of critic Lawrence Gilman in the front row of seats. The threat was symbolic. Cowell more than any other urged American composers of younger generations to fear nothing in bringing together the most diverse instruments and traditions into an American music increasingly free of traditional European ideology and method.

"The only warning I wish to give you," he said to young composers, "is against the feeling that any single style, any single technique, is the only possible one, or the only good one, or the only important one. That kind of thinking is the source of all sterility." And he said in Tokyo: "Today no inherited style, no single acquired technique, will enable a composer to live in the twentieth century."

The danger in this way of thinking is exemplified by the music of the Japanese composer Michio Miyagi, who wrote in this century a music of mixed Japanese and European mannerisms: for the ancient bamboo flute (*shakuhachi*) a composition requiring the technical dexterity of the Western transverse flute, Viennese waltzes for an orchestra of *shakuhachis* and *kotos*—even a jig! He also used such Western instruments as the violin.

Miyagi's musicianship was eclectic and derivative, overloaded with the jaded arpeggios and melodious affects of Western sweet music. Yet one should not underrate Miyagi, who revived the popularity of the traditional Japanese instruments in competition with the rise of Japanese symphony orchestras by showing that musicians of the native tradition need not be deprived of new westernizing ideas.

Younger Japanese composers, among them Toshiro Mayuzumi and Toshi Ichiyanagi, the former an admirer of Varèse, the latter at one time a member of the New York experimental group which has learned from Cage, have carried back to Japan a more contemporary mingling of Western and Oriental means, ideas, and instruments. Mayuzumi, a sophisticated composer who has written a great number of scores for the Japanese film industry, composed in his *Nirvana Symphony* a large work for chorus and orchestra incorporating the traditional chanting of Buddhist monks and the sound of temple bells. Both composers are at ease in electronic music, indeterminacy, and the more extreme effects of sound-composition. Ichiyanagi mixes Western and Oriental instruments in indeterminate designs of random sound, yet his music remains intrinsically Japanese. He has a remarkable feeling for minimal and marginal sounds. The quality of his musical line suggests the alternatively smooth and rough edges of Japanese ink-brush painting.

In America a composer of Chinese ancestry, Chou Wen-chung, has brought to Western instruments a music subtly conveying the rhythms and colors of Chinese poetry and painting. Halim El-Dabh, from Egypt, more recently musical adviser to the Emperor of Abyssinia, wrote a large ballet, *Clytemnestra*, for Martha Graham, combining European and Egyptian idioms.

American Negro singers, instrumentalists, and eventually composers created the natural idioms and forms of shout, spiritual, blues, and jazz. Negro singers have been conspicuously successful in performing Western European music; several today sing leading roles with European operatic companies. Rather few Negro instrumentalists have succeeded in winning a similar place—not for lack of gift, as their leadership in jazz abundantly demonstrates. Negro composers have not yet found an idiom of large scope natural to their inheritance. When such an eminent jazz composer as Duke Ellington composes at symphonic length, the result is formless, if not pastiche, without content. The fault lies in trying to commingle the styles of jazz with the styles of European tradition, instead of exploring an idiomatic consistency enforcing its own style. One may speculate about sociological reasons, but Ellington has enjoyed incomparably greater opportunity than Ives.

Debussy and Ravel heard the Javanese *gamelan* at the Paris Exposition, and a new sense of color entered European music. Mahler and Puccini wrote imitation Chinese melodies, based on authentic sources, that imparted a fresh color to their harmonies. The whole-tone scale, in its brief empirical reign, opened ears to other coloristic combinations, temporarily exciting and as easily rationalized. Josef M. Hauer developed a serial method of twelve-tone music, as some like to say, "before Schoenberg," which brought from Schoenberg an offer to collaborate in a book, the chapters to be written alternately by each composer, defining their differences and the most important common elements. Alois Hába, a Czech composer interested in folk music, propagandized for and composed in quarter-tones (twenty-four-note scale). Hába was one of the heroes of John Cage's musical pantheon, because his quarter-tone composing went beyond the convention of twelve notes. When during a visit to Prague the mature Cage at last encountered Hába, he rushed to introduce himself to the master whom he admired. "Why do you write such horrible music!" was all Hába replied.

What was taken for granted as common theoretical knowledge about Bach, Beethoven, Berlioz, and Brahms was almost as mysterious in the minds of young musical practitioners as the equally real facts they were trying to grasp about the practices of Debussy, Strauss, Scriabin, and Stravinsky. The necessary rationalizations had to be learned as dogma and needed constant adjustment in usage. No amount of theoretical knowledge could enable anyone to create a new work in the style of Bach, Beethoven, Berlioz, or Brahms, but one could attempt to re-create Debussy, Strauss, Scriabin, and Stravinsky; nearly three decades passed before composers and the more attentive listeners became aware that this also was impossible. Composers then embraced, for the wrong reasons, the iconographic self-sufficiency of twelve-tone serial composition; the new practitioners refuted Schoenberg, who had declared that the tone-row is not a compositional method. A great part of the confusion throughout music at the present time can be understood by recognizing the consequences of many overlapping time-lags in musical education, in the experience and habituation of composers and audiences, in the rationalizing efforts of musical theoreticians and critics to defend their beliefs against the encroachments of irreconcilable new information and new practices.

A Canadian-born composer, Colin McPhee, returned to the United States after spending several years in Java and Bali during the 1930s. He transcribed Indonesian music for piano and composed in Indonesian idioms, using of course equal temperament instead of the correct Indonesian scales. McPhee's book *A House in Bali* and subsequent writings, culminating in *Music in Bali*, told much about the Indonesian music and the companioning traditional dances. In 1936 he composed, at the suggestion of the Mexican composer Carlos Chávez, his best-known orchestral work, *Tabuh-Tabuhan*, bringing together what he called a "nuclear *gamelan*" consisting of two pianos, celesta, xylophone, marimba, glockenspiel, Balinese cymbals and gongs with the traditional symphony orchestra.

Inspired in part by the example of McPhee, the elaborate combinations of percussion instruments in the works of Varèse, and the far-off cry of Marinetti's Futurist Manifesto, John Cage and fellow composers Lou Harrison and William Russell put together a homemade *gamelan* of percussive sound-producers. For the exactly pitched bronze bars and pots of the *gamelan* they substituted such musical means as Ford Model A brake drums, gloriously resonant but with no exact pitch; a set of brake drums arranged in microtonal sequence gives a resonant melodic instrument of quite arbitrary scale in narrow intervals. Substituting rhythmic for harmonic structure in this music which included microtonal or nontonal sound, Cage found corroboration for his ideas in Indian music, as well as in Satie and Webern. He conceived a music free of the European metrical and intervallic systems, prophesying his later development of indeterminate or aleatoric music.

Double-Music, composed in alternate sections by Cage and Harrison, imitates the accumulative effect of the *gamelan,* in quite different instrumental means. Cage's *Construction in Metal* incorporates numerical elements of form and rhythm derived from the music of India, and the instruments include a small authentic *gamelan.* Harrison wrote percussion *Simfonies* (his spelling), *Canticles,* and other pieces, among them a Mass for chorus, percussion, and bells, as the Mass is said to have been sung in the California Spanish missions. Several of Harrison's works include *gamelan* rhythms, among them the Suite for violin, piano, and small orchestra, the large chamber work *Solstice,* and the jewellike *Concerto in Slendro* for violin, tack pianos, celesta, and percussion. Other compositions employ Cage's Indian-derived schemata in a pitchless microtonal polyphony, which stands apart from the generally timbre-related character of the percussion literature. Harrison is a melodist, one of the most gifted of this century, but his conception of melody is preharmonic, linking the tone-row with the earlier Renaissance polyphony, exploring a Western elaboration of Oriental pentatonic scales.

For a while during the 1940s Cage followed Harrison in melodic exploration, the culminating work of this development his melodic-exotic sonatas and interludes for prepared piano. The ascendancy of discordant serialism with the breakdown of equal-tempered harmony and Cage's shift of direction to indeterminate-aleatoric and noise-music during the 1950s almost entirely distracted attention from the equally vital melodic-tonal alternative, so deeply rooted in music of all cultures and in preharmonic Western European music.

Harrison's sensitivity to the most subtle relationships of pitch and timbre had early convinced him that tonality should revert to the acoustically correct intervals of just intonation, that music should give up modulation and resume where the European polyphony of the fifteenth and sixteenth centuries ceased, at the start of the Harmonic Era. Throughout his compositions, whether written in equal temperament, in arbitrary microtonal intervals, or in just intonation, melodic inflection replaces harmonic modulation. As a student of Schoenberg he learned a thorough command of the tone-row, demonstrated in his Suite for Piano and *Schoenbergiana* (for string quintet, now arranged for wind sextet), afterwards adapting the row principles to his own concordant purpose. In pentatonic, diatonic, twelve-tone, or extratonal means he writes with a seeming simplicity which disarms theoretical routine. He has studied Korean, Japanese, Chinese, and Thai music and instruments and has written in Korean notation for the ancient medium of the Korean court orchestra. His *Nova Odo,* composed like many of his works in the open vowels of Esperanto, though performable in English, combines orchestra and chorus in just intonation with obbligato passages by a group of Korean oboes (*piri*) playing microtones. The microtones emphasize the higher partials of the overtone series in just intonation.

For the Festival of Music and Arts of This Century at the University of Hawaii, Harrison composed a *Pacifika Rondo* in seven movements, using a chamber orchestra of Western instruments with seven Oriental instruments and male voice. The musical techniques and styles of the movements reflect Korean and Japanese court music, Chinese chamber music, some Mexican and Spanish Colonial, and "one intrusion of common Atlantic 'modernism.' New serial techniques," he goes on to say in the program note, "have been used in movements in which the listener is least likely to suspect them. . . . I have been bold to try several of the ways in which I think classic Asian musics might of themselves, and together, evolve in the future, and have combined instruments of several ethnics directly for musical expression." It is a dangerous daring, a fresh exploration in the total field of sound Ives entered a half-century earlier.

Although the steplike progress of Cage's musical ideas, not imitating but continuing from the similar stepwise development of Schoenberg's musical ideas, has been for two decades the growing center of the American experimental tradition, one must keep clearly in mind the importance of Harrison's less conspicuous maturing—and the fact that the more obscure art of any period may be of primary importance in a succeeding period. Harrison and Cage stem from the same musical sources, European and American, but Harrison's roots spread more widely, and he is also linked more directly than Cage to the originators of the American tradition. While Cage rejected until recently the authority of Ives, Harrison has been, almost from boyhood, a propagator of Ives's music. He edited several of Ives's scores for publication, among them the Third Symphony, which he then conducted in its world premiere performance. He also directed in New York a performance of Ruggles's *Men and Mountains,* a decade and a half before Leonard Bernstein got around to repeating it. He has written short but important articles about the music of Ives, Ruggles, and Varèse.

Like Ives, Harrison composed in his early years a large pool of shorter works, from which he draws material for his maturer compositions. His composing emphasizes the fact that in the new sound-music just intonation will be no less important than noise, that concordant melodic polyphony is still a fertile area, and that microtonal intervals may be as free of exact acoustical relationship as the composer should be aware of it. He has shown that a composer need not aim at an all-embracing sound-polyphony but can try with equal pleasure many differing simpler combinations of sound.

Among his major works are a Symphony on G and a short opera, *Rapunzel.* His *Four Strict Songs* for eight baritones and orchestra and Suite for Symphonic Strings, both written to be performed in just intonation, were recorded by the Louisville Symphony, the former more accurately, the latter with varying degrees of intonational success. Several movements of the *Suite* parody, without reduction, the contrapuntal styles of senior contemporary composers, including a fugue with viola obbligato in unmistakably Schoenbergian wide intervals and a double fugue—in just intonation without dissonance—in the most elaborate style of Hindemith. His Second Suite for Strings, in nondissonant serial style, as recorded by the New Music Quartet, is an excellent example of just intonation in performance.

Hearing lately several more recent works by Benjamin Johnston—for instrumental groups with and without voice—also performed in just intonation, I would venture a distinction: with just intonation, wherever the human voice leads the music the gain of enriched sonority and tonal eloquence is unmistakable; but in strictly instrumental music, the loss of dissonance and discordance reduces the dramatic contrast we are accustomed to expect. This may be one reason, apart from the harmonic adaptation of the scale to fixed-pitch instruments, why composers, historically, with the increase of purely instrumental composing, began preferring the dramatic bite and contrast of a partly dissonant harmony to the blander sonority of just intonation. A similar criticism has been made of the effect of tone-row music when performed in exact equal temperament, as on a well-tuned piano: intonational uniformity reduces contrast. But the dramatic interest of Western European music is exceptional in the world's music, and the contemplative value of a more subtly colored, tonally uniform music is not yet so well appreciated as it may come to be, particularly as our awareness of the music of other cultures increases.

The probable outcome, already pointed by the example of Ives, is likely to be an increased utilization of the entire field of sound, bringing into relationship and contrast correct intonation, dissonance and discordance, microtonal intervals, and noise. Ives's most emphatic music is not his most characteristic, but rather the areas of subtly intertwining sound which offer no dramatic action.

Harrison's Mass, rewritten for unison chorus (alternating with occasional vocal solo), trumpet, harp, and strings, is distinguished by its restraint, the individuality of each section without recourse to drama, and the obbligato freedom of the vocal line, with no effort to display contrapuntal ingenuity. Composed in euphony, without key-harmony, modulation, or discordance, enriched like the late cantatas of Webern by preharmonic linear techniques, the Mass is a tower of tonal tone-emancipation in the postdodecaphonic landscape. (Another example is the large Symphony on G.) In a decade when the authoritarian Pierre Boulez had pronounced an interdict on all scalewise composition, the triumphant rise of the scale at the beginning of the *Alleluia* presents a decisive contradiction. Not less talented as musician and theorist than Boulez, with a natural, more widely ranging gift for composing, Harrison lacks only the propagandistic skill, or wish, to exploit his reputation. Work of art which exists apart from the contemporary fashion is not necessarily less prophetic or less skilled. Harrison withdrew many years ago from the competitive musical scene to continue his work in relative privacy, supporting himself much of the time by extramusical activities.

Another American composer, Alan Hovhaness, wrote his earlier works in poetic forms based on Near Eastern melodic traditions, especially those of his Armenian ancestry. He is an exotic rather than fundamentally an experimentalist; his skill enables him to devise fresh combinations by devices which give the effect of originality without going beyond what will be acceptable.

Hovhaness is not a setter of folk tunes. He has traveled, studying the native music, in Greece, India, Japan, and Korea, seeking to create a self-sustaining, long melodic line which furnishes its own harmonic coloration—a goal already achieved, without reference to borrowed material, by Carl Ruggles.

A prolific composer, Hovhaness disdains no commission that will allow him to write what he believes to be a suitable music. Among his recent works are a Seventeenth Symphony using entirely metallic instruments for the American Metallurgical Congress, and a Cantata on the opening verses of the Gospel of Saint John for a national Methodist conference. His music extends itself by long, rather simple melodies through a figuration of diverse instrumental timbres, in stylistic modes that reach back to the early Christian and the medieval, to ancient and to modern Asia. A Japanese critic wrote that Hovhaness's compositions are "like Japanese scrolls. As they are rolled out, they reveal new images and their message bit by bit. Western classical music is in comparison like a photographic print." The music exists not as a discrete structure but as a series of discoveries among instrumental clangors, the voices participating in the harmonic resonances they evoke. Hovhaness has written, like Harrison, for combined Oriental and Western instruments, as in his Sixteenth Symphony.

Certainly there are dangers of misconception or failure in any attempt to mingle instruments and ethnic musical habits until recently deemed incompatible. Yet the trend in this direction is becoming stronger. At the Ethnomusicological Institute of the University of California, Los Angeles, directed by Mantle Hood, skilled young musicians from distinct ethnic cultures teach one another to play their related or unlike music and instruments; American students learn from them the varieties of Oriental music. The students rehearse and perform on two large and several smaller *gamelans;* a *gagaku* group learns and performs the ancient court music of Japan; and there are other groups studying and performing in North and South Indian, Ghanaian, Philippine, Mexican, Persian, Thai, and Balkan traditions.

It seems sure that the reaching of musical arts towards one another from many cultures and periods will generate an original music, which will be, no less than the electronic composition now increasing so rapidly among us, a part of the new, vastly enlarged field of sound-music we anticipate.

Peripheral to this development, the percussion instruments conceived and built by Harry Partch to perform music composed by him in the scale of forty-three tones to the octave reflect a knowledge of the *gamelan* and suggest to unfamiliar ears the *gamelan* sound, though his compositions contain an enlarged harmony and are not at all Oriental. Partch rejected equal temperament in any form, devising instead a scale of true just intonation in unequal intervals, based on the study of intonation expounded in his book, *Genesis of a Music*. Partch's scale dispenses with key-harmony and modulation in conventional terms, while permitting an expansion of harmonic relationships in degrees unobtainable with twelve tones. Even in dissonance the correct acoustical relationship of overtones enriches the sonorities.

With a scale of intervals so finely divided, one is able to speak to exact pitches as easily as sing. The artificiality of recitative is done away with—rejected by Purcell, recitative has never been satisfactorily domesticated to English speech. Instead, there is by the use of the forty-three-tone scale a continuous field of melodic and harmonic relationship among the degrees of spoken, intoned, chanted, sung, melismatic, and shouted vocal utterance, a tonal spectrum filling in the gap between the vocal coloration of opera and the spoken drama. Spoken melody may be taken over by the instruments and translated back again to chant and song.

By arranging the adjustable bridges under the strings of one instrument, the *harmonic canon,* consisting of two overlapping sets of forty-four strings, Partch can define the melodic, harmonic, and melismatic materials of a work in advance of composition. No musician since Adolphe Sax a hundred years before has invented and built so many new instruments: great marimbas made of planks or cubes of wood with heavy wooden resonators, tall kitharas in the shape of a Greek harp standing as much as seven feet high with uprising arms and banks of strings, rounded sections of Pyrex carboys suspended like bells from a frame, as well as adapted conventional instruments—viola, cello, guitar, harmonium. There is only one set of instruments, and the size of them prevents easy transportation.

In an age when instruments are mass-manufactured, old instruments "reproduced" from external measurements or assembled of materials which alter the sounding character of the intonation, we have lost appreciation of the rare skill to design and build new instruments which will sound. Minute acoustical deviations, requiring much adjustment and often past improving, make the final difference.

To perform Partch's compositions, musicians must learn to read the notation and play the instruments; singers and speakers must be trained to distinguish and produce unaccustomed intervals in a scale larger and more complex than our own. The composer must function as teacher, tuner, instrument repairman, technical adviser, and vocal and dramatic coach. Partch has been careful to record each of his works in a reasonably good performance, so that the survival of his compositions is ensured.

Partch believes that music should be a dramatic and visual rather than a merely auditory or absolute experience. The very appearance of his instruments is dramatic; in *Water, Water* several of them move about the stage; in his forthcoming drama, *Delusion of the Fury,* the instruments "are the set." (See Appendix B.) One may differ with him, citing the long history of purely instrumental music since the sixteenth century. He has on his side the longer and broader tradition of earlier Euripean and of nearly all non-European cultures, that the art of music begins in ceremony, dance, and drama, enriched by speech, chanting, shouting, noisemaking, and melismatic song. Despite his belief, Partch has written several works for instruments alone.

In the purely instrumental *And on the Seventh Day Petals Fell on Petaluma* (1966) he has composed 33 *Verses,* each about one minute long: a sequence of duets and one trio, then the duets combined, some as quartets, some as sextets, with a concluding septet. Except reed organ, the instruments are plucked strings or percussion. Thus the sound medium is emancipated from the orchestral tradition. By eliminating bowed strings and all but a modicum of sustaining wind, Partch has required himself to speak his native idiom, with no accustomed foothold on sustained tones to distinguish melody; the tones are almost continually in the "wrong" place. That these "wrong" notes happen to be, acoustically, the right ones adds a light of comedy to aural misapprehension. The rhythm seems in similar manner to be downright as jazz and quite obviously never is.

His scale closes the operatic gap between song and speech. His major compositions include four full-length dramas. *Oedipus* is a dramatic and dance setting of the Sophoclean tragedy which can well bear comparison with Stravinsky's oratorio-like setting. *Revelation in the Courthouse Park,* an arrangement of Euripides' *The*

Bacchae, alternates dramatic scenes in Greek costume and mask with choral scenes and revels in midwestern American setting, the classical characters taking on contemporary roles. Text and music are made up of what Partch calls "Midwestern rituals," fragments of hymnlike and popular melody, rhythms ranging from rock-and-roll to staccato cries resembling those of a football cheering section, with choruses of Handelian eloquence. The verbal text is made up in the same way of short statements (anacoluthons) of wide religious and popular implication, the same fragment having sometimes both a sacred and a popular significance: "Holy joy and get religion!" The mingling of archaic and modern ritualistic terms—*The Bacchae* is in origin a Dionysiac ritual of sacrifice—juxtaposes psychological with religious characterization of the dramatic events. Modern popular dance furnishes the revels. Partch is his own librettist.

Water, Water, a comedy, continues Partch's habit of composing libretto and music from significant fragments of contemporary speech, rhythm, melody, and tune. He writes "in the style of" but does not quote. *The Bewitched* is an evening-long ballet with vocal interjections, the satirico-fantastic action set forth in a detailed libretto by the composer. A shorter semidramatic work, *U. S. Highball,* is a spoken, sung, recited, chanted conversation among hoboes going east on a freight train out of San Francisco, the talk interspersed with melismatic chanting of the names of stops and states along the route. During the depression 1930s Partch himself hoboed for eight years.

He has set to music the spoken texts of poems, newsboys' cries, and hobo graffiti. No composer is more indigenously American. Accustomed to equating our native rugged individualism with the frontiersman or the self-made businessman, we do not so easily recognize the same qualities when these appear in a present-day artist or composer. Partch offers a new musical system as valid and self-consistent as that of the recent Western European tradition but with a larger harmonic range. Those who believe music has advanced from pentatonic to diatonic to twelve-tone should recognize that Partch's has been a more far-thinking leap. Although Partch has worked in several universities, he has never been invited to join a music faculty as teacher or theorist.

Any worker in the new electronic sound who believes himself far ahead of Partch's medium is quite wrong. Generations of electronic composers may be needed to accomplish a range of tones and timbres as practically and subtly interrelated in acoustical correctness and as firmly at the composer's command."

We describe as "unpopular" any music which lacks a sizable public, yet one need only think back to our slight knowledge of the work of Anton Webern before Robert Craft brought out the recorded album of the *Complete Music,* to our unrelieved incomprehension of the progress of John Cage before the appearance of the recorded album of his *25-Year Retrospective Concert* made in 1958. It is not unreasonable to suppose that a more practical distribution of Partch's records might have a similar result. At the present time, the records must be obtained from the composer, after one has found out where he is living. There are also three short films with scores by Partch; in one of these he demonstrates his instruments, concluding with a synchronized performance on several of the instruments at once.

Henry Brant, a Canadian, with excellent academic training and a long experience as orchestrator and arranger of dance, film, and radio music, has composed works of unorthodox instrumentation with conspicuously fanciful titles: *Angels and Devils* for solo flute with an orchestra of flutes; a piece for tin whistle and orchestra called *Chico, Groucho, and Harpo; Ice Age* for the chilly combination of clarinet, glockenspiel, and piano; a large theatrical-performance composition marvelously entitled *The Grand Universal Circus;* and a succession of *Galaxies* for varied combinations. Like Riegger, with whom he studied, he makes up a lack of melodic individuality by an uncompromising craftsmanship. He rejected his earlier compositions to experiment in more individual methods and styles.

Brant uses for some compositions a "polyphony of tempos." As Gilbert Chase describes it, "each separated group or instrument [in a composition for diverse instrumental groups] has not only its own particular time signature, but also its own independent tempo. For example, in *Millennium 2,* in one place, there are as many as twenty-one different tempi heard simultaneously; but only one conductor is needed! In *Antiphony 1,* on the other hand, five conductors are required."[2]

In this, as in his practice of distributing the forces of a large composition at different levels around a concert hall, Brant takes after father and son Ives. Unlike their European counterparts, the American experimental composers do not conspicuously advertise themselves, their creative innovations, or their theories. Brant, a thorough all-round musician, conductor, and performer on several instruments, has been a major contributor to what I have called the fourth dimension of music, a theatrical-performance music as game or play involving audience participation. (See Chapter 32.) Brant has brought the audience into the work by creating it around them, so that they sit in the midst of visible and invisible sound-sources all performing at once, an experience now more familiar in the use of multiple loudspeakers. Because of the forces required and the unusual conditions, there have been few performances of Brant's larger works, and it is difficult to estimate their effectiveness. Recording or broadcast cannot do them justice. With the present widespread rise of theatrical-performance music in this country and abroad, Brant's larger compositions need and deserve much more performance than they have been granted. It is in encouraging and implementing such performances, as well as the more routine concerts of contemporary music, that the arts councils and the foundations should give leadership.

✽ Esthetic consistency is, by my definition, content, but in writing about certain composers one tends to give the impression that the many media of expression are in themselves the heart of the matter, that the composer adapts himself, with whatever technical consistency, to the media, rather than informing the media, or means, with his unique content. Thence arises the romantic manner of appreciation, which tries to describe, in a variety of ways, what the composer is writing *about,* or the analyst's contrary conviction counting only the notes.

In reading such a book as this, as well as writing it, one must recognize that among composers, some (Beethoven, Schoenberg, Cage) almost too sharply present themselves in what seems a logical progression by steps, whereas others animate a landscape of many diverse aspects (Berlioz, Ives, Harrison). Some (like Piston, Sessions, Carter, or Dahl) have realized themselves in a few works, asserting a common tradition that is in their work fully but not uniquely individualized; these are likely to be confused with the large body of academic composers whose skilled esthetic dissertations seldom achieve individuality. Others (Brant, Hovhaness, Partch, and again Harrison) require a special field of reference, which may be confined or diffuse but requires an extensive particularized knowledge to be done in words.

I place this note here as a warning that all estimations should not be reckoned by number of name entries, length of space devoted to the individual composer, or an appearance of conclusiveness in summary. A considerable part of the influence of Cage and the somewhat lesser authority of Boulez and Stockhausen results from modes of presentation which may be ephemeral; the essentials of Partch's creative work may have to survive by recording, for lack of a duplicate set of instruments and the skill to design, build, and use them. And it has not been possible for me to have the personal acquaintance with Brant's work that I have with the work of Partch. To cover such inequities by an apparent uniformity of scholarship or presentation seems to me dishonest and unwise.

30

AN INTRODUCTION TO JOHN CAGE

A former music librarian of the Los Angeles Public Library, Gladys Caldwell, told me that around 1924 a young but commanding voice spoke to her over the telephone: "My name is John Cage. I am twelve years old. I play the piano. I wish to find a violinist who will play the Beethoven sonatas with me. Can you find me one?" The authority of the young voice was not to be denied; she found the violinist.

A few years later, the still adolescent Cage was visiting house-wives in his neighborhood of Santa Monica to invite them to attend a series of lectures on contemporary music he intended to offer, himself when possible performing the music. Learning that the pianist Richard Buhlig, in Los Angeles, had been among the first to perform Schoenberg's *Three Piano Pieces*, opus 11, Cage went to Buhlig's residence at noon; no one was there. When Buhlig returned at midnight he found the young man waiting and indignantly refused the request to play for him. Cage afterwards studied piano and composition with Buhlig and gave him a painting of part of a house, seen realistically at an angle with an effect of cubist abstraction. Cage has not continued a possible career in painting, but his ideas have had decisive influence on the developments in American painting during the last twenty years, while inducing at the same time a strong and sublimating abstract-expressive (nonrepresentative) visual element into music, as exemplified by the works of Morton Feldman and Earle Brown, and a regard for the visual score itself as an esthetic object.

Cage devised a method of composing which "dealt with the problem of keeping repetitions of the 25 individual tones within a two-octave span as far apart as possible": no voice "introduces a repetition until all 25 tones have appeared." This method, like that of Carl Ruggles, is independent of the tone-row. Cage attended Henry Cowell's classes and worked with the American composer Adolph Weiss, who prepared him for study with Schoenberg. Cage studied with Schoenberg for two years, then went on to discover his own means. In earlier writings and lectures Cage afterwards denied the structural value of the tone-row: "The tone-row does not offer a structural means; it is a method, a control, not of the parts, large and small, of a composition, but only of the minute, note-to-note procedure." He also put aside the work of Ives: "He did do things in space and collage, and he did say, Do this or this (whichever you choose), and so indeterminacy which is so essential now did enter into his music" —as the verbal practice of Gertrude Stein is evident in Cage's sentence. "But his meters and rhythms are no longer any more important for us than curiosities of the past like the patterns one finds in Stravinsky."[1] Cage now praises both Schoenberg and Ives.

When I first encountered Cage, in 1939, we argued all evening, he insisting that Stravinsky was the great rhythmist of contemporary music, myself arguing that there are many other types of rhythm, citing Schoenberg's rhythms and that of Mozart's little *Gigue.* The remarkable quality of Cage's intelligence in early years did not show in his opinions, which were often uninformed and incorrect, but in the searchlight exclusiveness of his perceptions which lit so clearly for him the next step of his own progress. If he was critically fallible, his prophecies have seldom failed to be correct.

Cage learned from Marinetti, Cowell, and Varèse, from Indian and Indonesian music, the principles which he embodied in a new music for percussion; he learned from Satie and Webern, whose work was still generally unknown, and from the French Dada artist Marcel Duchamp an art of minimum statement that plays with its own elements for amusement as seriously as one plays a game of chess. Influenced by Carlos Chávez's book, *Toward a New Music,* and Cowell's *New Musical Resources,* he proposed eliminating the performer and his variable interpretation by composing directly on a record. In this way he created in 1939 his *Imaginary Landscape No. 1* (see page 14). *Imaginary Landscape No. 2* (1942) combines percussion instruments, buzzers, and an amplified coil of wire. In *Imaginary Landscape No. 3* (also 1942) he combined percussion with electrical and mechanical devices: audio-frequency oscillators, variable speed turntables, variable frequency recordings and "generator whines," and a buzzer. In these three compositions he realized the potentiality of indeterminately pitched electronic sound.

Imaginary Landscape No. 4 (1951) has become famous as the "Concert for 12 Radios and 24 Performers": one performer for the station dial and one for the volume dial, each following his own score; the rhythmic structure in changing tempi held together by a conductor beating chronological instead of metrical time; the notation "in space," a half-inch equaling a quarter-note. The first performance occurred much later in the evening than had been planned; programs were different and some stations had gone off the air. Unthinking critics haw-hawed that the performance had therefore gone wrong, since everything that was heard was unexpected. Cage was delighted and went on to glorify the failure in his new doctrine of music by chance. Critics better gifted with mathematical knowledge than musical imagination pointed out that this was not pure random chance but only relative chance; Cage renamed his new doctrine "Indeterminacy." To this one may object that his compositions by indeterminacy are exceedingly determinate. The rules of the game determine the nature of the play and the shape of the end-product. If it were not so, each composition by indeterminacy would be equally indeterminate, haphazard, unrecognizable, and shapeless. (This has indeed been the result of some of Cage's more extreme ventures, although even experienced critics might differ concerning which ones. The failure is more noticeable among his imitators.) All that has in fact been changed is the means of arriving at, and the location or shapeliness of, the shape. Form, in these days, need no longer be determined by outline or surface in depth; we understand nuclear structure not by what it looks like, which we guess, but by what it does. "Action painting" or a Calder mobile are examples of determinate form arrived at by indeterminacy and continuously fluid. Cage composed the score which accompanies a well-known documentary film of Calder mobiles.

Imaginary Landscape No. 5 is the first major sound-composition on tape: ". . . a score for making a recording on tape, using as material any 42 phonograph records. Each graph unit equals three inches of tape. . . . Differences of amplitude (1–8) are given. The rhythmic structure is 5 times 5. The composing means involved chance operations derived from the *I-Ching*."[2] Cage's performance version is merely one example of this do-it-yourself composition. Cage quickly realized that the value of such composition is in part the ability to cheat the rules or change the terms. Instead of forty-two records, any sounds or actions, or the absence of them, will do as well—or a few sounds indefinitely extended by recording them at very low frequency—mixing up the elements of graphic space, pitch frequency, event, and time. There is a point at which the audience—if there is to be one—may be simply bored, however impelled by cultural fashion to be present, or discouraged from continuing the effort of attention. Chaos is for Cage a positive, not a collapse of meaning but a source of unpredictable events.

I have written that one may think of John Cage as a philosopher, who uses instead of arguments esthetic *instances*. He is a thinker who will not be confined within esthetics, for whom the doings of music and words and poetry reach out into and affect a larger context than the appreciative. He is concerned with the event, not with its meaning; with the digits and their arrangement, not with the total number or the sum. His concentrated attention to what the work of art is doing at any moment, disregarding tradition, formalistic convention, precedent, links him with Gertrude Stein and Ludwig Wittgenstein. (The latter observation, when first made, drew Cage's notice to Wittgenstein's writings, which he had not read, and he was grateful.) Cage's attitude is charged with a morality of intense esthetic observations; he directs us to observe the commonplace miracles, not only the creations but the breakdowns, which are happening everywhere around us, sounds, noises, comments, visual occurrences, contradictions of expected happenings, that require us to examine freshly what we have been taking in all the time—like a fish tasting the water in which it lives and breathes. Many esthetes prefer an unnatural environment, like a fish swimming in wine.

Cage's esthetic instances include words as well as music. He performs and has recorded a lecture, called *Indeterminacy*, in which he tells ninety stories at the rate of exactly one a minute, speaking faster or more slowly as necessary. He has on occasion extended the lecture to 180 minutes. His principal writings and lectures have been collected in a book, *Silence;* they are compositions in the same manner and by the same means as his music: "When M. C. Richards asked me why I didn't one day give a conventional formal lecture, adding that that would be the most shocking thing I could do, I said, 'I don't give these lectures to surprise people, but out of a need for poetry.' As I see it, poetry is not prose simply because poetry is one way or another formalized. It is not poetry by reason of its content or ambiguity but by reason of allowing musical elements (time, sound) to be introduced into the world of words. Thus, traditionally, information no matter how stuffy (e.g. the sutras and shastras of India) was transmitted in poetry."[3]

A graphic verbal instance prefaces the book:

written in
response to
a request for } instantaneous   and unpredictable
a manifesto on
music, 1952 } nothing is accomplished by writing a ⎫
                    piece of music
              nothing is accomplished by hearing a ⎬ our ears
                    piece of music   are now in
              nothing is accomplished by playing a ⎭ excellent
                    piece of music   condition

His best discussion of what he has been doing is a poem, *45′ for a Speaker,* spoken to exact time including the pauses and accompanied by indicated gestures: *Cough. Laugh. Slap table. Hold up hand, gargle. Etc. Where Are We Going? And What Are We Doing?* consists of one part which he reads aloud and three other parts speaking in his voice from three loudspeakers. One voice, two voices, three voices, four voices, like a Renaissance motet, each speaking an unrelated text, falling silent, starting again, the microsecond differences in speed among the three tape turntables (which cannot be completely synchronized) providing the effect of higher and lower polyphonic parts. Listening, released from the preconception that *music must be notes,* the whole is heard as music. (The morning after first hearing it, I read through the text and recognized nearly every word. Who would expect to do as well after hearing four voices sing a four-part motet?) I have heard this performed by four readers reading simultaneously, but in my opinion the effort fails in confusion.

Some of these compositions are a type of glorified play, for example *Cartridge Music*. Phonograph-needle cartridges are attached to an overhead boom and the edge and center of a table, chosen for the resonance of its vibration when shoved back and forth across the floor. Cage and a companion, each following a different graphic pattern of events by chance, insert slinkies, pipe cleaners, miniature flags, even a tiny birthday candle which is then lighted, into the needle slots of the cartridges and agitate them, producing noises in the loudspeakers, which accompany the performance with low-frequency vibration sounds culled from records of his music. One watches the actions of the two performers as in other days one watched the actions of the clowns circulating around the three rings of the circus, and the more one relaxes into uninhibited attention the funnier it gets. The action, like great farce, treads with dangerous steps, as if unaware how narrowly it avoids the precipitous inane.

During the thirty years of John Cage's public career his name has seldom been mentioned or his latest performance been reviewed in the public prints without accompanying mockery and the distortion of observable facts. His own generation of composers and musicians, with few exceptions, holds him in disdain. For one example, in the Spring 1963 issue of the magazine *Perspectives of New Music,* Cage's name keeps popping up like the Devil in Punch and Judy, to be batted down each time by verbal bludgeon or flung brick. The rejection culminates in a review of *Silence.* The scholarly reviewer tries to be objective, to be accurate, to be amusing but not disrespectful; in the last paragraph he can no longer hold himself.

"In short, something seems to be missing. Mr. Cage is devoted, even dedicated to his art; he has no lack of talent, invention, sense of dramaturgy, care for performance, or musical *joie de vivre*. Perhaps what Mr. Cage's career as a composer lacks is a certain kind of hard work. . . . It is that peculiar labor of art itself, the incredible agony of the real artist in his struggles with lethargy and with misplaced zeal, with despair and with the temptations of his recent successes, *to get better*."

Thus the one who aspires to art and suffers with his aspiration chides the one to whom the gift comes naturally. I remember

Schoenberg telling me, when we were speaking of his String Trio, that the mark of genius is the ability to complete a whole work rapidly; and he said proudly that he began the String Trio on August 20 and completed it September 23, 1946. To a critic who will concede the entire measure of spontaneous ability and then try to qualify it by the need *to get better* one cannot explain, by exhibiting the names of Beethoven and Mozart, what Schoenberg means by "genius," the authority, the pride. (For Cage as for Stravinsky, the name "Beethoven" symbolizes all that is lumped together in misuse of the word *genius*.) The musical growth of John Cage has been as exact, exacting, and creatively logical as that of Beethoven or Schoenberg.

When I first knew John Cage he was stubborn, gifted, argumentative. As the gift took hold he became more silent, preoccupied with himself and the growing of his thought. He entered the room like a *bodhisattva*, floating. After he had studied the Japanese Zen philosophy and learned by it to master himself he became, as he has remained, the man of the great smile, the outgoing laugh, willing to explain but not, in my recent experience, to argue, tolerant of misconception, self-forgetful, and considerate. Around him everyone laughs.

To summarize: Cage invented the percussion orchestra; though others had worked with the idea (Varèse—culminating in *Ionisation*, the first masterpiece of the new medium, Cowell, Strang, Milhaud, Chávez), he formed the group that gave it a literature. Cage first put to use the sine continuum, source of subsequent electronic composition. Cage invented the prepared piano, carrying out his belief that when Schoenberg had emancipated the dissonance he should have gone farther and emancipated music from its notes. Cage challenged the concept of musical order with his music by chance or indeterminacy (random operations), now dignified as *aleatory music* and widely employed. He was the first to create an effectively sustained noise-music. His *Concert for Piano and Orchestra* and *Atlas Eclipticalis* may be called an antimusic, as a scientist speaks of antimatter. The many motives do not harmonically draw together but are mutually rejecting, an expanding not a contracting sound-universe, emphasizing silence—a more satisfactory means than the mingling of extraharmonic sounds and silence in that type of *Klangfarbenmelodie* which tries to combine the technical logic of Webern and the multiple-note tone of Messiaen with aleatory freedom. Cage is

also a master of prose, which he raises to the level of poetry, as
Gertrude Stein and James Joyce did, a gifted propagandist, and
one of the great showmen of his time. He has been the most influential composer, worldwide, of his generation. His influence
on American dance, particularly in collaboration with Jean Erd-
man and Merce Cunningham, both of whom have contributed to
his development; on American painting; and more obliquely in
poetry and theater, has been only less than his musical influence.

Though he was born in Los Angeles, the other side of the
American continent from New England, John Cage is, in appearance and mind, as in spirit and habit, the transcendental Puritan. The power that infused Emerson and Thoreau, the religious necessity that inspired William Miller to Adventism, that
lifted Joseph Smith from gold-dowser to Mosaic prophet of a
marching people seeking a new land, that drove Susan B. Anthony to the emancipation of women and Mary Baker Eddy to
establish a church upon the denial of ill-health by knowledge of
her *Key to the Scriptures;* the pragmatical-experimental Yankee
curiosity of Henry James, Sr., of father Ives, of Bronson Alcott,
C. S. Peirce, Willard Gibbs, who could project a mathematical
conclusion which afterwards became a product, of William
James's philosophy, and Cage's own father's inventions; ruminating on the unknown, speculating on the unknowable at the
edge of chaos, putting together self-consistent systems like so
many workable objects, unconcerned by theoretical completeness;
importers from the Orient, whale-hunters, merchants, philanthro-
pists, and well-wishers of mankind; the philosophical rational-
ism of the rural New England Athens: all reappear in the writing
and creative leadership of Cage. He does not hesitate to follow
other contemporary thinkers and embrace their theories, without
fear for the independence of his own course.

The face, long, lined beside the heavy jaw, resembles that of
the cartoon Puritan—the killjoy, *Prohibition*—but the lines lift
upward, not downward, around a smile like a cavern. Determined
as an abolitionist upon the emancipation of art, he has also an
abolitionist recklessness for the social consequences, but with a
Puritan distaste for physical or emotional excesses, drink or drugs.
He could not restrain his delight in telling how, in India, when a
cow enters an intersection, even where there are traffic lights,
traffic waits. The cranky, creative amateurism of the inventor
whose first thought is not for the refinement or appearance of the

machine but to make it work is disciplined by competence in a number of well-defined skills, among these electronics, the professional joinery of musicianship, and a capability of simple statement, in both melody and words, a rhetoric which seems to route rhetoric in prose, poetry, and music.

An anti-esthete like Ives, he now likes best in Ives's music, as he said to me, "the mud." Ives learned from the masters and rejected what he knew of the contemporary music; he composed in sound objects individual and substantial as fieldstones, for which there was no purchase. Cage rejects the masters and the thought of "object"—though all his scores can be purchased—to concentrate on the momentary, the event, in a frame and without frame. Like Ives he disregards art or money, his intention being a total awareness, "celebration"; but he is at the same time a philanthropist, concerned with the performance of other artists, and an organizer of complex purposes, who will spend months of effort on a single tape assemblage and has established and led the financing of a Foundation for Performance Arts in collaboration with a group of younger successful painters. For many years he has traveled throughout America and more recently abroad and around the world as music director, as well as occasional bus driver and cook, for the Merce Cunningham dance troupe, never letting increased fame or demand for his own services interfere with this service.

The projection of his musical development is as logical as his successive meanders through philosophy, esthetics, and religion are not; his theoretical rationalizations after the event are as treacherously deceiving as Schoenberg's, yet glow with a like wisdom. In Cage's most recent phase—or perhaps because so many persons hang on his occasional latest word—the philosophy always more than latent in his creative workmanship has become more prominent than the continuing need to exercise his craft, now esthetically emancipated as a broad, colorless field, infiltrated with humor, to which the audience must bring, as participants in the action, a willing, patient sensibility to the implications of whatever occurs. The seeming shortcuts offered by this attitude supply too many followers with too many quick, objective, easily rationalized productions; like Schoenberg's tone-row these become, beyond the composer's control, art-generating mechanisms; claiming to dispense with art, these solutions in fact employ the customary machinery for the customary self-exploitive purpose. But the inspiration of Cage's presence and example goes beyond the deceptive simplicity of these solutions.

He wrote me in a letter (August 4, 1953): "It becomes gradually clear to us dull-witted musicians that sound has other determinants than frequency: timbre, duration, amplitude, and (as magnetic tape makes evident) attack and decay, call it morphology, how a sound begins, continues, and dies away. And the path we are in is not a path, not a linear, but a space extending in all directions. Because it is no longer a case of moving along stepping stones (scales of any degree), but one can move, or just appear to, at any point in this total space. By changing just one of the 5 determinants the position of the sound in total space changes. And needless to say, each sound is unique and is not informed about European history and theory . . . Keeping one's mind on the emptiness, on the space, one can see that anything can be in it, is as a matter of fact, in it. That it is only our thinking and caution that keeps holding things up, that would, if we took our hands away, take care of themselves perfectly . . . I see now by many slow transitions, one of which is tempo like streams (varying and not varying), that as long as one distinguishes as I formerly did problems remain; if one stops thinking, all those things distinguished spring back suddenly into one thing: sound in space. Needing no excuse."

One may feel that this serenity, as of nature, has been invaded by a confusion of arbitrary *happenings*, of disorderly noise-producers; that it is nature no more but urban raucousness, rejecting nature; that the release from thinking has become a dogmatic rejection consummated in the slogan "purposeful purposelessness."[4] One may believe that this now world-embracing phenomenon is at a point of crisis: it has been so before but never so largely, and the solution of the crisis—or possible breakdown of the phenomenon—will be of significance, whether the outcome seem, at first reaction, positive or negative. For John Cage, unlike his contemporary Jean-Paul Sartre, is not only spinning existentialist theories and esthetic instances but living them.

31

ELECTRONIC AND COMPUTER MUSIC

"Wee have also Sound-Houses, wher wee practise and demonstrate all Sounds, and their Generation. Wee have Harmonies
which you have not, of Quarter-Sounds, and lesser Slides of
Sounds. Diverse Instruments of Musick likewise to you un-
knowne, some sweeter then any you have; Together with Bells
and Rings that are dainty and sweet. Wee represent Small Sounds
as Great and Deepe; Likewise Great Sounds, Extenuate and
Sharp; Wee make diverse Tremblings and Warblings of Sounds,
which in their Originall are Entire. Wee represent and imitate all
Articulate Sounds and Letters, and the Voices and Notes of
Beasts and Birds. Wee have certaine Helps, which sett to the
Eare doe further the Hearing greatly. Wee have also diverse
Strange and Artificial Eccho's, Reflecting the Voice many times,
and as it were Tossing it; And some that give back the Voice
Lowder then it came, some Shriller, and some Deeper; Yea some
rendring the Voice, Differing in the Letters or Articulate Sound,
from that they receyve. Wee have also meanes to convey Sounds
in Trunks and Pipes, in strange Lines, and Distances."–Sir
Francis Bacon, *New Atlantis* (dated 1624)

The unalterable fact during the first half of the twentieth
century was the emancipation of the dissonance. By 1950 only the
most reactionary musicians had failed to accept it. Such acceptance did not include corollary acceptance of the tone-row or

serial method. Schoenberg himself said seriously, with a glint of
humor, "That twelve-tone method—it was really six-plus-six." By
1960 the movement away from strict twelve-tone principle was
accelerating, in part because composers were outgrowing that
period of Schoenberg's composition, formalized by Berg and
Webern but incorrectly focused on *Pierrot Lunaire,* which centered around the relatively diagrammatic structure, and had not
yet come to terms with the fully achieved, freely inspired, larger
compositions of Schoenberg's later maturity. Apart from Schoenberg's new classicism, composers were exploiting atonality by a
great variety of individual methods and means. Serialism was
already academic.

The unalterable fact for the second half of the century is what
John Cage called "the emancipation of music from its notes." No
system of serial composing in notation can confine or define that
art which has abandoned notation in reaching towards the full
potentiality of the field of sound. Sir Francis Bacon, writing in the
first half of the seventeenth century, had estimated the present
situation of music so precisely that scarce anything needs to be
added to bring his prediction up to date. The new art is inherent
in the medium and required only the invention of electrical
means to produce it. But so long as people sing, strum string
instruments for pleasure, clap hands, and beat drums, electrical
means will not confine the art of music.

The long argumentation which followed the emancipation of
the dissonance resulted in an ambiguity that was not generally
understood or accurately stated. Schoenberg declared that the
twelve notes of the scale, as emancipated, exist as twelve precise
sounds divided by equal half-step and whole-step intervals, the
agreed artificial language of music. The acoustical incorrectness
of the intervals is to be disregarded, and with this the acoustical
presumptions which link these notes to any system of key-relationship. The intervals of the row furnish, in vertical relationship,
the grammar of music, apart from the harmonic laws which
formerly determined how the notes should be combined; the
extension of the row provides its syntax. A single row will suffice,
if properly constructed, for a composition of any size or complexity, and all relationships within the composition will partake of
the row in its unique coherence and consistency of notes and
intervals.

Schoenberg furnished grammatical and syntactical rules to

prevent an unwanted occurrence of key-relationship in the new order. He said plainly and repeatedly that these rules are not a method of composing music, as the grammar and syntax of key-related harmony are not a method of composing music. Poets and authors accept the rules of grammar and syntax which govern the usage of their language, but these rules do not provide subject, content, idiom, or style; a skilled author conceals rather than exposes knowledge of the rules; correctness of grammatical or syntactical construction is to be presumed, not praised.

To demonstrate the strict application of his newly conceived grammar and syntax Schoenberg composed several large works, notably the Wind Quintet, the Suite for Seven Instruments, the Orchestra Variations, the operas *Von Heute auf Morgen* and *Moses and Aron,* the Third and Fourth Quartets, the Violin and Piano Concertos, and the String Trio, the strictness gradually relaxing as he was able to divert his attention from the rules to the compositional procedure. Of these new compositions, the Wind Quintet, being the first complete presentation of the new mode, is the most difficult, being the most bound by the new rules and therefore, in relation to all precedent music, the most completely released from habitual expectation.

Schoenberg did not intend that tone-row music should forever exclude any other type of music. After the new mode had been learned and exhaustively applied, composing by this means would be simply a further extension of the musical tradition, to the study of which he continued to refer his pupils. In his teaching and opinion, composers should master that tradition before trying their creative ability in the new dimension. Soon after the Wind Quintet, in the little canon for voices *The Parting of the Ways,* Schoenberg demonstrated how plain harmony and the new extreme harmony could be satisfactorily combined. Such later compositions as the Suite for Strings, the Variations for Wind Band and for Organ, and several works for chorus showed his pleasure in being able to move at will between the traditional harmony and the new. Indeed, some of the last choruses are as free of either convention as sixteenth century polyphony.

The new generation of tone-row enthusiasts objected to this ambiguity. "Schoenberg Is Dead," Pierre Boulez caroled in the title of a tasteless article declaring that Schoenberg had betrayed his discovery by resuming the old-fashioned harmony.

One could prove, as Nicolas Slonimsky had earlier demonstrated, by treating the extraharmonic notes of Schoenberg's *Little Piano Piece,* opus 33a, as acciaccaturas and removing them, that the substratum of the piece is made up of Wagnerian harmony. Schoenberg might have pointed out that his disposition of these extraneous notes made precisely all the difference. The tone-row provided a new order exclusive of any key-relationship, but the disposition of tones and intervals in the row would allow for all traditional intervallic combinations, as the composer might wish to use them, so that the dissonant extension of the new art would not exclude the internal consonant relationships that enrich the sound. (The tone-row takes up fugal composition where J. S. Bach left it with the *Art of Fugue,* plus the experience of late Beethoven and Schubert.) Schoenberg could not understand why composers, instead of making music, should insist so much on the sterile legality of his new rules. He did not think of musical composition as a game of rules, but this exactly was what the tone-row devotees and serialists wished to make of it. Even during Schoenberg's lifetime, uncomprehending devotees of the new quick-and-easy formula for the production of difficult music made a habit of reviewing new Schoenberg scores in search of "mistakes," where he had perhaps deviated by a note from an exact disposition of the row. Schoenberg believed that true composing would require such deviation, that it was the very proof of musical art, though in general he took pains to avoid it.

Schoenberg had not abandoned his twelve-tone syntax and grammar: "This seems the most attractive feature of the method of composing with 12 tones: that, from the very beginning, to a certain degree, coherence is assured. . . . There will probably be various attempts at promoting coherence through this method, but I hope successors will not forget that it is not only 12 tone, but that the accent is on 'composing.' "[1]

Many successors thought otherwise, and musical evolution entered a period during which the substratum of simple harmonic relationships was determinedly excised in favor of an uncompromising discord. Schoenberg had contended that the "coherence" of tone-row music depends on its relation in all degrees to a single row of notes. The new enthusiasts, as early as Alban Berg in *Lulu,* preferred multiple rows and complex systems of row interchange, until a great part of serial composition, as they now preferred to call it, existed as a complete design in score, which the listener could seldom re-create while listening. Aleatory methods, borrowed from John Cage, after an initial fierce resistance, further complicated the procedures. Such complexities needed explanation; the production of explanatory articles and introductions to the music became an art in itself. Pierre Boulez wrote an article, in advance of composing his Third Piano Sonata, which elaborately tied his compositional method to that of James Joyce in writing the book *Ulysses;* the resulting work did not at all strictly follow this explanatory *précis.* Stockhausen explained his new techniques in profusion; informed criticism exposed some of these techniques as verbal bluff. The Argentinian composer Mauricio Kagel, a member of the Cologne group in Germany, explained in a lecture that the written or spoken preamble to his composition, sometimes longer than the succeeding page of music, is in fact part of the composition.

As a result, the tone-row became one of a variety of compositional devices, each in need of explanation, composers playing a cerebral, in-group game, which at its height of fashion threatened to transform music from an essentially audible to an essentially analytical art.

Schoenberg's argument that dissonance is merely an extension of consonance was carried to the further degree that discordance is only an extension of dissonance. Until this time composers had always been aware of the distinction: discord is an unacceptable degree of dissonance, which eighteenth century composers called "the Wolf" and permitted occasionally for emotional affect. The wider the harmonic base from which it proceeded, the more acceptable would be the occasional discordance, as Schoenberg and Ives amply demonstrated. A composition made up almost entirely of discord resembles an opera made up of screaming; there is no alternative of repose, except to scream very softly or keep silent. One hears the consequence already in Berg's opera *Lulu.* But such works in total discordance as *Sequence* by Jean Barraque and *Echoi* by Lukas Foss reach a nearly unendurable extreme: not an extremity of liking or disliking but an extremity of listening. By contrast, George Perle, author of a basic text on twelve-tone composition, preserves a rich tone-texture in such works as his *Serenade* and Quintet for Strings.

Discord, being composed of discrete notes, tangles and cancels the overtones in such a way as to eliminate or distort sonority, so that one hears mainly the jangling fundamentals. Noise, by contrast, comprises a chaotic mixture of resonances and sonorities unrelated to the specific audible reference of discrete tones. The trend to discordant composition ensured discovery of the superior audible richness of noise-composition. But noise for itself presents textural and structural problems similar to those raised by discord. Except silence, there is no dramatic or expressive point of rest.

The cancellation of instrumental timbres by the overtone conflicts of discord made more tolerable the new sounds produced by electronic generation. Although it is possible to imitate the timbre of an instrument by electronically generated means, experienced opinion agrees that the imitation still lacks much of the intrinsic quality of the original instrument. Exploration of the entire *sound situation* which creates the full timbre of an instrument is still in a relatively incomplete state, though knowledge of the necessary components is progressing rapidly. An increasing number of sound laboratories, most of them in universities, led by the pioneering work of RCA-Victor Synthesizer and the Columbia-Princeton group, by the Bell Laboratories in New Jersey, by the Experimental Music Studio at the University of Illinois, by the San Francisco Tape Music Center (now located at Mills College), and by members of the ONCE group in Ann Arbor, is exploring every so-far conceived aspect of electronic sound-production.

Lejaren Hiller, director of the Experimental Music Studio, initiated the use of the computer as a composing instrument. Hiller and Leonard Isaacson reported the new technique in a book, *Experimental Music*, published in 1959, a technical landmark for those who can read it, like the first upthrusting volcanic cone of a seismic evolutionary process which will soon transform the conceptual landscape of the art of music. Hiller's *Illiac Suite* (1957) is the first musical work of any size composed by means of a computer. The four movements consist of four sets of instructions given to the Illiac computer; the resolution of each set of instructions produced the technical data of one movement. The data was then transcribed as notes on musical staves and performed by string quartet. Any one movement of the *Illiac Suite* holds attention; the four movements in sequence eventuate in increasingly vague responses. That this is so is not the composer's "fault"; the movements are a type of problem-solving, in which the composer, having given the machine its preliminary instructions, did not intervene to "make it sound better." The *Suite* has had many performances.

A recent and more adequate work is Hiller's *Computer Cantata*, composed with Robert Baker, for voice, instruments, and electronic tape. It has been documented by a book of twenty-two double-spaced typewritten pages, plus an equally long appendage of bibliography and examples. I read such documents with incomprehension and awe, as I listen to the musical product with patience. Some composers try to transfer the incomprehension and awe to the product as esthetic value. Hiller knows better than to do this.

Reading from the book, the *Cantata* "presents the result of a series of studies in computer music composition carried out in the spring of 1963 . . . to test the efficiency and ease of MUSICOMP (MUsic SImulator-Interpreter for COMpositional Procedures), a completely generalized programming scheme for musical composition intended for use with an IBM 7090 computer. . . . Since [the] primary purpose was to demonstrate the flexibility and generality of MUSICOMP, the *Computer Cantata* presents a rather wide variety of compositional procedures, some of which proved of greater esthetic value than others, and many of which could be improved by more sophisticated logic. . . . It also includes two studies of computer synthesis carried out with a second computer, the CSX-1 . . . that permits compositional results to be converted directly into computer generated sound."

"We included," Hiller continues, "representative examples of the various significant categories of electronic sound": a theremin (an electronic musical instrument); a "harmonic tone generator" built in the Experimental Music Studio by James Beauchamp; the three basic periodic signals, sine tone (fundamental tone without overtone), square wave (fundamental tone plus odd upper partials—resembling a clarinet), and sawtooth wave (fundamental tone plus all upper partials—resembling an open string); plus two types of noise, white noise (the undifferentiated sound spectrum—resembling white light) and "ordinary noise" ("represented by eight characteristic recorded concrete sounds designated in the score by the mnemonic signs, CLICK, CLACK, SISS, CRACKLE, SNAP, POP, BANG, and BOOM").

"The texts . . . are five stochastic approximations to spoken English derived from a synthesis by a computer of stochastic phoneme sequences . . . prepared with the ILLIAC, the original

University of Illinois electronic digital computer . . . based on the statistical analysis of a corpus of English text drawn at random from the publication, *PLAYS, The Drama Magazine for Young People.* . . . Zeroth through fourth-order transition frequencies for the phonemic structure of this material were computed" by several professors.

Example for *Strophe I* (*Zeroth-order Approximation*): "shhlkächg # # mlthālnôĕ # ēŭdáôăshĭsnĭ # ĭôzhvmpäthy" etc. (for which a pronunciation key is given to help the vocalist).

The first strophe is exciting; then, as with the *Illiac Suite,* attention begins laboring. The abundance of data which enter into the composing, for instance a section modeled on Charles Ives's *Three Places in New England,* does not triumphantly proclaim itself. Is it a work of art? It is a work of superlative craftsmanship and skill.

One should understand that use of the computer as a problem-solving instrument, *without* attached sound-generating equipment, is distinct from the use of a computer *with* sound-generating equipment; the latter produces on tape a complete "composition" or realization in sound of the instructions. (The *Computer Cantata* employs both types.) This latter method may completely alter our conception of the art of music by its ability to produce, at present with severe limitations, any sound-combination or sequence of sounds, far beyond the capacity of present-day instruments, which the composer can imagine. The ability to create by this means rhythms beyond the possibility of any live musician being able to perform them will be restricted only by the listener's gradually increasing ability to distinguish and hear them. The same is true of the use of microtonal scales.

Any failure, any musical accomplishment belongs to the composer; the computer, though capable of unimaginable speed and exactness in computing any distinctions or random sequences the human mind can conceive as necessary to potential music, is as incapable of improving the instructions the composer gives it as an organ of correcting the organist's performance. The computer never finds out that it is composing music. The information which it feeds into the sound-conversion system or returns to the composer for notation has nothing to do with the art of music.

In listening to such music all of our normal expectations are displaced. If the composition is not wallowingly dull—as such compositions often are, and only their makers can take pride in them—the flair of the unexpected sharpens our attention to the microtonal detail; we listen with an unresting acuteness which is for some nervous agony, for others a protracted boredom. Few persons enjoy the experience at a first hearing. With repeated experience the agony and the boredom dissipate; one begins to be able to tell oneself with fair confidence: it's good; it's bad; it's not so bad; this is extraordinary—he's done it! One becomes able to deal with arbitrary sound-patterns as with notated tonal compositions, growing aware of the relationships which are beauty and of those which fail of beauty. The listener should be careful not to discover as beauty only those passages which in some way resemble or suggest traditional music.

I might say to the fearful that experience in listening to the *edges* of microtonal sounds or to the fine distinctions among noises and to their multidimensional sound-shapes improves and in no way diminishes one's ability to appreciate the art of our own or any other musical tradition. At the same time one becomes painfully aware of the vague and confused tonality which seems good enough for many orchestras, one rejects the acoustical noise and distortion caused by poorly designed concert halls, one evaluates downward much of the merely exact note-production which passes for musicianship. One's awareness of fine discrimination in tone-production and in the placement of successive tones, one's feeling for the transparency, texture, and shape of well-produced instrumental timbre, and a steadily growing appreciation of the distinctions in quality between real and assumed musicianship more than make up for what one feels one loses. Much that has been thought good will disappear forever, but what survives will be more accurately valued.

The entrance of the computer as an instrument capable of controlling the entire field of sound will eventually render obsolete the intervening method of altering recorded sound on tape, the principal method of composing music on tape until the present time. But this time-consuming art will not soon cease to fascinate composers and listeners. The use of single- or multiple-channel tape offers conveniences for which a computer is too inaccessible and complicated.

Such elaborate tape compositions as Karlheinz Stockhausen's *Children's Voices,* made from the voice of a child reading the story of the children in the fiery furnace from the Book of Daniel plus altered and generated sound, and Edgard Varèse's *Electronic*

Poem are landmarks of creative achievement in a musical art where mechanical and electronic skill are generally more evident than original musical ability. Composing on tape is a game many can play, and performance is guaranteed by no more than running back the tape through one's own machine.

Gerald Strang, composer, acoustical and electronics expert, who learned computer composing at the Bell Laboratories, said to me recently, "What we need in electronic music, to enable it to speak its own language, is to have many more skilled amateurs and far fewer musically trained professionals."

The pioneers in electronically altered tape composition rather cautiously compiled sound collages, which were called by the French term *musique concrète*. Such work has been done by Pierre Schaeffer and his group in Paris and by Vladimir Ussachevsky and Otto Luening in America. The basic idea of these composers and of their more radical successors, among them Henk Badings, Karl-Birger Blomdahl, Ernst Krenek, Milton Babbitt, Mario Davidovsky, Mel Powell, Aurelio de la Vega, and many others, is to continue producing "music," the new sound-means serving to extend the traditional conceptions. Reputation and performance still reward this approach.

Others more positively favor the belief that electronic-sound composition should not be used to imitate or extend traditional music but should be developed as a distinct medium: among them Richard Maxfield, James Tenney, the ONCE group in Ann Arbor with Robert Ashley, Gordon Mumma, and others, the University of Illinois Experimental Music Studio with Hiller, Herbert Brün, and James Beauchamp, the San Francisco Tape Music Center with Morton Subotnick, Ramon Sender, and many more. The lines are by no means clearly drawn, and it is not unlikely that several of the composers whom I have listed would deny an exclusive attachment to either practice.

Participation in electronic musical activity or use of the computer does not exclude a composer from using more conventional means. Most of those I have named are also skilled in composing for instruments and voice.

It is not unreasonable that electronic music should partake of the nature of the field of sound rather than imitate instrumental or notated music. Yet all the devices of conventional music, including tone-row and serial procedures, may be and in practice have been applied to it. Milton Babbitt has been a leader in this development. Such basic differences in procedure signify more than the literary fusses over design details which take up most of the space in professional writing about contemporary music. Rhythmic refinements in notation which now seem problematic or insuperable may soon find an easy solution by reference to the computer and mathematical or graphic *ossia* to indicate the exact proportions. Composers should keep in mind that exact mathematical divisions do not phrase a complex passage, that, as Boulez has demonstrated in conducting his own music, a free movement between two fixed points may be rhythmically more effective than a fractionally exact placement of the individual tones.

John Cage, with prophetic accuracy, wrote in 1937: "I BELIEVE THAT THE USE OF NOISE TO MAKE MUSIC WILL CONTINUE AND INCREASE UNTIL WE REACH A MUSIC PRODUCED THROUGH THE AID OF ELECTRICAL INSTRUMENTS. Most inventors of electrical musical instruments have attempted to imitate eighteenth- and nineteenth-century instruments, just as early automobile designers copied the carriage. . . . The special function of electrical instruments will be to provide complete control of the overtone structure of tones (as opposed to noises) and to make these tones available in any frequency, amplitude, and duration. WHICH WILL MAKE AVAILABLE FOR MUSICAL PURPOSES ANY AND ALL SOUNDS THAT CAN BE HEARD. . . . THE PRESENT METHODS OF WRITING MUSIC, PRINCIPALLY THOSE WHICH EMPLOY HARMONY AND ITS REFERENCE TO PARTICULAR STEPS IN THE FIELD OF SOUND, WILL BE INADEQUATE FOR THE COMPOSER, WHO WILL BE FACED WITH THE ENTIRE FIELD OF SOUND."[2]

Cage did not at the time appreciate the contrary fact, that increase of noise and breakdown of the conventional language of music in equal temperament will vastly increase the importance for musical sound of acoustically correct temperament, the principal means of producing a true sonority. Systems of just temperament can be realized by computer in a variety of exact scales, the majority of them not previously tried in performance. One can also program a computer to give exact just intonation.

Cage's method of composition by chance, which became indeterminacy, has been divided by increasing technical usage into two distinct conceptions: *aleatory*, depending on more or less controlled choices of alternative actions or materials in composing or performance or both; and *random*, where all choices, whether made by the computer used as a composing instrument or by the performers, are equiprobable on the average. Although the difference is clear, composers and performers in practice continually travel between or muddle the two types. At this stage of rapidly expanding information, the confusion is not surprising.

Bertrand de Jouvenal points out that the world of social affairs is different from the world of a game of chance. Throwing dice, one knows beforehand every situation which can occur without knowing what will happen next throw. In social affairs one may hope to foresee but cannot know the probable alternatives. The imagination can construct one possible future, and alternatively another, and another, and so on, without ever explicating all possible futures, one of which will in the meantime have arrived, influenced by something not now evident, or changing so gradually we assume everyone is aware of it, or so suddenly that we are sure everyone must see it.

A very interesting offshoot of electronic music has appeared in a large body of compositions for instruments, lying between discordance for the sake of formalistic design and altered, distorted, or arbitrarily produced intonation approaching the condition of electronically altered sound. The composers who practise these devices are usually skilled as well in electronic composition. When listening to tapes of compositions by Richard Maxfield, for example, it would be hard sometimes to decide, without supplementary information, whether the resulting sound has been naturally, instrumentally, or electronically produced. Maxfield's *Steam* is a sound-photograph of steam issuing from a radiator. Robert Ashley's *Heat*, consisting of both throat sounds and electronic sounds on tape, verges at some points on instrumental timbres. Two effective tapes in my possession record live performances of instrumental music by Toshi Ichiyanagi which have the advantage of instrumental timbre in registers often suggesting electronic production. This area of composition has been useful in carrying to extremes, whether or not totally enjoyable, the exploitation of instruments to produce sounds they were not made for, with a consequent expansion, perhaps towards destruction, as some prefer to believe, of performance techniques. A great quantity of such music has been composed, and even more improvised or flung together by various chancy means. What survives of it, for the most part on tape, is not so much a literature as a guide to and a means of aural self-education. Whether heard in live performance or via tape, instrumentally altered music is, in my opinion, with some decisive exceptions, a better guide to the future of electronic sound than electronic sound itself in its present limited development.

Median between outright tonal distortion and the preservation of exact pitches, another rather distinct type of music is appearing: a close-ordered composition of tones, sliding pitches, and microtones, discordant in fact but at its best free of the discrete assertion of fundamental pitches which exaggerates "the Wolf." I would list as outstanding examples a string quartet of close-intervalled instrumental sound, interspersed with decisive silences, by Witold Lutoslawski; a microtonal quartet for three instruments in close-ordered microtones and piano-playing chords, *Majority* by Malcolm Goldstein, on a collage of fragments from the music of Ives; and a Mass by Joseph Byrd for small vocal chorus singing close intervals very softly, with occasional increased emphasis of isolated phrases, as unique in unpretentious style as Satie's *Mass of the Poor.*

I doubt that there has been, in the entire history of music in any culture, a more totally fascinating period of development than the twenty years following the end of the Second World War (1945–1965). During this period formal music has been vastly enlarged in its ideas by the belated authority of Schoenberg and of Ives. Formalists have driven their conceptions of musical design to a satisfaction which comes near dispensing with the contemporary limitations of notated sound. Visual presentations of music as a notated design in score to be enjoyed more when read than when performed have been matched by graphic representations suitable (and in some opinions more pleasurable) for framing. Instruments and those who play them have been forced to previously unimaginable extremes—and have sometimes gone beyond, as when LaMonte Young stuffed a violin with concert programs and burned it in public performance, or when David Tudor attacked a piano with chisel, rubber hammer, and bicycle chain, and on another occasion with a saw.

The field of sound has expanded to include any type, kind, or quality of sound which may be obtained by electronic means on tape, or for that matter by any other device which has occurred to anyone as worth exploiting. To match Cage's *4'33''* ("Silent Sonata") there is LaMonte Young's work for some thousand equal strokes with a wooden spoon on a cast-iron frying pan—or with any type of beater on any object. (I have performed both of these in my own way with pleasure and a not unfavorable audience response.) The extensibilities of the scale in equal temperament and in just temperament and just intonation have opened up an important area of sound increasingly talked and written of by theoretical specialists since Helmholtz. And by aid of the computer the entire field of sound, in infinite complexity of mixture and rhythmic intricacy, has been brought within reach.

But apart from the electrical inventions that have made possible realization of Sir Francis Bacon's prophecy, we have added nothing to the scope, in exquisite and formidable detail, of his precise imagining. What has been done was not ridiculous but, as he predicted three centuries ago, was waiting to be done.

THEATRICAL-PERFORMANCE MUSIC

DRAMA, THEATER, RITUAL, GAME, OR PLAY

In the fourth dimension of music, to state it very simply, an action takes the place of a note.

Max Neuhaus plays *The King of Denmark*, by Morton Feldman, very delicately with fingertips on a large assemblage of percussive sound-producers supported on metal-pipe frames. Elusive music, at the threshold of silence, ending gratefully without change of dynamics. Then follows *Everything Max Has, Including Beforehand and Afterward*, a composition attributed to Philip Corner. Rushing before the audience, his hands in black gloves, Neuhaus pulls apart his equipment and its frames, dumping the pieces into traveling boxes and cases, wrapping the more frail parts in cloth containers, a display of energy, rattles, bangs, whishes, and purposive actions, which the audience, pushing forward from its seats, watches with amused but undeviating attention, then applause. Enjoying it is like standing on the sidewalk to watch the furniture movers. Corner's composition, a scheme of instructions, gives the actions a rationale, to direct notice to them.

In Cage's *Theater Piece*, "parts are provided for 1 to 8 performers (musicians, dancers, singers, et al.) to be used in whole or part, in any combination. This is a composition indeterminate of its performance. Time-brackets are given within which any action may be made. These actions are from a gamut of twenty nouns and/or verbs chosen by the performer. This gamut changes at given points, so that each part involves a performer in a maximum of 50 to 100 different actions. Means are supplied for the answering of four questions with regard to the activities within any one time bracket. The composing means were the material of *Fontana Mix*."[1] Here, specifically, actions replace sounds.

Repeating what I wrote earlier (Chapter 2): The fourth dimension (of sound), dance, drama, play, theatrical action, and audience participation, though as ancient as the use of sound for any musical, ritualistic, or dramatic purpose, has to do with the nature of the sound as a means of group relationship and not with its nature or quality as a sound.

When in ceremony or in church we sit, stand, kneel, sing, give responses, we are in the theatrical, the ritualistic, the celebrative dimension of art. It has been for all peoples at all times the most necessary dimension—with masks of many kinds, tangible or invisible, creating superreal presences; music, dance, drama, liturgy, oratory, rhetoric, representation emerged from it as separate arts. "The first common quality between play and religion, according to Huizinga [*Homo Ludens*], is the possibility of seriousness. . . . play becomes more intense and imbued with ideals of perfection. Second, it is the separate space that reminds the player or the prayer that he is momentarily in a world of its own rules and sanctions . . . unbounded in the imagination. Third, the holy and the make-believe have pretense and illusion in common . . . special language. Thus religion and ritual are both play . . . For Plato saw this when he asked, 'What, then, is the right way of living?' and then answered, 'Life must be lived as play, playing certain games, making sacrifices, singing and dancing, and then a man will be able to propitiate the gods, and defend himself against his enemies, and win in the contest.' "[2] This superreal expressiveness of the imagination has been civilized into narrative (mythical or fictional), representative, esthetic, and semiscientific channels; we seek it through psychology and anthropology, in ruins and museums. The product has been institutionalized, commercialized, regularized by the imposition of rationalizing theory, debased to the excuses of entertainment and the "old-town" alleyways of gambling and astrology.

Human beings brought together in this way can rise to intense potency, in worship, in heroism, in vatic rites, where the group chanting stimulates the oracle to prophesy, in response to demagoguery, or as a shouting mob. We have seen all these in our society in our lifetime.

The objection is that so far the theatrical-performance composers have had small success in creating situations which bring the onlooker into the activity, except by indirection—as the majority of the accompanying examples indicate.

If an action can replace a note, a sound can do the work of an action. The performer can raise his hand, turn his head, stamp his foot, play the note *sotto voce* (the tone that is not a tone). Sir Thomas Beecham, conducting Haydn, snatched away what seemed as if it should be the last note of a descending scalewise passage and hid it in his fist under the tails of his dress coat. I have heard Glenn Gould convey the same effect rhythmically three times in one Beethoven concerto; the gesture becomes a mannerism, like the abrupt short crescendo of some earlier twentieth century pianists. In music, as in rite or farce, the act need not be descriptive; it can be the act itself. The impossible can happen, not because we lend to it the strength of illusion but—as in the magical instants of the old two-reel motion picture comics —because it does happen. As Debussy wrote of the Annamese drama, "A small clarinet passionately directs the emotion, a tam-tam creates a terror . . . and that is all!"

Now there is an urgency to recover the lost dimensions of imagination, by the artificiality of art and the collaboration of chance, and with the insistent immediacy of a group of picketers with their placards. The slogans summon angels and raise the devil—in sociopolitical instead of religious terms.

During the last century the drawing together of mixed arts has occurred in two conflicting theatrical modes: the *Gesamtkunst-werk* (whole or unified art work), of which Wagner's *Ring of the Nibelungs* and *Parsifal* are inspired exemplars; and the action, event, or object which would give the effect of occurring out of the unconscious like dream or nightmare. The two modes are less far from each other than from the commercially rational social image the composer wished to subvert. Society has instead tied them up as art object and entertainment in its display places.

Schoenberg joined the two modes in *Die glückliche Hand,* an overt cry of despair by the artist against his society, bringing together during its short passion visual and symbolic action, a score for the stage lighting, expressionistic dancelike movement, a chorus speaking interior thought, a superreal monster.

Some composers, among them Luciano Berio and Luigi Nono

from Italy, prefer the combinatory *Gesamtkunstwerk* of live and recorded music, actors and projected slides, motion pictures, colors, exemplified by Nono's *Intolerance*. Such composition is purposed communication, by large means.

Others, like the composing team of the Dutch work *Labyrinth*, disagree: ". . . in the modern form of the total theater all elements retain their own separate expressive values, which make the whole 'senseless,' multidimensional and multi-interpretable. This openness to various interpretations gives scope for the creativeness of an audience."[3] Henry Brant's *Grand Universal Circus* is such a work.

Unfortunately, the exigencies of our inherited theater too often reduce the multidimensional and multi-interpretable values to what seems no better than anarchy, a mere excitement with the absurd. And the theatrical-performance idea stirs two confusing types of imitation: the illiterate and the merely anarchic. The illiterate believes that the result can be achieved without adequate preparation and without self-discipline. The merely anarchic holds that anything is as good as anything else. After the first excitement, the "happening" is too often predictable. There is a lack of foresight in developing what happens, in the skill to perform it, in starting, pacing, overlapping events, in knowing where, when, and how to stop. But occasionally the real thing does occur, and the ability to share in it, as meaningful experience, has been increasing.

In the circumstances of present-day esthetics, it is not astonishing that the fourth dimension of sound should be breaking the proscenium or stage barrier between performance and audience to overturn habituated expectation and create new opportunities for esthetic realization. Whether this is progress, advance and not regression, whether the consequent overturning and destruction of established values is, in the long view, creative, is not the question.

We have seen that a war-blasted nation can rise from the disaster advantaged by the removal of obsolete structure which contained the necessity for and justified retaining obsolete practice. We have been awed, too, by the care of these nations in restoring cultural and religious buildings during a period when one might have expected that all available money and effort would be used to rebuild industry and housing; the inherent morality of their culture, which had been suspended, has not broken down. We have observed that nations less thoroughly devastated soon suffered in competition with the destroyed industry of nations they had thoroughly defeated, because of the ideological drag of obsolescent practice in unchanged surroundings.

An unprecedented worldwide revolution against cultural habit is destroying cherished esthetic landmarks and inhabited values: the trader's metal hatchet replacing the New Guinea tribesman's stone axe (with its magical connotations); medicine increasing the chance of human life (upsetting the ecological balance of life, death, and food supply); democracy among tribal or depressed populations breaking up the authority of their tradition to replace it with the abuses of nationalism; religion conferring the liberating discovery of the individual soul (apart from the tribe) and its accompanying moral disease which we call "alienation"; the most civilized nations destroying their resources with a wasting, mechanized efficiency.

In our specialized view, we have seen Western European music and its counterpart, American commercialized music, replacing the native musical traditions, and our own taste being now rapidly altered by discovery of the values in what had been almost destroyed.

It is possible that we are becoming able to distinguish, by fresh spiritual and esthetic awakening, as well as by the new techniques of musicology, the values creatively implicit in music as an art from those values we have created by our modes of temporary habituation. Music is an art of abstract messages transmitted by signs: by notation, by actions, by gestures, by moments of relative silence, therefore played, danced, enacted, performed, improvised. It is not and can never be an art of exact communication or representation. It is a game of rules and signs which vary with the play. Computer music will not convey a more exact message than a beaten hollow log; telegraphic meaning is not the purport of this art.

Theoretically, we should now direct our efforts towards a more perfect art of music; in fact we do not know what a more perfect art would be; we invent new modes of temporary esthetic habit.

Art, like religion and politics, concerns itself with human actions resulting from thought; engaging with these is the great privilege of being human.

Much art today is religiously and politically urgent, because it tries to help us break out of the dead rule of accepted and institutionalized intellectuality which binds us. It is a searching after wisdom, rejecting the authorities we cling to.

Informational systems are likely to guard their methods as an asset and to resist contrary ideas which discredit them. Church, government, education, arts and sciences, the established informational systems, are being continually assaulted and disturbed by the international dissemination of news and propaganda—facts and misinformation, speculation and opinion. The increase of all-embracing informational systems can only be countered by an increase of religious, esthetic, scientific, and in a practical sense political imagination. The imagination does not fight the new informational techniques but the habituated information which persists by means of them. Thus the religious thinker becomes a theologian, even to denying deity; the scientist predicates humane philosophy; the artist becomes a technician experimenting in communications systems; and the student protests in the streets.

Imaginatively, the problem is to break down the accreditation of accepted knowledge (ability to do by thinking in accepted modes) so that new modes of thinking and doing can be achieved more rapidly than in the past. Esthetically, the problem is to explore chaos in pursuit of unpreconceived order. But the form of this new order, like the form of the universe since Einstein initiated the beliefs of relativity, may be quite unlike anything we have considered orderly. Human experience of conjunctions in time, causality, perception, psychology, and society may soon be astonishingly unlike those of our present acceptance. As we have made the air a means of travel, so we shall be cultivating food crops in the sea.

With such awareness we may now comprehend performance experiments designed as it seems for the express purpose of breaking up all habituation by predetermined criteria. Here is an example from the San Francisco Tape Music Center. The four glass sides of a tropical fish tank are painted with a musical staff and with squares indicating *arco, pizzicato,* etc., or "make a vocal sound." Four instrumentalists sit one at each side. Six fish, white or black, placed in the water, swim behind staves and boxes to furnish notes and instructions. Several weeks of practising were needed to enable the players to keep up with the fish. One might describe this as *art accustoming itself to events in a nonesthetic landscape.* A strong element of humor and of play is involved, but the fun is serious.

The character of a wisdom literature consists in advice and contradiction, the habit of all oracles. Knowledge is ability to do, but wisdom, which should govern knowledge, is in oneself—in art, the esthetic consistency or content. The oracle returns the question to the questioner to be answered by himself, but in the process the alternatives have been channeled, even by nonsense, in a poetic or irrational language which says, Proceed to this or that consequence. The student demonstrating in the street does not have the answer to what provokes him: as citizen he must himself, eventually, provide some answer; anarchy is a term in recognition of the problem.

When John Cage borrowed from the ancient Chinese *Book of Changes* (*I Ching*) both an attitude and a method of composing music by chance means (throwing dice, pulling straws, noticing imperfections in the paper), he was not rejecting practical reality but seeking wisdom in himself. Though he delights in the breakdown of practical reality (machinery, systems), Cage is an eminently practical person. He would not delight in a plane crash. Like many sincere political, religious, and esthetic leaders today, he wishes to release anarchy and yet control it, as in nonviolent demonstration. The initiative of theatrical-performance art and music, which had been for a long time in formulation, seems to have been redefined, after Dada and surrealism, by his guidance; the practice has spread widely, revealing new aspects and fresh possibilities not only in music but in painting, sculpture, literature, dance, and drama. If information can be systematized and channeled into learning systems, it can also be liberated so that it recurs in constantly fresh patterns resembling free association. The audience reacts not *to* but *within* the current pattern, unhelped by habituation, indeed "crossed-up," as one might say, by a complex of events deprived of their expected sequences and connotations, as seemingly random as accident. The audience must explore the conflation of events as if it were a dream or ritual of unknown significance, or like an anthropologist in a village, at once playing along with it and in search of meanings.

But as an accident is not in fact random but an elaborate configuration of causes and effects, depending upon coincidences in chronological time, so the theatrical-performance event cannot occur haphazard. However comic, or farcical, however disturbing, seemingly purposeless, or incomprehensible the outcome, the purpose is intensely serious, a positive rather than the prevailing negative of Dada or the exciting illusion of surrealism. The art is concerned with *what occurs,* not with what *should* happen, but it begins in careful preparation and does not intend that "anything goes." We think too much *of* a work of art and not often enough *in and through* it. The artists of this new mode reject the more abstract *comprehending of* works of art and wish to provoke us, instead, to see and hear, that is, to *participate in and through* them. This art contains elements of game, information theory, dead-pan comedy, and ritual, as well as the entire field of sound and any performance means one can invent. Though the conception is at its best very strict in its requirements, the makers profess to reject all rules and, preferably, explanations. To quote Max Kaplan again: "In the sphere of play we can forget social rules and prescriptions, for here is a world within a world, with its own concepts of right and wrong, good and bad." And Bertolt Brecht: "Nobody who fails to get fun out of his activities can expect them to be fun for anybody else."[4] (See Appendix C.)

Cage rejects the idea of relationship, holding that each object should be seen completely for itself, apart from what it may signify or represent.

> Theater takes place
> all the time wherever one is and art simply
> facilitates persuading one this is the case.
> —*45' for a Speaker*

The theatrical-performance art directs notice to each event as it happens, as to each play of a ball game or the concentration of a move in chess, but the effect may be that of the diffused attention one gives to the concurrent events in the three rings of a circus, to magazine advertisements, to a scene of television, or as one passes through a landscape.

Some of the most representative demonstrations of theatrical-performance music, or "spectacular-performance music" as its makers call it, have been occurring at the festivals of the ONCE group in Ann Arbor, Michigan. In their words: ". . . the dynamics of recent musical evolution have led creative artists to consciously explore those performance elements which extend beyond the realm of 'pure music' and sound.

"These performance elements can be included in the category of 'theater,' and include *dance* (physical activity, human gesture, and movement of all sorts), *staging* (lighting, the juxtaposition and manipulation of stage properties), *natural sounds* (the artistic integration of stage-activity sounds and speech), and the *spatial disposition* of performance (the means of involvement and confrontation of the audience-spectator with the performance activities).

". . . The primary dramatic issues are those of the entire program: where the work of one composer ends and the next begins is of less significance than the context of the whole experience." They do not intend masterpieces.

✿ Or one might better say it this way. They do not intend masterpieces but put the best workmanship they are able to into each job as a job, whether it's a solo or concealed electrical wiring or promotion, because they know that by such common effort the single artist who may be capable of producing masterpieces is given the same help that Shakespeare had, and if one of them is that artist his work will be better than if he were struggling with his untried medium in isolation. It does not detract from their argument to point out that the artist struggling with his untried medium may be an Ives or that they would not have the facilities to produce his larger work. Some may believe that idiosyncratic edges may be smoothed by conformity in collaboration; that is why they don't smooth them and therefore some work turns out to be, or seem to be, unsuccessful.

At ONCE all performances are done with care; one cannot tell from the presentation how the performers estimate the worth of what they are doing. Providing opportunity for local composers, almost without restriction, and for works by outside composers, well known and unknown, the group leaders refuse judgement on any work they present. The group will try anything once. They admit many failures (without distinguishing them), changes of taste and sophistication, representing communal growth. They never apologize and seldom explain.

In Los Angeles I had watched Cage and Tudor perform Cage's *Variations IV* for three hours in an art gallery, each operating a portable phonograph, tape players, and radio, through speakers located at various points in the building, the musical selections and sounds at random, while the listeners moved about.

At ONCE, performing the same composition, the theatrical possibilities were emphasized. On a small platform an interview was being mimed (an American composer interviewing another American composer), while a tape of the actual interview, taken from a broadcast, played through an inconspicuous loudspeaker. The interviewee blasted several of his more popular contemporaries, saying many things about musical conditions and personalities as true as embarrassing, while the mimed "feedback" turned it all to parodic comedy, the audience laughing at truth and parody together. Meanwhile a girl was being tied to a table and elevated by two men to the top of a metal pole. Firecrackers were exploding, an automobile running outside an open door. A man appeared, bemused and carrying a baton, as if expecting an orchestra. A girl approached him with a scarf, wound it around his neck, returned with an overcoat to put it on him, returned to exchange his glasses for dark glasses, to outfit him with a piano accordion, finally to replace his baton with a blind man's white, red-tipped cane. The image of the reduced conductor was led up the aisle, bleating his accordion. An allegory of "the end of music as we have known it"!

One cannot judge the effectiveness of such events by reading about them; a new sense of theater in the audience responds to them. At the Judson Memorial Church in New York, a group of dancers, musicians, and such other artists as painter Robert Rauschenberg, who has been a leader in theatrical-performance activities, share in mutually conceived extradance adventures. A dancer sits while another brushes her hair, one stroke of the brush spread over several minutes, surrounded by distracting but visually insignificant dance actions. The core of time is brought to a slow focus. One "dance" offers the nondrama of an audience assembling to watch a motion picture, watching while portions of an actual picture are shown, rising for an intermission, resuming, and then breaking up to leave. The audience, which also has been watching the motion picture, sees not itself mirrored but itself. San Francisco dancer Ann Halprin's group moves slowly among heaps of colored clothing and objects, the dancers bending to drape themselves in still another colored cloth or headpiece, until the slow heaping of color takes on the resonance of a visual saraband. In many of Merce Cunningham's dances the accompanying sound has no relation to the dance movement.

In *Play* by Morton Subotnick, the rules are as definite as those of Parcheesi: in certain places, according to what happens, certain things are done; you move ahead or go back and so on. "Play" as a general motivating principle replaces "beauty" or "communication" as the term of esthetic relationship. There is of course much "play" in such a strict discipline as the art of canon.

In compositions by Christian Wolff the general principle resembles a game: for example, the action of one musician, whenever he initiates it, setting off the action of another musician; and the game reciprocates, regardless of the consequent overlapping of sounds. Wolff does not theorize about the effect of his music but instructs how it is to be done. Asked about the amorphic succession of planless sound which results, he says that is what he likes. A scholar of the classics faculty at Harvard, Christian Wolff creates with an authority not to be disregarded.

Mauricio Kagel, who claims that his introductory verbal explanation is one composition with the resulting music, has also composed a theatrical-performance comedy, *Sur Scène,* with musicians, actors, mimes, mocking the effort of a lecturer to explain.

The motion of art is circular, beginning and ending with the creative skill and purpose of those who make it and the perceptive skill and patience of those who receive it; the performer, as intermediary, must be at the same time skillful, creative, and perceptive.

We should keep in mind that the arts are, in effect, a many-sided trial of life, that whatever the work of art may include of reasonableness and seemingly exact description will have been set off, balanced or unbalanced, by its own esthetic-experimental needs. A practical sculptor, preparing a three-dimensional mock-up of Leonardo's *Last Supper* to be shaped in vinyl plastisol, discovered that the anatomy of the figures follows not nature but Leonardo's graphic design. What Leonardo wished to be seen through his composition was not his ability to compose anatomy correctly but the design of expressively related heads and hands and torsos, even of concealed thrusting feet beneath the table, by which each viewer would compose his unique awareness of the event. In one direction creative design drops off to *narrative formalism* (Napoleon on a white horse at whatever battle), in the other to *abstract formalism* (of which during the last half-century we have seen too much). The trial is in the effort of the creative mind to wrest life to its purpose; in the judgement of this purpose upon life; and in the judgement of life upon the purpose. Our knowledge (ability to do) as partakers in art is perpetually in question, even as we question the artist's knowledge (or ability to do), and both are questioned by what we think to be real life.

Theatrical-performance music has come into prominence while still very partially conceived. Unlike those artists whose change of term within the musical medium brought down general reprobation and a time-lag in comprehension often lasting many years, the theatrical-performance composers have won rapid acceptance and no more than tentative rebuke. They evade criticism, because they have changed not some rules of the game but the game itself. They do not regard their works as creations built to last but as opportunities for mutual action which may be repeated or discarded. They question the usefulness in any community of having little more than "the best music by the best musicians."

In correspondence with Gordon Mumma of ONCE I asked him whether he could provide some definitions applicable to their work. He answered: "We have always felt that the definitions need only apply to the *social* problem of creating communities of artistic *activity*, and not to artistic esthetics as such. Personally, I *insist* that the problems at hand find their solutions by doing rather than talking, that an open forum of activity for the contemporary performance arts must be established, nourished, and spread far and wide."

We equate the professional performer with repetition of the professionalized classics, reiterating their "values," as critically adumbrated (meaning "vaguely shadowed forth"), which the audience receives and compares with the "values" of other performances or reads about in newspaper reviews. Therefore any new work is expected to present similar "values" which may be compared with other "values," a stifling requirement. When a community opens a Center for the Performing Arts, the local directors seldom turn to the community to provide those arts; they rent and import what they believe the community cannot create. It is a modern, negating, destructive attitude, productive of false values, the sin of *acedia*—sloth, torpor, apathy. The common denominator of these "values" is entertainment; the obverse of entertainment is boredom.

Therefore many artists today, reacting against entertainment, impose boredom as an esthetic discipline. So in the waning of medieval faith, as Huizinga writes, ascetics publicized for merit amid luxury their rags, sores, and stink.

The artist is expected to make his reputation elsewhere, in the "big city" or abroad, before his own community can value what he offers. And he may not return to it, preferring the big city or to live abroad.

In music, this is not the tradition of Palestrina the merchant, of the Couperins, of the Bachs, of Haydn; it is not what Dr. Burney found in his travels through Italy and Germany. There the communities were proud of their musicians, the composers no less than the performers. But in Haydn's later years he became the man internationally sought after, the composer liberated from routine duties. Beethoven and Berlioz struggled to establish themselves on the same ground; Liszt, Wagner, and Strauss did so successfully. The artist now measures his success in part by his income and his independence of employment. His reputation, tossed among many mouths, renders him a mountebank. It is a dangerous measure, product of propaganda, destructive of real values, putting in disesteem the resident artist, retarding his growth and preventing his leadership in the community, forcing him in isolation to aim at masterpieces instead of putting his art immediately to use.

Even a minor artist, living in the respect of his community, will be a source of benefit and light. The romantic notion of the artist as an isolate, a wolf running wild against society, an idea some artists cultivate, has been forced on the artist. An artist is not a renegade but a workman. The critical and creative independence of the artist is not improved by making him an outcast—or by expecting him to teach for a living. The artist at his best speaks like saint and prophet for revelation and conscience against complacency and conformity. He earns the persecution of hate and rejection by the unwise; they have in themselves nothing he can speak to. We should honor him even when we disagree with him, as we should honor any hardworking public figure. We should also respect his creative privacy.

Critically we should seek the artist for what he does, not for his temporary prestige, his popularity, his ability to get on and up in the world of vogue. We should pay him for doing his own work among us.

You and I are the public; we should learn what we are denied and then assert our right to it. Without this, our arts councils, our performance centers, our wire-pulling machinery of awards and grants which misleads youth by easy benefits and honors merit only in age, our restless official striving to build up the professional performing arts, while the proportion of amateur artists is steadily increasing, would be better done away with. The official, the administrator, the committee too often stand between the living composer—in music, theater, dance, poetry—and his public: those who might learn to cherish and love his work, if they could know it.

Any first-rate composer must expect an undue share of incomprehension and misrepresentation—and may be expected to give back some of his own. The more his art and medium deviate from the conventional, the more he may expect the incomprehension to be published in the ugliness of hatred, and the misrepresentation to become untruth, even malignant lying. The conventional mind, in composer, critic, or performer, cannot admit any serious alteration of the craft it knows. Only frequent performance can awaken appreciation and dispel the falsehood. Infrequent performance is considered by ignorant critics to be proof of an impersonal divine judgement on the composer and his art. Thus the most creative composer suffers most bitterly both the spiral of neglect and severe resistance and rejection at each occasional performance. This truth, known to all, is consistently disregarded.

To keep art in growth we should keep it constantly in trial—not on trial—by frequent performance and repetition of new works. The national and local publicity machines war with this need; the entertainment industry labors to distract notice from its urgency. Public apathy is satisfied by entertainment which diverts disturbing thought. Anarchy and atheism are still concerned; apathy concerns itself with nothing.

If the theatrical-performance practice, by upsetting apathy, by establishing an attitude which does not depend upon the masterpiece and "values," can revive the communal ability to play art seriously together, it will have accomplished, all other values aside, its revolutionary spiritual purpose. The official, the administrator, the committee should be the servants of the artist and the community, instead of setting themselves up as arbiters. In this era of increasing leisure we need to break down the barrier between the professional performer and the inert audience. The amateur should not displace the professional but seek his leadership and learn to share his skills. We know that a well-led community recreation center can break through neighborhood *acedia* and overcome delinquency.

It is by common participation in a common rite that a community establishes what it thinks sacred. In the cathedral at Strasbourg the altar stands, as formerly, almost out of sight at the far end of the chancel (the space reserved by tradition for the clergy). At Cologne, when the cathedral was restored, the altar was moved forward to the central position where the transepts and nave cross, with the congregation on three sides. Among us, entertainment, boredom gilded by "values," has been held sacred. The shock of theatrical-performance participation may be curative.

If the theatrical-performance idea seems too simple, in contrast to what art specialists prefer to call "art," the answer might be given in the sentence composer Morton Feldman, waking out of a sound sleep, spoke to John Cage: "Now that things are so simple, there's so much to do." —

APPENDIXES

NOTES

INDEX

APPENDIX A

IVES'S "ANTICIPATIONS"

To demonstrate how much "anticipation" Ives could pack into a movement, I quote from *The Avant-Garde Character of Charles Ives's Music Exemplified in Representative Vocal, Chamber, and Symphonic Works*, an M.A. dissertation for Mount St. Mary's College, Los Angeles, by Sister Emily Marie Bryant, SP.

"A summary of Ives's devices used in the second movement (of the Fourth Symphony) yields the following observations:

"1—Like Schoenberg, Ives used the twelve tones of the scale freely in dissonant counterpoint. Unlike Schoenberg, whose polyphony is composed of single lines, 'Ives for the first time in history establishes . . . a polyphony of groups, in which the elements are not lines but full musical entities which carry within themselves their harmonic and contrapuntal life.' [Quoted from Reti, see p. 267.]

"2—Like Stravinsky's, Ives's incredible rhythms are held together with an infallible sense of climax. Alternating bars of varying meter, cross rhythms, and dislocation of the accent by means of intricate patterns of syncopation are frequent.

"3—Like Stravinsky, Cowell, and Bartók, Ives uses cluster chords for percussive effects.

"4—Like Bartók and Ruggles, Ives employs notational freedom regarding mixtures of sharps and flats, expanding the conventional scale by successive enharmonic equivalents to form synthetic scales.

"5–Like Mahler, Schoenberg, and Webern, Ives's dynamic specifications and relative intensities are subtly annotated. His occasional delicate use of the strings and the metrical discontinuity strengthened by rhythmic and motivic independence parallel Webern's pointillistic patterns.

"6–Like Messiaen and Carter, Ives introduced rhythmic counterpoint and, like Stravinsky, employs prominent piano parts in his Symphony.

"7–Like Brant and Stockhausen, Ives specified a divided orchestra, requiring more than one conductor, and stereophonic and antiphonal effects."

APPENDIX B

EXTRACTED FROM HARRY PARTCH'S DESCRIPTION OF HIS MUSICAL DRAMA *DELUSION OF THE FURY*

The following material has been extracted from Harry Partch's description of his new musical drama, *Delusion of the Fury*.

"I do not disdain the idea of concert music, but theater work is the compulsive direction of my mind; it is what I want to do; it is the vehicle for whatever vision I possess. The two acts of *Delusion of the Fury* have this in common: both convey the mood that reality is in no way real, despite the very different locales, subject matter, and the very different paths toward the awareness of unreality.

"Act I, on the recurrent theme of Japanese Noh plays, is a music-theater portrayal of release from the wheel of life and death. I am not trying to write a Noh play. Act I is actually a development of my own style in dramatic music. The instrumental sounds (except my koto) are not Japanese, the scales I use are not Japanese, the voice usage is different, costumes are different. Its *daimon* is American.

"Act II, based on an Ethiopian folk tale, is a reconciliation with life . . . a tongue-in-cheek understanding, attained through irony, even through farce. Again, and despite the use of much percussion, the tone is American.

"Dialogue as such is never present. I feel that the mysterious, perverse qualities of these story ideas can be conveyed through music, mime, lights, with more sureness of impact than with spoken or sung lines. . . . There are exactly ten recognizable English words, spoken or intoned, in Act I, not counting repetitions . . . and exactly forty-four in Act II. . . .

"The instruments must be on stage, and they must not be pushed back into corners. They *are* the set. . . . The clichés of modern dance must be avoided, and I believe that the impedimenta of instruments will prove an effective deterrent. The vigorous movers . . . will simply learn to avoid instruments. . . . The principals must be actors, mimes, and—in another strange sense—dancers. They must be able to move with firm dramatic or theatrical purpose. . . .

"The approximately 20 musicians (with conductor) *are* the Chorus. There are 21 instruments on stage (not counting small hand instruments), but never do the 21 play simultaneously. The tacit musicians may thus become actors and dancers, moving from instruments to acting areas as the impetus of the drama requires. Where necessary, instrumentalists must memorize (musical) parts (so that lighting of the music stands will not detract from the stage lighting). They must be in costume, not suggesting anything that is either Japanese or Ethiopian. The basic garment is a huge pair of pantaloons, wrapping around the waist. In Act I they also wear a poncho-like garment—a single, full piece of cloth with a neckhole. During Act II the musicians are naked from the waist up. Each musician will wear a different fantastic headpiece. The three principals wear more imaginative costumes and make-up, wigs but no headpieces.

"At the end of Act I the stage darkens, but there is no intermission; music is continuous."

APPENDIX C

ON THEATER

"It seems indeed that where simplicity and order reign, there can be no theater nor drama, and the true theater, like poetry as well, though by other means, is born out of a kind of organized anarchy after philosophical battles which are the passionate aspect of these primitive unifications."[1]

I had not read these words from *The Theater and Its Double* by Antonin Artaud, nor the book itself, until I had completed writing my chapter on *Theatrical-Performance Music*. My experience came from what I had seen and heard and my thought after these encounters. I have no great regard for manifestos, preferring to observe what is done. It is too easy to be convinced by frenetic language and the word "Absolute."

Reading Artaud's proposals one must admit that the greater part of them have now been taken up by the theatrical craft; too often the result merely exaggerates a stultifying stagecraft by elaborating a spectacle to entertain an audience.

There is a complete antithesis between the traditional disciplines of the Balinese and Japanese theatrical arts which Artaud praised and the traditionless spectacles by which he would have had us attempt to free ourselves from masterpieces. The Balinese and Japanese traditional theaters are already masterpieces, not expecting change—as if our art of music had settled in permanence in the Italian and French operatic styles of the seventeenth and eighteenth centuries.

Artaud wished to overwhelm the audience by the multifarious dissonances of his theatrical passion. Bertolt Brecht, in contrast, preferred that the audience should remain outside the action, dispassionately considering its judgement of these events.

John Cage, accepting as theatrical whatever occurs, dismisses both passion and judgement in favor of a consummate and termless attention. The events of the theatrical occasion are not more significant and should not be more focused than other events which occur before or after or accidentally peripheral to the occasion. He enjoins "game" or "play," calling it instead "celebration." (Compare Josef Pieper's "The soul of leisure . . . lies in 'celebration,'" in *Leisure the Basis of Culture*.) Cage's theater closely resembles the total awareness that Jiddu Krishnamurti would not permit to be called "religion," because he rejected the word and all its accompanying words.

Any statement of an absolute renders itself unassailable by rejecting or qualifying terms. An ultimate religion or esthetics can only repeat its proposition. I once questioned Krishnamurti about his denial of esthetic values. His vehement reply swept me like a spiritual flame. I was awed and chastened, as if I had committed sin. It was—in ten minutes—an experience of absolute value, forbidding any possible discussion.

Each of these spiritual creators has been a master of words. Each holds that using other means than words will free us from verbal intellectuality. These other means we may call, generically, "signs." Marshall McLuhan believes that such signs, replacing the linear continuity of print, are already established and engrained in our communications systems. What Buckminster Fuller speaks of as "the third parent, television," is displacing the book at the age when the child learns most, when his still undirected imagination is challenged, when his habit of reality is formed. Television educates children to think without boundaries in intercommunicating time, so that for them events become history even as they are visualized, and the conceptual limitation of difference ceases to exist. One consequence may be *indifference:* between battle scene real and battle scene enacted, between emotion caught in vital moment and emotion simulated, wrenching pathos followed by the patter of a commercial, the event like a headline visually focussed in its prejudice, without geography, depth, or contrast—fact, speculation, propaganda, and advertisement given equal suburban throwaway status, anything seen and nothing seen for what it is.

Certainly we are no longer bound to time and place like a peasant who is born and dies in the same village. And many villagers are now caught up, as passionately as Artaud, in "rhythmic repetitions of syllables and particular modulations of the voice, swathing the precise sense of words," which we know to be not poetry but propaganda. The enduring "Evil" Artaud prophesied in 1933 was already breaking the cosmic seams; theater today cannot attempt to match that dissonance.

The desire to promulgate a belief capable of overwhelming deliberate and conscious thought, whether generated by Nietzsche or by Hitler, by the French military mystique or by Artaud, by the psychologies of Freud, Jung, and Pavlov, or by the cults of nationalism, is a narrowing rebellion against the totality of experience it claims for its own.

If theater should be, as Artaud wished, a "digestive" experience, it cannot succeed by heaping before us mountains of unprepared food or by advising us that all experience is equally theater. A total awareness is the vanishing-point of esthetics and religion.

The purpose of a work of art is to prepare the food and serve it in digestible portions, according to the skill and judgement of the artist. Excesses of technique do not make up the deficiency of imagination. The present esthetic revolution, like the worldwide cultural revolution, is a search for new food, for a new ordering of experience. The purpose is not to produce a giant spectacle—that the world itself presents—but to educate the imagination to adapt to the altering realities of the world it lives in. The new ordering will be theatrical, political, spiritual.

Though our acts may disappear from history, we can appreciate them as drama. To appreciate is both to set a just value and to raise the value. By learning to give a just value to our acts we raise their value. The purpose of theater, indeed of art, is not to escape but to teach us a dispassionate appreciation of the drama of our mutual acts, which of themselves arouse our passions.

Schoenberg's *Moses and Aron*, in the many-voiced ordering of its significances, is the most complete model our century has given of this all-questioning drama. I refer not to its stagecraft but to its thoughtcraft. All means subserve the intangible: the mixed speaking-singing in contradictory messages of the Thornbush, the ritualistic arguments and sacrificial excesses, the all-embracing verbal contradictions thrown in conflict as much by discordant apprehension of their sound as by precedent or subsequent comprehension of their meaning.

Partch's dramas of Midwestern word and music rituals, heavily beaten incantatory dances, dramatized instruments (some of these seven feet high, as Artaud wished), Partch's musical art which permits all gradations of expression from speech to chant to song to shout to scream, his use of verbalized sounds as often as words—his newest drama, *Delusion of the Fury*, will have a vocabulary of only some fifty words—respond to Artaud's desires; but Partch is his own prophet. Those elements of Partch's dramatic works which often stir contempt, because they lack that type of professionalized difference from ordinary life and speech the stage-accustomed intelligence expects, are the elements he shares with Artaud's prophecies. His theater excites emotion by the realization of emotion in the primitive terms to which he, like Artaud, appeals. But it is easier to play around uncritically with Artaud's hallucinating prose than to appreciate the coarse rub of reality in Partch's concrete usage.

If the theater is to give thought to Artaud, to Brecht, to Cage, to Schoenberg, if we are to grasp the nub of Fuller and McLuhan in these regards, we must no less give thought to the dramatic works and teaching of Partch.

Among these at once mutually reinforcing and contradictory doctrines, we shall be wiser and more knowledgeable if we listen to each separately and learn from it what we can use, than if, in anarchic enthusiasm or rejection, we confuse them.

"It seems indeed that where simplicity and order reign, there can be no theater or drama," Artaud insisted, but the Balinese theater existed among the villagers in such conditions and did not subsist on Indonesian political confusion. The "true theater" is not "born out of . . . organized anarchy" but out of "philosophical battles," the religious, esthetic, and political experience of mankind, in which anarchy is but one term.

NOTES

CHAPTER 1. *Music and Sound*

1. The useful term, mutable tone, is borrowed from Ll. S. Lloyd and Hugh Boyle, *Intervals, Scales and Temperaments* (New York, St. Martin's Press, 1963.)
2. Edward Greenfield, in *High Fidelity-Musical America*, Vol. 16, No. 5 (May 1966), p. 157.
3. Ferruccio Busoni, *Sketch of a New Esthetic of Music*, in *Three Classics in the Aesthetic of Music* (New York, Dover Publications, Inc., 1962), p. 91.
4. Letter to Joseph Yasser, in Josef Rufer, *The Works of Arnold Schoenberg: A Catalogue of His Compositions, Writings, and Paintings*, trans. Dika Newlin (New York, Free Press of Glencoe, Inc., 1963), p. 143.
5. *Ibid.*, p. 143.
6. Roberto Gerhard, "Some Lectures by Webern," *The Score, A Music Magazine*, No. 28 (January 1961), p. 27.
7. Note on the manuscript page of *The Fourth of July*. Quoted from John Kirkpatrick, *A Temporary Mimeographed Catalogue of the Music Manuscripts of Charles Edward Ives, 1874–1954*, given by Mrs. Ives to the Library of the Yale School of Music, September 1955; compiled in 1954–1960; mimeographed at Yale University for the Library of the Yale School of Music. Copyright 1960 by John Kirkpatrick.

CHAPTER 5. *Harmony*

1. Paul Hindemith, *A Composer's World: Horizons and Limitations* (Cambridge, Harvard University Press, 1953), pp. 55–56.

CHAPTER 7. *An Introduction to Arnold Schoenberg*

1. *Arnold Schoenberg: Letters*, ed. Erwin Stein, trans. Eithne Wilkins and Ernst Kaiser (New York, St. Martin's Press, Inc., 1965), pp. 245–46.

2. Compare the translation of this passage in the *Letters*. The more forceful and idiosyncratic translation which I reproduce was made under Schoenberg's exacting supervision, to be sent, with the original in German, to non-German friends.

3. Igor Stravinsky and Robert Craft, *Themes and Episodes* (New York, Alfred A. Knopf, Inc., 1966), pp. 105–6.

CHAPTER 8. *Idiom, Content, Style*

1. Norman Malcolm, *Ludwig Wittgenstein* (New York, Oxford University Press, 1959), p. 50.

2. "How To Make Our Ideas Clear," from *Values in a Universe of Chance, Selected Writings of Charles S. Peirce (1839–1914)*, ed. with an introduction and notes by Philip P. Wiener (Garden City, N.Y., Doubleday & Company, Inc. [Anchor Books], 1958), p. 122.

3. Peter Yates, *An Amateur at the Keyboard* (New York, Pantheon Books, 1964), p. 235.

CHAPTER 10. *The Five-plus-Two Idiomatic Origins of Twentieth Century Music*

1. James Roy Newman, *Science and Sensibility*, Vol. II (New York, Simon and Schuster, Inc., 1961), p. 139.

CHAPTER 11. *"A New Language . . . the Fight Against Routine"*

1. Jay Leyda and Sergei Bertensson, eds., *The Musorgsky Reader* (New York, W. W. Norton & Company, Inc., 1947), p. 367.

2. Victor Seroff, *Debussy, Musician of France* (New York, G. P. Putnam's Sons, 1956), p. 97.

3. Hugo von Hofmannsthal, *Correspondence Between Richard Strauss and Hugo von Hofmannsthal, 1907–1918* (New York, Alfred A. Knopf, Inc., 1927), p. 79.

4. Igor Stravinsky, *An Autobiography* (New York, W. W. Norton & Company, Inc., 1962), p. 43.

5. Schoenberg, *Letters*, p. 282.

6. Leyda and Bertensson, *The Musorgsky Reader*, p. 113.

7. *Ibid.*, pp. 419–20.

8. *Ibid.*, p. 408.

9. *Ibid.*, p. 192.

10. Charles Ives, *Essays Before a Sonata* (New York, Knickerbocker Press, 1920), pp. 99–100.

11. Claude Debussy, *Monsieur Croche the Dilettante Hater*, quoted in Seroff, *Debussy*, pp. 131–32.

CHAPTER 12. *An Introduction to Claude Debussy*

1. Seroff, *Debussy*, p. 128.

2. Edward Lockspeiser, *Debussy* (New York, Farrar, Straus & Giroux, Inc., 1952), p. 18.

3. *Ibid.*, p. 26.

4. *Ibid.*, p. 27.

5. Seroff, *Debussy*, p. 99.

6. *Ibid.*, p. 99.

CHAPTER 13. *The Neoclassicists*

1. Étienne Gilson, *Painting and Reality* (New York, Bollingen Foundation, 1957), p. 87.

2. Victor I. Seroff, *Maurice Ravel* (New York, Holt, Rinehart and Winston, Inc., 1953), p. 53.
3. Robert Craft, "Music and Words," in Minna Lederman, ed., *Stravinsky in the Theatre* (New York, Pellegrini & Cudahy, 1949), p. 86.
4. Rollo Hugh Myers, *Erik Satie* (London, Dennis Dobson Limited, 1948), p. 130.

CHAPTER 14. *The Art of Musical Parody*

1. Myers, *Erik Satie*, p. 119.

CHAPTER 15. *Stein-Thomson*

1. Virgil Thomson, in *The New York Review of Books*, Vol. 4 (June 3, 1965), p. 3.

CHAPTER 16. *The Popular Art of Melodrama*

1. Mosco Carner, *Puccini: A Critical Biography* (New York, Alfred A. Knopf, Inc., 1959), p. 135.

CHAPTER 17. *The Dictatorship of Popularity*

1. Susanne K. Langer, "The Social Influence of Design," in Laurence B. Holland, ed., *Who Designs America?* (Garden City, N.Y., Doubleday & Company, Inc. [Anchor Books], 1966), pp. 38–40.
2. Igor Stravinsky, in an interview for *The New York Review of Books*, quoted from Stravinsky and Craft, *Themes and Episodes*, pp. 102, 107.

CHAPTER 18. *Scriabin, Rachmaninoff, Prokofiev*

1. Claude Debussy, *Monsieur Croche the Dilettante Hater*, in *Three Classics in the Aesthetic of Music* (New York, Dover Publications, Inc., 1962), p. 18.
2. Sergei Prokofiev, *S. Prokofiev, Autobiography, Articles, Reminiscences* (Moscow, The Foreign Languages Publishing House, 1959), pp. 36–37.
3. Lawrence and Elisabeth Hanson, *Prokofiev: A Biography in Three Movements* (New York, Random House, Inc., 1964), p. 145.
4. Prokofiev, *S. Prokofiev*, p. 37.
5. *Ibid.*, p. 40.
6. *Ibid.*, p. 257.

CHAPTER 19. *Useful or Practical Music*

1. Hindemith, *A Composer's World*, p. viii.
2. Aaron Copland, *Music and Imagination* (Cambridge, Harvard University Press, 1952), pp. 99–100.
3. *Ibid.*, p. 107.
4. *Ibid.*, p. 108.
5. Hindemith, *A Composer's World*, p. 5.
6. *Ibid.*, pp. 11–13.
7. Saint Augustine, *Confessions*, Book X, sections 25 and 34. Reprinted from *The Essential Augustine*, ed. Vernon J. Bourke (New York, Mentor-Omega, New American Library, 1964), pp. 85, 92.
8. Copland, *Music and Imagination*, p. 104.
9. *Ibid.*, p. 109.
10. *Ibid.*, p. 105.

CHAPTER 20. *The Integrity of Compromise*

1. James Day, *Vaughan Williams* (Farrar, Straus & Giroux, Inc., 1961), p. 83.
2. Ralph Vaughan Williams and Gustav Holst, *Heirs and Rebels: Letters Written to Each Other and Occasional Writings on Music,* ed. Ursula Vaughan Williams and Imogen Holst (New York, Oxford University Press, 1959), p. 99.
3. *Ibid.,* p. 97.
4. *Ibid.,* p. 55.

CHAPTER 21. *The Isolated Aristocratic Composer in a Commercialized Environment*

1. Heinrich Wölfflin, *Principles of Art History* (New York, Dover Publications, Inc., n.d.), p. 63.
2. Max Wilcox, "An Afternoon with Artur Rubinstein," *High Fidelity,* Vol. 13, No. 7 (July 1963), p. 28.
3. Busoni, *A New Esthetic of Music,* in *Three Classics,* pp. 84–95.

CHAPTER 22. *An Introduction to Béla Bartók*

1. Halsey Stevens, *Béla Bartók,* rev. ed. (New York, Oxford University Press, 1964), pp. 41–42.
2. *Ibid.,* p. 199.
3. *Ibid.,* p. 192.
4. *Ibid.,* p. 194.

CHAPTER 23. *The Morphogenesis of Ideas*

1. Arnold Schoenberg, *Style and Idea* (New York, Philosophical Library, 1950), p. 50.
2. Olivier Messiaen, *The Technique of My Musical Language,* trans. John Satterfield (Paris, A. Leduc, 1956), p. 52.
3. Schoenberg, *Style and Idea,* p. 49.
4. Messiaen, *Technique,* p. 55.
5. Schoenberg, *Style and Idea,* p. 151.
6. Messiaen, *Technique,* p. 55.
7. *Ibid.,* p. 56.
8. Eric Salzman, in *High Fidelity-Musical America,* Vol. 16, No. 4 (April 1966), p. 92.
9. Schoenberg, *Style and Idea,* pp. 40–41.
10. Craft, "Music and Words," in Lederman, ed., *Stravinsky in the Theatre,* pp. 91–92.

CHAPTER 24. *An Introduction to Igor Stravinsky*

1. Walter Piston, "Stravinsky's Rediscoveries," in Lederman, ed., *Stravinsky in the Theatre,* pp. 130–31.
2. Stravinsky, *Autobiography,* p. 108.
3. Busoni, *A New Esthetic of Music,* in *Three Classics,* pp. 76–85.
4. Stravinsky, *Autobiography,* p. 75.
5. Egon Wellesz, *Arnold Schönberg* (New York, E. P. Dutton & Co., Inc., 1925), p. 17.
6. Stravinsky, *Autobiography,* pp. 50–51.

7. *Ibid.*, pp. 115–16, 117, 119.
8. Arthur Schopenhauer, *The World as Will and Idea,* Book III, section 52.
9. Debussy, *Monsieur Croche,* in *Three Classics,* p. 34.
10. Stravinsky, *Autobiography,* pp. 53–54.
11. Schoenberg, *Style and Idea,* p. 192.
12. *Ibid.,* p. 113.
13. *Ibid.,* pp. 113–14.
14. Stravinsky, *Autobiography,* p. 125.
15. Igor Stravinsky, "Schoenberg's Letters," *High Fidelity-Musical America,* Vol. 15, No. 5 (May 1965), p. 136.

CHAPTER 25. *The Proof of the Notation*

1. Ludwig Wittgenstein, *Philosophical Investigations,* trans. G. E. M. Anscombe (New York, The Macmillan Company, 1953), pp. 212e, 227e, 230e.
2. Schoenberg, *Letters,* p. 74.
3. Earle Brown, written statement to author.
4. John Cage, *Silence: Lectures and Writings* (Middletown, Conn., Wesleyan University Press, 1961), p. 14.

CHAPTER 27. *An Introduction to Charles Ives*

1. Ives, *Essays Before a Sonata,* pp. 122–23.
2. Henry and Sidney Cowell, *Charles Ives* (New York, Oxford University Press, 1955), pp. 19–20.
3. *Ibid.,* p. 20.
4. Ives, *Essays Before a Sonata,* pp. 97–98.
5. Cowell, *Charles Ives,* pp. 23–24.
6. *Ibid.,* p. 24.
7. *Ibid.,* p. 32.
8. John Kirkpatrick, *A Temporary Mimeographed Catalogue of the Music Manuscripts of Charles Edward Ives.*
9. See *ibid.* Ives wrote on the manuscript of *The Housatonic at Stockbridge:* "River mists, leaves in slight breeze—river bed—all notes & phrases in upper accompaniment . . . should interweave in uneven way, riverside colors, leaves & sounds—not come down on main beat . . ."
10. Cowell, *Charles Ives,* p. 114n.
11. *Ibid.,* pp. 43–44.
12. *Ibid.,* p. 156.
13. *Ibid.,* pp. 156–57.
14. Rudolph Reti, *Tonality in Modern Music* (New York, Collier Books, 1962), pp. 172–73.
15. Cowell, *Charles Ives,* p. 165.

CHAPTER 28. *The American Experimental Tradition I*

1. For an example: measures 66–74 of the second movement of the Second String Quartet.
2. Charles Seeger, "Carl Ruggles," in Henry Cowell, ed., *American Composers on American Music, a Symposium* (New York, Frederick Ungar Publishing Co., 1933, 1961), p. 30.

CHAPTER 29. *The American Experimental Tradition II*

1. Ives, *Essays Before a Sonata*, p. 94.
2. Gilbert Chase, *America's Music* (New York, McGraw-Hill Book Company, 1955), p. 584.

CHAPTER 30. *An Introduction to John Cage*

1. Cage, *Silence*, p. 70.
2. John Cage, *Compositions* (New York, C. F. Peters, n.d.), p. 37.
3. Cage, *Silence*, p. x.
4. "An Interview," *Tulane Drama Review*, Winter 1965, p. 70.

CHAPTER 31. *Electronic and Computer Music*

1. Letter to G. F. Stegmann, 1949, in Schoenberg, *Letters*, p. 267.
2. Cage, *Silence*, pp. 3–4.

CHAPTER 32. *Theatrical-Performance Music*

1. Cage, *Compositions*, p. 42.
2. Max Kaplan, *Leisure in America* (New York, John Wiley & Sons, Inc., 1960), pp. 152–53.
3. Quoted from *Forum voor architectuur en gebonden kunsten* (Amsterdam), issue of May 6, 1964.
4. Those who practice this art should be wary that it treads a dangerous path between aimless farce (the daily fictional brutality of television) and the faceless cruelty of a de Sade or an Eichmann who denies responsibility for his actions.

APPENDIX C. *On Theater*

1. Antonin Artaud, *The Theater and Its Double*, trans. Mary Caroline Richards (New York, Grove Press, Inc., 1958), p. 51.

INDEX

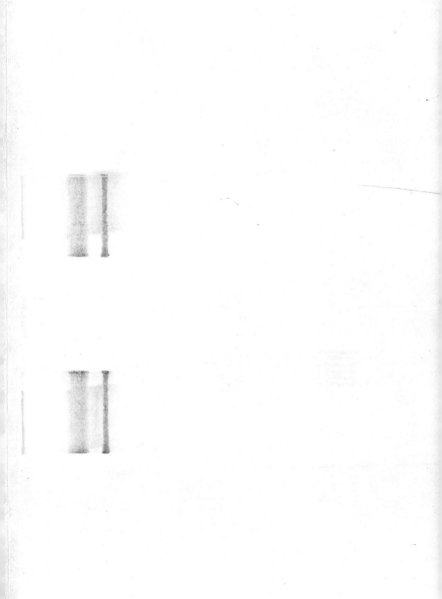